Managing Immigration and Diversity in Canada

Managing Immigration and Diversity in Canada

A Transatlantic Dialogue in the New Age of Migration

Edited by
Dan Rodríguez-García

Queen's Policy Studies Series
School of Policy Studies, Queen's University
McGill-Queen's University Press
Montreal & Kingston • London • Ithaca

SCHOOL OF
Policy Studies

Publications Unit
Robert Sutherland Hall, 138 Union Street
Kingston, ON, Canada K7L 3N6
www.queensu.ca/sps/

In partnership with

The contents of this publication are the result of the *Managing Immigration and Diversity in Quebec and Canada Forum,* organized by CIDOB (Barcelona Centre for International Affairs) on 22–23 October 2008.

Library and Archives Canada Cataloguing in Publication

Managing immigration and diversity in Canada : a transatlantic dialogue in the new age of migration / edited by Dan Rodríguez-García.

(Queen's policy studies series)
Includes bibliographical references.
Includes some text in French.
ISBN 978-1-55339-289-7

1. Canada—Emigration and immigration—Government policy. 2. Social integration—Canada. 3. Québec (Province)—Emigration and immigration—Government policy. 4. Social integration—Québec (Province). I. Rodríguez García, Dan, 1971- II. Queen's University (Kingston, Ont.). School of Policy Studies III. Series: Queen's policy studies series

JV7233.M36 2012   325.71   C2012-902273-XE

Catalogage avant publication de Bibliothèque et Archives Canada

Managing immigration and diversity in Canada : a transatlantic dialogue in the new age of migration / edited by Dan Rodríguez-García.

(Queen's policy studies series)
Comprend des réf. bibliogr.
Comprend du texte en français.
ISBN 978-1-55339-289-7

1. Canada—Émigration et immigration—Politique gouvernementale. 2. Intégration sociale—Canada. 3. Québec (Province)—Émigration et immigration—Politique gouvernementale. 4. Intégration sociale—Québec (Province). I. Rodríguez García, Dan, 1971- II. Queen's University (Kingston, Ont.). School of Policy Studies III. Collection: Queen's policy studies series

JV7233.M36 2012   325.71   C2012-902273-XF

Copy editor (English): Joanna Freedman
Copy editor (French): Sandrine Fuentes

CONTENTS

PART II
MANAGEMENT OF IMMIGRATION FLOWS

PART III
IMMIGRATION AND THE LABOUR MARKET

PART IV
CITIZENSHIP, SETTLEMENT, AND SOCIO-CULTURAL
INTEGRATION

ACKNOWLEDGEMENTS

This book has its origins in a multilateral government-funded international symposium, the *Managing Immigration and Diversity in Quebec and Canada Forum*, held in Barcelona, Spain, in October 2008. As Founder and Director of the symposium, an event that took about two years to orchestrate, I would like to thank all of the participating institutions and individuals, from both sides of the Atlantic, for their contributions to this memorable event. I specifically extend my thanks to CIDOB, the Barcelona Centre for International Affairs, for its involvement in organizing and supporting the Forum.

I particularly thank all of the authors who contributed to this volume, for the high calibre of their chapters as well as for their continued patience and co-operation throughout this project.

I am also very grateful to the anonymous reviewers of the initial manuscript, whose reports aided the deliberations of the Aid to Scholarly Publications Program (ASPP) Committee (administered by the Canadian Federation for the Humanities and Social Sciences). The reviewers' positive feedback offered great encouragement, and their thoughtful and useful comments undoubtedly have helped to make this book a stronger contribution to research. In addition, I would like to express my gratitude to Arthur Sweetman and Keith Banting, former and current Senior Editor, respectively, for the Queen's University Policy Studies Series, for the support and guidance they have provided along the way; to Mark Howes, Publications Coordinator for the Queen's School of Policy Studies, for his ongoing assistance in overseeing the publication process of this book; and to Valerie Jarus, of the Publications Unit, for her patience, helpfulness, and careful work during the typesetting process.

Finally, I would like to thank Joanna Freedman and Sandrine Fuentes, the respective English and French copy editors of the manuscript, for their truly excellent work.

Special recognition goes to Joanna Freedman, not only for her outstanding editorial expertise and meticulous proofreading, but also for her brilliant and constant feedback during all phases of this complex undertaking. I tremendously appreciate her extraordinary dedication to this project, from its very embryonic stages, more than five years ago, to its successful culmination. It is greatly thanks to her that this book was born.

PREFACE

This volume brings together the contributions of participants at the *Managing Immigration and Diversity in Quebec and Canada Forum*, a two-day international symposium that took place in Barcelona, Spain, in October 2008. The conference was founded and directed by Professor Dan Rodríguez-García (Autonomous University of Barcelona) and was organized by the Directorate General for Immigration (formerly the Secretary of Immigration) of the Government of Catalonia (*Generalitat de Catalunya*) and by CIDOB (Barcelona Centre for International Affairs). Other collaborating institutions included the Ministry of Labour and Immigration of Spain, the Canadian Embassy in Spain, the Canadian Foundation (Canadian Ministry of Foreign Affairs), and the Québec Government Office in Barcelona. The contributors to this book have revised and updated the content of their respective chapters where possible.

INTRODUCTION

Managing Immigration and Diversity in the New Age of Migration: A Transatlantic Dialogue

DAN RODRÍGUEZ-GARCÍA, *Professor of Social and Cultural Anthropology, Autonomous University of Barcelona*

Without a doubt, the management of immigration and diversity is one of the most important questions of the present historical moment. Human migration itself is not a new phenomenon. Indeed, there have been tremendous migratory flows in the past, significantly the massive European emigration that took place in the 19th and early 20th centuries. Nevertheless, the current period of migration, which is similarly characterized by extremely high levels of international migration, is distinct in that the movement of people across borders now occurs on an unprecedented global scale and in an increasingly complex manner (Castles and Miller 2009).

Since the mid-1970s, and especially from the 1980s onward, the acceleration and diversification of mobility worldwide, owing in large part to the internationalization of the labour market and other globalization processes, have substantially transformed the global landscape, as different continents, countries, and regions have become more and more interconnected and interdependent (Fröbel, Juergen, and Kreye 1980; Basch, Glick Schiller, and Blanc-Szanton 1994; Sassen 1988, 2007). The

Managing Immigration and Diversity in Canada: A Transatlantic Dialogue in the New Age of Migration,
ed. D. Rodríguez-García. Montreal and Kingston: Queen's Policy Studies Series, McGill-Queen's University Press.

number of international migrants in the world (people living outside their country of origin) has nearly tripled since 1970, reaching an estimated 214 million in 2010 (UN DESA 2009; IOM 2010, 115). And there seems little likelihood of considerable reduction in volume given rising population trends, ongoing emigration pressures in poorer countries, environmental degradation, and the increased globalization of the economy (Castles and Miller 2009; IOM 2010, 2011; OECD 2011a).

Notably, unlike in previous decades, there is no longer a single predominant immigrant profile or type of migration, but increasingly a diversity of them: migrations not only south-north, but also south-south, the latter of which have already reached proportions similar to the former; migrations of people coming from both poor and rich countries; immigrants of urban origin in similar proportions to those of rural origin; both male and female immigrants, including greater numbers of women with independent migratory projects; working-age adults, but also youth—many of whom are international students, and an increasing number of whom are non-accompanied minors—as well as retired people, who more and more often migrate as long-stay/seasonal tourists; people who migrate voluntarily, and others who are forced to migrate, as in the case of refugees and environmental migrants, the latter of whom have increased dramatically in number; legal immigrants, but also undocumented immigrants; low-skilled workers, but also highly qualified professionals; and paid workers, but also self-employed workers or entrepreneurs, whose activities and occupational sectors are becoming increasingly diversified. In general, too, there are greater numbers of migratory projects that give rise to movements of very variable duration, from temporary or circular migrations, for example, to long-term or "permanent" migrations. In addition, many of the present migrants are transnational migrants; that is, they live in or maintain multi-dimensional links (social, cultural, political, economic, familial, etc.) in several countries simultaneously, facilitated greatly by advances in transportation and communication technologies that connect people and places globally. This reality of immigrant transnationalism entails not only physical mobility in itself (the crossing of national borders), but also other aspects, whether legal or political (e.g., multiple citizenship), economic (e.g., remittances, international consumption of goods, international investments), or socio-cultural (e.g., intercultural values, models, and practices) (Glick Schiller, Basch, and Blanc-Szanton 1992; Basch, Glick Schiller, and Blanc-Szanton 1994; Smith and Guarnizo 1998; Levitt and Glick Schiller 2004; Vertovec 2010). Paradoxically, these trends of growing and diversified global mobility have been accompanied, especially in the last decade, by increasing restrictions on international migration—such as stricter immigration and border control policies (for non-EU nationals in the case of the European Union)—as well as mounting anti-immigrant sentiment (see Cornelius et al. 2004; Collett 2011b; Düvell and Vollmer

2011; Fargues et al. 2011, 11-14; see also Papademetriou and Terrazas 2009; OECD 2011a; and Massey and Pren 2012).

This set of complex migration phenomena of our contemporary world calls for fresh approaches to conceptualizing immigration and to understanding its effects (Massey et al. 2009, chapter 1). Countries being rapidly changed by the demographic and social impacts of international migration, together with long-standing countries of immigration, both are contemplating—perhaps with differing degrees of urgency—new theories, models, and/or practices to address the enormous variety and complexity of issues arising in this new migration era.

SHIFTING MIGRATION PATTERNS IN EUROPE: THE CASE OF SPAIN

Within this global context of growing international migration, Spain is an exemplary case of a country whose population composition has been transformed by recent large-scale immigration. The speed at which Spain has moved from being a country of emigration to one of immigration is unprecedented in Europe's demographic history, and perhaps worldwide. Whereas in Northwestern European countries such as England and France, this change took place over several decades, primarily between the 1950s and the 1970s, in the case of Southern Europe, which principally includes Spain, Italy, Portugal, and Greece, the change in migratory patterns occurred much later and much more quickly (King, Fielding, and Black 1997).

Among its Southern European counterparts, Spain experienced this transformation most rapidly and remarkably. The country's economic boom during the latter part of the 1980s served to create jobs and attract immigrants in an ongoing manner; large numbers of foreigners entered the country as workers, mostly with temporary permits, and filled low-wage jobs mainly in the agricultural, construction, and domestic service sectors (Muñoz and Izquierdo 1989; Izquierdo 1996; Arango 2000; Calavita 2007). In addition, while Spain had primarily been a transit country for immigrants moving to traditional destinations in Northwestern Europe, Spain's incorporation into the European Union (formerly the European Community) in 1986 greatly contributed to the country's transition to an immigrant-receiving area itself. Notably, there were some years documented during the 1980s when Spain was technically defined as a net immigration country (albeit showing only minimal net gains), mostly because of return migration by native Spaniards who had been living outside the country during less prosperous times. However, it was really in a span of *less than ten years* that Spain's migratory balance clearly and unwaveringly—and also, unexpectedly—changed from one of net loss to net gain: For consecutive years in the late 1980s and early 1990s, Spain still recorded more emigration than immigration, but by the mid- to late

1990s, Spain had become a country of immigration, with population gains that were indisputably because of continual foreign immigration to the country (see Arango 2000).

From that time onward, most markedly since 2000, the steady immigration growth has been enormous. Spain went from having about 1 million legal immigrants in 2000 (representing 2 percent of the total population in the country) to having 5.7 million in 2010 (representing 12 percent of the total population) (Eurostat 2011; INE 2011a, 2011b). To put these radical increases in foreign-born population into perspective, it can be noted that since 1998, Spain has received the highest net inflows of immigrants annually among all European Union member states, and in some years during the past decade, it has received *almost half of the entire immigrant population that arrived in the EU* (Eurostat 2008). Furthermore, Spain has been second only to the United States in terms of intensity of annual migration flows on a world scale, receiving well over 600,000 immigrants each year between 2003 and 2008. In 2007 alone, Spain absorbed nearly 1 million immigrants (ibid., 2). Notably, newly legalized immigrants—that is, foreign-born undocumented workers residing in Spain who obtained legal immigrant status through government regularization programs (most significantly in 2005)—have also been included in these annual immigration numbers (see Arango and Finotelli 2009). Only from 2009 to the present have immigration rates in Spain experienced a slight decline, coinciding with a period of global economic downturn and serious financial crisis in Spain (INE 2011c).[1]

Within Spain, the autonomous region of Catalonia,[2] now populated by approximately 7.5 million inhabitants, is the area that has received the largest number of immigrants: Catalonia currently accounts for about 21 percent of Spain's foreign-born population (Idescat 2011; INE 2011a). In contrast to Spain as a whole, though, Catalonia has always been an (im)migrant-receiving region, with very high migration inflows, importantly from southern France between the 16th and 17th centuries and then from other regions of Spain from the early 20th century until the end of the 1970s (Cabré 1999; Pascual, Cardelús, and Solana 2000; Bayona, Domingo, and Gil 2008). In fact, immigration, because it has been so essential to population growth in Catalonia, has been considered a central structural component of "the Catalan modern reproduction system" (Cabré 1999, 28). The argument could be made, then, that the large-scale international immigration experienced by Catalonia in recent years is a continuation of normal patterns (see Bayona, Domingo, and Gil 2008). However, the contemporary migrations to this region have been unique in many ways, particularly because of their sudden and unexpected volume, intensity, and diversity, all of which have had a tremendous impact on the demographic composition of the Catalan population (ibid.). In the span of only ten years, more than 1 million people from other countries arrived in Catalonia, thus increasing the number of immigrants from 3 percent of the total regional population in 2000 to 16 percent of the population in 2010, as well as rejuvenating the region's population and making it much more ethnically diverse (Idescat 2011; INE 2011a). All of these rapid changes have made Catalonia an exceptional immigration case within the already unique Spanish context.

While the internal cultural and linguistic pluralism of Spain is a defining aspect of the country (various regions in Spain, including Catalonia, have distinct cultural traditions and officially recognized languages), the perceptibly greater ethnocultural diversity now found in Catalonia and in Spain overall is one of the more pronounced and novel effects of Spain's recent immigration boom. The variety of immigrants' countries of origin has increased dramatically. It is no longer the case that foreign-born persons living in Spain are mainly from Northwestern European countries (e.g., the United Kingdom) and the Maghreb. Virtually all regions of the world, including Eastern Europe, South America, Asia, and sub-Saharan Africa (with Senegal as an important sending country in the last case), are represented in the modern-day flows. According to the Spanish Population Register, the foreign nationalities that in 2011 were shown to be most numerous in Spain corresponded to countries as diverse as Romania, Morocco, Ecuador, Bolivia, Argentina, Italy, Germany, the Ukraine, China, and Pakistan (INE 2011a, 2011b), among others; and significantly, the immigrant groups from many of these sending countries are often characterized by great internal heterogeneity. In this way, the diversification of immigration source countries, leading to substantially higher levels of ethnocultural diversity in Spain, can be considered a salient feature of Spain's current immigration landscape.

In summary, if there is something that has structurally changed Spanish society in the past decade, it is, undoubtedly, immigration. It is clear now that this phenomenon is not an isolated or transient event, but a reality with long-term and profound demographic, economic, political, and socio-cultural effects. What is more, because continual large-scale international migration to the country has been an unexpected and very new trend, a national legal framework for planning for and managing immigration had heretofore largely been absent in Spain. The first modern immigration law, the *Ley de Extranjería* (*Ley Orgánica 7/1985*), a measure to deter irregular immigration, was passed only in 1985 and was essentially a precondition for Spain's 1986 entry into the European Community (Arango 2000, 265; Maas 2010, 241). Since then, further immigration policies have been introduced, including a quota system, established in 1993 and subsequently modified, for the purpose of issuing temporary and "stable" work permits to recruited foreign workers, as well as legalization—most often called "regularization"—programs, designed to address the realities of illegal immigration (in many cases, the overstaying of work visas). However, these laws have predominantly been short-term strategies and have not taken into account larger questions of long-term immigration needs or effective measures for integrating immigrants into Spanish society.[3] Only more recently have policy-makers in Spain come to understand that immigration is a force of enduring social transformation in the country, requiring comprehensive and carefully thought-out policies, which are now beginning to emerge. The management of immigration and diversity is, therefore, one of the most crucial and urgent issues on the Spanish political agenda today.

TRANSATLANTIC PERSPECTIVES: WHY LOOK AT CANADIAN APPROACHES TO THE MANAGEMENT OF IMMIGRATION AND DIVERSITY?

In a globalized world, it is clear that to face the challenges posed by immigration and growing ethnocultural diversity at the local or national level, it is necessary to have a global and outward-looking perspective. It is important to look outside the domestic context, to analyze a variety of governance approaches to immigration and integration, to see the limitations and potential of different experiences, and to adapt the aspects that can be useful from one context to another. And this comparative perspective, if it is to prove most fruitful, must be not only international but also transatlantic.[4]

Obviously, models for the management of immigration and diversity are not transferable en bloc, as they respond to the particular characteristics—historical, demographic, economic, political, geographical, and cultural—of each country or region. But, again, it is evident that the concrete experiences of one place and the knowledge of what has worked better or worse can be of assistance to the policy development of other places.

In this respect, Canada, often referred to as a "traditional country of immigration" (along with countries such as the United States, Australia, and, to a lesser extent, New Zealand), deserves special attention: Not only is it one of the countries that receives the most immigrants and has some of the greatest cultural diversity in the world, but also, it is often taken as a point of reference because it seems to have been more successful than most other countries in resolving the management of immigration and diversity. For this reason, Canada's tested immigration practices—the country's successes in this area, as well as its shortcomings—can be particularly instructive to decision-makers in fast-growing "new countries of immigration," like Spain, or in rapidly changing immigrant-receiving regions, like Catalonia, where leaders must tackle new and improved immigration policy initiatives and try to forecast outcomes. This search to find solutions to immigration challenges is all the more pressing given the tremendous importance that the Spanish public and Europeans in general are now placing on this matter: Public opinion survey results show that immigration policy is currently ranked as the second highest priority subject (level with health policy, and slightly after economic and monetary policy) in the European Union (European Commission 2011). While this book gives particular emphasis to the Spanish case, as Spain's specific immigration circumstances and internal regional dynamics (discussed further in the following sections of this Introduction) uniquely lend themselves to productive transatlantic dialogue and pointed comparisons with Canada, it should be noted that interest in the Canadian system is not confined to Spain and Southern Europe; countries like Sweden are also closely looking at Canada's achievements in immigration and are considering what policy elements could be adopted (see Adahl and Hojem 2011).

Canada, a country whose founders include its diverse Aboriginal populations and the French and British peoples who established permanent settlements as far back as the early 1600s, is largely considered a nation formed by immigrants. Its original colonizers migrated from Europe; it has historically relied on large-scale immigration in order to populate and farm its land (see chapters 2 and 4 of this book); and based on its current demographic profile, Canada clearly continues to be a country of immigration. Each year, this country of about 34 million inhabitants receives approximately 250,000 new immigrants; notably, in 2010, Canada welcomed 280,636 permanent residents, the highest number admitted in more than 50 years (Citizenship and Immigration Canada 2011a). The effect of this continual immigration has been that the foreign-born in Canada constitute a relatively large proportion of the country's population: In the 2006 census year, almost 20 percent of Canada's population consisted of immigrants (people born outside Canada)—a percentage of foreign-born population exceeded only by Australia (22.2 percent)—while in Toronto, one of the three largest metropolitan areas in Canada, close to one-half of the city's people were foreign-born (Chui, Tran, and Maheux 2007; see also Anisef and Lanphier 2003). Significantly, a large proportion of Canada's immigrants are from places other than Europe and the United States, a growing pattern since the 1970s (ibid.; see also chapters 4 and 5 of this book). Between 2001 and 2006, almost 60 percent of newcomers to Canada were born in Asian countries, including the Middle East (Chui, Tran, and Maheux 2007, 9), and this trend has continued into present years, with China, India, and the Philippines being the top three source countries, respectively, in both 2008 and 2009 (Milan 2011, 5). Furthermore, Canada's increasing ethno-racial diversity has not been kept a "quiet" aspect of the country's evolving immigration history: Since 1971, an official policy of multiculturalism has been in place (see chapters 1, 8, 9, and 10), which acknowledges and supports the great cultural diversity of the country's people.

In spite of Canada's high immigration levels and ethnically diverse metropolises, neither Canada, in general, nor Toronto, in particular, seems to have had more problems with immigration than European countries or large European cities. Very much to the contrary, in fact: Canada is one of the most prosperous and least segmented societies in the world, and often it is put forward as a model of an advanced and cohesive society. In the United Nations' *Human Development Report 2010*, Canada was ranked eighth in its quality of life out of 182 countries. Moreover, based on the results of the 2011 OECD (Organisation for Economic Co-operation and Development) Better Life Index, a comparative index that profiled the 34 OECD member countries across 11 topics of well-being (life satisfaction, housing, income, jobs, community, education, environment, governance, health, safety, and work-life balance), Canada ranked within the top three countries in most of the areas and was rated as the second-best country in terms of life satisfaction (OECD 2011b). In addition, a 2007 survey carried out by the BBC, for which 28,000 people were interviewed in 27 different countries, found that Canada was the country perceived most positively by people around the world.[5] Further, in the *Economist*'s February *2011 Global Liveability Report* on the world's most livable cities, three Canadian cities were ranked in the top five out of 140 cities in the world, with Vancouver holding the *number one* position. Toronto and Calgary were ranked fourth and fifth, respectively (Economist Intelligence Unit 2011). Significantly, these internationally esteemed Canadian cities are also some of the places in Canada that are home to the greatest number of the country's immigrants, with Toronto and Vancouver having the largest number of foreign-born people in the nation (Chui, Tran, and Maheux 2007). Hence, the case of Canada continues to be a good example of the fact that immigration and incorporation processes are more a problem of conception and management than of the volume or degree of diversity itself.

Canada's accomplishments, nevertheless, do not mean that this country has found solutions to all of the challenges related to immigration and diversity or that Canadian society has indisputably achieved full social equality for all of its members (discussed in chapters 1, 4, 6, 7, 8, and 9). Forms of exclusion and inequality still exist, as evidenced, for example, by persisting social divisions, differential statuses, and discriminatory treatment of immigrants regarding access to the labour market[6] (see Reitz and Banerjee 2007; Picot, Lu, and Hou 2009). Many things can be improved and are in the process of evolving—some for the better, and some, perhaps, for the worse. In response to new challenges and the country's changing circumstances, Canada itself has begun to rethink aspects of its immigration model (see chapters 1, 2, 4, 6, and 8), in general placing a greater focus on meeting immediate or short-term employer and labour market needs and reconsidering policies that affect not only the country's economic immigration system but also the processing of refugee claims (CIC 2012b; CIC n.d.-a) and the sponsorship of certain family members (CIC n.d.-b). Under Canada's current Conservative government, the admission process for bringing over the parents and grandparents of immigrant families seems to be moving in a direction that grants these close relatives temporary, rather than permanent, residence. Moreover, immediately prior to this book's publication in 2012, the Canadian government had proposed some new specific changes to Canada's economic immigration program that included, for example, "eliminating the backlog of old applications in the federal skilled worker category," "reforming the federal skilled worker point system used to select immigrants," "creating a new Federal Skilled Trades program," and introducing more stringent language criteria (i.e., English or French) for certain categories of applicants ([sic] CIC 2012a). Notably, many of the contributors to this book, in their respective chapters, comment on and view with a degree of caution some of the more recent policy changes, such as the growing number of temporary foreign workers admitted to Canada (CIC 2011b) in accordance with the country's more market-oriented immigration objectives (see also Fudge and MacPhail 2009; Reitz 2010; Siemiatycki 2010). It can be observed that the use of temporary workers (or "guest workers") has been the predominant immigration strategy in Spain and in much of Europe, a pattern that Spain is now re-evaluating because of the socio-cultural and political problems this approach has entailed. Such types of competing transatlantic trends show at once how important local contextual factors are to immigration decisions, but also that outside experiences can sometimes illuminate local and domestic situations and bring a fresh perspective at crucial moments of decision-making. Just as the Canadian experience and record of successes can provide insight to policy-makers and immigration researchers in Spain, so too can an understanding of the European situation help immigration experts in Canada to re-evaluate and possibly reorient current policies and trends.

Whatever weaknesses may presently exist in the Canadian system and whatever future setbacks may arise from newer, less tested policies, it is nonetheless apparent that, somehow, policies for managing large-scale immigration and social accommodation in Canada have thus far generally been more successful than in other Western democracies, many of which are now experiencing growing xenophobia and a pronounced backlash against multiculturalism[7] (see especially chapter 8 of this book for a discussion of Canada's record on immigrant integration). Canadian approaches have resulted in less social isolation of immigrants and fewer social conflicts; brought about higher degrees of comfort and security for foreign-born populations; produced high levels of immigrant educational attainment and traditionally led to greater possibilities for the upward social mobility of immigrants and their children; garnered strong public and political support for immigration; and generated considerable enthusiasm for multiculturalism (except, to some extent, in the province of Quebec, where a policy of "interculturalism" has been adopted instead, and where there has been more heated debate over issues of "reasonable accommodation" for minority cultures; see chapter 9 of this book) (Aydemir and Sweetman 2008; Banting and Kymlicka 2010; Rodríguez-García 2010b;

Huddleston and Niessen 2011; Reitz 2011). It should not be overlooked that Canada outperformed Australia, the United States, and almost all 27 EU member states in its policies for successfully integrating immigrants, as determined by the Migrant Integration Policy Index (MIPEX) for 2010, which ranked Canada third among the 33 countries studied (see Huddleston and Niessen 2011). Furthermore, and perhaps of even greater significance, a Statistics Canada longitudinal survey released in 2005 (also discussed by Jack Jedwab in chapter 7) stated that about three-quarters of recently arrived immigrants reported being satisfied with life in Canada; four years later, when interviewed again, over two-thirds of the study participants reported that their expectations of life in Canada had already been met or exceeded (Statistics Canada 2005; Schellenberg and Maheux 2007; see also Bloemraad 2006, chapter 4). Given these favourable outcomes, the Canadian experience should be taken into account by countries seeking improved strategies for the integration of immigrants.

Admittedly, the success of what is often called "the Canadian model" can partially be attributed to the country's continual need for labour, the flexibility of its job market, and the effectiveness of Canada's immigrant selection policies. In addition, Canada's geographical isolation, which limits illegal immigration and enables greater control of flows, has likely been a helpful factor for Canada. As a point of comparison, Spain faces significant migration pressure and a high volume of irregular immigration because of the proximity of its southern maritime borders—which also constitute external EU borders—to Africa; Italy similarly grapples with this issue. This reality creates a distinct set of concerns for countries' immigration programs, often calling increased attention to border control practices, to methods to deter unauthorized migration and control the underground economy, and to the viability of using regularization programs as migration management and immigrant integration strategies (see Carling 2007; Zapata-Barrero and de Witte 2007; Castles and Miller 2009, 111-112, 184-186; Maas 2010; Collett 2011b).

Even though Canada may have a greater advantage in this respect, the country's successes can also largely be explained by some of the basic principles Canada has put into practice in its management of immigration and integration, particularly during the latter part of the 20th century. Notable features of the Canadian model include immigrant access to core social programs, such as universal health care and education (which similarly, to varying degrees, is a right for immigrants in many European countries); a generally proactive approach to immigration; a policy of open but planned and controlled immigration; a focus on effective inclusion (versus exclusion), which advocates the relatively rapid acquisition of citizenship (in three years) and the possibility of immigrants' full participation in the social, political, and cultural life of the country; the continual institutional fight against racism and other forms of discrimination; the active promotion of pluralism as well as of social cohesion; a balance between decentralization and coordination in the institutional management of immigration, which requires co-operation between different levels of government (federal, provincial, municipal); and the promotion of strategies of transversality, participation, and negotiation between government administrations and community and social agencies (associations, businesses, cultural institutions, foundations, non-profit organizations, etc.), a set-up that also gives great importance to knowledge transfer between academics, policy-makers, and front-line community service workers. What is more, to a great extent, all of this is possible thanks to the fairly solid overarching management structure in place in Canada and the expectation that "reasonable" resources will be allocated to immigration planning, programs, and services.[8]

Rapidly changing new countries of immigration could learn a lot from these experiences. Models and innovations are needed. In the case of Spain, where large-scale international migration to the country is a relatively new phenomenon, the design of a comprehensive policy for the management of immigration is still at an early stage—a situation that is also true of other countries in Southern Europe. It must be taken into account, as stated earlier in this Introduction, that Spain did not pass its first immigration law, the Foreigners' Law (*Ley de Extranjería*), until 1985, just prior to, and as a necessity for, joining the European Economic Community (Arango 2000, 265; Maas 2010, 241). Furthermore, that law was mainly concerned with the control of immigration flows, rather than with aspects of immigrant integration. Since then, new immigration laws have come into effect, but the move toward establishing a more comprehensive national system for managing immigration—a policy framework that addresses the integration and rights of immigrants, as well as the management of flows and border security issues—really goes back only to 2000 (see Cachón 2002), if not, more concretely, to 2004 (Bruquetas-Callejo et al. 2011). Increasingly, efforts in Spain have been stepped up to establish wide-ranging management plans, the most recent national one being the 2011–2014 Second Strategic Plan for Citizenship and Integration (*II Plan Estratégico de Ciudadanía and Integración 2011–2014*) (MTAS 2011), which, in comparision with its 2007–2010 predecessor, places stronger emphasis on immigrants' social integration.

With respect to immigration policy developments in Spain, certain of the country's autonomous communities have distinguished themselves for the unique advances they have made. Catalonia, in particular, merits special mention. With its 2005–2008 Citizenship and Immigration Plan (*Pla de Ciutadania i Immigració 2005–2008*), the Government of Catalonia (*Generalitat de Catalunya*) presented a program that reflected a more extensive management approach and that expressly incorporated the common principles for integration approved by the Council of the European Union in 2004 (European Commission 2005, 4-5). Some specific objectives stated in the plan were the introduction of a "first welcome" protocol (e.g., in schools); the implementation of mediation, cultural awareness, community-building, anti-discrimination, and occupational training programs; and the application of interculturalist principles in the business sector (Generalitat de Catalunya 2005). The more recent 2009–2012 Citizenship and Immigration Plan (Generalitat de Catalunya 2010b) has gone even further in formulating, implementing, and strengthening concrete policies for integrating immigrants. Moreover, the Government of Catalonia's 2009 National Agreement on Immigration (*Pacte Nacional per a la Immigració*, Generalitat de Catalunya 2009), in effect until 2020, and the autonomous region's 2010 Integration Law (*Llei d'Acollida*, Generalitat de Catalunya 2010a) have been regarded as pioneering initiatives in matters of immigration and integration, not only among the various regions of Spain, but also throughout Europe.

The progress stemming from this improved planning and legislation is reflected in Spain's performance on the aforementioned international Migrant Integration Policy Index (MIPEX) for 2010 (see report by Huddleston and Niessen 2011). Out of 33 countries, Spain ranked ninth, with an overall score of 63 on a 100-point scale, as compared with Canada's third-place score of 72. Both Canada and Spain received high marks for their promotion of family reunification and immigrant economic integration (on the basis of legal access to the job market, workers' rights, and access to supports), and Spain also achieved favourable results—up from its 2007 scores—for its policies of offering improved security and rights to long-term residents.[9] However, while the criticisms bringing down Canadian scores were almost entirely related to the country's backlog for processing immigrant applications, the failure to extend voting rights to non-citizen residents (although access to nationality/citizenship itself was rated highly), and the lack of official opportunities for immigrants to inform integration policy through immigrant consultative bodies, Spanish integration policies did not score well in some particularly important and diverse areas, such as access to nationality, educational supports for newcomers, and anti-discrimination mechanisms. Like Canada, Spain also lost points for not providing immigrants with sufficient opportunities for official political participation. In this way, even though Spain has made advances in the realm of integrating immigrants, the country's policies evidently require further consideration and development.

Significantly, a country's economic circumstances can affect the best of intentions, and here is where it should be noted that the MIPEX measures policies, not necessarily real practices or outcomes. More time and research are usually required to assess how effectively immigration and immigrant integration policies have been implemented and whether they have led to the anticipated results. In recent years, Spain's serious financial crisis has had a significant impact on the projected funding for immigration; budgets were substantially reduced in 2010, and further reductions were in place as of 2011 and 2012. These budgetary cuts may ultimately make it difficult for certain integration initiatives to be put into action, in spite of the fact that this policy area has been acknowledged as an especially important one (see Arango and González 2009; Aja, Arango, and Oliver 2011; Collett 2011a, 16; Aja, Arango, and Oliver 2012, 14, 22).

The reality is that investment in immigration by the Spanish government is still very new. The country's administrative infrastructure for managing immigration continues to mature and be consolidated, requiring additional knowledge and strategies, adequate resources, and firm collaborative relationships. Nonetheless, national and regional governments in Spain, in order to adapt to a society that has dramatically changed in size and composition as a direct consequence of extensive international immigration, have, no doubt, given increased priority to the creation of coherent, comprehensive immigration policies and to the necessity of having a strong administrative management structure in place. Specifically, there has been the awareness in both Spain and Catalonia that it is crucial to equip public services (education, health care, culture, etc.) with new resources—although some of these investments are now being rethought by the Spanish government that assumed office on 21 December 2011—as well as to reinforce transversality and coordination between collaborating institutions.

Before concrete strategies or managing tools can effectively be implemented, however, basic principles or conceptions must lead the process. The transforming of public and political attitudes towards immigration and diversity in Europe seems to be a fundamental component of creating and bolstering immigration policies and integration programs that are more likely to lead to successful results. In this area, there are lessons to be learned from the other side of the Atlantic, namely Canada, where immigration tends to be seen more positively, both in economic and social terms (see Banting and Kymlicka 2010, 57-60; Reitz 2011). Notably, public support for immigration is considerably stronger in Canada than it is in the United States (ibid.; Canada FAAE 2009). While Americans, on the whole, demonstrate significant tolerance for cultural diversity and continue to take pride in being "a nation of immigrants," they do not exhibit the same preference for high levels of immigration (Citrin and Sides 2008; see also Rosner 2009) that Canadians have generally expressed. In the States, over the past two decades, a number of restrictionist immigration policies—both restrictive legislation and enforcement operations—have been introduced, reflecting, and also reinforcing, pronounced public anger over undocumented immigration and an increase in anti-immigrant sentiment, especially directed towards certain groups (ibid.; and in particular, see Massey and Pren 2012). Canadian attitudes to immigration, however, have been far less ambivalent.

Some recent evidence of the positive outlooks on immigration that prevail in Canada is provided by the Environics "Focus Canada" public opinion survey, conducted in November 2010, which showed that the majority of Canadians across the country are in favour of Canada's long-standing high levels of immigration (Reitz 2011, 1, 11). In his study analyzing this survey, Jeffrey G. Reitz states that "two important sources of [Canadian] pro-immigration sentiment are belief in immigration as an economic benefit and pride in Canadian multiculturalism" (2011, 1). Reitz points out that at the time of the survey, in the midst of "considerable international economic instability," "most Canadians—82.0 percent ... — agreed that immigration had a positive impact on the economy. Relatively few—25.0 percent—thought that immigrants would 'take away jobs' from other Canadians" (ibid., 13). This support is shown to be widely distributed across Canada, and Reitz mentions that even unemployed Canadians make some positive connections between immigration and the economy: Among this group, "68 percent see immigration as having a positive effect on the economy" (ibid.).

In contrast to countries like Canada—where immigration has been central to the project of nation-building and where immigrants have most often been conceptualized as, and traditionally admitted as, permanent residents and prospective citizens (see chapters 2, 4, 6, and 8 of this book)—European nations have generally not been inclined to promote a proactive vision of immigration, one that considers it as an opportunity and a contribution to society, rather than as a "problem" or threat (Arango 2006; Papademetriou 2006; Calavita 2007; Rodríguez-García 2010b; Reitz 2011, 3, 21). Many countries in Europe have continued to view immigration as a temporary phenomenon and to hold onto the 1960s/1970s notion of immigrants as visiting "guest workers" who will go back to their home countries. Such a model constructs immigrants' involvement with the host country as consisting of nothing more than the circumstantial contribution of labour; consequently, "foreigners" are not perceived as belonging to the society or as likely citizens (Bauböck et al. 2006; Rodríguez-García 2010b). The reality, though, is that immigrants do not exist only on the basis of labour-related and economic inputs: They generally maintain social and cultural attachments with their societies of origin, and they also generally form permanent attachments in the host society (Levitt and Glick Schiller 2004; Penninx 2005). As Swiss writer Max Frisch noted in the aftermath of the Second World War when speaking of the guest worker program in Switzerland, "We asked for workers, and we got people instead." The "immigrant-as-guest-worker" philosophy that has predominated in Europe, therefore, has impacted negatively on public perceptions of immigrants and on countries' immigrant integration initiatives.

That is not to say that temporary migration programs, which are sometimes practical for both immigrants and the receiving/recruiting country, may not have a place in countries' larger immigration plans—with the caveat that such programs ensure workplace protections, fair wages and contracts (including health coverage and fair opportunities for contract/permit renewal), and equitable treatment for immigrants. However, perpetuating the "temporary worker" model as a primary immigration strategy is more likely to lead to the (continued) segregation and exclusion of immigrants—not to mention, their economic exploitation and impoverishment—rather than to desirable outcomes of equity and social cohesion. Kitty Calavita, in her discussion of immigration laws and policies in Spain and Italy, states, "[L]aws that inhibit the full incorporation of immigrants ... by limiting their ability to put down permanent roots ensure their continued marginality" (2007, 10).[10] In that case, in order for countries to address more successfully the issue of immigrant integration and social inclusion, a more welcoming, less restrictive, and longer-term approach to immigration will be a crucial and preliminary step in the process.

It is particularly important to take this longer-term view into account in a context of global economic downturn like the one at present.[11] Spain, for example, has been hard hit by the recent financial crisis, and in the ensuing domestic environment of high unemployment (occurring at an even higher rate among Spain's immigrant population[12]), substantial cuts to government spending, and state-created "voluntary return" programs for non-EU immigrants, the country has seen some new restrictionist immigration policies that affect, for instance, family reunification and universal access to health care (see note 9) and has also experienced rising trends of economic nationalism (i.e., "Spanish jobs for Spanish workers")[13] and xenophobia.[14] Here, the report *Transatlantic Trends: Immigration 2010* (German Marshall Fund of the United States 2011) is especially pertinent. This report presented the findings from a large international public opinion survey about immigration and integration, and it aimed, in part, to evaluate the effect of the economic crisis (which began in 2008) on North American and European attitudes toward immigration; the countries surveyed included both Canada and Spain. The results showed that in 2010, about 50 percent of Europeans considered immigration to be more of a problem than an opportunity. In the case of Spain, 53 percent of Spaniards held this view. In contrast, Canadians were, by far, the least likely among all of the countries surveyed to hold this opinion (only 27 percent). Furthermore, 52 percent of the Spanish respondents believed that immigrants bring down the wages of citizens; for Europe overall, this percentage was 44 percent, and for Canada, it was much lower, at 30 percent. Moreover, only 33 percent of Spanish respondents agreed that immigrants help create jobs through setting up new businesses in the country. This number contrasted notably with the European average (43 percent) and greatly with the opinions expressed in Canada, where 67 percent of the survey respondents commented favourably on the job-creating potential of immigrants. Similarly, a separate research study by Cea D'Ancona and Valles (2009) found that almost half of the Spanish participants expressed a rejection of immigration. As a final example, the results of a 2011 large-scale survey conducted in Catalonia (CEO 2011) showed that 85 percent of respondents considered the current volume of immigration to Catalonia to be "excessive" or "too high"; 39 percent felt that immigrants take more than they give; and 41 percent regarded immigration, in general, as negative (for the case of Spain, see also Zapata-Barrero 2009).

Low levels of public support for immigration surely make matters of management even more challenging and complex for governments. No matter what public opinion may be, though, the reality is that immigration has been a fundamental engine of economic and social dynamism in Europe (OECD 2010a; Fargues et al. 2011, 1-8) and in Spain (Solé 2001; Sebastián 2006; Moreno and Bruquetas-Callejo 2011). A variety of national and international studies report that, on balance, immigrants contribute more to the state than they receive from it. Immigration is also shown to have brought more flexibility to the labour market, to have contributed to surpluses in public budgets, and to have improved individual wealth in the population as a whole (see, for instance, Moreno and Bruquetas-Callejo 2011). Moreover, in spite of the current economic crisis, which has led to high levels of unemployment among immigrant populations in Catalonia, Spain, and the European Union in general, all projections show that the European Union will need more immigrants and that immigration will continue to be key to long-term economic growth (Oliver 2006; CeiMigra 2010, 51; OECD 2010a; Pajares 2010; Aja, Arango, and Oliver 2011; Fargues et al. 2011; see also Borjas 1995).

Bearing this in mind, it becomes all the more important for countries to have a proactive, versus reactive, approach to immigration—a perspective of "triple gain," or win-win-win. That is, if the process is well managed, everybody will benefit: the native population, immigrants, and the societies—both of origin and of destination—as a whole. Above all, while controls over immigration are needed to protect both the receiving society and immigrants themselves, it is necessary for decision-makers and the public not to act guided by fear.

The Canadian positive outlook towards immigration, which underlies the country's policies, then, can serve as a much-needed example for Europe. As mentioned earlier, the majority view in Canada is that immigration is a phenomenon that gives more than it takes away. That is, immigration is more often seen as representing an essential contribution to the host society and as being a mutual opportunity, both economically and socially. Interestingly enough, immigration is almost never an election issue in Canada—various authors in this volume point out that all of the Canadian political parties advocate pro-immigration policies—and members of the native-born population generally support the country's multiculturalism policy (see Banting and Kymlicka 2010) as well as the rapid acquisition of citizenship for immigrants. Myer Siemiatycki further explains in his chapter of this book that "the government department responsible for immigration in Canada … is called 'Citizenship and Immigration Canada,'" which, he argues, is reflective of the nation-building and inclusive principles that for many years defined Canada's immigration policies (see chapter 8). As a point of comparison, it could be noted that in Spain, responsibility for the management of immigration lies with the Ministry of *Labour* and Immigration (an observation also made by Maas 2010, 241); moreover, immigrants—even permanent residents—typically have their documents processed through the discouragingly named Office for *Foreigners*.

The above arguments are not intended to imply that immigration should be regarded or promoted as a panacea to solve countries' population or labour shortage problems. Immigration can be one area of national investment among many. If countries like Spain worry about declining or stagnating birth rates, especially in light of an aging population, then it is necessary for governments to increase support measures for families, maternity leave, and child care. If a more qualified workforce is needed, then additional investments in education, training, and key labour sectors are required. Still, a positive conceptualization of and approach to immigration can complement these measures, can prevent immigration programs from breaking down, and can also help to bring about a more just and harmonious society. Such an outlook will involve a shift in thinking on the part of European nations and a break with the "*us* versus *them*" dichotomy that tends to surround immigration and that conceives of immigrants as only temporarily attached to the host society. Fear of jeopardizing "static" national (or regional) cultures will have to be supplanted by a view of societies as being in continual evolution—as being works-in-progress that benefit from the contribution of all of their inhabitants, who coexist, interact, and negotiate a shared civic community (see Rodríguez-García 2010b).

In summary, there is a growing awareness among European policy-makers and publics, especially in Southern Europe, that immigration is an event with profound structural effects and long-term implications. It is in this context that the Canadian immigration model—notable for its proactive, welcoming approach to immigration; comprehensive policies for managing immigration and diversity; and demonstrated successes in integrating immigrants, supporting ethnic diversity, and achieving overall social cohesion—may be instructive for countries seeking to overhaul, innovate, or expand their immigration programs.

PURPOSE AND STRUCTURE OF THE BOOK

As the Preface of this book mentions, this volume is a compilation of the revised and, where possible, updated contributions made by the Canadian presenters at the *Managing Immigration and Diversity in Quebec and Canada Forum*, a two-day symposium that took place in Barcelona in October 2008, organized by CIDOB (Barcelona Centre for International Affairs) and the Secretary of Immigration of the Government of Catalonia.[15] The Forum brought together Canadian and Spanish academic experts on immigration and diversity, policy-makers from Catalonia and other parts of Spain, representatives from Canadian and Quebecois government institutions, and Spanish government officials at both national and regional levels. The principal objective of the symposium was to learn from Canada's experiences, as well as from Quebec's specific experiences, of managing immigration and diversity given Canada's leadership role and significant successes in this area; the Forum had the ultimate goal of producing information that would help to bridge the research-policy divide in the immigration sphere. The basic rationale underlying the project has been explained in the previous section of this Introduction: Expert information and tested policies coming from a "classic" country of immigration like Canada are of vital importance to "new" countries of immigration like Spain, where governments are under tremendous pressure to respond to recent dramatic demographic changes affecting all societal levels; this pressure equally applies to regional governments, especially in the case of quickly changing high-immigration regions like Catalonia.

This current publication, then, derived from the aforementioned conference, is intended to be a body of comprehensive information on the Canadian immigration experience and, as such, to serve two main purposes. On the one hand, the book provides scholars, policy-makers, and other professionals working in the area of immigration and diversity in Europe, Spain, and Catalonia with access to valuable information that can help them to reflect on and positively redirect domestic immigration and social incorporation policies. On the other hand, this volume is designed as a resource to assist researchers, students, and practitioners engaged in work or study related to immigration in Canada or to comparative migration studies, for whose purposes it will be useful to have a thorough, up-to-date summary and analysis of topical Canadian and Quebecois immigration issues. Achieving a two-way benefit, therefore, is one of the fundamental aims of this transatlantic collaboration.

The book is divided into six parts, or sections, which correspond to six key thematic areas pertaining to immigration today: (1) government jurisdiction over immigration and diversity; (2) management of immigration flows; (3) immigration and the labour market; (4) citizenship, settlement, and the socio-cultural integration of immigrants; (5) linguistic policies and linguistic pluralism; and (6) partnerships and knowledge transfer between government, universities, and civil society. Many of these subjects are very closely connected; for example, management of flows cannot easily be separated from labour needs, and in the case of both Catalonia and Quebec, linguistic matters inevitably form a part of any discussion on immigrants' socio-cultural incorporation. Furthermore, it is not possible to analyze the linguistic sphere without referring to education and schooling, so this latter topic also ends up receiving considerable attention in this book.

Chapter 1 is an overview chapter. After that, each thematic part of the volume is comprised of two chapters: one that is dedicated to Canada as a whole, and one that addresses the specific case of the province of Quebec. The final section of the book, Part VI, which looks at knowledge transfer issues, follows this same format but has three chapters instead of two: one chapter that offers a national perspective, and two chapters that focus on provinces—one on Ontario, and the other on Quebec.

The decision to juxtapose Canadian and specifically Quebecois viewpoints is twofold. First, in order for this book to serve as a comprehensive reference on immigration in Canada, it endeavours to balance national and provincial experiences and to include the knowledge of both anglophone and francophone immigration experts in the country. Moreover, Quebec's "interculturalist" integration model and the province's agreements with the federal government concerning the management of immigration are distinct in many ways within Canada; for this reason, the Quebec chapters provide information and perspectives that might otherwise not be sufficiently conveyed.

The second reason is that the parallels between the Canadian province of Quebec and the Spanish autonomous community of Catalonia are of great interest to a Spanish audience, or, indeed, to readers from any country that is characterized by internal cultural pluralism. In considering what immigration models or policy features might work best in the Spanish or Catalan context, it is essential to note that Spain, like Canada, is a country that grapples with simultaneous processes of multiculturalism and what could be called "multinationalism." The former stems from significant immigration from diverse countries and continents, and the latter is the historical legacy left by the country's founding peoples, whose distinct cultures and traditions have given a national character to different regions. Just as Canada's cultural diversity across its provinces and territories has been shaped, at a fundamental level, by the country's Aboriginal, French, and English founders, Spain is a country composed of and administratively divided into historical autonomous "communities" or regions, some of which have their own officially recognized languages (e.g., Catalan, Basque, Galician), varied cultures, and a strong sense of "national" identity. For this reason, like Canada, Spain faces specific challenges in addressing pronounced regional concerns when contemplating immigration programs.

A political affinity has existed for a number of years in particular between Catalonia and Quebec (in fact, a Québec Government Office was established in Barcelona in 1999) because Catalonia's circumstances and its relationship with the central Spanish government are similar in many ways to the experience of Quebec within Canada. There are some important distinctions, of course, between the two regions: Catalonia proportionally absorbs a significantly higher percentage of Spain's immigrants—more than 20 percent, and more than any other region in Spain (INE 2011b)—than Quebec does within Canada. Quebec is home to close to 14 percent of Canada's foreign-born population, as compared with the province of Ontario, which is where almost 55 percent of the country's immigrants live (Chui, Tran, and Maheux 2007). Moreover, Catalonia has until recently been a relatively more prosperous region—with higher economic growth—within Spain than Quebec has been within Canada.[16] While these differences warrant mention, the similarities between the Spanish autonomous community and the Canadian province are especially noteworthy. Both Quebec and Catalonia are considered "distinct" societies in their respective countries because of unique historical, cultural, and linguistic developments, and both places have been governed by nationalist or sovereigntist political parties for significant periods in the course of their histories. With respect to language, both societies are deeply concerned with protecting and promoting dominant regional languages. In Quebec, French, not English, is recognized as the majority language, whereas Catalan is a co-official language of Catalonia, along with Spanish. Because Spanish researchers and politicians have noted the commonalities between Quebec and Catalonia, Quebec's specific perspectives and strategies regarding immigration and integration hold a special interest for scholars, policy-makers, and other professionals working in the field of immigration in Spain, in general, and in Catalonia, in particular. For all prospective readers of this book, however, whether audiences are international or Canadian, it is hoped that the Quebec chapters will provide greater insight into how immigration issues in Canada are coordinated between the various levels of government—that is, between central and provincial governments.

OVERVIEW OF THE CHAPTERS AND THEMES:
A TRANSATLANTIC DIALOGUE[17]

In the opening chapter by Jeffrey G. Reitz (*Managing Immigration and Diversity in Canada and Quebec: Lessons for Spain?*), he raises the question of whether there are lessons to be learned from Canada for Spain and other European countries. To begin with, the author identifies and discusses "the three pillars" of Canadian immigration policy: the point (or points) system used for the selection of skilled immigrants, a multiculturalism policy that recognizes cultural diversity and the rights of minority groups, and provincial autonomy. On examining these cornerstones of the Canadian model, Reitz contends, however, that in themselves, "their impacts are uncertain and limited." He also looks at some changing realities, emerging problems, and associated recent policy responses related to Canadian immigration. Ultimately, the author argues that more than the value of specific policies themselves, the most important feature of the Canadian immigration case is "the national commitment to the immigration project itself," the fact that Canadians, in general, support immigration and are convinced of its benefits. This attitude, according to Reitz, appears to be crucial to success.

Notably, in contrast to Europe, where most people think of immigrants as being temporary workers and short-term residents, rather than as forming part of the mainstream population, Canada has had the goal of using immigration to expand the country's economy, society, and numbers, an objective that is reflected in its very large-scale immigration program (proportionally, Canada takes in more immigrants than the United States and than most European countries). Therefore, in order for specific Canadian policy approaches such as skill- and education-based selection and multiculturalism even to be considered and tested in outside contexts, it would seem that such policies first must be based on the idea of offering permanent settlement to foreigners. This fact brings us back to Reitz's argument concerning the importance of seeing immigration as an opportunity for the country. The question, then, is how in Europe we might transform public and political attitudes towards immigration.

Part I of the book deals with *government jurisdiction over immigration and diversity*. In a context of federalism, it seems obvious that the effective management of public services requires both a degree of decentralization—with an efficient distribution of powers and duties between the different administrative and jurisdictional levels (i.e., federal, provincial or "autonomous,"[18] and municipal)—and shared guidelines and standards, in addition to high levels of coordination between different government levels.

With respect to the management of immigration, experience tells us that it is essential, for instance, to have sufficient autonomous or provincial input concerning immigration levels and the management of flows—that is, in the selection process itself, rather than only in the integration or post-arrival aspects. To decide upon, or at least to know with adequate time in advance, the quantitative aspects of immigrant flows is crucial to predicting and organizing the necessary resources for the newly arrived people and their families. To a great extent, immigrants' successful integration at all levels (workplace, educational, linguistic, social, etc.) will depend on the availability of these resources and services.

In Catalonia, the transfer of jurisdiction over certain aspects of immigration, described and implemented in the new *Statute of Autonomy* (passed in 2006), is still taking place. There are some areas, though, in which the process has already advanced considerably. For example, the hiring of temporary foreign workers (i.e., the initial authorization of work permits, so that the number of foreign workers entering the Catalan labour market in a given time period is controlled) is a jurisdictional domain that was effectively transferred to the Government of Catalonia in October 2009. This arrangement was a pioneering political measure in Spain. Nevertheless, the coordination of this area between the two levels of government administrations (central and autonomous), as well as the completion of the whole jurisdictional restructuring, which must take into account the general European Union directives to which Spain is subject, is still a big challenge.

Regarding jurisdictional responsibilities in Spain, the local level is also gaining an increasing amount of importance in the development of strategies for managing immigration and diversity, as cities and communities are where most of the social action takes place. It seems clear that in all immigrant-receiving countries, central and regional governments need to make sure that the local institutional network (e.g., municipal governments, neighbourhoods, schools, community and trade associations, etc.) is equipped with the necessary authority and resources for carrying out certain tasks.

The question then arises, How are immigration matters coordinated and legislated in Canada, a country with an advanced federal structure? In Peter S. Li's chapter (*Federal and Provincial Immigration Arrangements in Canada: Policy Changes and Implications*), he first reviews the fundamental historical stages of immigration policy development in Canada and then goes into greater depth about the legislative agreements on immigration that have existed in recent decades between federal and provincial governments and have served to grant provinces a greater say in the selection and settlement of immigrants. Particular attention is given in the chapter to the Provincial Nominee Program (PNP) that is now incorporated into most federal-provincial agreements.[19] Li explains how the program is used to give priority processing to a specified number of immigrant applicants based on provinces' differing economic and regional needs. Notably, the PNP admission criteria, which are established separately by each of the provinces, usually vary from the federal point system criteria used to admit most economic immigrants to Canada.

The PNP is an interesting prospect for the autonomous regions of Spain, as there has been enormous debate over the jurisdictional need for different regions to exercise a greater voice and more control regarding the number, type, and distribution of immigrants admitted to the country. However, while Li recognizes the legitimate need of provinces "to make regional decisions regarding the type of economic immigrants that best suit the development of provinces," he also warns of the possible negative consequences that could arise from the excessive regionalization of the selection system. He argues that the expansion of the PNP could lead to a "multi-tiered system of immigrant selection" that is unpredictable in its economic and labour market outcomes (namely because provincial nominees might move to other places in Canada), likely more costly and complex to administrate, and lacking in a national standard.

In Louise Fontaine's chapter on immigration arrangements affecting Quebec (*L'action du Québec en matière d'immigration*), she begins by indicating that the current policy framework in Quebec for the management of immigration is the Canada-Quebec Accord. This agreement between the governments of Canada and Quebec was signed in 1991, and it grants Quebec exclusive jurisdiction over the selection of immigrants to the province, while the federal government retains sole control over admitting immigrants. The author points out that Quebec is the only province in Canada that has the power to determine both the volume and the composition of permanent immigration to the province. Fontaine explains that Quebec also has jurisdiction over the creation and implementation of linguistic and socio-economic integration programs for permanent residents in the province, a task for which the Quebec government receives funding from the federal government. When discussing the province's services for immigrant integration, Fontaine specifically mentions Quebec's objective of promoting the "francization" (*francisation*) of immigrants residing in Quebec and highlights the province's establishment of diverse programs and courses that facilitate immigrants' knowledge and use of the French language. Quebec's socio-cultural goals in this respect are similar in nature to those of Catalonia, where government services for immigrants are designed to encourage the everyday use of Catalan, not Spanish, among the region's inhabitants. However, with reference to matters of linguistic integration, an important difference between Quebec and Catalonia is that many immigrants now arrive in Quebec already knowing French (see chapters 5 and 7), as the province, through its ability to select most immigrants destined for Quebec, is able to attract and select immigrants from countries where French is a first or second language. Clearly, Catalonia could not have this same advantage, regardless of what jurisdictional arrangements may evolve, seeing that Catalan, with very few exceptions, is a language that is spoken only locally (including in Valencia, the Balearic Islands, Andorra, and, to a lesser degree, the Pyrénées-Orientales or Rousillon region of southern France).

Part II of this book examines the *management of immigration flows* in Canada and Quebec. Immigration management is a critical issue because it inherently determines many other aspects of a country's or region's immigration policy, and, in turn, it affects social incorporation outcomes.

Since migratory movement very often has an economic basis (i.e., the supply and demand of labour), the management of immigration flows is intimately related to the labour market and, consequently, to policies surrounding the hiring of immigrants and their incorporation into the workforce. Decisions have to be made regarding whether to promote a policy of admitting workers as permanent residents (or, at least, as permanent-residents-in-waiting) or whether to adopt or reinforce a program of recruiting temporary workers, whose duration of residence is intended to be determined by their (short-term) work contracts. As stated earlier, many countries in Europe have continued to hold onto the 1960s/1970s conception of immigration as a temporary phenomenon. However, using this restrictive approach as a primary immigration management strategy has led to a variety of problems, such as the socio-economic segregation of immigrants and relatively poor integration outcomes; the separation of families; the later need for mass regularization (amnesty) programs; and difficulties for immigrants in adapting to changing labour market needs.

It seems that an effective policy of managing immigration flows—for a variety of pragmatic as well as humanitarian reasons—needs to have a longer-term and bigger-picture outlook. An important policy element to consider is the promotion, rather than discouragement, of family migration. Family immigration or reunification is a crucial aspect of the whole migratory process because the family unit/network influences all levels of immigrant social incorporation (economic, social, cultural, etc.). Maintaining the immigrant family unit has traditionally been a central principle governing the Canadian management of immigration flows; accordingly, the volume of family immigrant admissions (both under the Family Class and as dependants of Economic Class immigrants) has always been very significant. Actions announced in late 2011 by Canada's current government suggest, however, that the sponsoring of parents and grandparents to come to Canada as permanent residents may be made more difficult in the future, although temporary family reunification will be expedited (for eligible applicants) through the newly created "Parent and Grandparent Super Visa," which allows these family members to stay in Canada for up to two years at a time and is valid for up to ten years (CIC 2011c; CIC n.d.-b). The need to keep families together to improve the well-being and socio-economic outcomes of immigrants has also received greater attention in Spain in recent years and should continue to be viewed as a priority area for future policy-making. Notably, while the fourth reform to Spain's Foreigners' Law, approved in October 2009, made it easier for spouses/partners and adult children—that is, nuclear family members—to immigrate to Spain, this amendment also limited family reunification with respect to bringing over parents/grandparents and other relatives.

Furthermore, the management of immigrant flows is directly linked to immigrant selection criteria, which, in turn, are closely related to labour market considerations. The advantages of employing selection standards that call for high levels of human capital are well known, since a more skilled and educated population not only is more adaptable to changing labour market conditions but also increases the competitiveness of the workforce and benefits the country's economic growth. Nonetheless, an extremely restrictive policy that recruits only highly qualified immigrants may leave other fundamental labour niches with a shortage of workers.

Finding a balance between using a quota system, as has been used until now in Spain, and employing a criteria-driven point system, as has been used in Canada for the admission of (federally selected) economic immigrants, is one of the challenges that Spain currently faces.

Finally, another important principle to be applied toward the management of flows is the coordination of efforts between governments of sending and receiving countries: working together to shape practices that are guided by concerns for co-development, equality, and the respect for human rights. This area of focus includes how best to tackle the problem of illegal immigration and the associated situations of immigrant exploitation, an issue that particularly impacts on Spain because of its extensive maritime borders and its geographical proximity to the African continent. Jeffrey Reitz points out in his chapter that illegal immigration is also becoming more visible in Canada.

In examining the management of immigration flows to Canada and/or Quebec, both chapters in this section of the volume indicate the comprehensive planning involved in the process and the coordination that takes place between the different levels of government. These management approaches appear to be especially important in the current global context of great acceleration, diversification, and complexity of flows. It should be noted that the admission of immigrants to Canada on humanitarian grounds (i.e., refugees, displaced persons, asylum seekers) receives some discussion in this section of the book, as well as in the chapters by Peter Li, Louise Fontaine, Yves Poisson, Jack Jedwab, and Myer Siemiatycki.

In their chapter (*Managing International Migration: The Canadian Case*), Monica Boyd and Naomi Alboim begin by characterizing Canada as a "nation that was forged ... by immigration," where the current migration inflows remain very important and contribute greatly to the country's population growth. The authors point out the change in the national origins of migration flows to Canada over the past several decades and explain that the significant shift to non-European, especially Asian, source countries is related in large part to changes to Canadian immigration policy that took place in the 1960s. As observed earlier in this Introduction, a diversification of origin countries is now also the pattern in Spain, where some of the top immigration source countries presently include Romania, Morocco, Ecuador, China, Brazil, Poland, and Pakistan (INE 2011a, 2011b).

After describing how Canadian immigration legislation has evolved over the past 100 years, Boyd and Alboim draw attention to how Canada's annual immigration numbers have been determined and to changes in the socio-professional characteristics of immigrants entering Canada. First, more permanent residents are now admitted under economic criteria (i.e., mostly in the federal "skilled worker" category, with principal applicants assessed according to Canada's point system), rather than under the Family Class. Second, whereas previous immigration policy in

Canada had emphasized economic immigrant selection based on specific occupational demand, more recent legislation (prior to an amendment made in 2008) has generally placed increased importance on the human capital (skill and educational level, as well as official language ability) of immigrant applicants. These assets possessed by successful applicants, however, are frequently undervalued and underutilized once immigrants actually arrive in Canada—a paradox that is discussed by the authors. Boyd and Alboim also note that an exception towards this trend of admitting economic immigrants with higher human capital has occurred in the case of certain immigrants who enter through Provincial Nominee Programs (see also Peter Li's chapter); these fast-tracked applicants include greater numbers of immigrants with lower educational attainment and skill levels, and the authors argue that these programs, for which "there is no overall national framework," may prove to create longer-term difficulties for the labour market incorporation of these immigrants. The authors further explain modifications as of 2008 to immigration legislation and policy and allude to extremely recent and still developing policy changes—both of which place a stronger emphasis on current labour market needs and the role of employers. Such reforms to Canada's immigrant selection system may yet again shift the composition (educational, occupational, etc.) of economic immigrants to the country.

The latter part of this chapter is devoted to outlining and critically analyzing some of the relatively new initiatives in the management of immigration at the federal level, namely the expanded power granted to the Minister of Immigration to determine priorities for the processing of applications; the greater involvement of provinces in immigrant selection and settlement (although federally funded settlement programs in all provinces except Quebec will return to being managed by the federal government); the increasing reliance on and admission of temporary workers; and the recruitment of permanent residents from temporary workers and from international students graduating from Canadian post-secondary institutions. The chapter makes it clear that immigration policy and management strategies are variable.

While Boyd and Alboim mention that certain established temporary worker programs in Canada tend to be tightly controlled, thus making it difficult for these employees to stay on illegally, given the trend of rising temporary admissions to Canada, the country surely faces potentially growing numbers of immigrants with illegal status. It will be interesting to see how Canada deals with this likely situation, a problem that is much more common and at the forefront of political debate in other countries, including Spain.

In his chapter (*Le Gouvernement du Québec et la gestion de l'immigration : un spectateur passif devenu un acteur de premier plan*), Gérard Pinsonneault provides an overview of the historical, socio-demographic, and political specificities of Quebec within the Canadian context. He explains how both population and provincial identity factors have impacted on Quebec's particular relationship with immigration and on the province's increased concern with developing and managing its own immigration plan. In discussing the Canadian federal government's devolution of more powers to Quebec with respect to the management of immigration and integration, a process of transference that began in the early 1970s, Pinsonneault details the terms of the (still current) 1991 Canada-Quebec Accord and assesses the outcomes and benefits that such agreements have had for Quebec. It can be noted that, on the one hand, the province's considerations regarding immigrant selection, as well as the general characteristics of post-1971 migratory flows to Quebec, are consistent in many ways with the overall trends for Canada described by Boyd and Alboim. Quebec's experience similarly has included, for example, changing emphases in the selection of economic immigrants; debate over whether immigrant selection criteria should prioritize more immediate labour market needs or human capital factors, the latter of which may give immigrants greater long-term adaptability; growing importance given to temporary labour migration (see also chapter 3); and a significant diversification of immigrant origins, with many more immigrants to the province coming from non-European countries. On the other hand, the author makes it clear that Quebec's considerable control over its immigration program in the past few decades has produced specific results that uniquely meet the province's needs and objectives. One of the aspects that has been crucial to Quebec's relative success in managing its immigration flows, Pinsonneault ultimately argues, is the province's ability, based on its own point system, to give priority selection/admission to (qualified) immigrant applicants from the international Francophonie. In doing so, Quebec is able to maintain its French-speaking majority, and the immigrants selected are more likely to become better integrated into francophone Quebecois society and, therefore, to continue residing in Quebec, rather than moving to other predominantly anglophone Canadian provinces.

As a point of comparison, while the inter-regional geographical mobility of immigrants in Spain has not been a widely studied area, curiously, language appears to be a less significant—or, at least, a less evidently significant—determinant than in the Canada-Quebec context. There is little documentation concerning immigrants' expressed preferences—with regard to matters of linguistic and cultural integration—for settling in "exclusively" Spanish-speaking regions of Spain rather than in autonomous communities with distinct regional languages (e.g., Catalonia). However, Spain's 2007 National Immigrant Survey (ENI) offers some insights on this subject. As discussed by Antonio Caparrós, ENI data on immigrant workers living in the country indicate that "speaking Spanish fluently is not a relevant variable … that determines the probability of geographical mobility" (Caparrós 2010, 14-15). In other words, immigrant workers who speak Spanish, whether as a first or an additional language, and those who do not *both* move within Spain. And certainly, as previously explained, Catalonia is an area in Spain in which very large numbers of immigrants have settled; for that matter, so is the autonomous community of Valencia (INE 2011b), a region that also has a co-official language (Valencian, which is very similar to Catalan). Furthermore, four countries that have Spanish as an official language—Ecuador, Bolivia, Colombia, and Peru—are included among the top ten source countries for immigrants living in Catalonia (Idescat 2011). Some of the more observable, and often interconnected, determinants, then, of inter-regional mobility in Spain—which are frequently related to immigrants' economic integration—are wages (i.e., higher wage opportunities, balanced against the cost of moving, may make inter-regional migration more likely); age and marital status (movement is more likely among younger, unmarried immigrants); and education and country of origin (the probability of migration within Spain is higher among more educated immigrants and among immigrants from less developed countries) (Caparrós 2010).

Part III of this volume focuses on the *economic integration of immigrants and their incorporation into the labour market*, a topic that is very much related to the previous section on the management of immigration flows. The labour issue is of vital importance to immigration research since it is commonly the motive underlying migratory movement and it affects many other dimensions of immigrant incorporation.

The employment issues for countries are not always the same, but there are often overlapping areas of concern—some of which may be interrelated—such as evaluating whether immigrant applicants' skills and qualifications match the labour market needs of the country of destination; finding a balance between the selection of higher-skilled and less-skilled workers and determining the extent to which admissions of economic immigrants should be based on high human capital; working towards developing a more efficient system for the recognition of foreign-acquired credentials; establishing an appropriate balance between the recruitment/admission of permanent residents and temporary migrants; and successfully managing the entry and departure of temporary foreign workers.

It is greatly hoped that the economic aspects of immigration planning will also take into account equity issues. Feasible but fair work-related immigration management policies tend to combine principles of social justice (traditionally championed by left-of-centre political parties) with a consideration of labour market needs (traditionally advocated by right-of-centre political parties). The goal of creating fair conditions for all workers involves, for example, protecting their rights; fighting against discrimination in the job market, which in part requires identifying whether certain groups face greater barriers to employment; and preventing the conditions (in terms of wages, hours, safety standards, etc.) that exploit and marginalize immigrants (see Calavita 2005). Given the reality of free-market tendencies that increasingly take advantage of opportunities for cheaper labour, it cannot be counted upon that workplace conditions and practices will be equitable for immigrants joining the workforce in the host country. Temporary immigrants in low-skilled occupations are likely particularly vulnerable in this respect. Governments and employers should be encouraged to see that ensuring workplace protections and equitable social and economic treatment for all immigrant workers, whether temporary or permanent, is not only necessary because of evident humanitarian and ethical concerns, but also such policies and regulations surely are more likely to contribute to generally desired societal outcomes: better immigrant integration and improved social cohesion.

It is important to emphasize that many of the problems in the management of immigration originate in policies that concentrate only on short-term labour needs. The following example from the Spanish milieu illustrates some possible consequences that can arise from this type of planning. Spain's primary strategy for managing immigration flows has been a quota system, a policy that considers national and regional labour needs and sets a quota for the number of work permits (usually of fixed duration, though sometimes renewable) that can be issued to non-EU nationals. Foreign workers are then recruited and admitted to Spain exclusively on the basis of having a preliminary job offer/work contract in a given occupation. The viability of this system for managing immigration, however, has been called into question in recent years. In the current context of severe economic crisis and the decline of the real estate and housing market, many of Spain's immigrants who had been specifically recruited to work in sectors such as construction—formerly a booming industry—have become unemployed (see note 12). To address the problem of the very large number of legal immigrants (i.e., foreign-born persons with residence rights or valid permits) without jobs, the Spanish government launched the Voluntary Return Program in November 2008. In coordination with the main origin countries of unemployed immigrants in Spain (importantly Ecuador), the Spanish government has offered these immigrants voluntary repatriation to their countries, which would require renunciation of Spanish residence rights, in exchange for travel arrangements and two lump-sum payments of unemployment benefits—a type of "departure bonus." (It should be noted that the Voluntary Return Program applies only to workers who are eligible for unemployment benefits.) However, these types of programs have had only modest results (IOM 2010, 162; López and Davis 2011). Many immigrants have not wanted to return, fearing being back in a labour market in which their chances for employment and social mobility might be even more restricted, especially in dollarized economies, such as that of Ecuador; the Ecuadorean government has even offered microcredits as an incentive for immigrants to return. Furthermore, economic factors are not the only ones to be considered when immigrants contemplate returning to their country of origin, since their migratory projects generally involve the objective of social mobility not only in the labour sphere, but also in areas such as education and health, among others, especially for their children. Although the work contracts that brought immigrants to Spain may have been conceived with a time limit in mind, that intent does not mean that the immigrants who came to Spain arrived with the idea that they would stay only temporarily—that is, until the work in question was completed. The alternative for these immigrant populations, then, if they are to avoid the usually exploitative types of jobs that can sometimes still be found in the informal economy, is to find work in other labour sectors; but this will require significant government investment to improve skills assessment, retraining, and labour reinsertion programs in Spain. Partly because of the unenthusiastic response among immigrants to the financial incentives of voluntary repatriation programs, Spain and other European countries are now considering alternative measures (Ratha and Mohapatra 2009). In short, many of the problems that have resulted have their origin in the lack of broader and longer-term planning approaches—significantly, the failure to consider both the country's and immigrants' future needs and larger goals; the limited methods used for the selection/admission of immigrants and the country's fairly routine, and arguably ambiguous, practice of issuing temporary-but-renewable work/residence permits; and the failure to contemplate and commit to the longer-term economic and social integration of immigrants.

The perspective of a comprehensive and long-term policy approach generally seems to have been the one that has prevailed until now in Canadian society. However, many contributors to this book observe that the economic integration of Canada's immigrants has increasingly become a weaker point in the Canadian record. Notably, this situation has occurred despite the fact that recent immigrants to Canada often have university degrees, as Canada's selection grid has awarded more points to applicants with higher educational levels. The labour market and economic integration of immigrants is, therefore, also an area in which Canada is re-evaluating its planning and policies to date (including its selection policies) and looking to address current failings. In devising and implementing changes in this area, Canada would be well advised to take heed of the policy shortcomings of other countries. Likewise, countries that have taken a keen interest in Canada's point system, in general, and in the country's focus on human capital selection criteria, in particular, will be paying attention to new labour-related immigration strategies proposed by Canada, as well as to their outcomes.

In his chapter on the economic dimensions of immigrant integration in Canada (*Integrating Immigrants into the Canadian Labour Market: Findings from Public Policy Forum Research and Activities*), Yves Poisson identifies some of the specific challenges that both the Canadian immigration system itself and new immigrants to Canada are now facing. First, the author presents Canada as a place where immigration has been integral to nation-building and to the labour force growth of the country. He also looks at Canadians' attitudes—"mostly positive"—towards immigration. Poisson's chapter then concentrates on some of the shortcomings of the immigration system and on how these difficulties are being addressed. He notes that there has been a very large backlog of immigration applications, which until recently "had to be processed in the order in which they were received," and he comments, too, on the long processing times for applications. The author also argues that a crucial area that is impacting on the immigration program in Canada is the "lack of connection between applicants' skills and labour market needs." In terms of recent immigrants' degree of economic success in Canada, Poisson, along with other authors in this book, explains how immigrants' foreign-acquired education and lack of Canadian work experience, as well as other factors, can hinder their employment opportunities in Canada. Poisson discusses how these various problems have led the Canadian government to introduce new policy measures, which include a large increase in the number of temporary foreign workers admitted to the country; the expansion of Provincial Nominee Programs, which allow for the priority processing of immigrant applicants whose occupational skills are particularly needed in a region; the development of a Canadian Experience Class, which provides permanent residence opportunities for international students completing degrees in Canada and for temporary foreign workers with significant Canadian work experience; and greater powers given to the Minister of Immigration to determine which applications should be prioritized for processing—subjects that are also examined in this volume by Monica Boyd and Naomi Alboim (see chapter 4).

With respect to newly arrived immigrants to Canada, there is a concern that their economic integration has been poorer than that of previous immigrant cohorts. Poisson explains that even though these newcomers, when selected on the basis of human capital criteria, have a high level of educational attainment—proportionally higher than that of the Canadian-born population—recent immigrants have been experiencing significant problems of access to the Canadian labour market. Their unemployment rates are higher, and even when they do find jobs, they often must work in occupations that are "negative[ly] mismatch[ed]" to their educational backgrounds and earning capacity. This reality has led to higher levels of poverty among recently arrived immigrants and to a widening gap between the earnings of immigrants and the Canadian-born population.

In considering such problems and reflecting on Canadian immigration policy, Poisson stresses the need for an improved system for assessing and recognizing foreign credentials. He points to the importance of having better pre-migration screening of immigrants' educational/skill certifications (to determine the equivalency to Canadian standards) and language abilities (i.e., level of proficiency in English and/or French). Such measures would help to minimize the underutilization of immigrants' skills and training and would also create more realistic expectations for newcomers to Canada. The author additionally recommends continuing to invest in "employment assistance and bridging programs," which address educational or work experience gaps and thus help immigrants to integrate more quickly into the labour market. Poisson further suggests that the selection criteria for economic immigrants could be modified to "better reflect the labour market needs of receiving communities"; that the engagement of employers and communities in the immigration planning process, both of which hold important knowledge about "local realities," might contribute positively to the labour market (and overall) integration of immigrants; and that success in integrating immigrants "requires multi-stakeholder coordination at the local level."

Jack Jedwab (*The Economic Integration of Immigrants in Canada and the Quebec Difference*) explores in his chapter whether the economic integration of immigrants in Canada and Quebec "can be deemed a success." He reiterates the concern that recent waves of immigrants, who proportionally have higher levels of education than both the immigrant groups that preceded them and the Canadian-born population, seem to be encountering greater labour market integration difficulties than earlier immigrant cohorts. He proceeds to assess the economic condition of immigrants by providing both quantitative and qualitative data. In presenting and analyzing statistical evidence, Jedwab pays particular attention to two areas: (1) the educational attainment of foreign-born and Canadian-born populations in relation to, first, their respective rates of unemployment and, second, their earnings/income; and (2) differences in both educational level and employment rates between white and visible minority[20] populations as well as between different visible minority groups themselves. Examining the data, the author discusses perceptible "disparities in levels of employment" between immigrant and Canadian-born populations that have similar levels of education, observing, too, how certain visible minority groups in Canada appear to be particularly "vulnerable to situations of unemployment." He also looks at the widening income gap between Canadian-born workers and recent immigrants, the latter of whom are more prone to be underemployed. Jedwab, nevertheless, avoids offering easy explanations as to the causes of employment and earnings disparities, and he notes that the income gaps are less pronounced in certain regions of Canada. The author, like Yves Poisson, identifies the barriers posed by issues of foreign credential recognition and the requisite for Canadian work experience, together which may impede new immigrants from finding employment in their professional fields, and his chapter seems to suggest as well that societal discrimination may play a partial role in the difficulties that certain groups face in accessing employment. However, Jedwab, in searching for explanations, also considers other factors, such as the previously mentioned mismatch between recent immigrants' skills/training and current labour market needs; immigrants' lack of "a network of contacts" in Canada, which may make it harder for them to find work; and the amount of time that achieving economic integration really takes.

In spite of all of these difficulties concerning the labour market integration of new immigrants, Jedwab argues that the empirically observed economic conditions of immigrants are not the only indicator of their well-being in Canada. He draws attention to "the qualitative dimension of the immigrant experience," presenting evidence from a longitudinal survey (2001–2005) that found that life satisfaction levels are, in fact, quite high among many newcomers to the country. The results of the survey, Jedwab contends, provide important information about the overall integration and adjustment process of recent immigrants to Canada.

The second part of Jedwab's chapter shifts its focus to the province of Quebec, looking at how immigrants in this province have fared in terms of their economic/labour force integration. The author first discusses Quebec's considerable authority over immigrant selection and integration, highlighting the province's commitment over the years to increasing the percentage of immigrant arrivals who possess knowledge of French. He then shows that in spite of Quebec's assumption of these responsibilities, the economic and labour market outcomes for immigrants in this province have not been better than immigrant outcomes in other parts of Canada. In fact, study findings presented by the author indicate that Quebec's performance in this respect has been significantly poorer than Ontario's and that Quebec's visible minority immigrant populations in particular are facing challenges in finding employment. While Jedwab mentions that some recent improvements have been reported in Quebec with regard to immigrants' access to the labour market, his chapter suggests that it will nonetheless be important for Quebec to better understand and address the situations of unemployment and underemployment affecting its immigrants, especially given the province's plans to maintain higher annual immigration levels.

Part IV of this book is dedicated to the subject of *citizenship, settlement, and socio-cultural integration*. This is a key issue at present, particularly in new countries of immigration, many of which are experiencing not only increased immigration numbers but also higher levels of ethnocultural diversity owing to the much wider range of immigrant source countries. These recent countries of immigration previously had minimal policy provisions in place for the social integration of immigrants, who were generally viewed as short-term residents, existing outside the mainstream society.

With respect to this topic, a first point to be made is that if an immigration program is intended to foster social inclusion (and, evidently, not all programs are), it must enable immigrants to access basic social services and also to exercise their rights and responsibilities—most often, through the acquisition of permanent residence or citizenship. At an individual level, this means that immigrants would have equal access to resources such as education, health care, housing, work, and, in the case of citizens, political participation and representation. By extension, certain cultural rights of groups might also be included, provided that these rights do not violate the laws of the country.

Notably, traditional perspectives of mobility, especially in Europe, have focused on the purely individual and economic aspects of migration. The "guest worker" framework, discussed earlier in this Introduction, has created a logic that conceives of immigration entirely as an economic exchange and overlooks the fact that immigrants do not exist solely on the basis of their circumstantial contribution of labour. Furthermore, a crucial oversight in limited conceptualizations of migration is the failure to recognize that all *immigrants* are at the same time *emigrants*. And this fact implies, to a greater or lesser extent, the maintenance of cultural (territorial, familial, identity) bonds—that is, the existence of multi-dimensional affiliations/identities on local and global scales. Countries that are beginning to switch from policies of temporary immigration to longer-term approaches, the latter of which normally take into account the social and cultural aspects of immigrant integration, are opening themselves to the possibility that immigrants can identify with the host country and the society as a whole, but without relinquishing other ethnocultural identity affiliations; this perspective is sometimes arrived at through having observed certain shortcomings of assimilationist models (see Rodríguez-García 2010b).

Generally speaking, the current trend seems to be toward formulating management models that, to varying degrees and as adapted to the particularities of each country or region, reconcile cultural *diversity* with social *cohesion*. In other words, the attempt is to grant immigrants and minorities the same civil rights and obligations and the same socio-economic opportunities as the majority, and, at the same time, to value diversity, but with an approach that is mindful and critical of fragmented societies with "closed," segregated communities and also of unequal power relations, which may occur both between and within groups. While a great amount of debate still exists in this area, there is increasing consensus that the management of diversity in democratic societies should be an interculturalist process of bidirectional adaptation, or of mutual accommodation; it should be a process that promotes the full participation and civic engagement of, as well as the social exchange between, all members of society, beyond that of mere recognition and coexistence, in turn forming a plural and cohesive civic community.[21]

The Canadian case, as observed by onlookers as well as by the Canadian contributors to this volume, appears to have largely achieved this reconciliation of respect and support for plurality within a framework of national unity. The state is committed to playing an active role in the defence of cultural diversity and the rights of minorities, while it simultaneously promotes common "Canadian" values that encourage civic equality, a sense of shared belonging (reinforced by the relatively easy access to Canadian citizenship for immigrants), and the fight against discrimination. Significantly, the Canadian policy of multiculturalism[22] (1971), the first of its kind, and the complementary *Canadian Charter of Rights and Freedoms* (1982) together draw attention not only to the protection of ethnocultural differences, but also to the rights of many groups who have historically been discriminated against, whether on the basis of sex, sexual orientation, or disability, among other factors. Respect for diversity of all types, therefore, becomes a central value-and-practice that unifies citizens and contributes to social cohesion in Canada.

Across Canada, however, it appears that some different approaches, based on regional needs and circumstances, are taken to the socio-cultural integration of immigrants and minorities. This situation is true, too, of Spain, which is also a country characterized, on the one hand, by internal cultural and linguistic pluralism (in the cases, for example, of the historical autonomous communities of Catalonia, the Basque Country, and Galicia) and, on the other, by realities of multiculturalism, which result from international immigration. Within differing national and historical contexts, Catalonia and Quebec are similarly concerned with establishing immigrant integration policies that balance these distinct cultural considerations. Quebec, which respects and manages ethnocultural diversity around a model of "interculturalism"—rather than "multiculturalism" per se—has put a strong emphasis on achieving integration and social cohesion through French language acquisition, just as Catalonia, in its project of immigrant incorporation, has emphasized the learning of its regional language, Catalan.

Regional approaches and preoccupations in Canada are also highlighted by the recent and ongoing debate that has taken place particularly in Quebec surrounding the "reasonable accommodation" of religious and cultural diversity (discussed in depth in Maryse Potvin's chapter of this book). Indeed, the accommodation of cultural difference is a topical issue for all of Spain and Europe—where some very controversial and restrictive measures have been taken[23]—and so the manner in which both Quebec and Canada at large have experienced and continue to manage these questions is of significant interest to Europeans. While outside audiences could possibly get sidetracked by the widely reported (and media-hyped) social antagonism generated in Quebec by the subject of reasonable accommodation, the provincial government's formal appointment of an investigatory panel in 2007, the "Bouchard-Taylor Commission," to consider the input of a very large and diverse cross-section of participants, as well as some of the actual recommendations offered by the commission's report (e.g., the promotion of an "open secularism," in which the state itself is religiously neutral, but the lawful religious expressions of members of the society are permitted to enter into the public sphere or mainstream), can hold valuable lessons for other countries or regions looking to deal with inter-ethnic tensions.[24] Although the debate in Quebec and in Canada over the accommodation of diversity (principally religious diversity) continues and has even escalated in certain respects, there nonetheless seems to be a more dialogic process in place in *all* of Canada regarding this subject;[25] it could be argued that the country's expectation of dialogue around specific "accommodation" challenges, together with the high degree of importance that has been placed on protecting all forms of individual rights, has an impact on the public and political mood and somehow tempers legislative and policy decisions. We do not see in Canada the same kind of tendency towards adopting "absolute" or broad restrictive measures that we do in Europe, and the complex question of how best to foster equality and inclusion in society is often evaluated from a wider variety of perspectives than it is in European contexts.

Issues surrounding cultural diversity in Canadian society and the integration of immigrants in Canada and Quebec are further taken up and explained by the authors contributing to this section of the book. In his chapter (*The Place of Immigrants: Citizenship, Settlement, and Socio-cultural Integration in Canada*), Myer Siemiatycki defines Canada as a "classic country of immigration" and first provides a historical overview of the country's changing immigration model. Beginning with a critical discussion of the encounter 400 years ago between European colonizers and Canada's Aboriginal peoples, an encounter that had many devastating effects for the latter population, Siemiatycki then identifies three distinct approaches to immigration and diversity that Canada has adopted in its post-Confederation history: first (1867–1960s), a restrictive, assimilationist policy that admitted almost exclusively white, Christian, and, as much as possible, British immigrants; second (1960s–2000), a point system approach—which relied on human capital criteria, as opposed to race and nationality considerations, for the selection of immigrants—and a complementing national policy of multiculturalism; and third (2000–the present), a "more market-oriented approach to immigration," which increasingly relies on temporary foreign workers; this most recent epoch is also characterized by greater suspicion toward certain immigrant groups and by stricter security measures.

Siemiatycki then determines and explains six factors that have influenced the cultural and structural integration of immigrants into Canadian society: "immigrant settlement patterns; immigrant settlement programs; Canada's multiculturalism policy; human rights protection; Canada's citizenship policy; and inclusive public institutions." (A notable example given by the author of the last-mentioned item is Canada's, particularly

Toronto's, extensive public library system, which provides many useful resources and services specifically for immigrants. Such a development of the library system could be a worthwhile undertaking for different regions of Spain.) In his discussion of these key elements, Siemiatycki looks at how changing policies and attitudes, especially the introduction of multiculturalism as an official policy, have transformed national conceptions about immigrant integration: This process has become a "two-way street," which requires the mutual adaptation of both immigrants and the native-born (as well as naturalized) population.[26] The author also emphasizes that the promotion of citizenship acquisition in Canada is a vital aspect of encouraging immigrant inclusion, as becoming a citizen fosters a sense of belonging to the country and also makes political participation possible. While Siemiatycki draws attention to Canadians' "favourable attitude towards immigration" and the relative ease for immigrants in Canada to "[retain] ancestral homeland culture," both factors of which undoubtedly contribute to better immigrant integration and greater social cohesion, he also points out the fact that a multiculturalist approach to diversity does not mean granting social permission to particular cultural or religious practices that may compromise other human rights and/or be considered contrary to Canadian law. He gives the example here of how Sharia law, in addition to other religious-based laws, was rejected by the Ontario government as an option for arbitrating family law disputes.

The points that Siemiatycki makes about Canadian multiculturalism— its significant contribution to fostering immigrant inclusion; and Canada's constitutional ability, as a democratic society, to contain elements of diversity that do not find universal (i.e., majority) resonance within the multicultural civil sphere—are important ones for a European audience (see Rodríguez-García 2010b; see also Alexander 2006). In Europe, multiculturalism has often been connoted with its most negative and radical manifestations and has been misinterpreted as an ideology that somehow grants licence to "illiberal" practices, social polarization, and ghettoization (Rodríguez-García 2010b, 264, 268). These versions of the policy, however, clearly do not reflect the manner in which multiculturalism is lived out and managed—in general—in the Canadian context, and, here, it is crucial for critics of multiculturalism to ask what other social, political, or economic factors might be preventing other culturally diverse societies from achieving similarly positive and equitable outcomes.[27]

Finally, Siemiatycki identifies various empirical indicators of successful immigrant integration in Canada (e.g., intermarriage, cultural and political participation in mainstream society, high educational attainment). In a similar fashion, he then documents evidence showing the "shortcomings in immigrant integration in Canada" (e.g., lower economic performance, ongoing societal racism). While, on balance, Canada's record in integrating immigrants has thus far been strong in comparison with that of other countries, the author expresses a cautionary concern that new directions in Canadian immigration policy might undermine the important progress that has been made to date.

In analyzing the case of Quebec, Maryse Potvin (*Relations ethniques et crise des « accommodements raisonnables » au Québec*) looks at the place of immigrants in Quebecois society through closely examining the historical, political, and legislative circumstances that have helped to shape Quebec's approach to issues of socio-cultural integration. Her overview of this history calls attention, as the previous chapter did, to the impact of the French and British colonization of Canada on the country's Aboriginal peoples. An important point discussed by Potvin is Quebec's strained relationship with Canada's multiculturalism model: a tension resulting from a perception among certain Quebecers that in giving primacy and equality to *all* cultures/ethnic groups in Canada (apart from the fact that French is acknowledged as one of the two official languages of Canada), the policy of multiculturalism, reflected also in section 27 of the *Canadian Charter of Rights and Freedoms*, serves to overlook and undermine the particular history and cultural position of French Canadians within Canada—as one of the country's "two founding peoples."

Within this context—which is explored in much greater depth in Potvin's chapter, along with a discussion of the consolidation of Quebecois national identity and francophones' relatively recent "sociological passage" from a "minority" status group to a "majority" status group—Quebec asserted its own "interculturalism model" (« *modèle d'interculturalisme » québécois*). The author explains how Quebec, through various legislative measures, has strived to culturally and structurally integrate immigrants and, like the multiculturalism model, to protect their human rights and respect cultural diversity, yet within a framework of integrating them into a majority francophone Quebecois society. Because of the province's goal to protect its French majority identity—and Potvin points out that in the past, non-French-speaking immigrants with hopes of upward social mobility usually attempted to integrate into the smaller anglophone community—Quebec's current interculturalist model is premised on what Potvin refers to as a sort of "moral contract" between immigrants and Quebecois society: Immigrants are expected to respect the "common public culture" of Quebec and to understand that French is the common language of public life (and, therefore, that learning French, facilitated by the Quebec government's language programs, is a crucial measure for immigrant integration and participation in Quebecois society), and the province, for its part, is committed to protecting the human rights of individuals (within the law); showing openness to pluralism and striving for harmonious "intercommunity" relations; and welcoming immigrants and all "cultural communities" in Quebec to participate fully in the economic, social, cultural, and institutional life of Quebecois democratic society.

A good part of Potvin's chapter, which refers back to the above themes and continues to highlight identity issues, is devoted to the aforementioned debate surrounding the "reasonable accommodation" of religious and cultural diversity in Quebec.[28] The author sheds light on this debate and the related societal tensions through analyzing the media's handling of the issue and the discursive devices used; her chapter draws on findings from the expert report she wrote for the Bouchard-Taylor Commission, the panel set up in February 2007 by Quebec's premier, Jean Charest, to investigate and make recommendations on the subject of reasonable accommodation in Quebec. Potvin shows how the reasonable accommodation debate became a "social crisis" in the province, largely because of the media's sensationalistic misrepresentation of the issues, which created public confusion and alarm, indirectly forced the topic into the political arena prior to the 2007 Quebec provincial election, and contributed to increased expressions of polarization between provincial majority and minority groups. The author alerts us to a new type of "neo-racism" that has emerged, which places undue emphasis on the cultural *differences* of certain ethnic minority groups and which suggests the threat that these differences may pose to the common values of the majority; social disharmony is thus accounted for (if not, at times, augmented or produced) through culturalist interpretations. Through her analysis of the Quebec debate around reasonable accommodation, Potvin especially warns of the power that the media can have in shaping immigration and diversity issues and in affecting public opinion, a lesson that is particularly important for Spain and Europe, where the transformation of public perceptions towards immigration will be critical to the success of future immigration programs and policies.

Significantly, Potvin's discussion of Quebec's "moral contract" with its immigrants has particular resonance for a Catalan audience. The subject of linguistic policies, to which this Introduction will next turn, cannot be extricated from the topic of socio-cultural integration for any immigrant-receiving society, but the link is especially strong in contexts like that of Quebec or Catalonia. In Catalonia, learning Catalan is similarly envisioned as a vehicle that enables immigrants with long-term residence to access and participate in all aspects of the local society. This objective is nonetheless also underpinned by pressing demographic concerns: Catalonia's immigration policy, however more open it may become to expressions of cultural diversity, is inevitably informed by the project to ensure that Catalan, both practically and symbolically, will be the region's official public language. However, seeing that many people from other parts of Spain—a country in which the larger part of the population speaks Spanish as a mother tongue—move or have moved to Catalonia, and seeing, too, that so many immigrants to Catalonia are native Spanish speakers (e.g., immigrants from Latin America), the emotional and logistical issues surrounding language-as-a-tool-of-integration in Catalonia are extremely complicated. Native English speakers in Quebec, from the provincial anglophone minority or from other parts of Canada, have certain educational rights (e.g., the right to receive their education in English) that native Spanish speakers in Catalonia, even those from Spain, do not. Having said this, it must be understood that the emotional questions surrounding the protection of Catalan as a "majority" and privileged language within Catalonia are very complex. It is not "only" that Catalan has a history of being a marginalized and minority language within Spain; more significantly, it was actively and brutally suppressed and prohibited as a public language during the lengthy Franco dictator-ship (1939–1975). For this reason, the need to restore and maintain it as the dominant official language in the region—in the name of democracy and human rights as well as for cultural/nationalistic reasons—is looked upon with great importance.

Part V of this volume specifically looks at *linguistic policies and linguis-tic pluralism.* This thematic area is related both to issues of education and—as previously discussed—to the socio-cultural and labour market integration of immigrants. International immigration, which is often accompanied by a diversity of first languages and a strong need for im-migrants to acquire the host society's language(s) as quickly as possible, poses linguistic and educational challenges for all immigrant-receiving countries. But in all likelihood, host countries and regions striving to manage an already internally multilingual context—like Canada, where English and French are both recognized as official languages, or Spain, where Catalan/Valencian, Basque, Galician, and Aranese have co-official language status with Spanish (*castellano*) in certain autonomous com-munities—will find themselves all the more challenged by the complex set of language issues that immigration brings. Practical considerations must often be weighed with symbolic, personal, and cultural ones when developing language learning support for immigrants; in places like Quebec and Catalonia, a concern for protecting regional language rights inevitably shapes language and integration programs for newcomers.

As a general comment on language and education policies that affect immigrants, it seems that policy-makers must take into account various factors: (1) the functional and use-value realities of learning the language(s) of the receiving country or region, (2) the integration objectives of learning the language(s), and (3) the need to value the first languages of immigrants and to promote multilingualism. Both of the contributors to this section of the book convey the need for host societies and educators to support the second language learning—in one or both of the official languages—of immigrant children and adults; official lan-guage acquisition is needed for both the social integration and the success, whether academic or work-related, of newcomers. However, both authors also stress the importance of encouraging and supporting immigrants' first languages. First language maintenance has personal, community, and educational benefits for immigrants; and furthermore, it increases the human capital of the host society as a whole. Multilingualism must be recognized as an ever more valuable skill in a growingly diverse and globalized world.

In addressing the issue of second language acquisition for immigrants in Canada, Elizabeth Coelho (*Multilingualism in Ontario, Canada: An Educational Perspective*) focuses on the situation in the province of Ontario, an increasingly "multilingual and multicultural context." Notably, Ontario—a province in which English is the official language predominantly used[29]—includes the city of Toronto, the Canadian urban centre that receives the largest number of immigrants (Chui, Tran, and Maheux 2007). Coelho outlines the responsibilities of each level of government (federal, provincial, municipal) for the social, linguistic, and scholastic incorporation of immigrants in Ontario and explains how the different administrative levels collaborate in delivering services to newcomer children and adults. The author particularly concentrates on the forms of language support provided to immigrant children and youth in elementary and secondary schools. She notes that in recent years, the provincial Ministry of Education "has been paying increased attention to the needs of immigrant students and Canadian-born children whose first language is neither English nor French" and has implemented new policy measures to better accommodate these learners and to better equip their teachers. Coelho points out that apart from incoming immigrants, many Canadian-born students whose parents' mother tongue is other than English or French have had minimal exposure to the language of instruction when they first start school in Canada. A similar situation will likely become increasingly common in Catalonia and other parts of Spain.

In discussing differing designs of language programs in Ontario's (and Canada's) English-language schools, as well as educational outcomes for immigrant children, the author argues that English-as-a-second-language programs that provide focused language support for students while integrating them into the mainstream classroom (for subjects such as physical education, the arts, and math, for example) represent a constructive approach to fostering language skills and integration. In contrast, self-contained programs that keep language learners separated from their English-speaking age peers can disadvantage newcomers both linguistically and socially.

One of the key ideas emphasized in Coelho's chapter is the benefit—both cultural and academic—that students receive from maintaining their first languages. She explains that Canada supports this principle through facilitating and contributing funding to "heritage language" programs; these classes for instructing students in their (or in their parents') native languages "are available in many school districts across

Canada" and are housed mostly in local schools. At the high school level, students may be able to take courses in their first/home language for official academic credit.

In her chapter, Coelho also draws attention to the importance of "develop[ing] procedures for the reception, assessment, and orientation of newcomer students and their parents." To accomplish these goals, Toronto and most other sizable urban centres in Ontario have established actual "reception centres," at which immigrant students and their parents spend a day *before* registering in the local school. The centres' preliminary evaluation of students' language abilities (i.e., proficiency both in their first language(s) and in English) and of their mathematical background helps to place newcomer students in the appropriate program and provides teaching staff with a sense of the educational needs of incoming students. An innovative program of this type might have tremendous use in large immigrant-receiving areas in Spain and could certainly serve as a point of reference to help improve the reception strategies that are already under way in regions such as Catalonia.

In her chapter on Quebec (*Les services d'accueil, d'intégration scolaire et de francisation offerts aux immigrants au Québec*), Zita De Koninck shows how this province has also devoted a great deal of thought and resources to developing its welcoming and language programs for both newcomer children and adults. She notes the wide diversity of immigrant languages in the province, pointing out that 237 languages are spoken on the Island of Montreal. The author describes the different services and models for language learning that the Quebec government has put in place in schools and in the community to support the French language acquisition of immigrants of all ages as well as that of school-age children born in Quebec to non-French-speaking immigrant parents. In her discussion of "the pedagogical dimension"[30] of services for students in the Quebec school system, De Koninck seems to recommend, in agreement with the views stated by Elizabeth Coelho, a "Partial Integration Model," which enables immigrant students to receive intensive linguistic support in the second language (French) while being "progressively integrated into regular classes for a number of disciplines according to their age and their previous academic level." When outlining the government services available to immigrant adults for learning French—including full-time and part-time French courses that feature a "communicative approach" to language learning, as well as specialized classes for adults with low literacy—De Koninck provides details of the financial support (for child care arrangements, transportation expenses, etc.) that the Quebec government also offers to newcomers to make it possible for them to take these language courses. Other countries and governments can learn from this holistic policy approach, as economic and logistical factors may sometimes impede immigrants' socio-linguistic integration, which disadvantages not only them but the receiving society at large.

The chief difference in Quebec, De Koninck points out, is the importance of the socio-cultural and legal context in which these measures for immigrants' second language acquisition have developed. French has legally been the official language of Quebec since 1974. The author explains that policies regarding socio-linguistic integration have actively been changed in Quebec over the past several decades "in order to ensure the perpetuation of the French language." As international migration to Quebec increased and it was noted that non-francophone and non-anglophone immigrants had the tendency to prefer English as the language of use as well as English-language schools for their children's education, the provincial government created legislation, most significantly Bill 101, or the *Charter of the French Language*, passed in 1977, that would prevent and reverse this pattern. By law, as of 1977, immigrants to Quebec, except under fairly exceptional circumstances, have been required (in the public system) to enrol their children in French schools. Previous legislation had permitted parents, whether immigrant or Quebec-born, to choose the language—English or French—in which their children would be schooled. However, since 1977, in general, only people who themselves were educated in English-language schools in Quebec, along with other anglophone Canadians residing in Quebec, may send their children to schools where English is the primary language of instruction. Importantly, De Koninck addresses how official linguistic policies surrounding education and integration in Quebec have formed part of the province's broader legislative and "social project" to francize Quebec society and "make French the language of legislation, of justice and of public administration, ... and the language of commerce and business." The author observes that, by and large, Quebec's linguistic policies have ultimately been very successful in "ensur[ing] the development of French as the common language" in the province.

Notably, in Spain, the educational options in the Basque Country are more similar to Quebec's pre-1977 policies regarding the language of instruction in schools. In that region of Spain, parents are allowed to choose between three models of education for their children: (1) curricular instruction in Spanish (with Basque studied as a subject); (2) curricular instruction in Basque (with Spanish studied as a subject); or (3) a model of bilingual education, in which both Basque and Spanish are used as languages of instruction. There is also a trilingual model being developed, with English as the third language of instruction. The present-day educational model in Catalonia, however, bears greater similarity to the current approach in Quebec. In this autonomous community of Spain, except in certain "pilot project" cases (usually of trilingual education), Catalan is now almost always the exclusive language of instruction, with Spanish studied as a subject. A difference in Catalonia, though, is that the Catalan model applies equally to immigrants, a number of whom come from Spanish-speaking countries, and to *all* native-born Spaniards living in the region. That is to say, there is not an alternative system available even to families in which the parents or grandparents are native-born Spaniards who have moved to Catalonia from other "exclusively" Spanish-speaking parts of Spain. Therefore, unlike Quebec's English school provisions for its English-speaking Canadian-born minority (and perhaps *minority*, here, is the word to be emphasized), in Catalonia, even residents and citizens whose mother tongue is Spanish—more than 50 percent of the regional population (Idescat 2008)—are required to have their children's elementary and secondary schooling taught solely in Catalan, which effectively results in a mandatory "Catalan immersion" model for many students. The assumption is that this scholastic system will support and foster increased bilingualism in Catalan society, as Spanish, a language at home for many students, is studied as a subject area and is readily accessible in the local environment and through all forms of media and culture.

Some of the particular historical and political considerations regarding the maintenance of Catalan as the dominant official language in Catalonia have been discussed earlier in this Introduction. Regardless of political factors, though, the fact is that Catalan currently forms an important part of everyday life in Catalonia. It is the principal language of the Catalan government and the local authorities. It is widely used in public services, in mass media, and in the business sector (European Commission n.d.). For this reason, immigrants' knowledge of Catalan—not only of Spanish—is essential for their full integration into Catalan society. The decision to make Catalan the exclusive language of instruction in schools, therefore, can be said to have two objectives. On the one hand, this policy helps to perpetuate the use of Catalan in Catalonia, and, here, it should be noted that the percentage of people residing in this autonomous community who claim Spanish, rather than Catalan, as their primary "language of identification" is significantly lower than the percentage of residents who objectively identify Spanish as their "first language" (see Idescat 2008). On the other hand, Catalonia's educational project is premised on the understanding that proficiency in Catalan is a key element of inclusion and social cohesion for all migrants and immigrants to the region.

While the regional, linguistic, and historical contexts are different for Canada and Spain, both the Quebec and Ontario pedagogical experiences might nonetheless provide some useful insights for educators in Catalonia and Spain. Quebec's strategy of offering flexible and long-term (two to three years') support for non-francophone students' linguistic accommodation is something for other governments to consider. De Koninck notes that the academic success of these students in Quebec is encouraged through *not* placing them "in a situation of submersion." Moreover, in Coelho's chapter, she emphasizes the importance of using appropriate teaching techniques in language immersion contexts. A crucial factor leading to students' success in French Immersion programs in Canada, Coelho says, is that "teachers … are sensitive to the needs of their students as second language learners, and use second language teaching techniques to integrate language and content instruction."[31] A further instructive point that arises from these chapters is that while Quebec actively—and legislatively—promotes the need for all of its residents to learn French, it simultaneously, and in a manner similar to other regions in Canada, endorses the maintenance of immigrants' languages of origin. Like Ontario, Quebec has implemented heritage language programs in the province, and Quebec high school students of immigrant background similarly have opportunities to earn official credits for taking courses in their respective ethnic languages.

Part VI of this book is devoted to exploring the question of *partnerships and knowledge transfer between government, universities, and civil society.* The complex and far-reaching nature of immigration means that many diverse realms are affected: demographic, social, political, cultural, and linguistic areas; scholarly domains (methodologies, disciplines, etc.); and also, areas of policy-making, social programming, and social service provision. In this sense, policy-makers, researchers, and civil society are all involved, whether directly or indirectly, in the process of managing migration, and they share varying degrees of responsibility for whether the immigration process is handled well or poorly. A number of contributors to this volume have commented that an important element for achieving good results in managing immigration, diversity, and immigrant integration is the promotion of transversality, collaboration, and coordination both between different stakeholders and between different levels of government. A partnership approach is more likely to optimize resources and knowledge sharing, thereby producing better outcomes. In all of Spain, it is necessary to advance in the creation of policy-research structures that encourage direct and ongoing interaction between the various partners and in which all levels of government play a role.

The International Metropolis Project and its centres in Canada provide an excellent prototype for how a collaborative partnership of this nature can be accomplished and organized. Metropolis is a network of government bodies (involved in making law and policy), universities (academic researchers), and local entities (civil society, such as community groups and non-governmental organizations) that are committed to working together in the production, transfer, and application of knowledge related to immigration and diversity matters.

In his chapter on this topic (*The International Metropolis Project: A Model Worth Emulating?*), John Biles explains the evolution, structure (including sources of funding), changing mandate, and achievements/outcomes to date of the International Metropolis Project. He traces the development of this unique policy-research network, both national and international, from its inception in Canada in the early 1990s to its present form. Over the three phases of the project, Metropolis has grown enormously, whether measured by its numbers (over 8,000 members), its tremendous research output, or the great success of its two annual conferences, the International Metropolis Conference and the Canadian National Metropolis Conference. Through providing a clear explanation of the guiding principles, start-up, operation, and activities of the Metropolis Project, the author uses the benefits of hindsight to offer important lessons for other groups interested in establishing a similar enterprise.

At the heart of the Metropolis Project are its five Centres of Excellence, located in different provinces across Canada, including in the country's three largest immigrant-receiving cities: Toronto, Montreal, and Vancouver. The remaining two chapters of Part VI of this volume are contributed by the directors (current or former) of two of these centres. Joanna Anneke Rummens (*Creating Spaces: Linking Migration and Diversity Research with Policy/Practice Needs*) presents the case of CERIS – The Ontario Metropolis Centre,[32] located in Toronto; and Annick Germain (*Immigration et métropoles, Centre Métropolis du Québec (CMQ-IM) : une expérience de partenariat intersectoriel et interinstitutionnel réussie, en transition*) discusses the Quebec Metropolis Centre, situated in Montreal. These academic research centres, each one with unique characteristics and approaches, are knowledge production and translation networks that focus on pertinent immigration and settlement issues. Rummens and Germain explain how and why these centres were put into place, how they are organized and managed, their specific goals and challenges, and the types of knowledge creation and knowledge dissemination in which they are involved. Notably, "training and mentoring the next generation of researchers, practitioners, and decision-makers," as stated by Rummens, is of vital concern to both centres. The two authors further describe how the research conducted by the various Metropolis centres is structured around different policy-research domains or priorities, with the objective of ensuring that the research produced will be relevant to policy and practice and will support evidence-based decision-making in both local and national contexts.

Some key issues that are highlighted by the contributors to this section on knowledge transfer are the importance of dialogue, co-operation, and transference of information between academics/community researchers and government, whose work projects are often interconnected and whose collaborative partnerships can undoubtedly lead to improvements in policy and practice; the importance of securing human and financial resources to generate and sustain these synergies; the need to build trust between collaborating partners; the necessity of identifying priority topics to be addressed to make sure that the research projects undertaken are useful at the level of policy and practice; the importance of translating the research knowledge that has been produced (using a variety of formats for optimal results) so that it reaches its target audiences and may be used for its intended purposes; and the need for ongoing—although not excessive—evaluation of the process and outcomes.

This final section of the book, therefore, thematically takes us full circle to the starting point and aims of this entire collaborative project: to produce a collection of policy- and practice-relevant information about the Canadian immigration experience that might (a) provide a greater understanding of central immigration and diversity issues as they apply to Canada, and (b) assist immigration policy-makers and practitioners on both sides of the Atlantic in their efforts to assess and improve immigration programs in their respective countries and regions.

NOTES

1. Despite the fact that Spain can still be considered a country of immigration, in 2011, for the first time in over a decade, the country registered a negative net migration of roughly 130,000 persons (450,000 immigrants and 580,850 emigrants) (INE 2011c). The majority of the emigrants for the year 2011 were shown to be foreigners who had been living in the country, but a significant number of Spanish nationals—mostly high-skilled youth—also emigrated, mainly to Northern European countries and to North America, pushed by the serious effects of the economic crisis in Spain. Nonetheless, it is still too early to talk about a change or reversal in Spain's migration patterns.

2. Catalonia is one of the 17 "autonomous communities" that constitute Spain. Catalonia was officially recognized as such in the Statute of Autonomy of Catalonia (*Estatut d'Autonomia de Catalunya*) enacted in 1979, following the Spanish Constitution of 1978, the culmination of the Spanish transition from dictatorship to democracy. Catalan self-government operates in accordance with the Spanish Constitution and the Statute of Autonomy of Catalonia, the latter of which is Catalonia's basic institutional regulatory framework. The Government of Catalonia (*Generalitat de Catalunya*) is the system under which Catalan self-government is politically organized. Its members are elected by universal suffrage every four years. The Generalitat is comprised of the Parliament, which has 135 members, the President, and the Executive Council.

3. While the Spanish government has, arguably, taken some steps to promote immigrant integration prior to recent years (see Calavita 2007, 9-10), these measures have not been particularly comprehensive or impactful. Integration programs have been more visible in certain autonomous communities that have longer histories of significant migration inflows (e.g., Catalonia), but in the case of Spain overall, the first national policy framework for promoting immigrant incorporation did not really materialize until 2004 (see Bruquetas-Callejo et al. 2011).

4. Further evidence of the value of, and trend toward, transatlantic comparison has been the recent collaborative project "Improving EU and US Immigration Systems' Capacity for Responding to Global Challenges: Learning from Experiences" (2011), funded by the European Commission, and jointly directed at the Migration Policy Centre, European University Institute, Florence, Italy, and at the Migration Policy Institute, Washington, DC. The project's stated aims are to identify, through transatlantic co-operation, the ways in which EU and U.S. immigration systems can be improved in order

to address the major challenges confronted by policy-makers in both places. For more information, see http://www.eui.eu/Projects/TransatlanticProject/Home.aspx and http://www.migrationpolicy.org/immigrationsystems/.

5.   See http://news.bbc.co.uk/2/hi/6421597.stm.

6.   While immigrants have the *legal* right to work in Canada, a crucial problem for newcomers has been Canada's lack of recognition of foreign-earned professional credentials. This subject is discussed by various authors in this book (e.g., chapters 1, 4, and 6). Efforts on the part of the Canadian government to improve this situation were commented on in the Migrant Integration Policy Index (2010) report, which overall ranked Canada quite highly in the area of labour market integration policies for immigrants (see Huddleston and Niessen 2011).

7.   On the backlash against multiculturalism in Europe, see Vertovec and Wessendorf (2010). See also Rodríguez-García (2010b).

8.   It should be noted that Canada's Conservative government in its 2011 federal budget proposed significant cuts to settlement funding for immigrants, especially affecting a number of ethnocultural agencies serving particular ethnic groups (see Keung 2010; Pagliaro and Mahoney 2010). It is not yet known how this decreased funding may impact on future integration outcomes for certain newcomers to Canada.

9.   It is important to note that while Spain was rated highly for its family reunification policies, the country's fourth reform of its Foreigners' Law (*Ley de Extranjería*), approved in October 2009, had the effect of limiting eligibility for certain family members (e.g., parents/grandparents). Moreover, while Spain has improved its immigration policies for granting long-term residence to certain groups of immigrants, thus providing these residents with greater security and rights, new policies announced in April 2012 will significantly affect the integration and rights of other sizable immigrant populations in the country. As part of the current Spanish government's austerity plan, only legal immigrants will have full access to public health care services (see http://extranjeros.empleo.gob.es/es/NormativaJurisprudencia/), in contrast to Spain's previous health care provisions for all residents registered in the local municipality, regardless of their formal immigration status (Calavita 2007, 10).

10. See also Calavita (2005) for an analysis of how European laws that perpetuate immigrants' temporary legal status in the country (i.e., the issuing of temporary work permits) and that deny them access to permanent residence, combined with realities of labour market segmentation and the lack of work options available to immigrants, can lead to an outcome of immigrants being stuck in an underclass.

11. On the impact, both actual and anticipated, of the current global economic crisis on international migration and immigration policy-making, see Papademetriou and Terrazas (2009); and Koser (2010).

12. Several reports point out that the effects of the current economic crisis have been particularly devastating for Spain's immigrant population. By the end of 2010, the unemployment rate among immigrants in Spain had soared to over 30 percent, nearly twice the rate reported for native-born Spaniards (International Labour Office 2010, 72-74; Pajares 2010, 27-41; Aja, Arango, and Oliver 2011, and 2012, 37; Collett 2011a, 4, 15-16; OECD 2011a, 322).

13. When considering the growing tendency toward economic nationalism, it is important to note that immigrants in Spain, as in Italy, often "occupy the most precarious niches" in the workforce, "do[ing] the jobs, and under conditions, that most Spanish workers no longer accept" (Calavita 2007, 8-9).

14. The significant increase in support for the xenophobic *Plataforma per Catalunya* political party indicates the growing anti-immigrant sentiment in Spain (see Noguer 2011).

15. The Secretary of Immigration of the Government of Catalonia is now called the Directorate General for Immigration. For the Forum program, see http://im.metropolis.net/actualites/PROGRAM_Canada_Forum_Barcelona_2008.pdf. For a complete commentary on the Forum in Spanish, see Rodríguez-García (2010a).

16. Catalonia's economic productivity has slowed down in the past few years because of the economic crisis that has affected all of Spain since 2008. Catalonia, however, until very recently, has been one of the main contributors to the Spanish economy, with nearly 19 percent of Spain's GDP (an economic output that is higher than the European Union average and similar to that of countries like Portugal and Norway). Notably, this autonomous community is the second most populous region in Spain, and the economic dynamism of Catalonia has in part been due to the region's massive population growth over the past decade as a result of immigration. While Catalonia is currently facing serious financial difficulties, it has long been counted on to help support poorer autonomous communities in the country through taxes collected by the central Spanish government (OECD 2010b; Minder 2011). In contrast, Quebec, regardless of its large size and high population numbers within Canada, is a relatively less prosperous province in its country, as indicated by the equalization payments it regularly receives from the Canadian federal government (Department of Finance Canada n.d.-a and n.d.-b). Professor of Economics Serge Coulombe, in his study of provincial economic disparities in Canada, explains that Quebec's economy has been affected by a variety of factors, including "the westward shift of Canada's center of economic activity" (1999, 7).

17. The chapter summaries presented in this next section were written by the editor of this volume/author of this Introduction, permitting him to introduce the themes of the book, indicate where certain information can be located, and engage in dialogue with the chapters from a transatlantic perspective. Readers should go directly to the chapters themselves for a clear understanding of chapter content and for the purpose of citing facts or arguments presented by the various authors.

18. As Spain is jurisdictionally divided into autonomous regions or "communities" (e.g., Catalonia, Andalusia, the Basque Country) rather than into provinces, "autonomous" refers here to that which pertains to or is under the jurisdiction of a Spanish autonomous region.

19. Note that the Northwest Territories now also has a Provincial Nominee agreement with the Canadian federal government. See http://www.cic.gc.ca/english/department/laws-policy/agreements/index.asp.

20. As Myer Siemiatycki clarifies in his chapter of this book, "'Visible minority' is the official term for Canada's non-white, non-Aboriginal population" (see chapter 8); even Statistics Canada uses "visible minority" as a demographic

category. Canadian readers should note that this term is not widely used in Europe, where categorizations like "ethnic minority" or "ethnic group" are more common.

21. For a detailed discussion of this topic and a review of the related literature, see Rodríguez-García (2010b).

22. Canada's official multiculturalism policy, adopted in 1971, was reaffirmed in the *Canadian Multiculturalism Act* of 1988.

23. In 2004, France passed legislation that prohibited students in French public schools from wearing conspicuous religious symbols; this law had the pronounced effect of preventing Muslim girls from wearing the *hijab*, a head scarf that does not cover the face. In 2011, both France and Belgium legally banned the wearing of full-face veils (i.e., veils that show only the eyes) in *all* public spaces. These recent laws (enforceable mostly by fines) target the face coverings, like the *niqab* or full *burka*, worn by some Muslim women—only by a small minority of women in both of these countries—and have the effect of making it illegal for these women to go anywhere outside their own homes in their habitual mode of dress. Other European countries, such as Italy and the Netherlands, are looking into passing similar legislation. The issue has been hotly debated as well in Spain, although the proposal for this type of broad ban has been rejected thus far. In the city of Barcelona, however, legislation is under way to prohibit all headgear that impedes identification (e.g., the niqab, motorcycle helmets, face-covering hats) from being worn in the city's municipal buildings (e.g., government offices, public markets, libraries). It has been argued that this law addresses security, not religious, issues.

24. For details of the report, see http://www.accommodements.qc.ca/index-en.html.

25. A new, controversial law tabled in Quebec in 2010 has reignited the debate in the province—and in Canada—over what the limits of "reasonable accommodation" should be. Quebec's Bill 94, affecting Muslim women who wear the *niqab*, would require women who wear face veils to uncover their faces when providing or receiving public services (i.e., during the delivery of services). It is estimated that about 25 women living in the province currently wear the niqab. To be sure, the proposed legislation is a hardline measure, especially in the Canadian context, and especially depending on how broadly the Quebec government ends up defining "public services" or the length of time that women would have to remove their veils while dealing with a public service provider. However, in its initial conception, the law still shows a degree of restraint when compared with the debates and outcomes taking place in Europe. Through its focus on purportedly pragmatic questions of communication, identification, and security, Bill 94 could be said to be more similar in nature to the relatively "softer" laws regarding the niqab that have been adopted or proposed in a few cities in Catalonia, such as Barcelona (see note 23). Furthermore, Quebec's former Minister of Justice, Kathleen Weil, in a 2010 interview with NPR (National Public Radio), placed importance on consensus and on the dialogic process that would be needed to ultimately concretize and approve the law (for interview details, see NPR 2010). In terms of Canada at large, in late 2011,

there were continuing deliberations by the Supreme Court of Canada to determine whether a woman should be allowed to wear the niqab when testifying in court. Moreover, the federal Minister of Immigration announced that women would no longer be permitted to wear face coverings while taking the oath of Canadian citizenship (i.e., during this part of the ceremony); it is uncertain whether this proposed ban will be struck down on the basis that it violates human rights codes and the *Canadian Charter of Rights and Freedoms.*

26. Here, Siemiatycki cites Biles et al. (2008, 4) as a reference: Biles, J., M. Burstein, and J. Frideres. 2008. *Immigration and Integration in Canada in the Twenty-first Century.* Montreal and Kingston: McGill-Queen's University Press.

27. See also Banting and Kymlicka's (2010) discussion of the Canadian experience of multiculturalism, which the authors set against the backdrop of the global backlash against multiculturalism.

28. Potvin's chapter focuses on the time period from 2006 to 2008, particularly on the debate around "reasonable accommodation" that took place in 2006 and 2007.

29. It should be noted that the Ontario city of Ottawa, the capital of Canada, has a more bilingual (i.e., English and French) character. However, even in Ottawa, the majority of the city's inhabitants have English as their mother tongue and speak English most often at home (Statistics Canada 2007).

30. All quotes used are taken from an (unpublished) English translation of Zita De Koninck's chapter, which was provided directly by the author.

31. Here, Coelho cites Fred Genesee (1994) as a reference: Genesee, F. 1994. Integrating Language and Content: Lessons from Immersion. *Educational Practice Reports, No. 11.* National Center for Research on Cultural Diversity and Second Language Learning. Washington, DC: Center for Applied Linguistics.

32. It should be noted that CERIS – The Ontario Metropolis Centre was undergoing significant structural changes at the time of this book's publication. See http://www.ceris.metropolis.net/wp-content/uploads/pdf/about_us/Final_CERIS_Survey_Summer2011.pdf.

REFERENCES

Adahl, M., and P. Hojem. 2011. *Kanadamodellen: Hur invandring leder till jobb.* Stockholm: FORES.

Aja, E., J. Arango, and J. Oliver, eds. 2011. *Inmigración y crisis económica. Anuario de la inmigración en España. Edición 2010.* Barcelona: CIDOB.

Aja, E., J. Arango, and J. Oliver, eds. 2012. *La hora de la integración. Anuario de la inmigración en España. Edición 2011.* Barcelona: CIDOB.

Alexander, J. 2006. *The Civil Sphere.* New York: Oxford University Press.

Anisef, P., and M. Lanphier, eds. 2003. *The World in a City.* Toronto: Toronto University Press.

Arango, J. 2000. Becoming a Country of Immigration at the End of the Twentieth Century: The Case of Spain. In *Eldorado or Fortress? Migration in Southern Europe,* eds. R. King, G. Lazaridis, and C. Tsardanidis, 253-276. London: Palgrave Macmillan.

Arango, J. 2006. Europa y la inmigración. Una relación difícil. In *Migraciones: nuevas movilidades en un mundo en movimiento*, ed. C. Blanco, 91-111. Barcelona: Anthropos.

Arango, J., and C. Finotelli. 2009. Spain. In *REGINE. Regularisations in Europe*, eds. M. Baldwin-Edwards and A. Kraler, 443-458. Amsterdam: Pallas Publications.

Arango, J., and F. González. 2009. The Impacts of the Current Financial and Economic Crisis on Migration in the Spain-Morocco Corridor. CARIM Working Papers No. 39/09. Florence: European University Institute.

Aydemir, A., and A. Sweetman. 2008. First and Second Generation Immigrant Educational Attainment and Labor Market Outcomes: A Comparison of the United States and Canada. *Research in Labor Economics* 27: 215-270.

Banting, K., and W. Kymlicka. 2010. Canadian Multiculturalism: Global Anxieties and Local Debates. *British Journal of Canadian Studies* 23 (1):43-72.

Basch, L., N. Glick Schiller, and C. Blanc-Szanton. 1994. *Nations Unbound: Transnational Projects, Postcolonial Predicaments, and Deterritorialized Nation-states*. New York: Gordon and Breach.

Bauböck, R., A. Kraler, M. Martiniello, and B. Perchinig. 2006. Migrants' Citizenship: Legal Status, Rights and Political Participation. In *The Dynamics of International Migration and Settlement in Europe: A State of the Art*, eds. R. Penninx, M. Gerger, and K. Kraal, 65-98. Amsterdam: Amsterdam University Press – IMISCOE Joint Studies Series.

Bayona, J., A. Domingo, and F. Gil. 2008. Población extranjera y vivienda en Cataluña. Evolución reciente y previsión de la demanda. *Anales de Geografía de la Universidad Complutense* 28 (2):37-62.

Bloemraad, I. 2006. *Becoming a Citizen: Incorporating Immigrants and Refugees in the United States and Canada*. Berkeley: University of California Press.

Borjas, G.J. 1995. The Economic Benefits from Immigration. *Journal of Economic Perspectives* 9 (2):3-22.

Bruquetas-Callejo, M., B. Garcés-Mascareñas, R. Morén-Alegret, R. Penninx, and E. Ruiz-Vieytez. 2011. The Case of Spain. In *Migration Policymaking in Europe: The Dynamics of Actors and Contexts in Past and Present*, eds. G. Zincone, R. Penninx, and M. Borkert, 291-323. Amsterdam: Amsterdam University Press – IMISCOE Joint Studies Series.

Cabré, A. 1999. *El sistema català de reproducció: Cent anys de singularitat demogràfica* (The Catalan System of Reproduction: A Century of Demographic Uniqueness). Barcelona: Proa.

Cachón, L. 2002. La formación de la 'España inmigrante': mercado y ciudadanía. *Revista Española de Investigaciones Sociológicas* 97 (enero-marzo): 95-126.

Calavita, K. 2005. *Immigrants at the Margins: Law, Race, and Exclusion in Southern Europe*. New York: Cambridge University Press.

Calavita, K. 2007. The Immigration Conundrum in Italy and Spain. *Insights on Law and Society* 7 (2):7-10. At http://www.americanbar.org/content/dam/aba/publishing/insights_law_society/article2.authcheckdam.pdf (accessed 10 December 2011; same date hereinafter for all links unless otherwise indicated).

Canada. Standing Committee on Foreign Affairs and International Development (FAAE). 2009. *Evidence*, 40th Parliament, 2nd Session, 11 February, FAAE–03. Ottawa: House of Commons, Parliament of Canada. At http://www.parl.gc.ca/HousePublications/Publication.aspx?DocId=3676616&Language=E&Mode=1&Parl=40&Ses=2.

Caparrós, A. 2010. Geographical Mobility and Potential Wage Gain of Immigrants Within Spain. *Anales de economía aplicada*, XXIV.

Carling, J. 2007. Migration Control and Migrant Fatalities at the Spanish-African Borders. *International Migration Review* 41 (2):316-343.

Castles, S., and M. Miller. 2009. *The Age of Migration: International Population Movements in the Modern World*, 4th ed. Basingstoke and New York: Palgrave-Macmillan and Guilford Books.

Cea D'Ancona, M.A., and M. Valles. 2009. *Evolución del racismo y la xenofobia en España. Informe 2009*. Madrid: Observatorio español del racismo y la xenofobia (Oberaxe), Ministerio de Trabajo e Inmigración. At http://www.oberaxe.es/files/datos/4b26574eb2f66/Informe2009.pdf.

CeiMigra. 2010. *Informe anual sobre migraciones e integración 2009: Migraciones y crisis económica internacional*. Valencia: Generalitat Valenciana, Bancaja. At http://www.ceimigra.net/observatorio/images/stories/luis_pdf/Informe_Anual_2009_CeiMiga_vf.pdf.

Centre d'Estudis d'Opinió (CEO). 2011. *Dossier de premsa de Percepció dels catalans i catalanes sobre la immigració 2010*. Barcelona: Generalitat de Catalunya. At http://premsa.gencat.cat/pres_fsvp/docs/2011/03/14/10/10/04347dbe-82b4-479c-8c54-d8fd474d8e6a.pdf.

Chui, T., K. Tran, and H. Maheux. 2007. *Immigration in Canada: A Portrait of the Foreign-born Population, 2006 Census: Findings*. Catalogue no. 97-557-XIE. Ottawa: Statistics Canada. At http://www12.statcan.ca/census-recensement/2006/as-sa/97-557/index-eng.cfm.

Citizenship and Immigration Canada (CIC). 2011a. Canada welcomes highest number of legal immigrants in 50 years while taking action to maintain the integrity of Canada's immigration system. News Release, 13 February. At http://www.cic.gc.ca/english/department/media/releases/2011/2011-02-13.asp.

Citizenship and Immigration Canada (CIC). 2011b. *Facts and Figures 2010: Immigration Overview—Permanent and Temporary Residents*. At http://www.cic.gc.ca/english/pdf/research-stats/facts2010.pdf.

Citizenship and Immigration Canada (CIC). 2011c. Government of Canada to cut backlog and wait times for family reunification—Phase I of Action Plan for Faster Family Reunification. News Release, 4 November. At http://www.cic.gc.ca/english/department/media/releases/2011/2011-11-04.asp (accessed 7 May 2012).

Citizenship and Immigration Canada (CIC). 2012a. *Canada's Economic Action Plan 2012—Proposed Changes to Canada's Economic Immigration System*. E-newsletter. At http://www.cic.gc.ca/english/resources/enewsletter/ceap.asp (accessed 7 May 2012).

Citizenship and Immigration Canada (CIC). 2012b. Speaking Notes for The Honourable Jason Kenney, P.C., M.P. Minister of Citizenship, Immigration and Multiculturalism. At a news conference following the tabling of Bill C-31, *Protecting Canada's Immigration System Act*, 16 February. At http://www.cic.gc.ca/english/department/media/speeches/2012/2012-02-16.asp (accessed 7 May 2012).

Citizenship and Immigration Canada (CIC). no date-a. Backgrounder—Overview of Reforms to Canada's Refugee System. At http://www.cic.gc.ca/english/department/media/backgrounders/2012/2012-02-16.asp (accessed 7 May 2012).

Citizenship and Immigration Canada (CIC). no date-b. Sponsoring Your Family. At http://www.cic.gc.ca/english/immigrate/sponsor/index.asp (accessed 7 May 2012).

Citrin, J., and J. Sides. 2008. Immigration and the Imagined Community in Europe and the United States. *Political Studies* 56: 33-56.

Collett, E. 2011a. *Immigrant Integration in Europe in a Time of Austerity*. Washington, DC: Migration Policy Institute. At http://www.migrationpolicy.org/pubs/TCM-integration.pdf.

Collett, E. 2011b. *Emerging Transatlantic Security Dilemmas in Border Management*. Washington, DC: Migration Policy Institute. At http://www.migrationpolicy.org/pubs/securitydilemmas-2011.pdf.

Cornelius, W., T. Tsuda, P. Martin, and J. Hollifield, eds. 2004. *Controlling Immigration: A Global Perspective*, 2nd ed. Stanford: Stanford University Press.

Coulombe, S. 1999. *Economic Growth and Provincial Disparity: A New View of an Old Canadian Problem*. Commentary No. 122. Toronto: C.D. Howe Institute. At http://www.cdhowe.org/pdf/coulombe.pdf.

Department of Finance Canada. no date-a. Equalization Program. At http://www.fin.gc.ca/fedprov/eqp-eng.asp.

Department of Finance Canada. no date-b. Federal Support to Provinces and Territories. At http://www.fin.gc.ca/fedprov/mtp-eng.asp#Quebec.

Düvell, F., and B. Vollmer. 2011. *European Security Challenges*. Florence and Washington, DC: European University Institute and Migration Policy Institute. At http://cadmus.eui.eu/handle/1814/16212.

Economist Intelligence Unit. 2011. *Global Liveability Report*, February. At http://graphics.eiu.com/upload/Liveability2011.pdf.

European Commission. 2005. *A Common Agenda for Integration—Framework for the Integration of Third-Country Nationals in the European Union*. Communication from the Commission to the Council, the European Parliament, the European Economic and Social Committee and the Committee of the Regions, 1 September. Brussels: Commission of the European Communities. At http://eur-lex.europa.eu/LexUriServ/LexUriServ.do?uri=COM:2005:0389:FIN:EN:PDF.

European Commission. 2011. *Standard Eurobarometer 75: Public Opinion in the European Union*, Spring. Brussels: TNS Opinion & Social, Directorate General Research. At http://ec.europa.eu/public_opinion/archives/eb/eb75/eb75_publ_en.pdf.

European Commission. no date (last updated August 2011). Catalan in Catalonia. *The Euromosaic Study*. European Commission—Languages. At http://ec.europa.eu/languages/euromosaic/es51_en.htm#22.

Eurostat. 2008. *Population in Europe 2007*. Statistics in Focus 81/2008. Luxembourg: Eurostat. At http://epp.eurostat.ec.europa.eu/cache/ITY_OFFPUB/KS-SF-08-081/EN/KS-SF-08-081-EN.PDF.

Eurostat. 2011. Foreign citizens made up 6.5% of the EU27 population in 2010. New Release, 4 July. At http://epp.eurostat.ec.europa.eu/cache/ITY_PUBLIC/3-14072011-BP/EN/3-14072011-BP-EN.PDF.

Fargues, P., D. Papademetriou, G. Salinari, and M. Sumption. 2011. *Shared Challenges and Opportunities for EU and US Immigration Policymakers*. Florence and Washington, DC: European University Institute and Migration Policy Institute. At http://www.migrationpolicy.org/pubs/US-EUimmigrationsystems-finalreport.pdf.

Fröbel, F., H. Juergen, and O. Kreye. 1980. *The New International Division of Labour.* Cambridge: Cambridge University Press.

Fudge, J., and F. MacPhail. 2009. The Temporary Foreign Worker Program in Canada: Low-skilled Workers as an Extreme Form of Flexible Labour. *Comparative Labor Law and Policy Journal* 31: 101–139.

Generalitat de Catalunya. 2005. *Pla de Ciutadania i Immigració 2005–2008.* Barcelona: Secretaria per a la Immigració. At www.gencat.net/benestar/societat/convivencia/immigracio.

Generalitat de Catalunya. 2009. *Pacte Nacional per a la Immigració.* Barcelona: Secretaria per a la Immigració. At http://www.gencat.cat/.

Generalitat de Catalunya. 2010a. *Llei 10/2010, del 7 de maig, d'acollida de les persones immigrades i de les retornades a Catalunya.* DOGC-5629, BOE-139. At http://www.gencat.cat/eadop/imatges/5629/10126029.pdf.

Generalitat de Catalunya. 2010b. *Pla de Ciutadania i Immigració 2009–2012.* Barcelona: Secretaria per a la Immigració. At http://www.gencat.cat/.

German Marshall Fund of the United States. 2011. *Transatlantic Trends: Immigration—Key Findings 2010.* Washington, DC: German Marshall Fund of the United States. At http://trends.gmfus.org/immigration/doc/TTI2010_English_Key.pdf.

Glick Schiller, N., L. Basch, and C. Blanc-Szanton, eds. 1992. *Towards a Transnational Perspective on Migration: Race, Class, Ethnicity, and Nationalism Reconsidered.* New York: New York Academy of Sciences.

Huddleston, T., and J. Niessen. 2011. *The Migrant Integration Policy Index III (MIPEX).* Brussels: British Council and Migration Policy Group. At http://www.mipex.eu/.

Idescat (Catalan Statistics Institute). 2008. *Població de 15 anys i més segons llengua inicial, d'identificació i habitual. Catalunya. 2008.* At http://www.idescat.cat/de quavi/?TC=444&V0=15&V1=2&VA=2008&VOK=Confirmar.

Idescat (Catalan Statistics Institute). 2011. *Foreign Population. Series: Catalonia* (based on census data). At http://www.idescat.cat/poblacioestrangera/?b=0&lang=en.

INE (Spanish National Statistics Institute). 2011a. *Padrón Municipal de Población* (Municipal Register). Madrid: INE. At http://www.ine.es/inebmenu/mnu_cifraspob.htm.

INE (Spanish National Statistics Institute). 2011b. *Notas de Prensa* (press release), 4 April. Madrid: INE. At http://www.ine.es/prensa/np648.pdf.

INE (Spanish National Statistics Institute). 2011c. *Notas de Prensa* (press release), 7 October. Madrid: INE. At http://www.ine.es/prensa/np679.pdf.

International Labour Office (ILO). 2010. *International Labour Migration: A Rights-Based Approach.* Geneva: ILO.

International Organization for Migration (IOM). 2010. *World Migration Report 2010: The Future of Migration: Building Capacities for Change.* Geneva: IOM. At http://publications.iom.int/bookstore/free/WMR_2010_ENGLISH.pdf.

International Organization for Migration (IOM). 2011. *World Migration Report 2011: Communicating Effectively About Migration.* Geneva: IOM. At http://publications.iom.int/bookstore/free/WMR2011_English.pdf.

Izquierdo, A. 1996. *La inmigración inesperada. La población extranjera en España (1991–1995).* Madrid: Trotta.

Keung, N. 2010. Funding axed for Toronto immigrant agencies. *Toronto Star,* 23 December.

King, R., A. Fielding, and R. Black. 1997. The International Migration Turnaround in Southern Europe. In *Southern Europe and the New Immigrations*, eds. R. King and R. Black, 1-25. Brighton: Sussex Academic Press.

Koser, K. 2010. The Impact of the Global Financial Crisis on International Migration. *The Whitehead Journal of Diplomacy and International Relations* (Winter/Spring): 13-20.

Levitt, P., and N. Glick Schiller. 2004. Conceptualizing Simultaneity: A Transnational Field Perspective on Society. *International Migration Review* 38 (4):1002-1039.

López, M.P., and R.A. Davis. 2011. Immigration Law Spanish-Style II: A Study of Spain's Voluntary Immigrant Return Plan and Circular Migration. *Temple International and Comparative Law Journal* 25: 79.

Maas, W. 2010. Unauthorized Migration and the Politics of Regularization, Legalization, and Amnesty. In *Labour Migration in Europe*, eds. G. Menz and A. Caviedes, 232-250. Basingstoke: Palgrave Macmillan.

Massey, D.S., J. Arango, G. Hugo, A. Kouaouci, A. Pellegrino, and J.E. Taylor. 2009 [1998]. *Worlds in Motion: Understanding International Migration at the End of the Millennium*. New York: Oxford University Press.

Massey, D.S., and K.A. Pren. Forthcoming (2012). Unintended Consequences of US Immigration Policy: Explaining the Post-1965 Surge from Latin America. *Population and Development Review*.

Milan, A. 2011. *Migration: International, 2009*. Report on the Demographic Situation in Canada, Component of Statistics Canada Catalogue no. 91-209-X. Ottawa: Statistics Canada. At http://www.statcan.gc.ca/pub/91-209-x/2011001/article/11526-eng.pdf.

Minder, R. 2011. Deficits in regions compound fears about Spain. *New York Times*, 31 March. At http://www.nytimes.com/2011/04/01/business/global/01catalonia.html?_r=1&pagewanted=all.

Moreno, F.J., and M. Bruquetas-Callejo. 2011. *Inmigración y Estado de bienestar en España*. Barcelona: Obra Social la Caixa, CSIC, Col. Estudios Sociales 31.

MTAS (Ministry of Labour and Social Affairs). 2011. *II Plan estratégico Ciudadanía e Integración 2011–2014*. Madrid: Secretaría de Estado de Inmigración y Emigración, Dirección General de Integración de los Inmigrantes. At http://extranjeros.mtin.es/es/IntegracionRetorno/Plan_estrategico2011/pdf/PECI-2011-2014.pdf.

Muñoz, F., and A. Izquierdo. 1989. *L'Espagne, pays d'immigration*. Population 44 (2):257-289.

National Public Radio (NPR). 2010. Bill Seeks to Ban Muslim Veil in Quebec. Interview with Michele Norris (host) and Kathleen Weil, 12 April. At http://www.npr.org/templates/story/story.php?storyId=125866591.

Noguer, M. 2011. El partido xenófobo de Anglada quintuplica su resultado en Cataluña. *El País*, 24 May. At http://politica.elpais.com/politica/2011/05/24/actualidad/1306218355_467986.html.

Oliver, J. 2006. *España 2020: Un mestizaje ineludible. Cambio demográfico, mercado de trabajo e inmigración en las comunidades autónomas*. Barcelona: Institut d'Estudis Autonòmics.

Organisation for Economic Co-operation and Development (OECD). 2010a. *International Migration Outlook 2010: Migration Key to Long-term Economic Growth*. Paris: OECD-SOPEMI. At http://www.oecd.org/document/41/0,3746,en_2649_33931_45591593_1_1_1_1,00.html.

Organisation for Economic Co-operation and Development (OECD). 2010b. *OECD Reviews of Regional Innovation: Catalonia, Spain 2010.* London: OECD. At www.oecd.org/gov/regional/innovation.

Organisation for Economic Co-operation and Development (OECD). 2011a. *International Migration Outlook 2011: Migration in the Post-Crisis World.* Paris: OECD-SOPEMI. At www.oecd.org/migration/imo.

Organisation for Economic Co-operation and Development (OECD). 2011b. Better Life Index. At http://www.oecdbetterlifeindex.org/about/better-life-initiative/.

Pagliaro, J., and J. Mahoney. 2010. Funding cuts threaten immigrant agencies. *Globe and Mail,* 23 December.

Pajares, M. 2010. *Inmigración y mercado de trabajo. Informe 2010.* Madrid: Observatorio Permanente de la Inmigración 25, Ministerio de Trabajo e Inmigración.

Papademetriou, D.G., ed. 2006. *Europe and Its Immigrants in the 21st Century: A New Deal or a Continuing Dialogue of the Deaf?* Washington, DC: Migration Policy Institute and the Luso-American Foundation.

Papademetriou, D.G., and A. Terrazas. 2009. *Immigrants and the Current Economic Crisis: Research Evidence, Policy Challenges, and Implications.* Washington, DC: Migration Policy Institute.

Pascual, A., J. Cardelús, and M. Solana. 2000. Recent Immigration to Catalonia: Character and Responses. In *Eldorado or Fortress? Migration in Southern Europe,* eds. R. King, G. Lazaridis, and C. Tsardanidis, 104-124. London: Palgrave Macmillan.

Penninx, R. 2005. Integration of Migrants: Economic, Social, Cultural and Political Dimensions. In *The New Demographic Regime: Population Challenges and Policy Responses,* eds. M. Macura, A. MacDonald, and W. Haug, 137-152. New York and Geneva: United Nations.

Picot, G., Y. Lu, and F. Hou. 2009. Immigrant Low-income Rates: The Role of Market Income and Government Transfers. *Perspectives,* Catalogue no. 75-001-X. Ottawa: Statistics Canada. At http://www.statcan.gc.ca/pub/75-001-x/2009112/pdf/11055-eng.pdf.

Ratha, D., and S. Mohapatra. 2009. *Migration and Development Brief 9.* Washington, DC: Migration and Remittances Team, Development Prospectus Group, World Bank.

Reitz, J.G. 2010. Selecting Immigrants for the Short Term: Is It Smart in the Long Run? *Policy Options* 31 (7):12-16. Montreal: Institute for Research on Public Policy.

Reitz, J.G. 2011. *Pro-immigration Canada: Social and Economic Roots of Popular Views.* IRPP Study No. 20, October. Montreal: Institute for Research on Public Policy (IRPP).

Reitz, J.G., and R. Banerjee. 2007. Racial Inequality, Social Cohesion, and Policy Issues in Canada. In *Belonging? Diversity, Recognition and Shared Citizenship in Canada. The Art of the State,* Vol. 3, eds. K. Banting, T.J. Courchene, and F.L. Seidle, 489-545. Montreal: Institute for Research on Public Policy.

Rodríguez-García, D. 2010a. *Retos y tendencias en la gestión de la inmigración y la diversidad en clave transatlántica* [A Transatlantic View of Challenges and Trends in the Management of Immigration and Diversity]. Documentos CIDOB Migraciones, No. 21. Barcelona: CIDOB. At http://www.cidob.org/es/publicaciones/

documentos_cidob/migraciones/num_21_retos_y_tendencias_en_la_gestion_
de_la_inmigracion_y_la_diversidad_en_clave_transatlantica.

Rodríguez-García, D. 2010b. Beyond Assimilation and Multiculturalism: A
Critical Review of the Debate on Managing Diversity. *Journal of International
Migration and Integration* 11 (3):251-271.

Rosner, J.D. 2009. *The Politics of Immigration, and the (Limited) Case for New Optimism:
Perspectives from a Political Pollster.* Washington, DC: Migration Policy Institute.

Sassen, S. 1988. *The Mobility of Labor and Capital: A Study in International Investment
and Labor Flow.* Cambridge: Cambridge University Press.

Sassen, S. 2007. *A Sociology of Globalization.* New York: W.W. Norton.

Schellenberg, G., and H. Maheux. 2007. Immigrants' Perspectives on Their First
Four Years in Canada: Highlights from Three Waves of the Longitudinal
Survey of Immigrants to Canada. *Canadian Social Trends*, April. Ottawa: Sta-
tistics Canada.

Sebastián, M. 2006. *Inmigración y Economía Española: 1996–2006.* Madrid: Oficina
Económica del Presidente del Gobierno.

Siemiatycki, M. 2010. Marginalizing Migrants: Canada's Rising Reliance on
Temporary Foreign Workers. *Canadian Issues* (Spring): 60-63.

Smith, M., and L. Guarnizo, eds. 1998. *Transnationalism from Below.* New Brunswick, NJ: Transaction.

Solé, C., coord. 2001. *El impacto de la inmigración en la economía y en la sociedad
receptora.* Barcelona: Anthropos.

Statistics Canada. 2005. *Longitudinal Survey of Immigrants to Canada: A Portrait
of Early Settlement Experiences.* Catalogue no. 89-614-XIE. Ottawa: Statistics
Canada. At http://www.statcan.gc.ca/pub/89-614-x/89-614-x2005001-eng.pdf.

Statistics Canada. 2007. *2006 Community Profiles.* 2006 Census. Ottawa: Statistics Canada. At http://www12.statcan.ca/census-recensement/2006/dp-pd/
prof/92-591/index.cfm?Lang=E.

United Nations Department of Economic and Social Affairs (UN DESA). 2009.
Trends in International Migrant Stock: The 2008 Revision. New York: United
Nations. At http://esa.un.org/migration/index.asp?panel=1.

Vertovec, S. 2010. *Transnationalism.* London: Routledge.

Vertovec, S., and Wessendorf, S., eds. 2010. *The Multiculturalism Backlash: European
Discourses, Policies and Practices.* London and New York: Routledge.

Zapata-Barrero, R. 2009. Policies and Public Opinion Towards Immigrants: The
Spanish Case. *Ethnic and Racial Studies* 32 (7):1101-1120.

Zapata-Barrero, R., and N. de Witte. 2007. The Spanish Governance of EU Borders:
Normative Questions. *Mediterranean Politics* 12 (1):85-90.

OVERVIEW

CHAPTER 1

Managing Immigration and Diversity in Canada and Quebec: Lessons for Spain?

JEFFREY G. REITZ, *Professor of Sociology,*
R.F. Harney Professor and Director of Ethnic, Immigration,
and Pluralism Studies, University of Toronto

Managing immigration and diversity is among the most perplexing issues of the present era of globalization. While immigration brings huge economic opportunities for developed countries, with their low population growth and resulting labour shortages, it also brings problems of accommodating newcomers with diverse backgrounds and cultural differences. As the number of immigrant-receiving countries continues to expand, there has been an increasing focus primarily on the problems associated with immigration, namely, the economic, social, and political incorporation of immigrants. And in dealing with these problems, it is sometimes asked whether the long experience of the traditional countries of immigration—the United States, Canada, and Australia—contains useful lessons for newer immigration countries. Can Europeans—in particular, can Spain—learn from this experience?

The answer, in my view, is a qualified "yes." The case of Canada commands attention not only because of its comparatively positive experience managing immigration and diversity in recent decades, but it also has special relevance for Spain because the autonomy of Quebec, and to some

Managing Immigration and Diversity in Canada: A Transatlantic Dialogue in the New Age of Migration,
ed. D. Rodríguez-García. Montreal and Kingston: Queen's Policy Studies Series, McGill-Queen's University Press.

extent, of the other provinces, has a parallel with the regions of Spain. That Canada and Quebec have had real success with immigration is well known. This was recently marked by French President Nicolas Sarkozy at the 2008 Francophonie Summit, where he praised Canadian respect for diversity as well as Quebec's ability to defend its identity without rejecting others, which he called a "lesson to the world" (*Globe and Mail* 17 October 2008). Some speak of a "Canadian model" for immigration policy lying behind Canada's success. Some of the specific Canadian policy approaches to immigration, including selection, settlement and integration policies, multiculturalism, and provincial decentralization, deserve attention.

However, I will not suggest that existing Canadian policies deserve simply to be copied. There are at least three reasons. First, Canada's successes are not only due to its policies, whatever their merit; there are other reasons, including certain historical, institutional, and geographical circumstances unique to Canada (Reitz 2004). So at the level of specific policies, the lessons to be learned must be considered in light of particular circumstances. Each country presents its own distinctive issues, and local policies in Canada may not travel all that well. Second, circumstances that facilitated success in Canada in the past are now changing, and a number of new problems and challenges have emerged, requiring that Canada reinvent its own policy model. In considering Canadian experience, other countries should take these newly emerging Canadian problems into account. They may find it particularly interesting to consider how Canadians are responding to both the new realities and the lessons garnered from the country's own past experience.

And third, most importantly, I suggest that the most significant lesson to be gleaned from the Canadian case is actually at a broader level. Canadian experience suggests that the effort to address problems that accompany immigration should not neglect the opportunity side of the equation. Immigration has produced major benefits for Canada—and for all three traditional immigration countries—not only economic, but social and cultural. These benefits are an important reason why Canada, and also the United States and Australia, are successful nations in the modern world and why they continue to be attractive to new generations of immigrants. And to some extent, Canadian successes and the resulting benefits arise from recognition of immigration as an opportunity. In fact, Canada's attempts to reinvent its own policy model are aided immeasurably by the country's strong and continuing commitment to immigration and its positive opportunities.

Canada's immigration program is in a period of considerable change. Some changes have already been made, and further changes seem likely. These are related to evolving circumstances, as mentioned above, but they also stem from political change. The federal government recently introduced significant changes that provide the immigration minister with new powers to alter immigrant selection criteria, changes intended to respond differently to rapidly changing labour market needs. One such change is the introduction of the Canadian Experience Class. As these changes were being implemented, further question marks were added by the economic turmoil sweeping global financial markets, introducing huge uncertainties in labour markets and altering prospects for immigration and immigrant integration. As some of the new immigration policies were predicated on the idea of perpetual economic expansion and growth, they should be re-examined in light of economic circumstances.

CANADA'S IMMIGRATION POLICY MODEL

One of the most important features of Canada's immigration program is its large size relative to the country's overall population. It is justifiable to use the term "mass immigration" to describe the Canadian policy. As a percentage of the resident population, Canadian immigration has been relatively large for over a century, and an expansionist policy has been pursued more or less continually since the end of the Second World War. For more than 15 years, the explicit goal of Liberal governments was to take in a number of immigrants equalling 1 percent of the total population per year. The actual intake has fallen short of this target; at 200,000 to 250,000 annually for most years since 1990, the intake represents 0.75 percent of the population (see Figure 1). Even so, the Canadian program is still nearly twice the size of its American counterpart—even including illegal immigrants from Mexico as part of the American program.

As a result, and despite a certain amount of emigration or return migration, Canada has substantially more foreign-born residents as a percentage of the population than the United States and most European countries (see Figure 2). Australia is an exception; in the past, Australia was committed to mass immigration, but since the mid-1990s, the country has reduced its immigration flow considerably.

When Canada removed country-of-origin barriers to immigration in the 1960s, the origins of immigrants shifted to sources outside Europe (see Figure 3). The impact of the shift to non-European origins is well known in Toronto and Vancouver. Both major Canadian cities have gone from having populations of virtually entirely European origins in 1970 to having large non-European minorities today. Official projections say that within the next ten to 12 years, and based on current immigration patterns, the majority of the populations in those cities will be racial minorities (making them "majority-minority" cities). Immigration in Quebec has been lower than in other provinces (i.e., Ontario and British Columbia) because of economic problems linked to political instability, although recently, immigration in Montreal, the third major Canadian metropolis, is back up again (see Figure 4).

FIGURE 1
Numbers of Immigrants to Canada, 1980–2007, by Admission Category

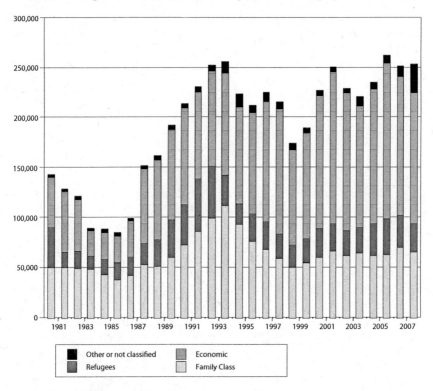

Source: Citizenship and Immigration Canada (various years).

FIGURE 2
Immigration Nations: Percent Foreign-born, 2005

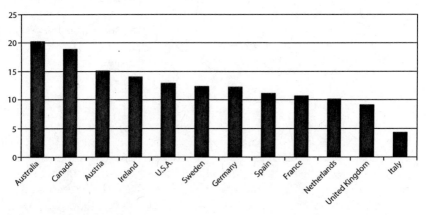

Source: United Nations (2006).

FIGURE 3
Birthplace of Immigrants by Period of Arrival, Canada 2001

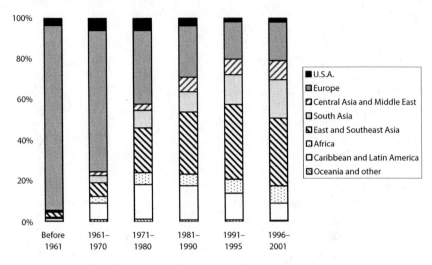

Source: Statistics Canada, Census of Canada (2005).

FIGURE 4
Immigration in 2005 As Proportion of 2001 Population, Canada and Provinces

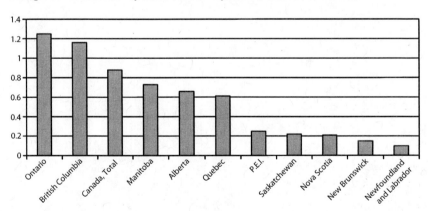

Source: Citizenship and Immigration Canada (2006); Statistics Canada (2005).

Canadian immigration has been unarguably successful in economic and social terms. The education-based skills level of immigrants is high, translating into a considerable degree of employment success, and the national celebration of cultural diversity seems to indicate a smooth social integration of minorities within distinct communities and in the wider society. The program is also successful in political terms, and this may be the most important success indicator. There is relatively widespread acceptance of and support for immigration policy in Canada, and relatively little of the acrimonious debate seen elsewhere (see Reitz 2011). Public opinion polls show that for the last several decades, in every year but one (1982, a recession year), a majority of the population has either supported immigration levels or has wanted them increased (Figure 5). In most countries, the reverse is true: There is less immigration, and a majority still wants reductions. Most telling, there is rarely any debate on immigration during Canadian election campaigns. Canadian political parties all espouse pro-immigration policies; the public rarely asks them to defend their policies. The word "immigration" is seldom, if ever, mentioned in the nationally televised leaders' debates. This was true in the election of October 2008, despite the significant changes to policy mentioned earlier. In the most recent debate, preceding the May 2011 election, a question on immigration and multiculturalism was posed by a voter, and the four debating prime ministerial candidates each attempted to put forward the most pro-immigration position, defending more accessible immigration and the interests of immigrants in Canada.

Internationally, Canadian success has been noticed, and as mentioned, there are frequent references to a "Canadian model" of immigration policy and immigrant integration. The implication is that Canadian success is

FIGURE 5
Canadian Public Opinion on Immigration Levels

"If it were your job to plan an immigration policy for Canada at this time, would you be inclined to increase immigration, decrease immigration, or keep the number of immigrants at about the current level?"

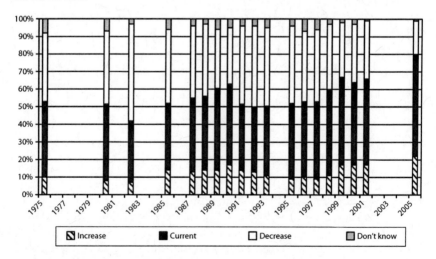

Source: Gallup Canada, Inc. (various years).

due to the country's policy model. But what exactly is this model? Briefly stated, there are three pillars of Canadian policy affecting the success of immigration: immigrant selection policy, immigrant integration policy, and provincial decentralization.

Regarding the selection of immigrants, the best-known feature is the skills-based selection criterion, the so-called "points system" for selecting skilled immigrants. There is also an increasingly important component of provincially controlled selection, particularly in Quebec, but now in every province.

Regarding integration policy, the best-known facet is the country's official policy of "multiculturalism," introduced in 1971 (and enshrined in the constitution in 1982, with further legislative mandate in 1988), and, again, with variations made for Quebec. In addition to these, however, there are a large number of other programs to encourage settlement and effective integration into local communities, including language training, fast-track citizenship, an array of human rights and equality guarantees, and efforts to promote better utilization of immigrant skills and improved recognition for foreign-acquired qualifications in the Canadian labour market.

Both selection and integration are, to some extent, decentralized, with provincial and even local autonomy. It is interesting that the basic designs for all three pillars of Canadian policy—the points system, multiculturalism, and provincial decentralization—were developed at about the same time, in the late 1960s and early 1970s, the period of the "Quiet Revolution" in Quebec that led to more provincial autonomy. All have been features of Canadian policy for nearly 40 years, and the emerging status of Quebec in Canada shaped them all.

Points System for Immigrant Selection

The points system has been effective in enhancing the employment potential of immigrants in Canada, and this has been a significant benefit to Canada. Introduced in 1967, it selects immigrants on the basis of education, knowledge of one of the two official languages, work experience, and other predictors of employment success. It has been essentially copied by Australia, and there have been influential advocates for its adoption in other countries. The points system in the Canadian case serves as a means for ensuring that large numbers of immigrants will have minimum qualifications for survival in a modern economy. For Canada, with its goal of mass immigration, the points system responds to the desire to make large-scale immigration contribute to the development of the Canadian economy. Simply stated, skilled workers are needed in the kind of knowledge economy Canada aspires to develop.

From the standpoint of public perception, this selection system feeds directly into one of the basic reasons why Canadians so strongly support immigration, namely the belief that immigration contributes to the economy (see Reitz 2011). To this basic rationale, national leaders add further reasons. There is rhetoric about nation-building, and about Canada's vulnerability as a small country with a low fertility rate located next to a world superpower. Some say that immigration supports Canada's status as a multicultural country, a proud point of presumed distinction from our southern neighbour. Many people in Canada believe that immigration helps offset population aging; by and large, demographers do not support this sentiment—illustrating that Canadian enthusiasm for immigration sometimes ignores expert opinion.

In recent years, popular emphasis has been on the immediate economic benefits of immigration. This is a second example where the Canadian enthusiasm for immigrants has disregarded expert opinion, since economists in Canada (as elsewhere) have not tended toward the view of immigration as a substantial economic benefit. The consensus in economics is that immigration adds to economic growth, but only to a small degree (Economic Council of Canada 1991; Borjas 1999). However, Canadian policy-makers—and the general public—have ignored this. They support immigration as a boon to the economy, not only for meeting labour shortfalls, but as a source of economic stimulation. They believe immigrants support the economy by adding size, new ideas, creative potentials, international awareness, and linkages critical in a global economy. Rather than listening to economists, they prefer the views of the American geographer Richard Florida (2002). Florida—now an immigrant himself in Canada—emphasizes the economic role of what he calls the "creative class," with immigrants as a significant component of that creative class.

As evidence of the Canadian view of immigration as a huge economic boost, one might notice that areas of the country that are not now the major areas of immigrant settlement—places other than Toronto, Vancouver, and Montreal—are hoping to attract immigrants. Not surprisingly, these include Alberta, a province where the oil industry during the economic boom has created an insatiable demand for workers of all kinds. Less obvious is the bid for immigrants by Atlantic Canada, where there are relatively few jobs and immigrants are sought as a way to create them.

The points system with its focus on employability contributes to this perception of immigration as an economic boon. However, it also has definite weaknesses; it does not completely satisfy the desire for highly skilled immigrants. This weakness is a direct result of the large numbers sought. When the intake is large, the selection standard declines, and there is a need for compromises and trade-offs. Indeed, the essential idea of the points system is to reduce such trade-offs to a simple formula. Most points are given for high levels of education, but without a university degree, sufficient points for admission may be scored by other indicators of employability, such as an arranged job or relative youth. Although most immigration officials want immigrants with a four-year university degree, because of the large numbers sought and taken, over 20 percent of the points-selected immigrants in 2005 did not have a four-year university degree.

The desire for large numbers is a reason for a points system, as well as its basic weakness. If a country wishes to admit a smaller number of skilled immigrants, there are other ways to administer selection to get better results. The United States uses an employer nomination process with government certification that no native-born Americans are suitable, which, when coupled with a minimum education standard of a four-year university degree, ensures high skill levels. Australia also emphasizes employer nomination, with smaller overall numbers. Some countries adopting a "points systems" in Europe are borrowing the Canadian label but not the Canadian policy, since they are not seeking mass immigration. For example, what the United Kingdom calls a points system has very high selection criteria, but small (or non-existent) numerical goals. The U.K. system is open to the admission of top scientists or similarly accomplished individuals, but the country seems unlikely to get demographically significant numbers using this scheme.

Multiculturalism

Multiculturalism policy has been labelled part of the Canadian success story. It, too, has been exported, including to Australia and Europe. As U.S. sociologist Nathan Glazer (1997) says, "We are all multiculturalists now." With respect to the United States, Glazer describes a particular variant of multiculturalism that not only recognizes minority cultures but attempts to promote cultural relativism and displace mainstream values. This theme also runs throughout the writings of critics of multiculturalism including the American historian Arthur Schlesinger (1992), and political theorists Brian Barry (2001) and Samuel Huntington (2004), among others. In Europe, there has been a retreat from multiculturalism, partly related to problems of integrating Muslims and the issue of terrorism. Multiculturalism has been criticized as promoting radical cultural relativism; if multiculturalism is implemented, opponents say, the basic values of democracy and Western culture will be disrespected, compromised, and devalued, including principles of free speech and gender equality. Amartya Sen (2006a, 2006b; see Kelly 2002) discusses multiculturalism as a Canadian import that promotes if not cultural relativism then a form of cultural isolation, what he calls "plural monoculturalism."

But none of this really reflects multiculturalism as the term applies in Canada. Whether or not multiculturalism as implemented in other countries represents an attack on mainstream values, in the Canadian context, this use of the term would certainly be an exaggeration. The Canadian policy was first formulated by Prime Minister Pierre Trudeau in 1971, in a speech to Parliament where he equated multiculturalism with cultural freedom. At the same time, he specified four specific "supports" that emphasize the connection of minority groups to the whole: (1) promoting contribution to Canada, (2) full participation in Canadian institutions, (3) interchange between groups in the interest of national unity, and (4) acquisition of an official language. These objectives make it quite clear that Canadian multiculturalism is not tantamount to cultural relativism or to cultural decentralization, much less to the displacement of mainstream values. There is little in Canadian discourse to call forth such interpretations.

There is, of course, some variation in Canadian concepts of multiculturalism. Canadian philosopher Will Kymlicka has argued, most notably in *Multicultural Citizenship* (1995), that although multiculturalism emphasizes recognition of the cultural distinctiveness of minority groups and, as such, champions group rights, it is not really a departure from political liberalism, which traditionally emphasizes individual rights. In his view, governments need multiculturalism to offset an otherwise virtually inescapable tendency to favour a dominant ethnic group. However, the specific policies he identifies as part of multiculturalism include not only recognition for cultural minorities but a variety of others, including affirmative action policies in employment and measures to protect minorities from harassment, including physical and verbal abuse. These policies may be consistent with Trudeau's list, which emphasizes equality of participation in mainstream institutions. Nonetheless, Kymlicka's list is somewhat arbitrary, and Canadians are far from united on all of these policies. In particular, affirmative action has been rejected as an employment policy in every Canadian province, without anyone suggesting that multiculturalism has been abandoned. Moreover, Trudeau's list includes many policies that without the commitment to group rights might look like assimilationism—such as promotion of the acquisition of English or French as official languages by minorities.

Do Canadian multicultural policies have any effect? Kymlicka, in his later book *Finding Our Way* (1999), takes a very positive view that multiculturalism works in Canada because immigrants are well integrated into society—especially since 1971. But in this discussion, the cause-effect logic is far from airtight. If immigrants are better integrated in Canada, this outcome has occurred for many reasons—including the immigrant selection system, which ensures relatively high levels of education and a degree of economic success. And when the focus is on immigrants at comparable levels of relative education, those in Canada are not better integrated than their counterparts in the United States, where there is no official multiculturalism. If as a result of the Canadian policy, as compared to the U.S. laissez-faire approach, there are differences between the countries in the formation of immigrant ethnic communities—in their retention of distinct culture or persistence over time, or even in the degree of their acceptance into the mainstream society—these are not dramatic ones. In fact, cross-national comparative research shows little difference (Reitz and Breton 1994). And are Canadians actually more strongly committed to the idea that immigrants should be encouraged to maintain their distinct cultures? Not according to the political opinion data, which show that Americans are actually somewhat more sympathetic to this idea, particularly those with a more individualistic outlook. Tellingly, Canadians who support multiculturalism are often more interested in asserting a Canadian difference from the United States, suggesting that Canadian nationalism reinforces the espousal of multiculturalism (see Reitz 2011).

Despite widespread approval of multiculturalism, the policy has critics in Canada. Some say multiculturalism reinforces the lack of a distinctive Canadian identity (Granatstein 2007, 90-100); others allege that it perpetuates marginality and inequality. But such critics also lack evidence. Moreover, in response to the concern over whether multiculturalism undermines the welfare state, Banting and Kymlicka (2006) show in a comparison of over a dozen countries that it does not.

The reality is that most evaluations of multiculturalism, whether positive or negative, are not substantiated by convincing empirical evidence. Many of those who extol the virtues of multiculturalism in Canada point to the enthusiasm with which Canadians embrace the philosophy of multiculturalism, and the progressive ideals it embodies. What is missing is clear evidence that these ideas produce a difference from what happens in other countries whose citizens express their ideals of inter-ethnic harmony differently. The most convincing positive evidence comes from a study (by Bloemraad 2006) showing that government funding of ethnic community organizations produces higher citizenship acquisition rates in Canada. How this affects the social integration of immigrants is not known, however. If anything, the existing evidence suggests that official policies have little real impact in Canada, something that is not surprising given the small size of the official multiculturalism budget. It would be more surprising if a program costing about C$21 million a year could produce major social re-engineering.

Quebec and Provincial Autonomy in Immigration

There is considerable provincial autonomy in both aspects of the Canadian model—immigration selection and multiculturalism. Quebec has been leading the way, but other provinces are now involved. Both the points system and multiculturalism reflect the political decentralization of Canada. It should be remembered that multiculturalism was shaped by interprovincial relations and arose because of the need to accommodate Canada's English-French linguistic duality. The awakening of Quebec national identity in the 1960s, supported by a highly educated middle and upper-middle class, focused attention on the accommodation of inter-ethnic differences as a way of building society. A proposal to recognize French language and culture was examined by a national commission on "bilingualism and biculturalism," prompting objections from immigrant groups that even if bilingualism was needed, an officially bicultural country created the potential for their own marginalization.

Noting an inequity inherent in adopting cultural recognition for a national minority, immigrant groups in Canada requested *multi*-culturalism as a compromise. The compromise was accepted fairly quickly, although with reluctance among many francophone Canadians. They noticed the symbolic reduction in their own status in replacement of the "bi" in biculturalism—where they were one of two—with "multi," where they would become one of many. The reluctance of Quebec to fully embrace multiculturalism may seem odd to outsiders who see the English-French duality of Canada as its most obviously multicultural feature. French Canadians do embrace the idea of cultural pluralism, but they prefer the term *inter*-culturalism, which is more ambiguous as to the number of groups involved or their relative status. Multiculturalism is formulated differently in Quebec than in the rest of Canada to accommodate local requirements.

The same is true of immigration policy. About 70 percent of immigrants settle in one of three cities: Toronto, Vancouver, and Montreal. Provincial governments have their own integration policies, and the most variable are the provincial policies related to the selection of immigrants. Since 1971, Quebec has had an agreement with the federal government to coordinate immigration policy and to collaborate in the selection of immigrants. This agreement has been updated three times, most recently in 1991, with the Gagnon-Tremblay/McDougal Accord, intended to provide elements that would have been part of the Canadian constitution had earlier negotiations between Quebec and Canada succeeded (the 1987 failed Meech Lake Accord). Quebec's goals for the 1991 agreement were to preserve its demographic weight within Canada and to integrate immigrants in a manner respecting the distinct society of Quebec. Quebec has a formal role in advising about the number of immigrants it wishes to receive, keeping the number proportional to the population of the province. Formally, Canada issues the visas and conducts the official background checks on health and security matters, but Quebec administers its own points system, giving priority to the French language. Quebec is in charge of all integration services, with a particular emphasis on providing permanent residents with the means to learn the French language (Young 2004). One evaluation (Jean Renaud et al. 1997; Jean Renaud 2000; Victor Piché et al. 1999) shows that immigrants in Quebec have done well in terms of employment.

Since 1998, most other provinces have negotiated Provincial Nominee Programs (PNPs) in agreements covering a five-year period. In each case, the stated purpose of the PNP is to boost economic and industrial growth. Compared to Quebec's role in selection, these PNPs are small, and although expanding, the total number of immigrants admitted to Canada under these programs was less than 7 percent in 2007. The small size of the programs means that their greatest impact is likely in provinces like Manitoba, where relatively few immigrants settle. In any case, interprovincial migration favours the high-immigration provinces of Ontario and British Columbia, and these movements significantly offset PNP schemes. The Citizenship and Immigration Canada study of interprovincial migration (Citizenship and Immigration Canada 2000) among tax filers tracked in a specially prepared Immigration Database (IMDB) shows that immigrants to the relatively unattractive provinces tend to move toward those that are more attractive. Ontario and British Columbia experienced net gains as a result of interprovincial migration; Quebec lost the largest absolute numbers.

The provinces in Canada also play an important role in settlement programs. The federal government provides much of the funding, and dispute has focused on the Quebec agreement with the federal government, which guarantees minimum funding regardless of the numbers of immigrants going to Quebec. During the economic slump in Quebec, which persisted partly because of controversies over Quebec separation and sovereignty, fewer immigrants went to Quebec, and the funding per immigrant become quite high, four times higher than for Ontario, according to the Ontario government. An agreement between the federal government and Ontario was designed to address this disparity.

Settlement programs have not been evaluated, partly because they are decentralized to the provincial level and partly because many activities are proposed and operated by local community agencies with their own specific plans. Even without formal evaluation, however, it is evident that despite its substantially greater funding per immigrant to pay for settlement programs, Quebec does not appear to have had correspondingly more favourable results in terms of key indicators of immigrant success such as employment or language learning.

EMERGING PROBLEMS OF CANADIAN IMMIGRATION

Looking at the three pillars of Canadian policy—the points system, multiculturalism, and provincial autonomy—we can see that their impacts are uncertain and limited. They are limited in what they can accomplish: the points system because of the mass nature of Canadian immigration, multiculturalism because it is largely symbolic, and provincial autonomy because of interprovincial migration. Moreover, duplication at the provincial level limits what provinces are willing to do.

As suggested at the outset, the success of Canadian immigration is due as well to a variety of circumstances *other than these well-known policies*. These factors might be thought of as the institutional context of

Canadian society; they include features of Canadian labour markets and related institutions. Within this context, certain changes are producing concomitant changes in Canadian immigration.

Geography is part of the context. The geographic isolation of Canada from all countries other than the United States has limited illegal immigration and has made legal immigration more attractive. This factor has been important in sustaining the political perception of Canadian immigration as being controlled in the national interest. Yet a number of institutional factors, which might be summed up under the heading of "globalization," are creating greater opportunities for migration and a much more visible flow of illegal immigrants into Canada. As a result, the immigration program is facing significant political pressures. With respect to immigration, globalization is undercutting the previous benefits of Canadian geography.

Other things are changing too, and associated problems are emerging. Skill-based selection has not prevented a significant decline in the labour market performance of immigrants and a related increase in immigrant poverty. Furthermore, increased racial inequality is now evident, making it clear that despite their value and popularity, multiculturalism and other related policies have not in themselves resolved the ambiguous status of racial minorities in Canada.

If changing circumstances affect Canadian immigration and threaten the success of the "Canadian model" in Canada, we need to look at the implications for Canada and for other countries considering adoption of the Canadian model. To this end, I want to examine two issues: the decline in employment success of the most recent cohorts of immigrants and emerging race relations issues in the context of Canada and Quebec.

Declining Employment Success for Immigrants in Canada

Recognition of employment problems was somewhat slow in coming because general trends over several decades were masked by the ups and downs of the business cycle. But the 2001 census showed a serious problem, and Frenette and Morissette (2003) have documented a significant decline in the earnings of successive cohorts of new immigrants since the 1970s—virtually the entire period during which the points system has been in place (Figure 6).

The 2001 data suggest that the much-touted policy framework no longer ensures the employability of immigrants. This is puzzling to many, as major upgrades to selection policies throughout the 1980s and 1990s were expected to prevent the decline in immigrant employment success. For one thing, the points system was revised to maximize the proportion of immigrants selected on the basis of points and to minimize the proportion admitted for family reunification (refer to Figure 1). Changes in the points system and the shift towards more immigrants selected on

FIGURE 6
Earnings Trends for Immigrant Men, Canada

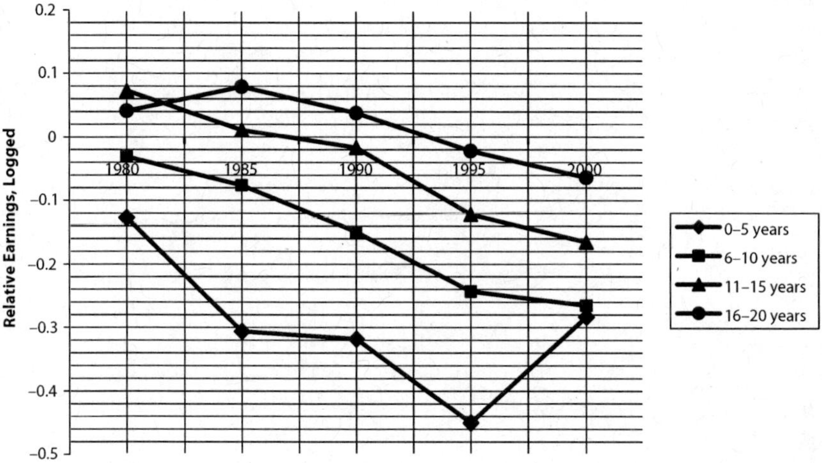

Source: Frenette and Morissette (2003).

points produced significant increases in the educational attainments of immigrants; by 2000, 45 percent of arriving immigrants had university degrees. Yet there was still a decline in employment success.

There is a debate about the causes of this trend, and the following factors have been cited as relevant: declining employment opportunity for all new labour market entrants; a shift in immigrant origins (which occurred in the 1970s and early 1980s, and so would not account for more recent changes); a shift to the "knowledge economy" and increased credentialism, with implications for the transferability of immigrant skills; a decline in the labour market value of foreign labour market experience for immigrants; and increased overall labour market inequality (Reitz 2007). The evidence supports some explanations more than others, but most explanations refer to broader institutional bases as causes, and in most cases, they do not lead to solutions based on elaboration or "fine-tuning" of the existing immigrant selection model.

Consider one item on the list that might seem less institution-related: the declining labour market value of foreign experience. The reasons for this trend are not clear. Some say that with technological change, foreign experience may be less relevant in Canada. Yet foreign education has not become any less relevant. Moreover, globalization should move us in the opposite direction, towards more cross-nationally consistent types of experience. Another possibility is that rising education levels in the native-born population are reducing opportunities for immigrants in the specific occupations in which they have experience, and as a result, they are being deflected to other occupations. Since the value of experience is occupation-specific, their experience is less valued in the occupations where they actually find employment. In this way, institutional change could at least partly account for the impact of the declining labour market value of foreign experience. Some hope for a selection-based solution, by putting greater selection emphasis on youth and less on previous employment experience. To some extent, this idea underlies the new Canadian Experience Class.

Most policy responses to the decline in immigrant employment success have been in the area of labour market reforms. There has been an effort made to increase the recognition and use of foreign-acquired skills in the Canadian economy. These include encouraging professional licensing agencies to remove bureaucratic barriers to the acceptance of foreign qualifications, providing bridge-training programs to "top-up" foreign-acquired skills and enhance their relevance in Canada, and setting up mentorship programs (a kind of apprenticeship for immigrants to "learn the ropes" and learn workplace-specific practices in Canadian firms). These programs are still under development. They may work, or they may turn out to be difficult and expensive.

If the mounting problem of immigrant poverty is an offshoot of the "knowledge economy" emerging in Canada, similar problems may be expected to surface in other countries as well. They certainly exist in the United States; skilled immigrants in that country have lower relative earnings than in Canada, and their earnings are in decline. One does not hear much about this from the U.S. because its focus is understandably on other problems, mainly at the Mexican border.

Some recent policy initiatives have placed less focus on education for the selection of immigrants and more on skilled trades (despite much talk of a "knowledge economy" and the new international competition for skills). Employers, particularly in the oil industry and construction, say they need workers in specific trades where the supply of native-born Canadians has been insufficient. They suggest that immigrants could fill the gap but cannot do so under the current system, with its focus on post-secondary education. The Canadian Experience Class is a new category in the selection system, introduced in 2008, which provides temporary immigrants, who have two years' experience in Canada, to apply for permanent status. Under this policy revision, not only university-trained workers but also persons trained in skilled trades, such as chefs, crane operators, carpenters, and electricians, would gain permanent admission to Canada, thereby becoming part of the immigration-generated workforce of the future.

The key difference in this selection method is that filling the demand for less-skilled immigration would be based on employer-driven selection. Employers would be the gatekeepers for initial admission to Canada and the gatekeepers for permanent residency. As this is done, the following two issues should be addressed.

The first is the question of the longer-term integration potential for less-skilled workers selected by an employer-driven scheme. Employer selection is based on immediate need, so there is a short-term advantage, in that such immigrants fare better than those who are better-trained but cannot find jobs. Yet even if a temporary worker survives in a job for two years, his or her longer-term success in employment might be less than for workers with broader skills and higher levels of education. If, as now seems likely, a recession occurs and some of these persons lose their jobs, they may be less able to find alternative employment than the better educated, points-selected immigrants. The points system gives points for an arranged job, but it demands higher levels of education for those without an arranged job, thereby taking advantage of the greater ability of the highly educated to recover from a reversal of economic fortune.

The second issue concerns enforcement. Meeting the need for less-skilled immigration by allowing employers to make selections essentially privatizes selection, and the integrity of the selection system is no longer guaranteed by the public accountability of government. An extensive array of documents mostly provided by employers is required, and this raises the question of the potential for fraud. Accountability must be built into the privatized aspects of the selection system to ensure that permanent visas are granted only for bona fide employment.

The employer demand for lower levels of skill is also shown by the increased visibility of illegal immigration. No one knows the number of illegal immigrants in Canada, but journalists have published estimates from activists indicating 200,000 or more illegal immigrants in Canada, mostly working in construction and other less-skilled occupations and trades. This is much smaller on a per capita basis than in other countries, but it is a growing issue in Canada. Arguably, since illegal immigrants are doing jobs that are necessary, or even critical, to the survival of large sectors of the economy, they should be granted amnesty and full permanent resident status.

In some ways, the distinction between employer-driven selection of less-skilled immigrants and illegal immigration is only the manner in which the immigrants initially gain admission to Canada: In the first case, they qualify as temporary workers, and in the second, they simply enter the country without a visa. In fact, many illegal immigrants may be temporary immigrants who have overstayed their visa. In both instances, solutions must address the long-term integration of less-skilled workers, as well as the enforcement of regulations to ensure the integrity of a partly privatized system of immigrant selection.

Racial Tensions and the Retreat from Multiculturalism

Despite multiculturalism, there are continuing concerns about racism and discriminatory treatment in key areas such as employment, housing, and policing. Although treated as a marginal issue by politicians, the impact of racism has been debated by researchers, and reports of discrimination are widespread among African- and Asian-Canadian communities. There is, in effect, a racial disagreement on racial discrimination in Canada.

Racial minorities in Canada have the lowest individual and family incomes. Not surprisingly, the declining employment situation for immigrants affects racial minorities more than other groups, and there is greater poverty among racial minorities in Canada. There are other mounting concerns, which compound the issue—for example, gun-related gang violence in some parts of the Black community, mainly in Toronto. A blue-ribbon report *The Roots of Youth Violence* (McMurtry and Curling 2008), released in 2008 by the Ontario government, documented these problems and noted their basis in racism, poverty, community isolation, and other interconnected features of Canadian society.

The idea that multiculturalism may not be the answer to all problems of inter-group relations is hardly news in Europe. Of course, much of this feeling (and the retreat from multiculturalism mentioned earlier) is related to security issues in the post-9/11 world, or the bombings in Madrid, 2004, and London, 2005. Yet Canadians tend to think that these issues do not really apply to Canada. Even when 17 alleged members of a purported Islamic terrorist cell were arrested in Canada in 2006, most Canadians—rightly or wrongly—discounted the threat.

The most important question here is not about security issues, but rather whether racial inequalities and discrimination as a domestic issue threaten the unity of the country, despite multiculturalism. Obviously, a number of the problems in Europe also have domestic sources: the disturbances in France in certain Maghreb communities with high rates of unemployment, to cite one example. In Canada, some prominent observers point to evidence of the marginality of minorities; inequality and poverty; the growing size of some minority communities and the concomitant possibility of social isolation; and emerging social problems in certain minority communities. They note that these problems happen despite multiculturalism. Although few predict a serious breakdown in social cohesion in Canada as a result of ethnic diversity or because of the policy of multiculturalism, concern has been expressed on both the Left and the Right: by advocates for minority rights (Lewis 1992; Omidvar and Richmond 2003) and by advocates for reductions in immigration into Canada (e.g., Stoffman 2002).

Concerns about racism and discrimination exist in Canada. The national statistical bureau, Statistics Canada, conducted a massive study called the Ethnic Diversity Survey (EDS) in 2002. Over 40,000 interviews, designed to provide a portrait of inter-group relations in Canada, were conducted. In particular, the survey looked at the attachments and commitments of individuals to the society as a whole, using indicators such as "sense of belonging," trust in others, feeling "Canadian," and becoming a citizen. It examined satisfaction with life in general. Finally, it assessed not only attitudes but relevant behaviours, such as participation in volunteer activities and voting in Canadian elections.

An analysis of the survey data, which I conducted with Rupa Banerjee (Reitz and Banerjee 2007), compares racial minorities with persons of European origins. It also compares persons by length of time in Canada, paying careful attention to the Canadian-born second generation, which, as experience shows, has a special significance for long-term integration. Most incidents of activism and violence in immigrant communities—including in Britain and France—have occurred on the part of those born in the host country. The overall findings of the EDS data are the following.

First, on most counts, visible minorities are less integrated into Canadian society than their white counterparts. Thirty percent fewer identify themselves as "Canadian," and 30 percent fewer bother to vote in federal elections—largely owing to lack of will rather than to lack of eligibility, because visible minorities actually become citizens more quickly than immigrants of European origins. Smaller, though quite significant, gaps exist with regard to life satisfaction and trust in others, differences that are partly related to the recent arrival of many racial minorities.

Second, the EDS shows that certain important differences for immigrants grow over time and with more experience in Canada. Perhaps surprisingly, the racial gap is greater for the children of immigrants—those born in Canada—than for the parents. This is true despite the high levels of education and employment success of the second generation. The analysis shows that the effect of minority status becomes more negative for those with longer experience in Canada, and for the children of immigrants. The trends for the second generation are most pronounced for Blacks, but they are prevalent among all racial minorities (see Figure 7).

These findings together with many other studies suggest that there are problems regarding the integration of visible minorities in Canada, and that these problems seem to be growing. As the survey data show, the impact of race on the social outlook of racial minorities is greater for the children of immigrants than for the immigrants themselves, and this is troubling. Whatever the impact of policies such as multiculturalism in paving the way towards the social integration of immigrants, they appear to have worked less well for racial minorities than for white immigrant groups. Over time and into the second generation, a racial gap has become evident in Canada.

Evidence from the Ethnic Diversity Survey also challenges some of the assumptions of multicultural policy about the impact of minority communities (Reitz et al. 2009). In fact, the relation between ethnic attachments and an individual's social integration into Canadian society is mixed. On the one hand, there are consistently *positive* relations between ethnic involvements and two indicators: sense of belonging in Canada and overall life satisfaction. In these respects, ethnic attachments make

FIGURE 7
Regression Effect* of Visible Minority Status on Selected Indicators of Social Integration, by Generation and (for Immigrants) Period of Immigration

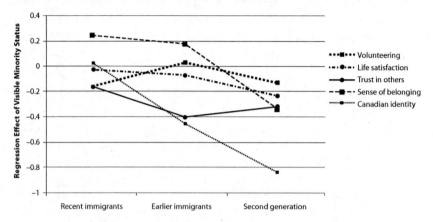

*Regression effects include statistical control for age and (for immigrants) years since immigration. Effects for Canadian identity, trust in others, and volunteering are based on logistic regression and are represented as odds ratios; regression effects for sense of belonging and life satisfaction are standardized OLS coefficients.

Source: Reitz and Banerjee (2007, 517-18).

a positive contribution to individual well-being. Further, those with stronger ethnic attachments are somewhat more likely to volunteer their time to participate in the community. On the other hand, ethnic attachments have a *negative* relation to the emergence of a "Canadian" identity and to the acquisition of Canadian citizenship. Even if involvement and commitment to a minority ethnic community yields some benefits for its members, for most of them it does not provide a strong link to matters that are explicitly "Canadian." Fostering a sense of belonging within Canadian society and fostering a sense of being explicitly "Canadian" are different. The first refers to a feeling of being connected to one's community, as a part of one's experience in Canada, and is positively related to ethnic attachments. The second refers to applying a label to oneself and is negatively related to ethnic attachments.

One way to summarize these findings is to observe that ethnic attachments are positively related to well-being within a circumscribed community context, but negatively related to some attachments to the broader society. This may be supported by another finding from the Ethnic Diversity Survey: Ethnic attachments have a negative impact on the sense of trust in others (Reitz et al. 2009, 39-40). This finding indicates that the potentially negative impact of ethnic community attachments is not only in relation to matters of national identity, but includes some of the social capital aspects highlighted in the American study by Robert Putnam (2007).

Ethnic communities have social benefits, but they also seem to promote a degree of social isolation. Thus, I suggest that multiculturalism in Canada might give more attention to working with ethnic communities to promote integration into Canadian society, and that at the moment certain ethnic communities have greater success with socio-cultural integration than others.

Regarding Quebec and the rest of Canada, the Ethnic Diversity Survey does not show major differences. Some have suggested that the controversy over "reasonable accommodation" in Quebec—really a debate about multiculturalism—reflects sensitivity to culture and discomfort with outsiders. The government commission assigned to investigate this matter decided that the issue had been blown out of proportion by the media, and the Ethnic Diversity Survey supports this view. The integration of minorities is no worse in Quebec than elsewhere in Canada, possibly even better.

LESSONS FOR SPAIN?

Looking over these aspects of Canadian immigration and integration, what are the lessons for other countries, such as Spain or other European countries? In summary, I think Canadian experiences carry implications for other countries. Canadian policies are partly—but only partly—responsible for the country's success, but I do not think these policies should simply be copied. This is partly because of the many differences in the situation of immigration in European countries such as Spain, compared to that of Canada. Policies must be adapted to the realities in each country. In fact, Canadians need to reinvent their own policies in light of new realities facing Canada, and they are in the process of doing this.

First, Canadian experience suggests that skill-selective immigration can be effective in promoting the economic integration of immigrants, with the caveat that foreign-acquired skills must be transferable. Unfortunately, this is not automatic.

Second, support for the integration of immigrants, from the traditional assimilationist perspective, including language instruction and assistance with employment and credential transferability, is an important component of Canadian policy that deserves attention from others.

Third, other countries should note that economic integration does not guarantee social integration. In Canada, more attention should be paid to the perceptions of the discriminatory treatment of minorities. Although existing approaches to multiculturalism are insufficient to address the problem, what is needed is not the abandonment of multiculturalism but policies to address equality issues directly and to address the isolation of minority communities from the mainstream. Canadian multiculturalism may not be for everyone, but other countries will find that immigrants and their descendants need to feel they have a meaningful place in the overall society. They must feel that they are fairly treated and that they are recognized and respected for their efforts. The inclusiveness of any society cannot be taken for granted, and both a policy and a reality of equal rights—including certain cultural freedoms—are essential. We need to find effective ways to promote equality that are supported by the majority and viewed as authentic by minorities.

These observations bring me back to the original point about immigration not simply as a problem but also as an opportunity. I have mentioned that Canadians support immigration. For a number of reasons, they believe in the value of immigration for national development. They see immigration as an opportunity for the country, and this outlook provides the country and its leaders with an enormous political resource, which is essential to finding solutions to the problems. A continued focus on opportunities is likely a good idea for both the mainstream population and immigrants: Both segments of society need to see something in it for themselves. It is crucial to ensure that the population retains its confidence in the value of immigration and in the contribution of immigrants to the society. Given that solving the problems of immigrant integration will require careful thought and significant resources, it is essential that both be available. Until now, Canada has managed to do this, but there are more challenges ahead.

In my view, the most distinctive feature of Canadian immigration, as much as or more than any of the specific policies I have mentioned, is the national commitment to the immigration project itself—the fact that Canadians want immigration and immigrants. Past policy successes have been based on this, and future success in dealing with current problems will not be possible without it. The success of Canada's efforts to deal with emerging problems depends on the commitment of Canadians to finding positive solutions. Immigration can be a major plus, as long as the population is convinced that it is necessary and positive, and remains committed to finding solutions to emerging problems.

REFERENCES

Banting, K., and W. Kymlicka. 2006. Introduction: Multiculturalism and the Welfare State: Setting the Context. In *Multiculturalism and the Welfare State: Recognition and Redistribution in Contemporary Democracies*, eds. K. Banting and W. Kymlicka, 1-48. Oxford: Oxford University Press.

Barry, B. 2001. *Culture and Equality: An Egalitarian Critique of Multiculturalism.* Cambridge, MA: Harvard University Press.

Bloemraad, I. 2006. *Becoming a Citizen: Incorporating Immigrants and Refugees in the United States and Canada.* Berkeley, CA: University of California Press.

Borjas, G.J. 1999. *Heaven's Door.* Princeton: Princeton University Press.

Citizenship and Immigration Canada. Various years. *Facts and Figures—Immigration Overview: Permanent and Temporary Residents*. Ottawa: Citizenship and Immigration Canada, Research and Evaluation Branch.

Economic Council of Canada. 1991. *Economic and Social Impacts of Immigration*. Ottawa: Supply and Services Canada.

Florida, R. 2002. *The Rise of the Creative Class: And How It's Transforming Work, Leisure, Community And Everyday Life*. New York: Basic Books.

Frenette, M., and R. Morisette. 2003. *Will They Ever Converge? Earnings of Immigrant and Canadian-born Workers over the Last Two Decades*. Analytical Studies Branch Research Paper Series, Catalogue no. 11F0019MIE—No. 215. Ottawa: Statistics Canada.

Fukuyama, F. 2007. Identity and Migration. *Prospect* 131 (February). At http://www.prospectmagazine.co.uk/2007/02/identityandmigration/ (accessed 5 July 2011).

Glazer, N. 1997. *We Are All Multiculturalists Now*. Cambridge: Harvard University Press.

Granatstein, J.L. 1998. *Who Killed Canadian History?* Toronto: Harper Perennial.

Hansen, R. 2007. Diversity, Integration, and the Turn from Multiculturalism in the United Kingdom. In *Belonging? Diversity, Recognition and Shared Citizenship in Canada. The Art of the State*, Vol. 3, eds. K. Banting, T.J. Courchene, and F.L. Seidle, 351-386. Montreal: Institute for Research on Public Policy.

Helliwell, J.F., and R.D. Putnam. 2004. The Social Context of Well-being. *Philosophical Transactions of the Royal Society of London*. B, 359: 1435-1446.

Joppke, C. 2001. Multicultural Citizenship: A Critique. *Archives européennes de sociologie* 42 (2):431-447.

Joppke, C. 2007. Immigrants and Civic Integration in Western Europe. In *Belonging? Diversity, Recognition and Shared Citizenship in Canada. The Art of the State*, Vol. 3, eds. K. Banting, T.J. Courchene, and F.L. Seidle, 521-350. Montreal: Institute for Research on Public Policy.

Kelly, P., ed. 2002. *Multiculturalism Reconsidered: Culture and Equality and Its Critics*. London: Polity Press.

Kymlicka, W. 1995. *Multicultural Citizenship: A Liberal Theory of Minority Rights*. Oxford: Oxford University Press.

Kymlicka, W. 1998. *Finding Our Way: Rethinking Ethnocultural Relations in Canada*. Oxford: Oxford University Press.

Lewis, S. 1992. *Report to the Office of the Premier*. Toronto: Government of Ontario.

McMurtry, R., and Dr. A. Curling. 2008. Review of *The Roots of Youth Violence: Findings, Analysis and Conclusions* (Volume 1). Toronto: Queen's Printer for Ontario.

Omidvar, R., and T. Richmond. 2003. *Immigrant Settlement and Social Inclusion in Canada*. Laidlaw Foundation Working Paper Series, Perspectives on Social Inclusion. Toronto: Laidlaw Foundation.

Piché, V., J. Renaud, and L. Gingras. 2002. Economic Integration of New Immigrants in the Montreal Labor Market: A Longitudinal Approach. *Population* 1 (57):57-82.

Putnam, R. 2007. E Pluribus Unum: Diversity and Community in the Twenty-first Century—The 2006 Johan Skytte Prize Lecture. *Scandinavian Political Studies* 30 (2):137-74.

Reitz, J.G. 2004. Canada: Immigration and Nation-Building in the Transition to a Knowledge Economy. In *Controlling Immigration: A Global Perspective*, 2nd ed., eds. W.A. Cornelius, P.L. Martin, J.F. Hollifield, and T. Tsuda, 97-133. Stanford, CA: Stanford University Press.

Reitz, J.G. 2007. Immigrant Employment Success in Canada, Part II: Understanding the Decline. *Journal of International Migration and Integration* 8 (1):37-62.

Reitz, J.G. 2011. *Pro-immigration Canada: Social and Economic Roots of Popular Views.* IRPP Study, No. 20, October. Montreal, Quebec: Institute for Research on Public Policy (IRPP).

Reitz, J.G., and R. Banerjee. 2007. Racial Inequality, Social Cohesion, and Policy Issues in Canada. In *Belonging? Diversity, Recognition and Shared Citizenship in Canada. The Art of the State*, Vol. 3, eds. K. Banting, T.J. Courchene, and F.L. Seidle, 489-545. Montreal: Institute for Research on Public Policy.

Reitz, J.G., and R. Breton. 1994. *The Illusion of Difference: Realities of Ethnicity in Canada and the United States.* Toronto: C.D. Howe Institute.

Reitz, J.G., R. Breton, K.K. Dion, and K.L. Dion. 2009. *Multiculturalism and Social Cohesion: Potentials and Challenges of Diversity.* Amsterdam: Springer.

Schlesinger, A. 1992. *The Disuniting of America: Reflections on a Multicultural Society.* New York: W.W. Norton.

Sen, A. 2006a. Two confusions, and counting. *Globe and Mail*, 6 August.

Sen, A. 2006b. The Uses and Abuses of Multiculturalism: Chili and Liberty. *The New Republic*, 27 February.

Statistics Canada. 2005. *2001 Census Public Use Microdata File—Individuals File*, User Documentation. Ottawa: Industry Canada, 95M0016XB.

Stoffman, D. 2002. *Who Gets In: What's Wrong with Canada's Immigration Program—and How to Fix It.* Toronto: Macfarlane, Walter and Ross.

United Nations. 2006. *International Migration 2006.* New York: United Nations Department of Economic and Social Affairs, Population Division, UN Publication Sales No. E.06.X111.

Young, M. 2004. *Immigration: The Canada-Quebec Accord.* Ottawa: Library of Parliament, Law and Government Division. At http://www.parl.gc.ca/information/library/PRBpubs/bp252-e.htm (accessed 5 July 2011).

PART I

GOVERNMENT JURISDICTION OVER IMMIGRATION AND DIVERSITY

CHAPTER 2

Federal and Provincial Immigration Arrangements in Canada: Policy Changes and Implications

PETER S. LI, *Professor of Sociology, University of Saskatchewan*

Canada's immigration system has several notable features: a relatively high level of admission every year compared to most OECD (Organisation for Economic Co-operation and Development) countries; a broad range of countries from which new immigrants originate; and an admission scheme based on labour market needs, family unification, and humanitarian consideration. Canada admits about a quarter of a million immigrants from over 200 countries of origin annually, according to 2005 and 2006 statistics (Citizenship and Immigration Canada 2006). In 2006, nationally, the immigrant population made up 19.8 percent of Canada's population,[1] and Canadians now report more than 200 different ethnic origins (Statistics Canada 2007, 2008). Many historical and contemporary factors contribute to shaping Canada's model of immigration, including the tension between the founding groups of the Confederation, the British and the French; the rising demand for human capital in the era after the Second World War; and the changing demographics of Canadian society.

Immigrants to Canada are admitted under three broad categories: Family Class, Economic Class, and Refugee Class (Statutes of Canada 2001, c. 27, s. 12). Individuals processed under these categories differ in

Managing Immigration and Diversity in Canada: A Transatlantic Dialogue in the New Age of Migration,
ed. D. Rodríguez-García. Montreal and Kingston: Queen's Policy Studies Series, McGill-Queen's University Press.

terms of selection criteria applied to them. Refugees are admitted based on the United Nations criteria for identifying refugees or on humanitarian grounds. Admissions under the Family Class are usually restricted to close family members of a resident or citizen of Canada, such as a spouse, common-law partner, child, parent, or other prescribed family member. In contrast, those admitted under the Independent or Economic Class are selected mainly on the basis of age, educational and occupational skills, or financial and investment capacity of the principal applicant. There are finer classifications within the Economic Class, which typically includes skilled workers, business immigrants (self-employed, investors, and entrepreneurs), and independent immigrants who are admitted as provincial or territorial nominees.

Historically, the federal government has assumed the authority and responsibility in framing the national immigration policy and in conducting the selection of immigrations. However, since the 1990s, there have been changes in the federal and provincial relationship regarding co-operation in immigration matters. This chapter focuses on recent policy changes and implications regarding the federal and provincial arrangements in selecting economic immigrants. Throughout the 1990s and early 2000s, the Canadian government and provincial governments have signed many agreements that give provinces greater control over the selection of economic immigrants under the Provincial Nominee Program. This chapter examines the features of these agreements in different regions of Canada and compares the characteristics of immigrants admitted under the Provincial Nominee Program and those admitted as other economic immigrants (see chapter 4 for a discussion on the admission of temporary or non-permanent residents).

LEGISLATIVE POWERS OF IMMIGRATION IN CANADA

The legislative powers of immigration in Canada are specified in the *Constitution Act of 1867* (*Constitution Act, 1867* [U.K.], 30 & 31 Vict., c. 3, formerly the *British North America Act*). Under the section that defines the distribution of legislative powers, the Parliament of Canada has the exclusive authority over matters regarding naturalization and aliens (s. 91). However, in matters relating to immigration, the Parliament of Canada and provincial legislatures have the right to make immigration laws, even though the federal government has the paramount power. Specifically, the act states in section 95,

> In each Province the Legislature may make laws in relation to Agriculture in the Province, and to Immigration into the Province; and it is hereby declared that the Parliament of Canada may from time to time make laws in relation to Agriculture in all or any of the Provinces, and to Immigration into all or any of the Provinces; and any law of the Legislature of a Province, relative

to Agriculture or to Immigration, shall have effect in and for the Province as long and as far only as it is not repugnant to any Act of the Parliament of Canada. (*Constitution Act, 1867* [U.K.], 30 & 31 Vict., c. 3, formerly the *British North America Act*)

It is difficult to separate matters related to aliens and immigration, and thus the division of authority between the federal government and the provinces on these matters was not clearly defined. Although section 95 allows provinces to make laws in relation to immigration, the condition of repugnancy and the exclusive rights given, in section 91, to the federal government over matters of aliens, in fact, give the federal government the paramount say in immigration matters. However, in practice, the division of authority between the federal government and provincial governments over matters of immigration has been unclear.

Several factors explain why immigration matters historically remained largely under the jurisdiction of the federal government. Immigration to Canada towards the latter part of the 19th century and the early 20th century was closely connected to Canada's expansion to the west and related agricultural settlement. Immigration was a component of Prime Minister Macdonald's National Policy,[2] which involved increasing tariffs to encourage domestic production and completing the transportation infrastructure to open up the West for agricultural settlement (Kelly and Trebilcock 1998, 110).

In 1869, Canada enacted the first *Immigration Act*, by which immigration agents were established in Canada, Britain, and elsewhere; but the act was silent on admissible classes (Manpower and Immigration 1974b). In practice, most immigrants were from Britain and the United States. Between 1867 and 1895, about 1.5 million immigrants, mainly from Europe, came to Canada (Statistics Canada 1983), most coming to work on the land but also in factories, mines, and other non-agricultural sectors (Manpower and Immigration 1974b, 5). The fact that the responsibility for immigration was initially placed under Canada's Department of Agriculture suggests that the government considered immigration to be important to agricultural development and land settlement.

British Columbia passed laws towards the latter part of the 19th century to regulate Chinese immigration to the province and to restrict the rights of those who were in the province. In 1872, 1874, and 1878, attempts were made to pass laws in British Columbia to tax the Chinese, but these acts were declared unconstitutional by the Supreme Court of British Columbia on the grounds that they interfered with the authority of the Dominion government (Woodsworth 1941, 26; Morton 1974, 63). The province again passed laws in 1884 (Statutes of British Columbia 1884, c. 3) and 1885 (S.B.C. 1885, c. 13) to prevent Chinese immigration, but these too were declared by the court as *ultra vires* because they were interpreted as interfering with the Dominion government's authority (Li

1998, 32). These court challenges that were either initiated or supported by the federal government indicate that the Government of Canada was quite determined to maintain its authority over matters related to alien control and immigration, which were seen as a part of the national plan for economic development.

Under the policy developed by Clifford Sifton,[3] Canada's Minister of the Interior responsible for land administration and immigration, Canada was again in favour of massive immigration for agricultural settlement, especially in the Prairie provinces. In the period between the "wheat boom" at the turn of the 20th century and the beginning of the First World War, Canada experienced the highest level of immigration in history, with 3 million immigrants coming to Canada between 1896 and 1914 (Li 2003, 19). Several factors contributed to the unprecedented growth of immigration: improved agricultural production in the Prairies, higher staple prices, declining transportation rates, higher European demand for Canadian produce, intensive industrialization, and a concerted national policy of immigration and settlement (Kelly and Trebilcock 1998, 111-163; Li 2003, 17-22). When the supply of emigrants from England and Western Europe was trailing behind the demand for workers and settlers, Canada began bringing in immigrants from Eastern and Southern Europe, such as Poles, Ukrainians, Hutterites, and Doukhobors. Canada's immigration policy for this period was well summarized by a government report in 1910:

> The policy of the Department (of the Interior) at the present time is to encourage the immigration of farmers, farm labourers, and female domestic servants from the United States, the British Isles, and certain Northern European countries, namely, France, Belgium, Holland, Switzerland, Germany, Denmark, Norway, Sweden and Iceland. On the other hand, it is the policy of the Department to do all in its power to keep out of the country undesirables ... those belonging to nationalities unlikely to assimilate and who consequently prevent the building up of a united nation of people of similar customs and ideals. (Manpower and Immigration Canada 1974b, 9-10)

The settlement of the West and the wheat boom created the conditions for the federal government to link the country's immigration policy to a national plan of economic development. In doing so, the federal government also took charge of setting immigration policies based on what it deemed to be desirable immigrants and harmful aliens.

When land settlement was completed in the first part of the 20th century, immigration to Canada became less related to agricultural development and more to urban development. By the end of the Second World War, provinces had shifted their earlier role of providing land settlement services to immigrants to a role that aimed at service delivery to the general population in the areas of health, welfare, and education (Manpower and

Immigration Canada 1974a, 54-55). A government report described the situation as follows: "... most provincial governments did not attempt to articulate in any detail their position on immigration problems as such, and policy development became very largely the concern of the central government" (Manpower and Immigration Canada 1974a, 55).

FEDERAL IMMIGRATION LAWS AFTER WORLD WAR II

The end of the Second World War is a watershed that demarcates a new era of immigration. Hawkins (1988, 3-5) identifies several features that mark this era: the end of free migration for the unskilled; the rising demand for skills and talents worldwide; and increased government intervention in international migration by receiving countries as a means to advance national interests. In Canada, the end of the Second World War saw the beginning of a new period of industrial growth and the framing of a postwar immigration policy that culminated in the adoption of a universal selection system in 1967. Canada's postwar immigration policy was framed by the then prime minister Mackenzie King in 1947 in his statement to the House of Commons:

> The policy of the government is to foster the growth of the population of Canada by the encouragement of immigration. The government will seek by legislation, regulation, and vigorous administration, to ensure the careful selection and permanent settlement of such numbers of immigrants as can advantageously be absorbed in our national economy ... Large-scale immigration from the Orient would change the fundamental composition of the Canadian population ... The government, therefore, has no thought of making any change in immigration regulations that would have consequences of the kind. (Canada, House of Commons Debates, 1 May 1947, pp. 2644-2646)

In his statement, King indicated that the government viewed immigration as a source of population and economic growth, but it did not wish to alter the racial composition of Canada's population by expanding immigration from Asia. In essence, this was a policy in favour of expanding the intake of immigrants from the traditional sources of Europe and the United States and maintaining a tight control of immigration from Asian countries.

In 1952, the Government of Canada passed the *Immigration Act*, which laid down the framework for managing Canada's immigration policy, gave sweeping power to specially designated immigration officers to determine what kinds of people were admissible, and empowered the Governor-in-Council to make regulations for carrying out the act (Hawkins 1988, 101-107). But a decision from the Supreme Court of Canada compelled the government to refine the categories of admissible people that were listed in an order-in-council, which excluded Asian countries as among those where immigration to Canada was permitted (Privy Council 1956-785). Further changes in the immigration regulations in 1967 finally resulted in a universal point system of assessment that was to be applied to all prospective immigrants, irrespective of country of origin or racial background (P.C. 1967-1616). Under the point system, an immigrant could apply either as an independent or as a nominated relative sponsored by a Canadian citizen or permanent resident. In either case, the immigrant would be assessed on the basis of his or her education, occupational demand, and age. The 1967 changes to the immigration regulations laid the foundation of a national immigration framework for selecting and admitting immigrants to Canada. Despite the emphasis on a national framework for immigration, the federal government also included in the 1976 *Immigration Act* a legal basis for entering into agreements with provinces for the purpose of framing immigration policies and facilitating immigration settlement (S.C. 1976–77, c. 52).

Although there were periodic modifications to the national selection grid, the point system adopted in 1967 to screen applicants essentially has been used as the framework for selecting immigrants. However, the point system only applies to the selection of economic immigrants; Family Class applicants are processed on the basis of close family relationship with citizens and permanent residents, and refugee claimants are assessed on humanitarian grounds.

In 2001, the Parliament of Canada passed the *Immigration and Refugee Protection Act* (S.C. 2001, c. 27), which replaced the 1976 *Immigration Act* (S.C. 1976–77, c. 52) and the more than 30 amendments that were made to the act. As in previous immigration legislation, the new act sets out the general framework and empowers the Governor-in-Council to make regulations pertaining to immigration and refugee matters. However, the act also requires the minister responsible for immigration to table before each House of Parliament proposed regulations for referral to appropriate House committees (S.C. 2001, c. 27, s. 4.2). The act clearly distinguishes between immigration and refugee protection, and it devotes a separate part of the act to each. As well, the act lists 11 objectives with respect to immigration and eight objectives regarding refugees. The first two objectives for the immigration program are "to permit Canada to pursue the maximum social, cultural and economic benefits of immigration" and "to enrich and strengthen the social and cultural fabric of Canadian society" (S.C. 2001, c. 27, s. 3.1). Thus, there is an emphasis on framing immigration in terms of its social and cultural features and in terms of Canada's national benefits. The importance of skilled immigrants and their economic benefits to Canada are explained in a document published by Citizenship and Immigration Canada to justify the new act as follows:

Canada needs young, dynamic, well-educated skilled people. It needs innovation, ideas and talents. Canadian employers want to take advantage of opportunities offered by the fast-moving pool of skilled workers. The global labour force can benefit Canadians through job creation and the transfer of skills. Immigration legislation must be adapted to enhance Canada's advantage in the global competition for skilled workers. (Citizenship and Immigration Canada 2001, 1)

In June 2002, the government finalized the immigration regulations to update the point system through an order-in-council (P.C. 2002-997). The new point system for selecting "skilled workers" or economic immigrants places an even greater emphasis on human capital in providing flexible skills to Canada's changing labour market.

FEDERAL AND PROVINCIAL AGREEMENTS ON IMMIGRATION

Despite the shared jurisdiction of immigration between the federal and provincial governments specified in the *Constitution Act of 1867*, historically the federal government has assumed the authority in setting the immigration policy as a national policy linked to the country's economic development. In recent decades, the role of provinces in immigration matters has increased. Quebec was the first province that signed an agreement with the federal government in the post-World War II era regarding immigration matters.[4] Between 1971 and 1991, several agreements were signed between Canada and Quebec, culminating in the 1991 Canada-Quebec Accord. One of Quebec's concerns was to have a proportional share of new immigrants and to be able to take control over integrating new immigrants in order to maintain the majority demographic and linguistic position of the French-speaking population in Quebec relative to the English-Canadian population. This objective is clearly specified in section 7 of the Canada-Quebec Accord as follows:

> Quebec undertakes to pursue an immigration policy that has as an objective the reception by Quebec of a percentage of the total number of immigrants received in Canada equal to the percentage of Quebec's population compared with the population of Canada. (Minister of Supply and Services Canada 1991)

The accord also gives Quebec the sole responsibility to select immigrants, while Canada retains the sole responsibility to admit immigrants. As well, Quebec, and not Canada, would provide programs for the reception and linguistic and cultural integration of permanent residents in Quebec, for which the province would receive reasonable compensation from the Government of Canada. These measures are to ensure that Quebec will have a large say in influencing the number and type of immigrants admitted to Quebec as well as the type of linguistic and cultural integration programs offered to new immigrants.

The devolution of power to Quebec in immigration matters arises in part from the constitution debate of the 1980s. Despite Canada's success in adopting the *Canada Act* and the *Constitution Act* in 1982, Quebec did not sign the 1981 agreement between provincial premiers and the prime minister to enable the repatriation of the constitution from the United Kingdom to Canada (Hogg 1988). The 1987 Constitution Accord, signed by the prime minister and the ten provincial premiers, was aimed at better accommodating Quebec within the federation, but it eventually failed in the final ratification in provincial legislatures. However, the abortive 1987 accord reflects a strong will to shift substantial authority in immigration matters from the federal government to the provinces (Garcea 1992), and it contains the key components that were later incorporated in the 1991 Canada-Quebec Accord.

Besides Quebec, several provinces have signed an immigration agreement with the federal government, including Manitoba in 1996, British Columbia and Saskatchewan in 1998, and New Brunswick and Newfoundland and Labrador in 1999 (see Table 1). By the time the *Immigration and Refugee Protection Act* was enacted in 2001, the relationship between the federal and provincial governments with respect to immigration was well clarified. Section 10 of the act states,

> The Minister must consult with the governments of the provinces respecting the number of foreign nationals in each class who will become permanent residents each year, their distribution in Canada taking into account regional economic and demographic requirements, and the measures to be undertaken to facilitate their integration into Canadian society. (S.C. 2001, c. 27, s. 10.2)

This clause institutionalizes the federal-provincial consultation process to give provinces a voice regarding the number and class of immigrants to be admitted each year, while allowing provinces to articulate their regional economic and demographic needs with respect to immigration and the settlement of immigrants. Another clause of the act gives the Minister of Immigration the power to sign immigration agreements with provinces, by which provinces may set up provincial criteria for immigrant selection (S.C. 2001, c. 27, s. 8, 9).

As of 2007, the federal government had agreements with eight provinces (British Columbia, Alberta, Saskatchewan, Manitoba, Ontario, Quebec, Prince Edward Island, and Nova Scotia) and one territory (Yukon). The titles of the agreements and the year that they were signed are given in Table 1. In addition, there are agreements in place with ten jurisdictions (the Yukon and all the provinces except Quebec) regarding the Provincial Nominee Program.

There are several notable features of the federal-provincial/territorial agreements. First, the agreements recognize the difference in local conditions in settling immigrants and the need of provinces to design

TABLE 1
Federal-Provincial Territorial Agreements

Province	Agreement	Year Signed	Originally Signed	Year Expired
Alberta	Agreement for Canada-Alberta Cooperation on Immigration	2007		Indefinite
British Columbia	Agreement for Canada-British Columbia Co-operation on Immigration	2004	1998	2009
Manitoba	Canada-Manitoba Immigration Agreement	2003	1996	Indefinite
New Brunswick	Canada-New Brunswick Agreement on Provincial Nominees	2005	1999	Indefinite
Newfoundland and Labrador	Canada-Newfoundland and Labrador Agreement on Provincial Nominees	2006	1999	Indefinite
Nova Scotia	Canada-Nova Scotia Co-operation on Immigration	2007		Indefinite
Ontario	Canada-Ontario Immigration Agreement	2005		2010
Prince Edward Island	Canada-Prince Edward Island Agreement on Co-operation on Immigration	2001		2007
Quebec	Canada-Quebec Accord Relating to Immigration and Temporary Admission of Aliens	1991		Indefinite
Saskatchewan	Canada-Saskatchewan Immigration Agreement	2005	1998	Indefinite
Yukon	Agreement for Canada-Yukon Co-operation on Immigration	2001		2007

Source: Citizenship and Immigration Canada, Annual Report to Parliament on Immigration (2007, 12).

particular settlement-related programs that will receive a level of federal funding. This idea was developed in the Canada-Quebec Accord, by which the federal government would withdraw from services related to reception, linguistic and cultural integration, and specialized economic integration services, and in return would provide compensation for such services provided by Quebec. This arrangement is now a standard feature in immigration agreements with provinces to enable them to deliver settlement services. For example, sections 4.1 and 5.1 of the Annex to the Canada-Manitoba Immigration Agreement specify the role of Manitoba and Canada with respect to settlement services as follows:

> Canada will play a continuing role by allocating to Manitoba a share of the funding available for settlement and integration services based upon an allocation determined by a model developed in consultation with Manitoba ... Manitoba will continue to design, administer and deliver and evaluate settlement and integration services with respect to immigrants and refugees residing in Manitoba... (Canada-Manitoba Immigration Agreement 2003, Annex)

Second, the agreements recognize the need to consult with provinces in developing general immigration policies and to take into account the provincial objectives and needs in developing immigration targets. This point is well illustrated in the Agreement for Canada-British Columbia Co-operation on Immigration, first signed in 1998 and again in 2004. Section 4 of the 2004 agreement states,

> Canada will establish general immigration policies, taking into consideration British Columbia's demographic, social and economic objectives and needs ... Canada will develop an annual delivery plan for federal immigration targets that may include, on agreement by both parties, specific targets for British Columbia. (Agreement for Canada-British Columbia Co-operation on Immigration 2004, s. 4)

Third, the agreements allow provincial and territorial governments to nominate immigrants who address local economic needs. This feature, too, originates from the Canada-Quebec Accord, although Quebec was given a much higher degree of autonomy in selecting immigrants. The Provincial Nominee Program allows provinces to choose a defined number of immigrants that meet provincial criteria and local needs, and these cases would be placed on a fast track by Citizenship and Immigration Canada in processing their applications. However, provinces tend to vary in selection criteria for the Provincial Nominee Program, depending in part on their share of immigrants to Canada and on their local economic needs.

THE PROVINCIAL NOMINEE PROGRAM

The three provinces with the largest share of immigration to Canada are Ontario, British Columbia (BC), and Quebec. These three provinces accounted for 87.5 percent of all immigrants to Canada in 2004, 87.2 percent in 2005, and 84.5 percent in 2006 (Citizenship and Immigration

Canada 2006). Ontario alone accounted for over 50 percent of immigrants to Canada between 1997 and 2006, while BC's share varied from 15 to 22 percent for the same period, and Quebec's share rose from 13 percent in 1997 to 18 percent in 2006 (Citizenship and Immigration Canada 2006). The disparity between Ontario and BC in their share of Canada's annual immigrants and the differences in these provinces' economic needs explain why the two provinces differ in their criteria for selecting provincial nominees and why Ontario tends to have more restrictive criteria compared to BC.

After Quebec, British Columbia was one of the first provinces to sign an immigration agreement with Canada and to adopt a Provincial Nominee Program. When British Columbia first signed the immigration agreement in 1998, it was given the entitlement to nominate 1,000 provincial nominees between 1998 and 2003, although the agreement also allowed the number to be changed if agreed by both parties (Agreement for Canada-British Columbia Co-operation on Immigration 1998, Annex A, s. 2.1). The 2004 agreement between Canada and British Columbia provides much greater detail regarding how the Provincial Nominee Program is to be conducted. The agreement recognizes that BC has the sole responsibility to assess and nominate immigrants to the province based on nominees' significant benefit to the economic development of the province, as defined in the province immigrant selection criteria, and on their strong likelihood of successfully establishing themselves. In accepting an immigrant nominee, BC would issue a nomination certificate to the mission where the candidate would apply for admission. Canada would accept the certificate as evidence that admission of the applicant would be of significant benefit to the province and would process the application expeditiously. Canada would make the final decision and would issue immigrant visas subject to applicants meeting legislative requirements including health, criminality, and security (Agreement for Canada-British Columbia Co-operation on Immigration 2004, Annex C).

The Provincial Nominee Program enables a province to specify categories for priority processing based on the province's economic needs. In the case of British Columbia, it accepts four categories of immigrants under the BC Provincial Nominee Program: (1) skilled workers who have an offer of employment in BC to work as a manager, professional, technologist, technician, or to work in a skilled trade; (2) trained doctors and nurses; (3) international graduates who recently graduated from a BC post-secondary institution and have a job offer in BC that is a skilled occupation related to the field of study; and (4) business people with experience and capital to develop a viable business that offers significant economic benefits to the province (Government of British Columbia 2008). The features of BC's immigrant selection criteria reflect the housing and economic boom in the lower mainland of BC that began in 2003 and the corresponding shortages in skilled workers. As well, the shortage of medical professionals and the interest in attracting international investors to BC also help to shape the provincial selection criteria.

In contrast, Ontario has a much larger share of annual immigrants to Canada to address its labour needs, and there is less pressure for Ontario to have to rely on the Provincial Nominee Program as a channel to fast-track new immigrants. Indeed, Ontario only developed a pilot Provincial Nominee Program with the federal government in 2005, with the objective of nominating 500 individuals under the program, not including their family members (Government of Ontario 2008). Ontario's pilot program is employer driven in that a prospective nominee can only apply if offered an approved job by an employer who has been pre-screened. Of the 500 potential immigrants year-marked annually for the pilot program, 450 are allocated to the "employer" category, and 50, to the "multinational investor" category. In the former case, a company employer who wishes to apply to the pilot program must demonstrate that the company has been in corporate existence for at least three years, with a minimum gross revenue of C$1 million and a minimum of five employees if the company is located in the Greater Metropolitan Area (GMA), or C$500,000 and three employees if located outside the GMA. A company may apply for up to five positions if the company is located in the GMA and has at least 25 employees, or for up to ten positions if it is located outside the GMA and has at least 30 employees (Government of Ontario 2008). These measures are to ensure that at least 50 percent of the nominees are reserved for employers outside the GMA. Regarding job positions, the program allows three types of positions within the employer category: (1) professional jobs that include eight occupations in the health sector and two occupations in the educational sector, (2) skilled workers in ten occupations in manufacturing and construction, and (3) international students who recently graduated from Canadian universities with a job offer that relates to their field of study.

The multinational investor category is designed to help major companies making sizable investments in Ontario to bring in key employees from outside Canada that will contribute to long-term investment successes. To be eligible for the program, a company has to make an investment of at least C$10 million and create a minimum of 25 permanent full-time positions. Under the program, a company may apply for up to five immigrants for each qualifying investment the company makes in Ontario, provided the position an immigrant is filling is a high-skilled occupation (Government of Ontario 2008).

It is clear that Ontario's Provincial Nominee Program is designed to help corporate employers to find skilled workers and professional personnel, with the objective of allocating a portion of the nominated skilled workers to outside the Greater Toronto Metropolitan Area, as well as linking the nomination of highly skilled corporate employees to sizable investments in Ontario. In contrast, British Columbia's Provincial Nominee Program is mainly designed to attract immigrants to fill labour shortages in skilled jobs and in the health profession, as well as to retain university graduates in BC. The Ontario program is more employer driven and investment driven, while the BC program tends to be job driven.

There are many variations in how other provinces have structured the Provincial Nominee Program. In the case of Manitoba, the 1998 addendum to the 1996 agreement indicated that the program was designed to meet critical skill shortages, to facilitate the immigration of key individuals of corporations wishing to locate in Manitoba, and to meet the province's specific industrial and economic needs, but not to raise capital for provincial investments (Addendum B: Provincial Nominees 1998). Manitoba was entitled to nominate up to 200 nominees each year between 1998 and 2001, but the number was raised to 1,250 for 2002 and 2003 (Canada-Manitoba Immigration Agreement 2003, Annex 3). The Manitoba program has several streams. The first stream, called "employer direct," allows workers who have been working for a Manitoba employer for at least six months and who have been given a job offer of long-term and full-time employment to be nominated. The second stream is to allow international students who have completed a post-secondary educational program in Manitoba and have obtained a job offer to apply. The third stream, known as "family support," allows a close relative in Manitoba to nominate a nominee by signing an affidavit of support. In addition, the "general stream" allows the nomination of those with family support or previous work experience in Manitoba (Government of Manitoba 2008).

Saskatchewan signed on a pilot Provincial Nominee Program in 1998, which allowed the province to nominate up to 150 applicants within two years, but this number was raised to 200 a year in 2002 (Canada-Saskatchewan Agreement on Provincial Nominees 2002). The Saskatchewan program has some unique features. Besides allowing skilled workers with a job offer from a Saskatchewan employer to be nominated, the province has nominee categories for entrepreneurs and for farm owners and operators, as well as for immigrant families living in Saskatchewan who wish to help their family members outside Canada to live and work in the province. The last feature is an innovative means by which Saskatchewan is trying to attract more immigrants to the province and to retain them.

Alberta signed the immigration agreement with the federal government in 2007 and adopted a Provincial Nominee Program that gave Alberta the entitlement to nominate 400 provincial nominees during the term of the agreement (Agreement for Canada-Alberta Cooperation in Immigration 2007, s. 4). The Alberta program is somewhat similar to the Ontario program in that it is employer driven, but it also differs in that it allows a self-employed farmer stream (Government of Alberta 2008). Under the employer-driven stream, employers in Alberta who are unable to fill skilled and semi-skilled positions may apply to the province for approval to recruit skilled workers, international graduates from universities, or semi-skilled workers in food and beverage processing, manufacturing, the hotel and lodging industries, and the trucking industry. Immigrants to Alberta account for over 7 percent each year of the total immigrants to Canada (Citizenship and Immigration Canada 2006), and Alberta's program reflects the desire to use provincial nomination to address labour needs in various industries, including farming and servicing, in a robust economy.

Nova Scotia and Canada signed an agreement on provincial nominees in 2002. Under the program, the province may nominate up to 200 immigrants a year, and as in the case of many other provinces, the agreement allows the targeted levels to be raised higher if agreed by both parties (Canada-Nova Scotia Agreement on Provincial Nominees 2002, s. 4). The subsequent agreement signed in 2007 simply indicates that the targeted levels may be exceeded at any time upon agreement by both parties (Canada-Nova Scotia Co-operation on Immigration 2007, Annex A).

Thus, since the early 2000s, a more flexible approach subject to mutual discussion and agreement has been adopted with regard to the number of nominees to which a province is entitled every year. This flexible approach results in higher levels of immigrant nominees going to provinces that traditionally have a relatively small share of annual immigrants to Canada. For example, immigrants to Nova Scotia accounted for less than 1 percent of all immigrants to Canada every year between 1999 and 2005, and for 1 percent in 2006 (Citizenship and Immigration Canada 2006), but the number of principal applicants admitted under the Nova Scotia Provincial Nominee Program increased from 23 in 2003 to 400 in 2006 and 405 in 2007 (Government of Nova Scotia 2008). The Nova Scotia program has a comprehensive set of categories of nominees who are qualified under the program, including (1) skilled workers with needed skills and with a permanent job offer; (2) family business workers, designed to help family-owned businesses to hire close relatives; (3) experienced managers and business owners; and (4) international graduates.

Similar to Nova Scotia, New Brunswick signed an initial immigration agreement with the federal government that entitled it to nominate up to 200 immigrants every year (Canada-New Brunswick Agreement on Provincial Nominees 1999, s. 4). But a subsequent agreement signed in 2005 simply indicates that the province "will develop an annual provincial nominee plan based on principles established by New Brunswick and shared with Canada" (Canada-New Brunswick Agreement on Provincial Nominees 2005, s. 5.4). The New Brunswick nominee program requires applicants to meet two criteria: a job offer and having a minimum score of 50 points measured in five factors that include age, language skills, education, work or business experience, and adaptability.

Under the Canada-Newfoundland and Labrador Agreement on Provincial Nominees, signed in 2006, the province of Newfoundland and Labrador adopts a nominee program similar to that of New Brunswick, but the Newfoundland and Labrador program only requires applicants to meet the criteria of having at least 50 points when an applicant applies for nomination as a skilled worker, an immigrant entrepreneur, or an immigrant partner (i.e., someone who proposes to make an investment in an existing company) (Government of Newfoundland and Labrador 2008).

Like other Maritime provinces, Prince Edward Island signed an agreement with the federal government that allows the province to nominate up to 200 immigrants every year (Agreement for Canada-Prince Edward Island Co-operation on Immigration 2001, Annex A). The P.E.I. nominee program has four categories: (1) the "immigrant partner" category, which requires an applicant to have a net worth of C$400,000 and to make an investment of at least C$200,000 in an eligible P.E.I. company; (2) the "immigrant entrepreneur" category, which requires an applicant to have the same net worth as above and to make the same minimum investment in a new enterprise; (3) the "immigrant connections" category, which requires an applicant to be nominated by a P.E.I. champion related to the applicant and requires that the champion will ensure that the person being nominated is integrated into the P.E.I. community; and (4) the "skilled worker" category, which requires an applicant to score 50 points on an assessment form and to have a job offer.

There are notable differences in how each province has set up selection criteria under the Provincial Nominee Program. The size of annual immigrant flows to the province and the specific economy features of the region explain these variations. Ontario, which has been receiving over 50 percent of annual immigrants to Canada, tends to be restrictive in limiting the number of provincial nominees and appears to be using the program as a specific means to attract investment capital and to divert skilled immigrants to companies outside the Greater Metropolitan Area. British Columbia takes in about 16 to 17 percent of annual immigrants to Canada, and its program emphasizes accepting nominees to address labour shortages in skilled and semi-skilled positions and in the health profession, as well as to attract business investments. Alberta, which receives about 7 to 8 percent of Canada's annual immigration, also uses a model that is employer driven, similar to that of Ontario. But unlike Ontario, Alberta also accepts nominees in semi-skilled positions in certain industries if qualified employers petition for these nominations. As well, Alberta accepts self-employed farmers as possible nominees.

For provinces with a smaller intake of immigrants, such as Manitoba, Saskatchewan, and the Maritime provinces, there is a greater emphasis on using the Provincial Nominee Program as a means to attract more immigrants to the province. For example, Saskatchewan's program accepts farm owners and operators as well as family sponsorship of relatives outside of Canada. The Prince Edward Island program has a feature similar to that of Saskatchewan to allow immigrant family in the province to act as a champion to sponsor other relations. Both New Brunswick and Newfoundland and Labrador use a model that requires applicants to have at least 50 points on the assessment scale, a level that is typically lower than what is required in the regular processing of economic immigrants by the federal government.

The federal government also tends to take a more flexible approach towards the number of nominees each province is entitled to under the new agreements. In some of the original agreements, the permissible number was relatively small, but later amendments often leave out the specific target levels and allow them to be modified upon mutual agreement. Thus, it appears that the federal government intends to expand the Provincial Nominee Program as a means to give provinces a greater influence in the selection of economic immigrants.

ECONOMIC IMMIGRANTS AND PROVINCIAL NOMINEES COMPARED

The selection of economic immigrants is typically made under a point system by which a visa officer assigns "points" or "units" to applicants using prescribed selection criteria. The system assigns substantial weight to educational and occupational factors. Under the assessment grid used to assess economic immigrants until 2001, 16 units could be assigned to education, 8 units to experience, 10 units to occupation, and 18 units to training (Li 2003, 39-41). The immigration regulations of 2002 established a new grid, whereby a maximum of 25 points could be given to formal education, 20 points to knowledge of official languages, and 25 points to a skilled worker's experience or 35 points to business experience for investors and entrepreneurs (Li 2003, 41). In this way, according to the 2002 regulations, between 70 to 80 points, depending on whether working experience or business experience is being assessed, can be allocated to factors related to human capital. The selection of economic immigrants, thus, places substantial emphasis on educational and occupational qualifications and on official language ability, as well as on age.

The changes in the composition of the three broad classes of immigrant admission between 1980 and 2006 are given in Figure 1. Before the early 1990s, Economic Class immigrants and Family Class immigrants fluctuated between 30 to 50 percent of all immigrants admitted every year. However, after the mid-1990s, economic immigrants rose to over 50 percent every year, while Family Class immigrants fell to below 30 percent. This divergence began even before the *Immigration and Refugee Protection Act* was passed in 2001 and before the new immigration regulations were adopted in 2002.

FIGURE 1
Landed Immigrants by Category, As Percent of Annual Immigrants Admitted to Canada, 1980–2006

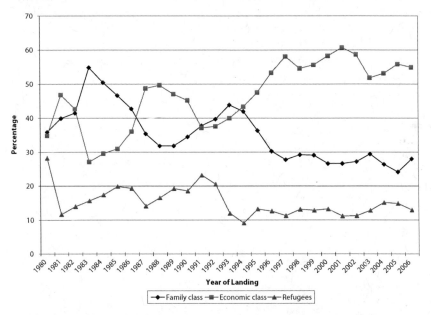

Source: 1980–2005 figures compiled from Citizenship and Immigration Canada, *Landed Immigrant Data System*, 1980–2005; 2006 figures compiled from Citizenship and Immigration Canada, *Facts and Figures 2006: Immigration Overview—Permanent and Temporary Residents.*[5]

One of the outcomes of the federal and provincial agreements on immigration, especially the component concerning the Provincial Nominee Program, is to give entitlements to provinces to select immigrants that suit the economic needs of the region. However, until the mid-2000s, provincial nominees only made up a small proportion of the total number of economic immigrants coming to Canada every year. Table 2 shows that prior to 2002, provincial nominees accounted for less than 1 percent of economic immigrants every year, even though the federal government and several provinces had signed immigration agreements in the late 1990s and adopted the Provincial Nominee Program. However, since 2003, the proportion of provincial nominees among economic immigrants has risen, from less than 5 percent in 2004 to 9.6 percent in 2006 and to 13 percent in 2007. If this trend is to continue, then admissions under the Provincial Nominee Program would constitute the fastest-growing admission category under the economic stream of immigration.

Despite the short history of the Provincial Nominee Program, available data indicate that there are differences between immigrants admitted as provincial nominees and other economic immigrants. Comparing only principal applicants admitted to Canada between 2001 and 2005, Table 3 shows that the average age at the time of immigration to Canada was slightly higher among provincial nominees (37.7 years) compared to other economic immigrants (35.7 years). But the level of human capital among provincial nominees tends to be lower than among other economic immigrants. For example, about 49 percent of provincial nominees, as compared to 81 percent of other economic immigrants, came to Canada with at least one university degree. Moreover, about 80 percent of economic immigrants speak either one or both of the official languages, compared to 76 percent among provincial nominees.

TABLE 2
Provincial Nominees Admitted to Canada, 1996–2007

Landing Year	Economic Immigrants	Provincial Nominees	% of Economic Immigrants
1996	125,370	233	0.19
1997	128,351	47	0.04
1998	97,911	0	0.00
1999	109,251	477	0.44
2000	136,292	1,252	0.92
2001	155,718	1,274	0.82
2002	137,864	2,127	1.54
2003	121,045	4,418	3.65
2004	133,748	6,248	4.67
2005	156,312	8,047	5.15
2006	138,251	13,336	9.65
2007	131,248	17,095	13.02
Total	1,571,361	54,554	3.47

Source: 1996 and 1997 figures compiled from "Canada—Permanent Residents by Category," in Citizenship and Immigration Canada, *Facts and Figures 2005: Immigration Overview—Permanent and Temporary Residents*[6]; 1998–2007 figures compiled from "Canada—Permanent Residents by Category, 1998–2007," in Citizenship and Immigration Canada, *Facts and Figures 2007: Immigration Overview—Permanent Residents and Temporary Foreign Workers and Students*.[7]

TABLE 3
Age at Immigration, University Degree and Official Language Capacity of Provincial Nominees and Other Economic Class Immigrants, Principal Applicants Only, 2001–2005 Landing Years

	Provincial Nominees	Other Economic Class Immigrants*
Mean age at time of immigration to Canada	37.7	35.7
% with university degree	48.9	81.1
% speaking either or both official languages	76.0	80.4
Total number of cases	7,237	273,090

*Economic and Business Class immigrants not admitted as provincial nominees.
Source: Compiled from *Landed Immigrant Data System*, 1980–2005, microdata file.

It is in the occupational profile of the two groups that differences are most pronounced. Table 4 indicates that about one-third of provincial nominees were in trades and skilled occupations in transportation and equipment operation, compared to only 3 percent of economic immigrants. In contrast, over half (55 percent) of economic immigrants and only 17 percent of provincial nominees were in professional and technical occupations in natural and applied sciences. Provincial nominees were less likely than other economic immigrants to be in professional and technical occupations in all sectors except health; occupations in the health sector accounted for 8.6 percent of all occupations among provincial nominees and for 5 percent among economic immigrants. There are also other notable differences. Provincial nominees were more likely to be in the primary industry (4.2 percent) and in senior and middle management (15.3 percent) than economic immigrants (0.4 percent and 5.7 percent, respectively). In general, the occupational profile of the two groups indicates that provincial nominees were more likely than economic immigrants to be in management, trades and skilled occupations, and the primary industry, whereas economic immigrants were more likely than provincial nominees to be in professional and technical occupations except the health sector.

TABLE 4
Occupation of Provincial Nominees and Other Economic Class Immigrants, Principal Applicants Only, 2001–2005 Landing Years

Occupation	Provincial Nominees %	Other Economic Class Immigrants* %
Senior management	3.0	0.4
Middle management	12.3	5.3
Professional/administrative in business and finance	4.9	11.9
Professional/technical in natural/applied sciences	16.9	55.4
Professional/technical in health	8.6	5.0
Other professional/paraprofessional	5.9	11.6
Clerical	1.5	1.1
Occupation in sales and services	4.3	5.5
Trades/skilled occupation in transportation/ equipment operation	32.7	3.3
Other trades, skilled and semi-skilled occupation	5.7	0.2
Occupation in primary industry	4.2	0.4
Total	100.0	100.1
[Number of cases]	[5,793]	[254,751]

*Economic and Business Class immigrants not admitted as provincial nominees.

Source: Compiled from Landed Immigrant Data System, 1980–2005, microdata file, for those with reported occupation.

POLICY IMPLICATIONS AND CONCLUDING REMARKS

Since the 1991 Canada-Quebec Accord, there have been changes in the immigration arrangements between the federal government and other provincial and territorial governments. The notable changes have to do with the signing of federal and provincial agreements on immigration that incorporate the Provincial Nominee Program. The program recognizes that regional demographic and economic needs of provinces vary and that these variations justify provinces having to make regional decisions regarding the type of economic immigrants that best suit the development of provinces. Thus, the program gives entitlements to provinces to set up selection criteria for provincial nominees and to use those criteria to nominate certain economic immigrants to the federal government for expeditious immigration admission. Most of the agreements signed in the 1990s have a small number of provincial nominees that a province is entitled to nominate each year, but subsequent agreements often allow both parties to raise the number of nominees each year as both parties see fit. As a result, the number of provincial nominees admitted to Canada has been increasing since 2002, and they accounted for about 10 percent of all economic immigrants in 2006 and for 13 percent in 2007. Besides granting provinces the right to nominate immigrants, the program also has provisions to allow provinces to deliver settlement programs to new immigrants with proper federal financial compensations.

Provinces vary substantially in how selection criteria for provincial nominees are set up. In general, provinces that have been receiving a large share of immigrants tend to have selection criteria that are more stringent and employer driven. In provinces with a relatively small population and a small share of annual immigration, such as the Maritime provinces and some Prairie provinces, the emphasis is to use the Provincial Nominee Program to attract professional, skilled, and semi-skilled workers; international graduates; and relatives outside Canada related to immigrant families in the province. These variations result in immigrants being selected as provincial nominees who may not meet the selection criteria of the federal government, or in immigrants being selected for immigration in one province but not in another because of differences in selection criteria.

In the long run, the expansion of the Provincial Nominee Program will likely result in a multi-tiered system of immigrant selection, with provincial nominees having a different occupational profile, human capital level, and age composition than other economic immigrants. If provincial nominees admitted to a province were to remain in the province-of-origin destination, they might serve to alleviate some of the skill and labour shortages of the region that the program is intended to address. However, the mobility rights of Canadians imply that provincial nominees, like other economic immigrants, will move to other regions of

Canada to maximize their economic and other returns. In other words, the selection criteria of provincial nominees are based on short-term needs of the province, whereas the long-term successful settlement of immigrants is influenced by national economic forces of supply and demand. Thus, if the Provincial Nominee Program is conceived of as a means to allow provinces to address short-term labour shortages, then the program would likely be able to accomplish such a goal if the number of provincial nominees admitted annually is substantial enough to produce an impact on the provincial labour market. However, in the long run, if provincial nominees were to become a large component of the economic stream of immigrants, then the program would alter the composition of economic immigrants to Canada. It is not clear how this altered com- position, devised supposedly to meet local needs, would affect Canada's labour market if provincial nominees begin to move to more prosperous areas where conventional immigrants tend to congregate. There is not yet enough evidence or understanding regarding how success in satisfying short-term immigration needs may negatively or positively affect the long-term interest of the nation.

The popularity of the Provincial Nominee Program also reflects the rigidity of the federal immigration selection system and the desire of provinces to be more flexible in bringing in new economic immigrants. By the time the immigration regulations were revamped in 2002, there were several predominant ideas regarding how Canada's immigration system should be modified. But these ideas resulted in a lopsided system of immigrant selection that over-emphasizes educational credentials at the expense of labour demands that require less qualification.

First, it was believed that a substantial portion of immigrants entering Canada should be composed of economic immigrants, since they are selected based on a point system that assesses their age, educational qualifications, occupational experience, and language capacity (Li 2003). Indeed, the statistics clearly indicate this changing mentality since the mid-1990s, as the proportion of economic immigrants rose and the pro- portion of family immigrants fell.

Second, it was believed that Canada's economy is technologically advanced and knowledge based and that the economy would require immigrants with highly trained human capital and not those without skills (*Canada Gazette* 2002). Hence, the revised national point system adopted for immigrant selection emphasizes educational credentials, work experience, and other human capital content (Li 2003). This change was in part a reaction to the old system of economic immigrant selection, which relied heavily on specific occupational demand based on a prior- ity list developed by Human Resources Development Canada. But the occupational list often became outdated by the time it was used to select immigrants, and even more so by the time that economic immigrants actually arrived in Canada. For this reason, the revised system of federal immigrant selection is premised on the thinking that immigrants with substantial educational credentials and qualifications would also possess generic skills suitable to Canada's knowledge economy.

In reality, the emphasis on selecting economic immigrants with substantial educational credentials creates a larger cohort of arriving immigrants with a university degree, but at the same time, it contributes to the mounting problem of well-qualified immigrants with credentials not being able to find jobs that fully recognize those credentials. Arrival statistics for new immigrants indicate that economic immigrants with a university degree accounted for less than one-fifth of all economic immigrants in the early 1990s, but this number rose to over 40 percent by the late 1990s and again to close to 50 percent by the early 2000s (Citizenship and Immigration Canada 2005). At the same time, provinces with a strong economy, such as Alberta and British Columbia, were having difficulties in finding certain types of workers, especially those in trades and semi-skilled professions. Thus it became apparent that the type of highly qualified immigrants admitted to Canada under the national system was insufficient to address the labour shortages in some regions.

The Provincial Nominee Program becomes a flexible means by which selection criteria can be relaxed and modified without having to revamp the national system of selection. Indeed, the differences between provincial nominees and other economic immigrants suggest that different types of immigrants have been selected under the two streams.

Since provincial nominees, like other types of immigrants or Canadian citizens, are entitled to mobility rights in Canada, they may choose to move to other regions of Canada after landing. The Provincial Nominee Program operates on the rationale that provincial nominees bring necessary skills and qualities that contribute to local development, but the success of the program hinges upon provincial nominees staying in the province of destination to meet certain labour needs. It remains to be seen whether this program alone is sufficient in creating the incentives to retain immigrants in regions that currently need immigrant labour but that historically have been unable to attract large numbers of immigrant arrivals.

In the long run, the proliferation of the Provincial Nominee Program will introduce substantial variations in immigrant selection and will produce a system of immigrant selection without much national uniformity. Ironically, the further the Provincial Nominee Program expands, the more the selection criteria of economic immigrants tend to be regionalized, and the more difficult it is to maintain a national standard. In the end, there will be as many sets of immigrant selection criteria as the number of provinces and territories, each one bearing some nominal relation to the national criteria. Consequently, there will be an increase in cost and complexity in managing the immigration system in Canada. Further evidence is needed to assess whether Canada will be better off economically from selecting economic immigrants under the Provincial Nominee programs as compared to using a uniform national system of selection.

NOTES

1. The immigrant population is made up of those who have been granted a landed immigrant status and live in Canada at the time of the census. A landed immigrant is a person who has been granted the right to live in Canada permanently by immigration authorities (Statistics Canada 2005).
2. John Alexander Macdonald served as the first prime minister of Canada from 1 July 1867 to 5 November 1873, and again as prime minister from 17 October 1878 to 6 June 1891.
3. Clifford Sifton served as the Minister of the Interior under Prime Minister Wilfrid Laurier, who was prime minister from 1896 to 1911. It was under Sifton that Canada expanded immigration to populate the West (Hall 1998).
4. The 1971 Lang-Cloutier Agreement was the first federal-provincial agreement in immigration matters. On 20 February 1978, Canada and Quebec concluded the agreement, commonly referred to as the Cullen-Couture Agreement, with regard to co-operation on immigration matters and on the selection of foreign nationals wishing to settle either permanently or temporarily in Quebec. On 5 February 1991, Canada and Quebec signed the Canada-Quebec Accord, relating to immigration and temporary admission of aliens.
5. See Citizenship and Immigration Canada, *Facts and Figures 2006: Immigration Overview—Permanent and Temporary Residents*, at http://www.cic.gc.ca/english/pdf/pub/facts2006.pdf.
6. See Citizenship and Immigration Canada, *Facts and Figures 2005: Immigration Overview—Permanent and Temporary Residents*, at http://www.cic.gc.ca/english/resources/statistics/facts2005/permanent/02.asp.
7. See Citizenship and Immigration Canada, *Facts and Figures 2007: Immigration Overview—Permanent Residents and Temporary Foreign Workers and Students*, at http://www.cic.gc.ca/english/resources/statistics/facts2007/01.asp.

REFERENCES

Canada, House of Commons. 1947. *Debates of the House of Commons*. 1 May, pp. 2644-9.

Citizenship and Immigration Canada. 2001. *Overview of Bill-C11 Immigration and Refugee Protection Act*. Released June 2001.

Citizenship and Immigration Canada. 2005. *Landed Immigrant Data System*. Microdata file.

Citizenship and Immigration Canada. 2006. *Facts and Figures*.

Citizenship and Immigration Canada. 2007. *Annual Report to Parliament on Immigration*.

Garcea, J. 1992. The Immigration Clause in the Meech Lake Accord. *Manitoba Law Journal* 21 (2):274-300.

Government of Alberta. 2008. Alberta Provincial Nominee Program. At http://www.alberta-canada.com/immigration/immigrate/international graduateemployereligibility.html.

Government of British Columbia. 2008. BC Provincial Nominee Program. At http://www.canadaspacificgateway.ca/en/live/immigrate/nominee.html.

Government of Manitoba. 2008a. Manitoba Provincial Nominee Program for Skilled Workers: Policy and Procedural Guidelines.

Government of Manitoba. 2008b. Provincial Nominee Program. At http://www2.immigratemanitoba.com.

Government of New Brunswick. 2008. New Brunswick Provincial Nominee Program. At http://www.gnb.ca/immigration/index-e.asp.

Government of Newfoundland and Labrador. 2008. Newfoundland and Labrador Provincial Nominee Program. At http://www.nlpnp.ca/gettingstarted.html.

Government of Nova Scotia. 2008. Nova Scotia Nominee Program. At http://www.novascotiaimmigration.com.

Government of Ontario. 2008. Ontario's Pilot Provincial Nominee Program. At http://www.ontarioimmigration.ca/english/PNPabout.asp.

Government of Prince Edward Island. 2008.Prince Edward Island Provincial Nominee Program. At http://www.gov.pe.ca/immigration.

Government of Saskatchewan. 2008.Saskatchewan Immigrant Nominee Program. At http://www.immigration.gov.sk.ca/sinp/.

Hall, D.J. 1998. Sir Clifford Sifton. In *The 1999 Canadian Encyclopedia World Edition*. Toronto: McClelland and Stewart.

Hawkins, F. 1988. *Canada and Immigration: Public Policy and Public Concern*, 2nd ed. Montreal: McGill-Queen's University Press.

Hogg, P.W. 1988. *Meech Lake Constitutional Accord Annotated*. Toronto: Carswell.

Kelly, N., and M. Trebilcock. 1998. *The Making of the Mosaic: A History of Canadian Immigration Policy*. Toronto: University of Toronto Press.

Li, P.S. 1998. *The Chinese in Canada*, 2nd ed. Don Mills, Ontario: Oxford University Press.

Li, P.S. 2003. *Destination Canada: Immigration Debates and Issues*. Don Mills, Ontario: Oxford University Press.

Manpower and Immigration Canada. 1974a. *Immigration Policy Perspectives*. Ottawa: Information Canada.

Manpower and Immigration Canada. 1974b. *The Immigration Program*. Ottawa: Information Canada.

Minister of Supply and Services Canada. 1991. *Canada-Quebec Accord Relating to Immigration and Temporary Admission of Aliens*. Cat. No. MP23-111/1991.

Morton, J. 1974. *In the Sea of Sterile Mountains: The Chinese in British Columbia*. Vancouver: J.J. Douglas.

Privy Council. 1956. 1956-785, 24 May, *Canada Gazette*, Part II, vol. 90, no. 11, 545-8.

Privy Council. 1967. 1967-1616, 16 Aug., *Canada Gazette*, Part II, vol. 101, no. 17, 1350-62.

Privy Council. 2002. 2002-997, 14 June, *Canada Gazette*, Part II, vol. 136, no. 9, 1-176.

Statistics Canada. 1983. *Historical Statistics of Canada*, 2nd ed. Ottawa: Minister of Supply and Services Canada.

Statistics Canada. 2005. *2001 Census Public Use Microdata File: Individual File User Documentation*, revised edition.

Statistics Canada. 2007. *The Daily*. 4 December.

Statistics Canada. 2008. *The Daily*. 2 April.
Statutes of British Columbia. 1884. *An Act to Prevent the Immigration of Chinese*, c. 3.
Statutes of British Columbia. 1885. *An Act to Prevent the Immigration of Chinese*, c. 13.
Statutes of Canada. 1976–7. *An Act Respecting Immigration to Canada*, c. 52.
Statutes of Canada. 2001. *An Act Respecting Immigration to Canada and the Granting of Refugee Protection to Persons Who Are Displaced, Persecuted or in Danger*, c. 27.
Woodsworth, C.J. 1941. *Canada and the Orient: A Study in International Relations*. Toronto: Macmillan.

CHAPTER 3

L'action du Québec en matière d'immigration[1]

Louise Fontaine, *Conseillère au sous-ministre adjoint à l'Immigration, Ministère de l'Immigration et des Communautés culturelles du Québec*

Cet exposé présente les responsabilités du Québec en matière d'immigration, les principaux leviers dont il dispose pour faire en sorte que l'immigration contribue au redressement démographique, à la pérennité du fait français et à la prospérité économique du Québec. Il signale aussi les axes d'intervention récemment choisis pour que les personnes immigrantes occupent une plus grande place et contribuent davantage au développement du Québec. Quelques grands chantiers sont également présentés afin de donner une image plus concrète des actions entreprises.

Rappelons d'abord qu'au Canada, l'immigration est un domaine de compétence partagé entre le gouvernement fédéral et les provinces, avec prépondérance du droit fédéral. Il y a plus de 30 ans, conscient de l'importance de l'immigration pour son avenir, le Québec a commencé à investir ce champ de responsabilités en signant, avec le gouvernement central, des ententes administratives successives.

Le Québec a ainsi acquis, au fil des ans, des responsabilités de plus en plus structurantes. La dernière des ententes, l'Accord Canada-Québec

Managing Immigration and Diversity in Canada: A Transatlantic Dialogue in the New Age of Migration, ed. D. Rodríguez-García. Montreal and Kingston: Queen's Policy Studies Series, McGill-Queen's University Press.

relatif à l'immigration et à l'admission temporaire des aubains, a été signée en 1991. Cet accord est d'une durée indéterminée et il ne peut être modifié sans le consentement des deux parties.

S'agissant d'immigration permanente, le Québec a la responsabilité exclusive de :

- déterminer les volumes d'immigrants qu'il désire accueillir;
- sélectionner les candidats à destination de son territoire, lorsque des critères de sélection s'appliquent (les réfugiés qui obtiennent l'asile alors qu'ils sont au Québec et les membres de la catégorie du regroupement familial sont exemptés de sélection) et d'établir les critères guidant cette sélection;
- gérer les engagements de parrainage, d'en déterminer la durée et d'établir les barèmes lorsque le droit fédéral prévoit que les capacités financières du parrain doivent être prises en compte.

En matière d'immigration temporaire, le consentement du Québec est requis pour que le Canada admette :

- certains travailleurs temporaires;
- les étudiants étrangers;
- les visiteurs qui viennent au Québec recevoir des traitements médicaux.

Pour sa part, le gouvernement fédéral a la responsabilité exclusive de :

- établir les volumes annuels d'immigration pour le Canada en prenant notamment en compte la planification québécoise;
- définir les normes générales de traitement et les catégories générales d'immigration (catégorie économique, regroupement familial et réfugiés);
- définir et appliquer les critères permettant à une personne d'entrer et de séjourner au pays, notamment les conditions relatives au séjour (ex. : durée, droit de travailler ou d'étudier) les critères d'interdiction de territoire (santé, sécurité, criminalité), les documents requis;
- admettre les immigrants et les résidents temporaires sur le territoire canadien;
- traiter les demandes d'asile au Canada;
- déterminer qui est un réfugié ou une personne qui mérite la protection du Canada;
- de procéder à des renvois.

Le Québec est la seule province au Canada qui a la possibilité de déterminer le volume et la composition de l'immigration permanente qu'elle souhaite accueillir. En fait, cette prérogative s'applique, pour la plus large part, à l'immigration économique, c'est-à-dire, là où l'acte de sélection est déterminant.

Le Québec est aussi la seule province à détenir des responsabilités exclusives dans la gestion du mouvement d'immigration. Ainsi, sous réserve de critères relatifs à l'interdiction de territoire, le Canada doit admettre à destination du Québec le ressortissant étranger qui aura satisfait aux exigences de sélection québécoises et il ne peut admettre, à destination du Québec, un candidat d'une catégorie d'immigration soumise à la sélection du Québec qui ne satisferait pas aux exigences de sélection québécoises.

Dans le cadre de l'Accord, le Québec a aussi, contre compensation financière, acquis la maîtrise d'œuvre exclusive de l'intégration socio-économique et linguistique des résidents permanents se destinant à son territoire. Il a toute marge de manœuvre pour élaborer et mettre en œuvre des politiques et des programmes d'intégration, selon sa propre lecture des enjeux en cause, en vue d'assurer l'intégration économique, sociale et linguistique des immigrants. La hauteur de la compensation versée au Québec tient compte du défi que représente la francisation des immigrants dans le contexte nord-américain.

En 2007, le Québec a accueilli quelque 45 000 nouveaux résidents permanents. Ce mouvement était composé à 62 pour cent d'immigrants économiques, 22 pour cent d'immigration familiale, à 13 pour cent de réfugiés et à 3 pour cent d'autres immigrants humanitaires. En 2007, il y avait aussi sur le territoire du Québec quelque 25 000 étudiants étrangers et 20 000 travailleurs temporaires.

La planification de l'immigration permanente est un élément clé de la politique d'immigration du Québec. Ainsi, La Loi sur l'immigration au Québec prévoit que le ministre responsable de l'immigration mène périodiquement des consultations publiques sur les orientations gou-vernementales en matière d'immigration permanente. La dernière consultation publique a été menée en septembre 2007. Elle portait sur la planification 2008–2010.

L'exercice réalisé a confirmé l'existence d'un large consensus, au sein de la société civile, en faveur de l'immigration et du rôle qu'elle peut jouer dans l'avenir du Québec. En effet, la grande majorité des participants à la consultation ont privilégié une hausse des niveaux d'immigration pour les trois prochaines années. Du même souffle, les avis entendus ont fait ressortir les défis de l'intégration, considérés comme plus nombreux et plus complexes qu'auparavant. On a entre autres relevé que dans plu-sieurs secteurs, il y a des besoins criants de main-d'œuvre alors qu'on observe un taux élevé de chômage et de sous-emploi chez les immigrants d'arrivée récente.

Le gouvernement a pris la décision de porter progressivement les vol-umes d'immigration permanente à 55 000, en 2010. Pour l'essentiel, cette hausse sera portée par l'immigration économique, plus particulièrement par les travailleurs qualifiés.

Toutefois, prenant acte des préoccupations exprimées, cette hausse des niveaux est accompagnée de deux plans de mesures afin de favoriser une meilleure intégration et un meilleur apprentissage du français chez les immigrants.

En francisation, trois objectifs sont poursuivis :

- franciser plus de personnes immigrantes, en rejoignant de nouvelles clientèles, notamment en milieu de travail;
- franciser plus tôt, à partir de l'étranger, en offrant aux personnes sélectionnées la possibilité d'apprendre le français avant leur arrivée au Québec;
- offrir des cours de français plus spécialisés afin de répondre aux besoins professionnels des nouveaux arrivants.

En matière d'immigration et d'intégration, les objectifs se déclinent comme suit :

- favoriser l'ouverture de la société québécoise à la diversité;
- accélérer l'insertion en emploi des immigrants;
- mobiliser les acteurs socio-économiques, notamment les employeurs, en matière de gestion de la diversité et d'intégration des personnes immigrantes;
- assurer une meilleure réponse aux besoins des employeurs;
- mieux soutenir les organismes communautaires et les partenaires municipaux et régionaux.

À titre d'exemples, voici quelques mesures d'intégration et de francisation qui sont révélatrices des préoccupations du gouvernement et de la société civile :

- promouvoir l'apport de l'immigration au développement du Québec;
- diversifier l'offre de service de francisation pour rejoindre une clientèle plus diversifiée et notamment mieux rejoindre les personnes parrainées dans le cadre du regroupement familial;
- accélérer la reconnaissance des compétences professionnelles des personnes formées à l'étranger;
- mieux accompagner les nouveaux arrivants dans leurs démarches vers l'emploi;
- mieux soutenir les employeurs en matière de gestion de la diversité.

S'agissant de mesures relatives à l'immigration, il faut rappeler qu'en 2006, le Québec a amorcé un virage en matière de sélection des immigrants se destinant à son territoire. D'un modèle basé pour l'essentiel sur le capital humain, il a visé un meilleur arrimage entre la sélection et les besoins du marché du travail.

À cette fin, la grille de sélection des travailleurs qualifiés a été modifiée pour accorder une importance accrue aux domaines de formation académique des candidats (ainsi, sur un seuil de passage de 59 points, un candidat peut obtenir de 0 à 12 points selon son domaine de formation). La pondération prend en compte les besoins à moyen terme du marché du travail, les difficultés particulières d'accès à l'emploi, par exemple, dans des professions régies par des ordres professionnels, ainsi que les volumes d'immigrants déjà admis au cours des dernières années dans les professions en cause.

On constate toutefois que si les règles ont changé, la demande est demeurée la même, avec une majorité de candidats de niveau universitaire, alors qu'on estime qu'une large part des besoins en main-d'œuvre se retrouvent et se retrouveront dans des emplois de techniciens et dans des métiers spécialisés.

En fait, à l'heure actuelle, trop peu de candidats (8 pour cent) ont les profils les plus valorisés sous l'angle du domaine de formation. Ces candidats doivent attendre, comme les autres, selon les territoires, parfois deux ans pour que leur demande soit traitée. Par la suite, ils doivent aussi attendre que le gouvernement fédéral traite leur demande.

Pour corriger cette situation, des modifications seront apportées à la réglementation pour que les demandes de certificats de sélection des travailleurs qualifiés soient traitées, non plus uniquement par ordre chronologique de dépôt, pour chacun des territoires, mais d'abord en accordant la priorité de traitement aux candidats dont le domaine de formation est prédicateur d'une insertion en emploi rapide. Nous sommes aussi en discussion avec le gouvernement fédéral pour qu'il fasse de même et que les dossiers traités en priorité par le Québec fassent eux aussi l'objet d'un traitement prioritaire par le gouvernement fédéral.

Cette approche sera accompagnée d'un effort de promotion ciblée.

Il faut rappeler que le Québec fait de la promotion de l'immigration dans les territoires où la demande a avantage à être stimulée. Au cours des dernières années, cette promotion s'est appuyée, en grande partie, sur la tenue de sessions d'information pour des groupes de personnes scolarisées, francophones ou francophiles, éventuellement intéressées à un projet d'immigration au Québec. Nous évoluons maintenant vers un modèle qui, en recourant à des études de marché et à de la veille sur le terrain, nous renseignera sur les bassins potentiels de candidats et nous orientera vers ceux qui ont les formations recherchées. Par le biais d'une promotion ciblée et en recourant à des partenariats, il nous restera à rejoindre ces candidats pour leur faire valoir les avantages d'immigrer au Québec.

D'autres mesures concernent davantage l'immigration temporaire.

Comme mentionné précédemment, le Québec n'a que des pouvoirs limités en matière d'immigration temporaire. Par ailleurs, cette facette du programme d'immigration a longtemps été considérée comme un enjeu mineur. Cette époque est révolue. À l'échelle mondiale, l'immigration temporaire prend une importance grandissante. C'est aussi le cas au Québec.

Le programme des travailleurs étrangers temporaires vise d'abord à répondre rapidement aux besoins des employeurs lorsqu'il n'y a pas de main-d'œuvre locale disponible. Il vise aussi à soutenir la performance des entreprises, des établissements d'enseignement ou des centres de recherche en accueillant des travailleurs stratégiques.

Depuis quelques années, la demande pour des travailleurs temporaires est en hausse au Québec et plus encore dans d'autres provinces canadiennes, particulièrement celles de l'Ouest. Ce programme prend de l'ampleur, du fait de l'accentuation des échanges internationaux, parce qu'il y a des secteurs économiques en pénurie de main-d'œuvre et que les délais d'admission pour les travailleurs permanents sont longs.

Il est donc prévu de faciliter davantage la venue de travailleurs temporaires spécialisés sans pour autant négliger le recours à la main-d'œuvre locale disponible.

À cet égard, le plan de mesures rendu public en mars 2008 prévoit le développement d'une offre de services pour les employeurs aux prises avec des difficultés de recrutement de main-d'œuvre spécialisée et qui souhaitent se tourner vers le recrutement à l'étranger.

Par ailleurs, la clientèle des étudiants étrangers est prisée par plusieurs pays. Les efforts déployés pour les attirer et les retenir sont de plus en plus importants. On reconnaît en effet que la venue d'étudiants étrangers contribue au rayonnement du Québec à l'étranger, permet de diversifier les équipes de recherche, de développer, chez les étudiants québécois et dans la population en général, une ouverture sur le monde. Elle permet aussi de contribuer à la vitalité des établissements et des communautés d'accueil.

Enfin, les étudiants étrangers et les travailleurs temporaires spécialisés présents au Québec constituent un bassin de choix en matière d'immigration permanente. S'agissant des étudiants, il faut rappeler que leurs diplômes sont immédiatement reconnus par les employeurs et que plusieurs d'entre eux ont acquis une expérience de travail québécoise. Pour leur part, les travailleurs temporaires spécialisés ont fait la démonstration de leur capacité à répondre à des besoins du marché du travail. Souvent, les employeurs sont intéressés à les retenir.

Le plan de mesures évoqué plus tôt prévoit donc une mesure qui consiste à favoriser le passage du statut temporaire au statut de résident permanent, par le biais d'efforts de promotion accentués et ciblés, et la mise en place de règles d'immigration davantage facilitantes.

En conclusion, au cours de la dernière décennie, le Québec a connu une hausse significative de son mouvement d'immigration. La poursuite de cette hausse nécessite que des efforts inédits soient déployés pour faire en sorte que l'immigration réponde davantage aux besoins du Québec et que l'ensemble des personnes immigrantes, qu'il s'agisse d'immigrants économiques, de réfugiés ou de membres de la catégorie du regroupement familial, puissent réaliser leurs aspirations et contribuer à l'avenir collectif. Il s'agit d'un grand défi qui interpelle non seulement le gouvernement, mais aussi tous les acteurs socio-économiques, dont le patronat et l'ensemble de la collectivité.

NOTE

1.   Note from the editor / Note de l'éditeur : This chapter was prepared by the author in late 2008, based on her presentation for the *Managing Immigration and Diversity in Quebec and Canada Forum* (Barcelona, October 2008). At the time, she was the Directrice des Politiques et des Programmes d'immigration at the Ministère de l'Immigration et des Communautés culturelles du Québec. / Ce chapitre a été rédigé par l'auteure en fin d'année 2008 et est basé sur sa présentation au *Forum sur la gestion de l'immigration et de la diversité au Québec et au Canada* (Barcelone, octobre 2008). À ce moment-là, elle occupait le poste de directrice des Politiques et des Programmes d'immigration au Ministère de l'Immigration et des Communautés culturelles du Québec.

PART II

MANAGEMENT OF IMMIGRATION FLOWS

CHAPTER 4

Managing International Migration: The Canadian Case

MONICA BOYD, *Professor of Sociology, Canada Research Chair in Immigration, Inequality and Public Policy, University of Toronto*

NAOMI ALBOIM, *Adjunct Professor, Chair of the Policy Forum at the School of Policy Studies, Queen's University*

This chapter presents past and present policy developments in Canadian immigration. Although the focus is on events prior to 2009, updates on new initiatives are provided through 2011. Many policy changes, however, even since late 2011, continue to be introduced.

INTRODUCTION

Today, with more than 300 years of settlement history, Canada is correctly described, alongside Australia and the United States, as a nation that was forged and developed by immigration. With a population one-tenth that of the United States, Canada admits a greater proportionate share of immigrants to North America. In the first four years of the 21st century (2000–2003), 20 percent of all immigrants destined for North America arrived in Canada. As a result of past and present immigration, close to one in five of Canada's inhabitants are foreign-born, compared with just

Managing Immigration and Diversity in Canada: A Transatlantic Dialogue in the New Age of Migration,
ed. D. Rodríguez-García. Montreal and Kingston: Queen's Policy Studies Series, McGill-Queen's University Press.
© 2012 The School of Policy Studies, Queen's University at Kingston. All rights reserved.

over one in ten of the United State's population. Only Australia has the distinction over Canada of having a higher percentage of foreign-born in its population (one in four).

Canada's current immigration system is the result of historical forces, the country's political system, and contemporary challenges arising from international politics and globalization. These factors all shape the goals that contemporary migration is thought to further, the apparatus—or bureaucratic organization—that guides migration policy-making and admits migrants, the actual demographic trends regarding migration, and the current issues and initiatives that exist with respect to Canada's management of migration flows.

THE HISTORICAL ORIGINS OF THE FUNDAMENTAL GOALS REGARDING MIGRATION

Unlike many European countries of today, which have switched from being countries of emigration to being countries of immigration, Canada has been a country of migrants from its very beginning. Even its Aboriginal populations are said to have crossed the land bridge from Asia to migrate to Canada. As a nation consisting of two major "charter" or founding groups, Canada is a place where migrants have been central to nation-building efforts. In the colonizing efforts by France and Britain during the 1600s and 1700s, migrants were solicited to literally populate new lands. The recruitment and settlement of these migrants was crucial to support the claims that each European country had on a vast dominion of land occupied by Aboriginal peoples. The resolution of these competing claims was decided in favour of the British as a result of the Seven Years' War. However, the loss of the French military to the British on the Plains of Abraham (Quebec City) in 1759, the capitulation of Governor Vaudreuil in Montreal a year later, and the official ceding of New France to the British in a 1763 treaty signed by the French did not mean the gradual disappearance of French Canada into an Anglo world. The continued use of French, the practice of Catholicism, geographical concentration, and high fertility rates helped to maintain a distinctive "nation."

After the end of the Seven Years' War, migration continued, but it was primarily from Britain, the United States, or European areas other than France. The creation of the (federal) Dominion of Canada in July 1867 meant the acquisition of new areas and the inclusion of new provincial members, all representing substantial nation-building and consolidation challenges. Immigration was central to meeting these challenges for three reasons. First, as settlers, immigrants would occupy and fill sparsely populated areas along the newly built railroad line that linked the western and eastern parts of the country. The second and third reasons for immigration were economic. As consumers, immigrants would stimulate demand for goods and services; and as workers, they could be employed in labour-scarce industries. However, care was to be taken with respect to who should be encouraged to enter Canada; immigrants from Britain were the most desired (Kelley and Trebilcock 1998). Although migrants often left Canada for the United States, the prevailing conceptualization then—as now—was that migrants would become permanent residents of Canada.

Eighty years later, in Prime Minister MacKenzie King's famous statement on Canada's long-term immigration objectives (1 May 1947), these goals of population growth and economic development were still in place. His statement contained six fundamental principles (Green and Green 1999; Hawkins 1972): (1) Immigration was to be used to increase population growth; (2) immigration was to further economic objectives; (3) immigration must be selective; (4) immigration must be related to Canada's economic conditions and thus to its absorptive capacity; (5) Canada is completely within its rights in controlling immigration, in particular in selecting the immigrants that Canada wants; and (6) immigration should not alter the composition of the Canadian population. This last principle rested on the argument that British and European migrants were preferred and that existing restrictions that prevented Asian migration should remain.

The relationship between Canada's economic goals and the recruitment of migrants is discussed in later sections of this chapter. However, inflows over nearly 150 years can be seen in Figure 1. The 20th century truly was a

FIGURE 1
Total Number of Immigrants to Canada (1860–2007)

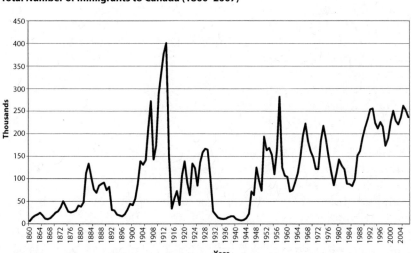

Source: Citizenship and Immigration Canada, *Facts and Figures 2002* (2002); Citizenship and Immigration Canada, *Facts and Figures 2007* (2007a).

time of mass migration, with the highest levels reached in 1911. Migration flows were reduced during World Wars I and II and the Great Depression of 1929 to 1933, but these numbers rose again after World War II (Figure 1). Overall, the inflow contributed greatly to Canada's demographic growth (Boyd and Vickers 2000), particularly as Canadian fertility rates began their precipitous decline in the 1970s. Today, Canada has a birth rate of 10.9 births per 1,000 population, or approximately 1.58 births per woman aged 15 to 44 (figures are for 2006). With fertility at below population replacement levels, immigration currently accounts for 60 percent of Canada's population growth between 1996 and 2007. Population projections show that international migration may become the only source of net population growth by about 2030 (Statistics Canada 2007).

CONTROLLING IMMIGRATION FLOWS AND COMPOSITION: THE MANAGEMENT STRUCTURE

From the 1800s to the 2000s, the management of immigration flows evolved from a laissez-faire system in which labour recruiters played a significant role in generating migration to a managed process under government jurisdiction. The *British North America Act*, now known as the *Constitution Act of 1867*, conferred the management of immigration to both federal and provincial governments, with paramount authority to the federal government. By 1874, it was evident that independent recruitment efforts by the provinces created waste and inefficiencies and in some cases conflicted with the recruitment efforts of the federal government; thereafter, the federal government assumed control of immigration recruitment (Kalbach 1970; Knowles 2007). Further, migration policy moved away from direct parliamentary control to being part of a government agency mandated to deal with migration issues. As agriculture was the dominant economic sector of the time and immigrants were primarily recruited to work on the land, immigration matters became housed in the Department of Agriculture in 1887, to be transferred at the end of the 1800s to the Department of the Interior, yet again, in 1917, to the newly established Department of Immigration and Colonization, and then to the Department of Mines and Resources in 1936 (Kelley and Trebilcock 1998). Thereafter, the management of immigration was part of the Department of Citizenship and Immigration (1950), the Department of Manpower and Immigration, then the Department of Employment and Immigration, and then Citizenship and Immigration in 1994.

The administrative management structure described above is noteworthy for three reasons. First, the administrative location of immigration management reflects the core economic and nation-building objectives of immigration that have existed from the very beginning of Canada as a nation. How these objectives are attained, however, is rapidly changing. Later sections of this chapter highlight the growing use of temporary labour and within-Canada recruitment from the temporary labour and student pool.

Second, in a parliamentary system, as compared with a congressional one, the management of immigration by departments means that migration issues are less subject to "capture" by public interest groups or spontaneous debate. Canadian party leaders typically maintain strong control over their party's elected members of Parliament. At the federal level, two governing bodies exist, an elected Parliament and an appointed Senate. Immigration legislation must be passed by both. The federal government department that manages immigration has its own minister, who is a member of the federal Cabinet. Immigration regulations are not enshrined in legislation, which simply states major guiding principles. As a result, alterations in immigrant admissions policies can occur with little visibility via Cabinet decisions and bureaucratic guidelines, rather than requiring continual legislative adjudication. Government departments also have discretion to fine-tune objectives. Overall, this arrangement for managing immigration allows for a more orderly process of planning. However, as discussed later in this chapter, recent legislative changes have given the Minister of Immigration power to issue instructions to visa officers without consultations or parliamentary review. These changes have the potential not only to diminish accountability but also to render the planning process less transparent.

Third, in little more than 100 years after Confederation, provinces are once again becoming part of the administrative structure of managing immigration. Although the federal government has the paramount authority to manage immigration, the 1976 *Immigration Act* mandated the practice of federal-provincial consultations, calling for provincial input into future immigration levels, the mix of immigrant classes admitted, and selection criteria. Several provinces took up the offer and signed agreements with the federal government. The most extensive agreement—one that granted powers in regard to selecting migrants—occurred with the province of Quebec (Kelley and Trebilcock 1998). In the wake of the 1976 election of the separatist Parti Québécois, the Quebec government was particularly keen to gain control over a system that many believed flooded the province with anglophones or allophones (whose language is neither French nor English). The Cullen-Couture Agreement, signed between Canada and Quebec in 1978, permitted Quebec to recruit more francophone immigrants to the province and allowed Quebec to select immigrants using a slightly different point system from the one used by the federal government (Kelley and Trebilcock 1998). In 1991, this agreement was replaced by the Canada-Quebec Accord, which has as its objective, among other things, the preservation of Quebec's demographic importance within Canada and the integration of immigrants to that province in a manner that respects the distinct identity of Quebec (Gouvernement du Québec 2000; Young 2004). The Canada-Quebec Accord grants Quebec the authority to set annual immigration targets and the responsibility for selecting immigrants in the economic category, as well as refugees from abroad. Quebec has its own point system, sends its own visa officers overseas, and gets a significant share of settlement funding provided by the federal government for the sole administration by Quebec government officials. The federal government remains responsible for establishing selection criteria for members of the Family Class and for determining the status of those claiming refugee status within Canada. The federal government also retains responsibility for health, security, and criminality checks of all immigrants and refugees and for defining immigrant categories, setting immigration levels, and establishing admissibility requirements under the *Immigration and Refugee Protection Act* (Citizenship and Immigration Canada 2008, section 2). Since the signing of the Canada-Quebec Accord, there has been growing involvement by other provinces in immigrant selection and integration processes; these new initiatives are discussed later in the chapter.

CONTROLLING IMMIGRATION FLOWS AND COMPOSITION: LEGISLATION AND REGULATIONS

Accounts of Canada's immigration history point to numerous pieces of legislation enacted to further the goals of population settlement and economic gain while controlling which individuals and groups would be allowed entry (Green and Green 1999, 2004; Kelley and Trebilcock 1998; Knowles 2007). Table 1 presents the major pieces of legislation in the past 100 years. As noted previously, Canada's parliamentary system allows for legislation to contain guiding principles; the specific implementation of these principles can occur via regulations that do not require a parliamentary vote.

A major change—done through regulations—did, in fact, occur in the 1960s. The 1952 *Immigration Act* had adopted national origin as the principle criterion on which people would be allowed legal entry and permanent residence; this allowed Europeans to migrate but excluded most of those from elsewhere in the world. By the 1960s, the civil rights movement in the United States, the role that Canada had played in the drafting of the Universal Declaration of Human Rights, and the leadership role that Canada was seeking in the British Commonwealth were making this criterion untenable. Regulations introduced in 1962 removed national origin as the primary selection criterion, retaining only one area of privilege for Europeans: Compared to non-Europeans, they could sponsor a wider range of relatives (Hawkins 1972, 125).

However, if national origin was no longer the criterion of admissibility, then other criteria had to be devised to regulate immigration. In 1967, an entirely new immigrant selection system was implemented, again through regulation. Included in this structure was Canada's point system, which applied to those who either lacked family in Canada or were not part of an immediate family, defined as spouses and children (Boyd 1976; Hawkins 1991), but who could be admitted on the basis of their potential economic contribution. This point system has become one of the defining character-istics of Canada's immigration system, sustained in the *Immigration Act* of 1976 (effective in 1978), and in later acts and amendments to the acts. Points were given for the principal applicant's age, education, knowledge of French or English (Canada has two official languages), and to other factors such as occupational demand and occupational skill (see Boyd 1976; Green and Green 1999).

TABLE 1
Significant Canadian Immigration Acts and Regulatory Changes, 1900–2008

1910	*Immigration Act*
1923	*Exclusion Act (Chinese Immigration Act)*—repealed in 1947
1952	*Immigration Act* passed (came into effect 1 June 1953)
February 1962	New regulations implemented that removed most racial discrimination by no longer basing admissions on national origin
October 1967	Point system introduced by regulation
November 1976	New Immigration Bill tabled—came into effect in April 1978
1981	Foreign Domestic Workers Program introduced; replaced in 1992 by the Live-in Caregiver Program
1989, 1992, 1995	Bills adopted that altered parts of the 1978 act
June 2002	New immigration act goes into effect; called the *Immigration and Refugee Protection Act* (IRPA)
8 June 2008	Bill C-50 passed, giving substantial discretion to the Minister of Citizenship and Immigration
17 September 2008	The Canadian Experience Class established

Source: Authors' compilation.

The 1962 and 1967 regulations were at odds with those stated in the 1952 *Immigration Act*. After a lengthy process, outlined by Hawkins (1991), a new *Immigration Act* was passed in 1976 and came into effect in 1978. By the time of these regulatory and legislative changes, out-migration from Europe was declining, stimulated by large improvements in European postwar economies. The removal of national origin as a criterion of admis-sibility, in combination with declining migration from Europe, changed the origin composition of immigrants living in Canada. By 2006, slightly more than 30 percent of the foreign-born permanently residing in Canada were from the United States, the United Kingdom, or other European countries; fifty percent were born in Asia; and the remainder were from other parts of the world, including Africa and Central and South America.

CURRENT MIGRATION GOALS

As had been the case from the very beginning, immigration remains part of Canada's nation-building endeavour. Immigration planning throughout the latter half of the 20th century has continued to rest on the principles that immigrants further demographic growth, stimulate the economy, and provide labour. Today, there are three main categories under which most immigrants enter Canada; each corresponds to a principle of admissibility. The three pillars of current Canadian immigration policy for permanent residence are family reunification, humanitarian criteria, and admission on the basis of economic contribution.

However, the comparative importance of each category of admissibility has varied over time since the 1950s, depending on the state of Canada's economy and the use, prior to the 1990s, of a "tap-on, tap-off" approach to regulating numbers of admissions by the authorized government department. Increasing or decreasing the numbers of immigrants to be admitted in any given year rested on the principle of fine-tuning immigration numbers to match Canada's "absorptive capacity." That is, immigration numbers in the economic category would be reduced during business cycle downturns when unemployment levels rose. In the late 1970s and the 1980s, admissions in the Family Class surpassed those in the economic category, partly because the introduction of a point system in the late 1960s made entry in the Economic Class more difficult (see Knowles 2007) and partly because during the recessionary period of 1982 to 1983, the Canadian government dramatically curbed the admission of those seeking to enter in the Economic Class.

From the early 1990s on, those entering in the Economic Class became a rapidly increasing share of all admissions for permanent residence (Figure 2). By 1995 and beyond, over half of immigrants entering Canada did so in the Economic Class (principal applicants and their accompanying dependants), rather than entering through family ties or on the basis of humanitarian concerns. Consistent with this trend, immigrants entering Canada during the 1990s on average were more educated than those arriving earlier. According to the 2006 census, two out of five of those immigrants had university degrees or higher; this rose to over half of those admitted between 2001 and 2006 (Figure 3).

The increasing proportion of immigrants admitted under economic criteria represents two fundamental shifts, one in policy and the other in the management of migration by Citizenship and Immigration. First, by the early 1990s, regulating the size of annual flows in accordance with the robustness of Canada's economy had ceased, signalling the end of

FIGURE 2
Permanent Residents by Category of Admissions, Canada, Annual Flows, 1980–2007

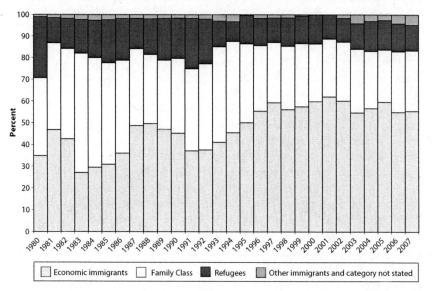

Source: Citizenship and Immigration Canada, *Facts and Figures 2004* (2004); Citizenship and Immigration Canada, *Facts and Figures 2007* (2007b).

FIGURE 3
Percent with University Degree or Higher, Non-Immigrants, Permanent Residents and Temporary Residents, Age 25 to 54, Canada 2006

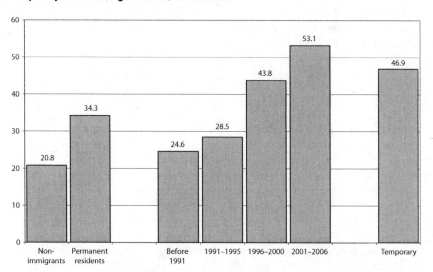

Source: Authors' tabulations compiled from Statistics Canada 2006 Census of Population: Data Products—Topic-based Tabulations—Immigration and Citizenship, Immigration Status, Item 12.[1]

the earlier "tap-on, tap-off" procedure in which volume was enlarged or diminished according to economic conditions. The in-migration of permanent residents was exceptionally high during the early 1990s, coinciding with one of Canada's worst recessions. Second, by the early 1990s, maintaining global competitiveness in knowledge-intensive activities had become the mantra of the Canadian federal government. Alongside the delinking between levels of immigration and economic downturns or upturns, Citizenship and Immigration Canada adopted a deliberate policy emphasis on increasing the flow of skilled workers. Tapping into the international movement of highly educated people is a major objective of Canada's current immigration policy. Contemporary shifts from a primary resource and manufacturing economy to a post-industrial service economy have created demand for skilled labour; however, low fertility rates since the 1970s have not only resulted in an increasingly aging population but also have reduced the numbers of new labour market entrants from the native-born population. Population projections for Canada show that if current immigration rates continue, immigration could account for virtually all net labour force growth as of 2011 (Statistics Canada 2007).

In the eyes of policy-makers, rising labour demand and demographic change make it necessary, indeed crucial, for Canada to recruit skilled workers in order to maintain its success in innovation and its economic growth and prosperity (Citizenship and Immigration Canada 2007; Gera and Songsakul 2007). As stated in the 31 October 2007 Annual Report to Parliament,

> Immigration will play an increasingly important role in supporting Canada's economic prosperity and competitiveness. ... Immigration can contribute to addressing both short- and long-term labour market needs by attracting people with the right mix of skills and talents to support economic growth today and in the future. With other industrialized countries confronting similar challenges with respect to sustaining population and economic growth, Canada will be operating in an increasingly competitive worldwide market for higher skilled workers. (Citizenship and Immigration Canada 2007)

For the most part, those entering Canada under the criterion of making an economic contribution are in the "skilled worker" category, representing three-fourths of all those admitted in 2007 in the Economic Class. However, during the 1980s, additional procedures were adopted not just to recruit workers but also to recruit those prepared to invest in business. The legacy of these changes is found in the most recent legislation, the *Immigration and Refugee Protection Act* (IRPA), which became effective in June 2002. The act includes provisions to "... facilitate the entry into Canada of immigrants who are better prepared to adapt to Canada's labour market needs and those who can make a contribution to the economy through investments and the establishment of new businesses" (Citizenship and Immigration Canada 2005).

For skilled workers, who represent the largest number of immigrants entering Canada under the criterion of economic contribution, the new legislation departed from earlier attempts to link the labour supply of applications to specific occupational demand. Prior to a 28 November 2008 amendment, which will be discussed later in this chapter, IRPA focused on selecting immigrants with human capital—that is, the flexible and transferable skills needed to succeed in a rapidly changing, knowledge-based economy—rather than on selecting those with qualifications for specific occupations.

The point system under the 2002 IRPA is provided in Appendix A; it applies to principal applicants who seek entry in the skilled worker category. The increased policy emphasis on recruiting workers with high generic levels of skill is evident in several ways. First, the points required to enter have been increased from 60 points to 67. Second, under IRPA, years of education may count for a maximum of 25 points, or 37 percent, of the minimum required 67 points; previously, educational achievements were allotted a maximum of 16 points, or 27 percent, of the total 60 points required. Similarly, under IRPA, having the highest levels of English and French language fluency counts for 24 points, or 36 percent, of the minimum of 67 points; prior to IRPA, linguistic fluency counted for 25 percent of the total minimum 60 required points. Third, would-be immigrants seeking admission as skilled workers must meet the following requirements:

1. Have at least one continuous year of paid, full-time work experience or the equivalent in part-time continuous employment.
2. Have work experience that must be Skill Type 0 (managerial occupations) or Skill Level A (professional occupations) or Skill Level B (technical occupations and skilled trades) on the Canadian National Occupational Classification (NOC).
3. Must have had this experience within the last ten years.

In addition, applicants with pre-arranged employment in occupations that are considered to be "skilled" occupations are awarded extra points.

The increasing emphasis in Canadian immigration policy on admitting skilled workers raises two readily identifiable issues. First, although the size of the Economic Class is increasing, it is inaccurate to assume that all who are admitted are destined to work or are highly skilled; spouses and dependants make up over half of those recently admitted in the skilled worker category, and these family members are not assessed on the point system. For example, between 1998 and 2007, 49 percent of those entering Canada on the basis of economic contributions were principal applicants; within the skilled worker category, 43 percent were principal applicants. Principal applicants in the skilled worker class represented slightly over 20 percent of all persons admitted as permanent residents in the period between 1998 and 2007, but this figure masks a downward trend over the ten-year period. In fact, in 2007, only 17 percent of all immigrants to Canada were assessed on the full skilled worker points system (Citizenship and Immigration Canada no date-a).

A second issue is the paradoxical situation in which nations seek high-skilled immigrants who then find their skills underutilized. The under-utilization of immigrant talents is at the core of two integration issues that are currently centre-stage in Canada: (a) the declining fortunes of recently arrived immigrants, particularly in relation to the experiences of earlier cohorts during their first years in Canada; and (b) the barriers to successful labour market integration that can arise when profession-ally trained newcomers must be re-accredited or re-certified to practise in their professions.

Research on the economic integration of recent immigrants during the 1990s shows that they are not doing as well as previous cohorts with respect to employment, avoidance of poverty, and earnings. Immigrants who entered Canada in the 1990s were less likely to be employed in 2000 compared to the Canadian-born or to immigrants who had arrived earlier. Compared to immigrant cohorts that arrived in previous decades, im-migrants who entered Canada in the 1990s also have higher percentages that fall below Statistics Canada's "low-income cut-offs" (Statistics Canada 2004a), which are commonly used as measures of poverty. Low-income rates rose throughout the 1990s for immigrants, but they have been high-est for those who have been in Canada for less than five years. In 2000, the low-income rates for these immigrants were 2.5 times higher than the rates observed for the Canadian-born (Picot and Hou 2003). Comparisons of the earnings of new arrivals across censuses from 1961 onward indicate that the relative entry earnings of those who arrived in the 1990s have declined over time (Aydemir and Skuterud 2005; Statistics Canada 2004b; also see Frenette and Morissette 2005, for comparisons of entry cohorts between 1981 and 2001). Further, the earnings gap between immigrant and Canadian-born men widened from 11 percent in 1980 to 33 percent in 1995, before declining to 22 percent in 2000 (Frenette and Morissette 2005; Warman and Worswick 2004). Studies also find that the time it takes for the wages of new cohorts to catch up to those of the Canadian-born is getting longer (Frenette and Morissette 2005). However, when classes of immigrants are disaggregated, those assessed on the basis of the point system—skilled worker principal applicants—consistently fare better than all other immigrant classes, and those with knowledge of one of the official languages do best of all.

As noted in a release by Statistics Canada (2004b) and in a 2005 review (Picot and Sweetman 2005), these trends cannot be explained by a single factor (also see Alboim, Finnie, and Meng 2005). Some studies suggest that the changing composition of immigrants does not play a direct role since educational levels have been rising among recent immigrants. Others find that knowledge of languages other than English or French and country of origin remain important factors underlying the deteriorating economic situation of immigrants (Galarneau and Morissette 2008). From a demand-side set of explanations, it does appear that employers may be increasingly discounting foreign education and work experience, treating immigrants as if they are new entrants to the labour force instead of being simply new arrivals in Canada. Ironically, under the criteria used to admit skilled workers, work experience is worth up to 21 points (Appendix A). In apparent response to this gap between policy and what is actually happening to immigrants, the federal government in 2011 proposed changes to the point system; the government recommends, along with making alterations in the points allocated to other selection factors, that points allotted to work experience be decreased from 21 to 15 points.[2]

Other factors behind the labour market difficulties of immigrants include the state of the economy and degree recognition difficulties. In the early 1990s, Canada experienced a severe recession, which impacted on Canadian new labour market entrants as well as on recent immigrants. Some researchers refer to the scarring effects of the early 1990s that entry cohorts continue to carry with them over time. The 2008–09 financial market declines and recessionary times will generate new scarring effects; yet the Canadian government admitted over 250,000 permanent residents in 2009 and another 280,000 in 2010, including nearly 154,000 and 187,000 immigrants in the Economic Class (Citizenship and Immigration Canada no date-b). The juxtaposition of economic recession and continued recruitment of skilled workers generates two questions for the future: (1) Do current economic conditions indicate the need to incorporate economic indicators into the planning of immigration levels? or (2) Will the numbers of skilled immigrants choosing to come to Canada during an economic downturn decline naturally? If the latter is answered affirmatively, then closing the tap now will make it harder to open it again when the economy improves. The most recent policy response to the high inflows juxtaposed against economic downturns was announced in June 2011; the number of skilled workers admitted without pre-arranged job offers will be capped at 10,000 as from July 2011. However, many of those destined to Canada's labour force also enter under the Provincial Nominee Program, discussed later in this chapter, and in the Family and Humanitarian classes, and these individuals remain unaffected by the new restrictions on skilled workers.

One obvious conclusion to be drawn from all of these studies is that having high human capital alone does not protect immigrants today from economic hardship. According to the 2006 census, 28 percent of men and 40 percent of women who had arrived within the past five years and who had university degrees were employed in jobs with low educational requirements, such as clerks, truck drivers, cashiers, and taxi drivers, compared to one in ten Canadian-born (Galarneau and Morissette 2008). Difficulties faced by immigrants in gaining recognition for educational and professional training, as well as for training in trades, is an issue that is now being extensively discussed among immigrants and non-governmental organizations (NGOs) and within government agencies.

In Canada, regulated occupations in certain trades, law, engineering, and health areas require certification and/or licensing. Such certification and/or licensing occurs primarily through professional regulatory bodies, who are often mandated to do so by provincial government statutes, the purpose being to ensure public health and safety. A recent study found that slightly over half of the foreign-trained who studied medicine are working as physicians, compared to over 90 percent of the Canadian-born. Further, more than half of the foreign-trained who studied engineering were employed in lower level technical occupations or in jobs unrelated to their training, compared to approximately one-fourth of the Canadian-born (Boyd and Schellenberg 2007). Yet, specialist physicians; general and family physicians; nurses; and mining, geological, and petroleum engineers are six of the 38 occupations identified as facing skill shortages and in demand of workers, and which were used to fast-track skilled worker applications made between 26 February 2008 and 26 June 2010 (Citizenship and Immigration Canada 2008; *Canada Gazette* 2010). Engineers were omitted in a reduced list of 29 occupations, issued on 26 June 2010, but approximately one-third of the 29 occupations are regulated by some or all of the provinces. Clearly, Canada's migration policies that admit immigrants on the basis of their potential professional contributions are not supported or complemented by provincial professional accreditation requirements. This conflict underlies ongoing discussions and government initiatives regarding immigrant re-accreditation; it also invites a re-examination of recent federal government actions to prioritize the admission of skilled workers on the basis of specific occupational expertise.

NEW INITIATIVES IN THE 21ST CENTURY

As Canada enters the 21st century, four important trends are evident in the management of immigration at the federal level: (1) increasing the flexibility for rapid change in policy decision-making through greater ministerial powers; (2) decentralizing and devolving more responsibility to the provinces for immigrant admission and settlement; (3) increasing the admission of temporary workers to meet short-term labour needs; and (4) recruiting permanent residents from temporary workers and international students studying in Canada.

Increasing Flexibility; Enhancing Ministerial Discretion

Recent federal legislation, passed on 9 June 2008, represents a major shift in the process of policy implementation. Previously, there were legislative requirements to conduct consultations on immigration levels and mix, as well as on proposed policy changes, and to table annual reports in the Parliament on the achievement of previous targets and on immigration plans for the coming year. This approach balanced the goals of government to manage the immigration program and the desires of citizens to participate in the decision-making process. Transparency and accountability were built into the process. However, Bill C-50, the 2008 *Budget Implementation Act*, contained within it amendments to Canada's most recent immigration act (the 2002 *Immigration and Refugee Protection Act*). These amendments gave complete discretion to the Minister of Immigration to process applications and requests made after 26 February 2008 "…in a manner that, in the opinion of the Minister, will best support the attainment of the immigration goals established by the Government of Canada." Further, the minister may give instructions to visa officers with respect to processing applications, establishing categories of applications, prioritizing the order, setting the number of applications or requests processed in a given year, and providing rules for repeat applications.[3]

The rationale for Bill C-50 is the need to have flexibility in the implementation of immigration policy in order to resolve the growing queues of applicants and to best serve the needs of the Canadian economy. However, the public reaction to Bill C-50 was extensive, and at least three major criticisms were raised. First, the method of passing amendments to the 2002 *Immigration and Refugee Protection Act* was highly unusual and without precedent. Rather than tabling amendments as a stand-alone parliamentary bill that would be subject to debate, consultation, and involvement by all political parties, amendments were inserted into a budget bill that was unlikely to face defeat since it would represent a vote of non-confidence, causing the dissolution of the Conservative government currently in power. Second, the amendments allowed for ministerial instructions to be issued at any time without consultation or accountability to Parliament and without transparency as to the underlying rationale. Third, by giving the Minister of Immigration the power to make changes at any time, immigration planning becomes more volatile. In the past, would-be immigrants, family members already resident in Canada who seek to sponsor relatives, or NGO groups willing to sponsor refugees could look to the targeted goals and selection criteria as providing information on the likelihood of success or the time required for gaining permanent residence. But the capacity of the minister to change levels suddenly or dramatically hampers such efforts. Even those seeking admission on the basis of their economic contribution will find it difficult to plan. For example, on 28 November 2008, the Minister of

Citizenship and Immigration announced that he was issuing instructions to visa officers to process from the federal "skilled worker" applications candidates in 38 high-demand occupations (out of over 500 occupations), such as health, skilled trades, finance, and resource extraction. These instructions were retroactive to 27 February 2008, the date specified by the Federal Budget. All other applications in the skilled worker category submitted since 27 February 2008 were returned unprocessed. Again, on 26 June 2010, a reduced list of 29 occupations was issued to be applied to all applications in the skilled worker category from that date forward. As indicated previously in this chapter, there is no guarantee that even the selected skilled workers in these demand occupations will be able to experience a smooth labour market entry in their fields given licensing requirements; moreover, given the current volatility of the Canadian economy, there is no guarantee that there will still be a need for these skilled workers by the time they arrive.

Delegating to Provinces

Provinces and territories are now partners with the federal government in the management of immigration. In addition to the Canada-Quebec Accord, at the start of 2011, Citizenship and Immigration Canada (CIC) had immigration agreements with all provinces (British Columbia, Alberta, Saskatchewan, Manitoba, Ontario, Quebec, Prince Edward Island, Nova Scotia, Newfoundland, and New Brunswick) and with two territories (Yukon and the Northwest Territories). However, the Ontario Immigration Agreement ended in 2011 and was not successfully renegotiated, and the agreements with Manitoba and British Columbia that transferred federal funds and responsibility for settlement services to those provinces will be terminated when they are up for renewal. In other provinces and territories, settlement program funding is administered by CIC regional offices, and services generally are delivered by third parties, such as community-based organizations.

Despite changing emphases, rationales, and programs over the years, the Canadian federal government, along with some provinces, has been a long-time funder of immigrant settlement activities. However, since the 1990s, the administration of settlement services has been increasingly decentralized. In the 1994 budget, the federal government indicated that it was no longer interested in being in the business of managing immigrant settlement policies and programs. Following a pattern of decentralization found in other policy domains, the federal government was interested in transferring funds to other agencies, including the provinces, as a cost-cutting measure. Only three provinces—Quebec, British Columbia, and Manitoba—were prepared to take on this role and allow the federal government to withdraw from its traditional mandate. In all three provinces, there are questions about whether the federal funds transferred are indeed being spent on immigrant settlement activities as intended.

Program assessment also is difficult. There is no centralized public list-ing of programs, expenditures, the numbers serviced, and the outcomes (or efficiencies) of the programs. Instead, descriptions are vague, and estimates regarding coverage are hampered by discussions that refer to levels of funding and number of services provided, rather than to clients served and the effectiveness of the services provided. This appears to be common in the settlement services realm. A 1998 report laments, "Not only are we unable to determine whether settlement funds are spent in an effective manner ..., but we have no information on who accesses these services, which would then allow us to determine whether these particular expenditures contribute in a positive or anticipated manner to the integration process of the individual immigrant" (Citizenship and Immigration Canada 1998).

In addition to federal-provincial agreements regarding settlement, the Provincial Nominee system is a mechanism by which provinces are al-lowed to select those who meet their special demographic or labour needs for admission as permanent residents in Canada. All provinces now have Provincial Nominee agreements. Ontario has a Pilot Provincial Nominee Program. The criteria for provincial nomination are determined by the individual provinces and territories, and they change over time. For ex-ample, in Alberta, which until recently had a strong oil-based economy, those selected as provincial nominees must have a full-time job offer from an Alberta employer, and they must have worked in industries including food and beverage, hotel and lodging, manufacturing, long-haul truck-ing, or foodservices. In British Columbia, provincial nominees must be managers, professionals, technologists and technicians, or in the skilled trades; or they must be registered nurses, midwives, registered psychiatric nurses, or physicians; or they must have worked in select occupations in the tourism/hospitality or food processing industry, or as long-haul truck drivers. As indicated in Figure 4, the number of admissions under the Provincial Nominee Program is growing over time. In 2010, the last year for which statistics are available, over 36,000 provincial nominees were admitted, or approximately 13 percent of all admissions in that year.

Although the intention of the Provincial Nominee Program is to meet the specific labour market needs of provinces, at least four problems exist in the current arrangements. First, most programs are short-sighted, fo-cusing on immediate labour market needs rather than on human capital characteristics of applicants, the latter of which would make them more adaptable to changing economic conditions. No attention is given to the unemployment and labour market difficulties that can occur when workers are admitted during economically prosperous times followed by recessionary periods. Second, because permanent residents have the right to live anywhere in Canada, allowing provinces to select (nomin-ate) migrants creates unanticipated consequences when workers leave for other provinces. Third, the program has the potential to undermine the overall planning process at the federal level, by admitting workers who normally would not be admitted in the skilled worker class (such as hotel workers). Until 2012 there were no ceilings to the Provincial Nominee Programs, yet these applicants have priority processing, ahead of any of the federally selected skilled workers. Fourth, there is no over-all national framework for the ten Provincial Nominee Programs, all of which have many subcomponents. They differ in eligibility criteria, costs, and processes. Further, basic language criteria are absent, although the federal government has indicated that they will be implemented, along with other changes, sometime in 2012. This makes it very complicated for would-be immigrants to understand the programs and does not allow for informed choices.

FIGURE 4
Canada, Provincial/Territorial Nominees, 1998–2007

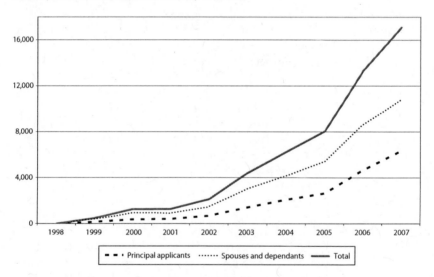

Source: Citizenship and Immigration Canada, *Facts and Figures 2007* (2007a).

Increasing Temporary Admissions

Temporary admissions cover a large range of circumstances and include refugee claimants, recently married spouses, international students who are studying in Canada, and persons explicitly admitted to meet labour shortages. Overall, the total annual flow of temporary migrants is comparable to the inflow of migrants admitted as permanent residents (Figure 5). However, because some temporary migrants have permits to stay for longer than a few days or months (students, refugee claimants, certain kinds of workers), the stock of temporary migrants—those in the country on a specific date—outnumbers the flow of temporary migrants (Figure 6). In fact, the gap between the inflow and the stock of workers

FIGURE 5
Canada, Annual Flow of Permanent and Temporary Residents, 1980–2006

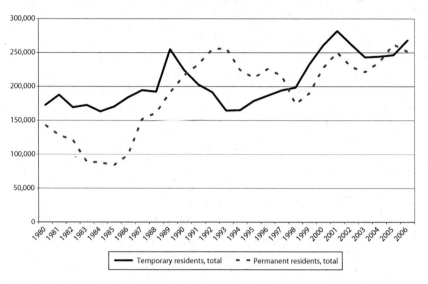

Source: Citizenship and Immigration Canada, *Facts and Figures 2006* (2006a).

FIGURE 6
Canada, Temporary Residents, Flow and Stock Data, 1980–2006

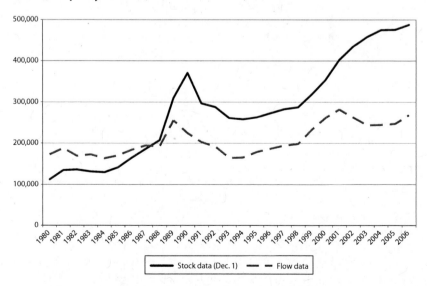

Source: Citizenship and Immigration Canada, *Facts and Figures 2006* (2006b).

has widened since 2001. Currently, the number of temporary migrants in Canada at the end of the calendar year is almost double the number admitted annually as permanent residents (Figures 5 and 6).

Persons who are explicitly recruited to meet Canadian labour market needs on a temporary basis usually enter under three main programs developed and managed by Citizenship and Immigration Canada: the Seasonal Agricultural Worker Program (SAWP), the Live-in Caregiver Program (LCP), and the Temporary Foreign Worker Program. The first two programs are highly gender-specific: The SAWP primarily recruits men, while over 90 percent of those admitted under the LCP are women.

The Seasonal Agricultural Worker Program began with bilateral agreements in 1966 with Mexican and Caribbean governments to provide seasonal employment in agriculture. The numbers have grown considerably since its inception. In 1968, there were fewer than 2,000 temporary agricultural workers; numbers rose to nearly 6,000 by the mid-1970s; and by 2001, close to 18,000 workers were admitted annually (Preibisch 2007). As a result, temporary workers are increasing their share of employment in select agricultural sectors. The work permit is valid only for a specified job, employer, and duration (eight months). Many are employed in tomato and fruit farms and in vineyards. Control over this program is tight; admissions are based on employer demand, with workers living in housing arranged by employers. There is little opportunity for workers to slip away; rates of return to their home countries are extremely high, as are the rates of return of the same workers to the same employers in Canada on an annual basis (Hennebry 2008; Preibisch 2007).

The potential for abuse is high for temporary workers in the Seasonal Agricultural Worker Program and takes three main forms. First, living and working conditions are often poor and pose health risks to workers, particularly those who do not speak or read English and may not be aware of the risks of the chemicals or machinery they are using or being exposed to (Hennebry 2008; McLaughlin 2008). Second, workers are vulnerable—their temporary status means they lack full permanent residency or citizenship rights, and they may have little recourse to services when difficulties arise. For example, while their employers are required to pay for their health coverage, individual accounts indicate that when they become ill, workers are pressured by contractors to return to their countries of origin. Third, workers are economically vulnerable. In recent months, the downturn in the Canadian economy has led to temporary workers in the SAWP losing their jobs and being told to leave; these workers pay into the employment insurance fund but are not eligible to collect benefits when they are laid off. Overall, the workers, their families and communities back home, and their home countries' economies are dependent on the workers' earnings and remittances, and the workers are often afraid to complain or assert their rights for fear that they will be returned to their home countries and not be invited back to work the following year.

The Live-in Caregiver Program admits caregivers to attend to children, elderly family members, or family members with disabilities. The migrant caregiver must live in the employer's home. Work permits may be issued for up to three years. A foreign live-in caregiver may apply for a permanent resident visa after working for a total of 24 months within a 36-month period; in April 2010, the requirement changed to a total of 24 months within a 48-month period. This capacity to transform a temporary status into that of a permanent resident has been unique until recently (see below) among Canada's temporary worker programs. This provision is the result of earlier programs in which domestic workers were admitted with no rights of residency but were allowed to stay for a number of years, coupled with intensive non-governmental lobbying on behalf of domestic workers. Like the SAWP, the Live-in Caregiver Program has received attention from non-governmental organizations that are concerned with the potential abuse of workers, ranging from poor living conditions, to being asked to work extra hours without pay, to sexual assault. The fact that the workers' homes are also their workplace contributes to their isolation and vulnerability.

The Temporary Foreign Worker Program was originally designed to admit workers, primarily at the high end, when Canadian employers could demonstrate that unsuccessful attempts had been made to hire Canadian workers. Recently, labour scarcities derived from the expanding oil-based industries in Alberta have allowed employers to hire workers at all levels of the occupational spectrum more easily. Not all temporary workers are admitted for lengthy periods; often, the duration of the work permit is only for days, in the case of entertainers, or for months, for international transferees. However, the growing numbers of temporary workers, particularly in low-skilled occupations, raises questions that are faced by all nations that import temporary workers. Is the overall program simply a way of bringing in cheaper labour? Are temporary foreign workers benefiting from the protections provided by provincial labour standards and laws, and what can be done about potential abuses and the denial of workers' rights? What are the long-term impacts of relying on temporary workers with respect to the wages and working conditions of Canadian workers? What happens to temporary workers during times of unemployment? Will workers return to their countries when their contracts are finished? What are the implications if they are not eligible for transition to permanent status and do not return to their home countries? And, will the Canadian reliance on temporary worker flows become institutionalized as part of an overall migration strategy?

Transforming Temporary Workers into Permanent Residents

As of 17 September 2008, the Canadian Experience Class (CEC) was established by formally amending the *Immigration and Refugee Protection Act*. The CEC is a new avenue of immigration for certain temporary foreign workers and for foreign student graduates with professional, managerial, and skilled work experience. This class of entry clearly is designed to take advantage of highly skilled workers who are already in Canada as well as foreign students who have recently received degrees, diplomas, or certificates from Canadian post-secondary institutions. The Canadian Experience Class allows an applicant's experience in Canada to be considered a key selection factor when immigrating as a permanent resident. A foreign graduate from a Canadian post-secondary institution needs a minimum of one year of full-time work experience. A foreign worker must have at least two years of full-time Canadian work experience in a managerial, professional, or technical occupation or in a skilled trade to qualify for the program. (This requirement will be lowered to one year in 2012.) Most temporary foreign workers currently in Canada working in lower-skilled jobs will therefore be ineligible for permanent status, potentially creating an underclass of "permanent" temporary workers with few rights, or an undocumented population of people without status who do not return to their home countries when their work permits expire.

The rationale for CEC is that applicants will have acquired Canadian experience or a Canadian academic credential and will have linguistic proficiency in English and/or French, which will allow them to integrate successfully into the Canadian labour market. Also, the expectation is that processing time will be reduced since most applicants are already in Canada, presumably employed. So far, the take-up rate has been slow; Citizenship and Immigration Canada's plans for 2009 allowed for the admission of 5,000 to 7,500 persons in this class, but only 2,500 were admitted, followed by 3,700 in 2010. Although it is very early in the implementation of the CEC, possible reasons for the unexpected low numbers include the downturn in the Canadian economy, with the result that applicants see themselves as competing with newly unemployed Canadians, and the requirement that applicants undergo a language proficiency test.

The development of the Canadian Experience Class is noteworthy in two respects. First, it creates a two-stage immigration process, thus potentially minimizing risk and cost to the government, since temporary workers and students are not eligible for federally funded services, and the initial costs for selection and settlement are borne by the employer, the educational institution, and the migrant. The message is, "Come to Canada as a student or as a temporary worker; establish yourself; and then apply for admission to Canada as a permanent resident." However, this two-stage process could have a significant negative impact on the long-term integration of the migrants, given their lack of access to early settlement interventions and their separation from their family members.

Second, this source of applicants indirectly relies on the criteria used to admit skilled temporary workers and students. As a result, candidates are the result of post-secondary college and university selections, provincial specifications for nominee programs, and employer-driven demand. This could result in potential immigrants taking advantage of the doors that are open in order to achieve their ultimate goal. For example, migrants could apply to Canada as students, not because they are particularly interested in a course of study, but because this avenue is perceived as a quicker, easier way to achieve their actual goal of immigration, thus adding to the strains currently faced by Canada's post-secondary education institutions. Canada has always viewed its immigrants as citizens-in-waiting. The question becomes, Is it appropriate to delegate the selection of Canada's citizens to agents (such as universities or employers) whose primary interest may not be the future of Canada as a nation or its citizenry?

CONCLUSION

Unlike many European countries of today, Canada has a long history of managing immigration, both with respect to numbers and composition. Consistent with the view that immigration is essential to Canada's nation-building and economic endeavours, a federal government department with its own Cabinet minister is responsible for setting immigration policy. What the numbers shall be and who shall be admitted have changed over the 20th century. Today, approximately a quarter of a million immigrants are admitted annually to become permanent residents; many have university degrees, and many are recruited on the basis of their potential economic contributions.

Immigration management is not static. Today, provinces are very active players in a variety of aspects of immigration. Most select specific types of workers under Provincial Nominee agreements, and a few currently manage federally funded settlement services, until their agreements with the federal government expire. Three other recent developments include the June 2008 enhancement of ministerial power to set criteria and to process applications; the increased admission of temporary workers; and the creation of a Canadian Experience Class, which will permit those highly educated foreign students and temporary workers in high-skilled jobs who are already in Canada to apply to become permanent residents. As of late fall 2011 and early 2012, additional policy modifications, not explicitly discussed here, which recentralize federal authority in certain management areas and continue on the path of giving greater priority to employer needs and market concerns, were reshaping many immigration programs, including those targeted at admitting skilled workers, investors, entrepreneurs, family members, refugees, temporary workers, international students, and workers in the Provincial Nominee categories. All of these changes bring new questions and new challenges to the ongoing study of Canada's immigration objectives and management strategies.

NOTES

1. See http://www12.statcan.gc.ca/census-recensement/2006/dp-pd/tbt/
    Lp-eng.cfm?LANG=E&APATH=3&DETAIL=0&DIM=0&FL=A&FRE
    E=0&GC=0&GID=0&GK=0&GRP=1&PID=0&PRID=0&PTYPE=8897
    1,97154&S=0&SHOWALL=0&SUB=722&Temporal=2006&THEME=72
    &VID=0&VNAMEE=&VNAMEF=.
2. See www.cic.gc.ca/english/department/consultations/fswp/part2.asp.
3. See www2.parl.gc.ca/HousePublications/Publication.aspx?DocId=
    3365116&Language=e&Mode=1&File=119#30.

REFERENCES

Alboim, N., R. Finnie, and R. Meng. 2005. The Discounting of Immigrant Skills: Evidence and Policy Recommendations. *Institute for Research on Public Policy Choices* 11 (2):1-28.

Aydemir, A., and M. Skuterud. 2005. Explaining the Deteriorating Entry Earnings of Canada's Immigrant Cohorts, 1966–2000. *Canadian Journal of Economics* 38 (2):641-672.

Boyd, M. 1976. International Migration Policies and Trends: A Comparison of Canada and the United States. *Demography* 13 (February): 83-104.

Boyd, M., and G. Schellenberg. 2007. Re-accreditation and the Occupations of Immigrant Doctors and Engineers. *Canadian Social Trends* 84 (September): 2-8.

Boyd, M., and M. Vickers. 2000. 100 Years of Immigration in Canada. *Canadian Social Trends*. 58 (Autumn): 2-12. At http://www.statcan.gc.ca/bsolc/olc-cel/olc-cel?lang=eng&catno=11-008-X20000025164 (accessed 21 September 2008).

Canada Gazette. 2010. Government Notices. Department of Citizenship and Immigration. *Immigration and Refugee Protection Act*. Updated Ministerial Instructions. Vol. 144, No. 26, 26 June. At http://canadagazette.gc.ca/rp-pr/p1/2010/2010-06-26/html/notice-avis-eng.html (accessed 30 September 2011).

Citizenship and Immigration Canada. 1998. *Medium Term Strategic Research Framework (June)*. At http://www.cic.gc.ca/english/resources/research/framework.asp (accessed 29 July 2008).

Citizenship and Immigration Canada. 2002. *Facts and Figures 2002*. At www.cic.gc.ca/english/pub/facts2002/immigration/immigration_1.html.

Citizenship and Immigration Canada. 2004. *Facts and Figures 2004*. At http://www.collectionscanada.gc.ca/webarchives/20060304013742/http://www.ci.gc.ca/english/pub/facts2004/permanent/1.html.

Citizenship and Immigration Canada. 2005. *Annual Report to Parliament 2005*. At http://www.cic.gc.ca/english/resources/publications/annual-report2005/index.asp (accessed 12 September 2008).

Citizenship and Immigration Canada. 2006a. *Facts and Figures 2006*. At http://www.cic.gc.ca/english/resources/statistics/facts2006/temporary/01.asp.

Citizenship and Immigration Canada. 2006b. *Facts and Figures 2006*. At http://www.cic.gc.ca/english/resources/statistics/facts2006/temporary/02.asp.

Citizenship and Immigration Canada. 2007. *Annual Report to Parliament 2007*. At http://www.cic.gc.ca/english/resources/publications/annual-report2007/section1.asp#1 (accessed 12 September 2008).

Citizenship and Immigration Canada. 2007a. *Facts and Figures 2007*. At http://www.cic.gc.ca/english/resources/statistics/facts2007/01.asp.

Citizenship and Immigration Canada. 2007b. *Facts and Figures 2007*. At http://www.cic.gc.ca/english/resources/statistics/facts2007/permanent/02.asp.

Citizenship and Immigration Canada. 2008. Backgrounder: Ministerial Instructions. At http://www.cic.gc.ca/english/department/media/backgrounders/2008/2008-11-28a.asp (accessed 10 December 2008).

Citizenship and Immigration Canada. no date-a. *Facts and Figures 2007—Immigration Overview: Permanent and Temporary Residents*. At http://www.cic.gc.ca/english/resources/statistics/facts2007/index.asp (accessed 20 December 2008).

Citizenship and Immigration Canada. no date-b. *Facts and Figures 2010—Immigration Overview: Permanent and Temporary Residents*. At http://www.cic.gc.ca/english/resources/statistics/facts2010/index.asp (accessed 30 September 2011).

Frenette, M., and R. Morissette. 2005. Will They Ever Converge? Earnings of Immigrant and Canadian-born Workers for the Last Two Decades. *International Migration Review* 39 (1):229-258.

Galarneau, D., and R. Morissette. 2008 (December). Immigrants' Education and Required Job Skills. *Perspectives on Labour and Income*. Statistics Canada. Catalogue no. 75-001-X: 5-18. At http://www.statcan.gc.ca/pub/75-001-x/2008112/pdf/10766-eng.pdf (accessed 20 December 2008).

Gera, S., and T. Songsakul. 2007. Benchmarking Canada's Performance in the Global Competition for Mobile Talent. *Canadian Public Policy-Analyse de Politiques* 33 (1):3-84.

Gouvernement du Québec. Ministère des Relations avec les citoyens et de l'Immigration. 2000. *Canada-Québec Accord Relating to Immigration and Temporary Admission of Aliens* (reprint of the 1991 agreement). At http://www.unhcr.org/refworld/pdfid/47c6bfd32.pdf (accessed 18 December 2008).

Green, A.G., and D.A. Green. 1999. The Economic Goals of Canada's Immigration Policy: Past and Present. *Canadian Public Policy* 25 (4):425-452.

Green, A.G., and D.A. Green. 2004. The Goals of Canada's Immigration Policy: A Historical Perspective. *Canadian Journal of Urban Research* 13 (1):102-139.

Hawkins, F. 1972. *Canada and Immigration: Public Policy and Public Concern*. Kingston: McGill-Queen's University Press.

Hawkins, F. 1991. *Critical Years in Immigration: Canada and Australia Compared*, 2nd ed. Montreal: McGill-Queen's University Press.

Hennebry, J.L. 2008. Mobile Vulnerabilities, Transnational Risks: Temporary Agricultural Migrants in Ontario. Presentation at CERIS – The Ontario Metropolis Policy Research Symposium, 19 October. At http://ceris.metropolis.net/research-policy/ResearRetreat/2008/Hennebry2008.pdf (accessed 10 December 2008).

Kalbach, W. 1970. *The Impact of Immigration on Canada's Population*. Ottawa: Dominion Bureau of Statistics (1961 Census Monograph).

Kelley, N., and M. Trebilcock. 1998. *The Making of the Mosaic: A History of Canadian Immigration Policy*. Toronto: University of Toronto Press.

Knowles, V. 2007. *Strangers at Our Gates: Canadian Immigration and Immigration Policy, 1540–2006, Revised Edition*. Toronto: Dundurn Press.

McLaughlin, J. 2008. Gender, Health and Mobility: Health Concerns of Women Migrant Farm Workers in Canada. *Focal Point* (Canadian Foundation of the Americas), Vol. 7, No. 9 (December). At http://www.focal.ca/pdf/focalpoint_december2008.pdf (accessed 16 December 2008).

Picot, G., and F. Hou. 2003. *The Rise in Low-income Rates Among Immigrants in Canada*. Analytical Studies Branch: Research Paper Series No. 198. Ottawa: Statistics Canada.

Picot, G., and A. Sweetman. 2005. *The Deteriorating Economic Welfare of Immigrants and Possible Causes: Update 2005*. Analytical Studies Branch: Research Paper Series No. 262. Ottawa: Statistics Canada.

Preibisch, K.L. 2007. Local Produce, Foreign Labor: Labor Mobility Programs and Global Trade Competitiveness in Canada. *Rural Sociology* 72 (3):418-419.

Statistics Canada. 2004a. *Low Income Cutoffs from 1994 to 2003 and Low Income Measures from 1992 to 2001*. Income Research Paper Series. Catalogue no. 75F0002MIE, No. 002. Ottawa: Statistics Canada, Income Statistics Division.

Statistics Canada. 2004b. Study: Why the earnings of new immigrants to Canada have deteriorated over time, 1966 to 2000. *The Daily*. 17 May. At http://www.statcan.gc.ca/daily-quotidien/040517/dq040517a-eng.htm (accessed 10 July 2008).

Statistics Canada. 2007. *The Daily*. 10 September. At http://www.statcan.gc.ca/daily-quotidien/070910/dq070910a-eng.htm (accessed 10 October 2008).

Warman, C.R., and C. Worswick. 2004. Immigrant Earnings Performance in Canadian Cities: 1981 Through 2001. *Canadian Journal of Urban Research* 13 (1):62-84.

Young, M. 2004. *Immigration: The Canada-Quebec Accord*. BP-252E. Ottawa: Library of Parliament: Parliamentary Information and Research Service. At http://www.parl.gc.ca/Content/LOP/ResearchPublications/bp252-e.pdf (accessed 18 December 2008).

APPENDIX A
Canada Skilled Migrant Category Selection Factors and Pass Mark

Factor One: Education	Maximum 25
You have a Master's degree or Ph.D. **and** at least 17 years of full-time or full-time equivalent study.	25
You have two or more university degrees at the Bachelor's level **and** at least 15 years of full-time or full-time equivalent study.	22
You have a three-year diploma, trade certificate, or apprenticeship **and** at least 15 years of full-time or full-time equivalent study.	22
You have a university degree of two years or more at the Bachelor's level **and** at least 14 years of full-time or full-time equivalent study.	20
You have a two-year diploma, trade certificate, or apprenticeship **and** at least 14 years of full-time or full-time equivalent study.	20
You have a one-year university degree at the Bachelor's level **and** at least 13 years of full-time or full-time equivalent study.	15
You have a one-year diploma, trade certificate, or apprenticeship **and** at least 13 years of full-time or full-time equivalent study.	15
You have a one-year diploma, trade certificate, or apprenticeship **and** at least 12 years of full-time or full-time equivalent study.	12
You completed high school.	5

Factor Two: Official Languages	Maximum 24
First Official Language	
High proficiency (per ability)	4
Moderate proficiency (per ability)	2
Basic proficiency (per ability)	1 to maximum of 2
No proficiency	0
Possible maximum (all 4 abilities)	16
Second Official Language	
High proficiency (per ability)	2
Moderate proficiency (per ability)	2
Basic proficiency (per ability)	1 to maximum of 2
No proficiency	0
Possible maximum (all 4 abilities)	8

... *continued*

APPENDIX A
(Continued)

Factor Three: Experience	Maximum 21
1 year	15
2 years	17
3 years	19
4 years	21

Factor Four: Age	Maximum 10
21 to 49 years at time of application	10
Less 2 points for each year over 49 or under 21	

Factor Five: Arranged Employment in Canada	Maximum 10
You have a permanent job offer that has been confirmed by Human Resources and Skills Development Canada (HRSDC).	10
You are applying from within Canada and have a temporary work permit that was:	
issued after receipt of a confirmation of your job offer from HRSDC; or you have a temporary work permit that was exempted from the requirement of a confirmed job offer from HRSDC on the basis of an international agreement (e.g., NAFTA), a significant benefit to Canada (e.g., intra-company transfer), or public policy on Canada's academic or economic competitiveness (e.g., postgraduate work).	10

Factor Six: Adaptability	Maximum 10
Spouse's or common-law partner's education	3–5
Minimum one year of full-time authorized work in Canada	5
Minimum two years of full-time authorized post-secondary study in Canada	5
Have received points under the Arranged Employment in Canada factor	5
Family relationship in Canada	5

Total	Maximum 100
Pass Mark	67

Source: Authors' compilation (2007) based on information from Citizenship and Immigration Canada, at http://www.cic.gc.ca/english/immigrate/skilled/apply-factors.asp.

CHAPTER 5

Le Gouvernement du Québec et la gestion de l'immigration : un spectateur passif devenu un acteur de premier plan[1]

GÉRARD PINSONNEAULT, *Chercheur associé,*
Chaire en Relations ethniques, Université de Montréal

1. INTRODUCTION

Le texte dont le lecteur s'apprête à prendre connaissance peut sembler ambitieux. Il prétend faire état de tout le mouvement d'immigration vers le Québec, depuis la Conquête britannique, au milieu du XVIIIᵉ siècle, jusqu'aux premières années du XXIᵉ, de même que des politiques qui ont, ou n'ont pas, présidé à sa gestion.

Il est bien entendu impossible de couvrir un tel sujet dans le cadre d'un article comme celui-ci. C'est pourquoi l'on ne fera qu'effleurer les deux premiers siècles de la période en question, juste assez pour saisir de quoi il retourne, mais en omettant de s'attarder aux nuances qu'il serait important de faire entre les concepts de colonisation, de migration et d'immigration. Ces nuances seraient indispensables si l'on voulait examiner sérieusement et en profondeur les mouvements migratoires qui ont marqué la période coloniale et les premières décennies de la Confédération.

Même si l'on ne s'attardera qu'aux décennies les plus récentes, il faudra, pour cerner adéquatement le sujet qui est le nôtre, d'abord décrire le cadre

Managing Immigration and Diversity in Canada: A Transatlantic Dialogue in the New Age of Migration,
ed. D. Rodríguez-García. Montreal and Kingston: Queen's Policy Studies Series, McGill-Queen's University Press.

constitutionnel et administratif dans lequel s'inscrivent les interventions gouvernementales en ce domaine et préciser ensuite quelque peu la nature des données qui seront utilisées pour illustrer notre propos. Tels seront les trois éléments contextuels abordés avant de plonger au cœur du sujet : les antécédents historiques, le cadre juridico-administratif et les conventions statistiques.

Une fois cette trame de fond ainsi dessinée à grands traits, on examinera de plus près l'évolution du mouvement d'immigration à destination du Québec pour tenter d'en déduire en quoi l'intervention distincte du gouvernement québécois en la matière a pu en infléchir le cours et le contenu.

2. UN PEU D'HISTOIRE : LE QUÉBEC FRANCOPHONE ET SON RAPPORT À L'IMMIGRATION

Le Québec moderne, province du Canada, membre fondateur de la fédération formée en 1867, constitue le legs le plus important laissé par le premier empire colonial français qui s'étendait sur la plus grande partie du continent nord-américain aux XVIIe et XVIIIe siècles. Après la Conquête par les Britanniques en 1760, les nouveaux maîtres du pays envisagèrent, par un afflux de colons britanniques, d'assimiler ces nouveaux sujets, de surcroît peu nombreux. Ils étaient en effet moins de 70 000, résidant pour la plupart sur les rives du St-Laurent, entre Montréal et Québec (Lacoursière et al. 2001).

Pour plusieurs raisons, heureusement ou malheureusement, selon le point de vue, ce projet assimilationniste a largement échoué. La principale de ces raisons est sans doute que dans un premier temps, les colons attendus ne sont pas venus en nombre suffisant (Cornell et al. 1968) et que, par la suite, il était trop tard.

En effet, grâce à leur très forte natalité, les francophones de ce qui allait devenir le Québec, formaient déjà, un siècle après la Conquête, une masse critique suffisamment importante (environ un million d'habitants) pour rendre difficile, sinon impossible, toute tentative d'assimilation. En outre, comme les immigrants admis au Québec avaient largement tendance à émigrer de nouveau, soit vers une autre province, soit vers les États-Unis, après un séjour de seulement quelques mois ou quelques années, la majorité francophone n'a jamais été sérieusement menacée.

Ailleurs au Canada, la situation a évolué bien différemment. On ne peut pas dire que les francophones y ont été assimilés, mais ils ont été très largement minorisés. Très tôt, ils ne formèrent plus qu'un faible pourcentage de la population des autres provinces. Au recensement de 2006, ils comptaient pour seulement 5 pour cent de leur population totale.

Mais que ce soit au Québec ou dans les autres provinces du Canada, les immigrants, traditionnellement, s'intégraient majoritairement au groupe anglophone.

Ce lien historique, décrit ici très grossièrement, entre l'immigration et le phénomène de la minorisation de la francophonie canadienne explique largement l'attitude longtemps manifestée par les francophones à l'égard de l'immigration : au mieux, ils s'en désintéressaient, au pire, ils entretenaient (et entretiennent encore parfois) à son endroit une certaine appréhension quant à son éventuel impact sur la situation linguistique et sur la place du français.

Même si la Constitution de 1867 reconnaissait aux provinces, dont le Québec, des pouvoirs importants en matière d'immigration, ce n'est qu'un siècle plus tard, au milieu des années 1960, que le gouvernement de la province a vraiment commencé à s'intéresser à cette problématique et à vouloir intervenir en ce domaine. On peut identifier au moins deux facteurs à l'origine de cet intérêt nouveau pour ce domaine d'intervention.

Le premier est d'ordre démographique. Au cours des années 1960, la plupart des sociétés occidentales ont vu leur natalité baisser fortement. Cette baisse a été particulièrement abrupte chez les francophones du Québec qui, jusque-là, affichaient l'un des taux de natalité les plus élevés du monde occidental. On a alors commencé à craindre que la majorité de langue française ne s'érode, particulièrement à Montréal, métropole économique et culturelle et lieu de destination de la très grande majorité des immigrants s'installant au Québec.

Cette chute de la natalité s'est produite en parallèle avec un second phénomène tout aussi important, bien que non quantifiable. Au cours des années 1960, les francophones du Québec, à la faveur de ce qu'on a alors appelé la Révolution tranquille, ont connu ce qu'on pourrait appeler une « mutation identitaire ». Ils ont progressivement cessé de se percevoir seulement comme une partie de la minorité francophone canadienne (ou continentale), pour se considérer davantage comme une majorité à l'intérieur des seules frontières du Québec. Ils ont peu à peu cessé de se dire « Canadiens-français » pour se désigner plutôt comme « Québécois ». Bientôt, ils allaient même vouloir étendre cette appellation à tous les habitants du Québec, sans égard à leur origine.

Se considérant désormais comme une majorité, mais comme une majorité fragile, ils en sont rapidement venus à ne plus accepter comme allant de soi que les nouveaux arrivants s'associent systématiquement à la minorité anglophone.

Pour infléchir cette tendance, des législations linguistiques successives ont été adoptées, dont l'objectif était d'établir et de préserver la prépondérance du français dans différents aspects de la vie en société : travail, enseignement, commerce, services, affichage, administration publique, etc.

On a aussi conclu qu'il fallait une gestion de l'immigration plus conforme aux intérêts de la majorité. Un ministère a été mis sur pied en 1968 et des pourparlers ont été engagés avec les autorités fédérales afin de permettre au Québec d'exercer davantage de pouvoirs en cette matière. Ces pourparlers ont mené à la conclusion de plusieurs ententes successives, en 1971, en 1975, en 1978 et en 1991. La plus récente, celle de 1991, appelée « Accord Canada-Québec relatif à l'immigration et à l'admission temporaire des aubains[2] » (Québec 1991) est toujours en vigueur et elle est la plus exhaustive. Chacune de ces ententes a permis au Québec d'accroître sa capacité d'intervention en matière de gestion de l'immigration.

3. L'AMÉNAGEMENT CONSTITUTIONNEL ET JURIDICO-ADMINISTRATIF

La Constitution de la fédération canadienne répartit la plupart des domaines de compétence entre les deux ordres de gouvernement (fédéral et provincial), chacun étant souverain dans les domaines qui lui sont reconnus. Par exemple, l'éducation relève exclusivement des provinces, tandis que la défense relève seulement du fédéral.

Par contre, l'immigration, comme l'agriculture, constituent des exceptions. Il s'agit de compétences « concurrentes ». Cela signifie que l'État provincial, comme l'État fédéral, peuvent légiférer en ces domaines comme ils l'entendent. Ce n'est qu'en cas de conflit que la législation fédérale est prépondérante. En pratique, un tel chevauchement, s'il n'est pas balisé par des textes précis convenus de part et d'autre, peut s'avérer très complexe à gérer et générer des contestations juridiques sans fin. C'est pourquoi l'Accord signé en 1991 prévoit un partage des responsabilités et non un partage des pouvoirs puisque juridiquement parlant, les deux gouvernements disposent chacun de pouvoirs premiers en cette matière.

En matière d'immigration proprement dite, c'est-à-dire relativement aux modalités de sélection et d'admission des candidats, l'Accord prévoit une répartition détaillée du rôle dévolu à chacune des parties. En matière d'intégration, le Québec s'est vu confier la responsabilité exclusive des interventions.

Mais préalablement à cette distribution des rôles, pour que l'Accord puisse fonctionner, il importait qu'il y ait consensus sur un certain nombre de principes de base. Ainsi, sans que cela n'apparaisse nécessairement en toutes lettres dans les textes, on constate que le Québec, comme le Canada :

- privilégient une immigration de nature permanente,
- utilisent des règles de nature universelle, sans référence à l'origine ethnique, raciale ou géographique des candidats,
- accordent une grande importance à la réunification familiale,
- reconnaissent l'importance d'assumer leur part de responsabilités en matière d'accueil humanitaire,

- reconnaissent le droit à la libre circulation au Canada des citoyens canadiens et des résidents permanents.

En matière d'immigration proprement dite, c'est-à-dire de gestion du mouvement, la répartition et l'articulation des responsabilités respectives se présentent de la manière suivante :

- au regard des niveaux d'immigration : le Québec établit le nombre d'immigrants qu'il souhaite accueillir au cours d'une année et leur répartition par catégorie; le Canada prend en considération ces données lorsqu'il procède à sa propre planification annuelle. Précisons que le concept de « niveaux » réfère à des « objectifs » qui, bien que chiffrés, ne constituent pas des quotas contraignants. En outre, ces objectifs ont trait aux catégories d'immigration (famille, humanitaire, économique) et non à la provenance géographique des candidats. Plus spécifiquement, en vertu de l'Accord, le Québec s'est engagé à poursuivre comme objectif d'accueillir un nombre d'immigrants correspondant au poids de sa population au sein du Canada. Le Canada s'est engagé en retour à poursuivre une politique facilitant l'atteinte ou même le dépassement de cet objectif par le Québec. Pour des raisons pratiques, ce volet de l'Accord de 1991 a eu peu d'écho dans la réalité des opérations et des statistiques. Jamais, depuis 1991, la part du Québec dans l'immigration canadienne totale n'a atteint un poids équivalent à sa part de la population canadienne (voir section 5.4 et graphique 1b);
- au regard des catégories : le Canada établit seul la définition des catégories générales d'immigrants : familiale, humanitaire et économique (travailleurs et gens d'affaires);
- au regard du regroupement familial : le Canada vérifie les liens de parenté ouvrant droit à la réunification familiale d'un résidant du Québec avec un candidat à l'immigration, ainsi que les catégories de personnes pour lesquelles un engagement financier sera requis de la part du résidant du Québec. Dans de tels cas, c'est le Québec qui est responsable de la fixation des normes financières requises, des engagements pris par les résidants du Québec et de leur suivi;
- au regard de la sélection : pour tous les candidats à l'immigration devant faire l'objet d'une sélection, c'est-à-dire, essentiellement, les travailleurs, les gens d'affaires et les réfugiés à l'étranger, le Québec est seul responsable de définir et d'appliquer les critères de sélection;
- au regard des demandes d'asile déposées par des ressortissants étrangers se trouvant au Canada ou se présentant à ses frontières : le Canada est seul responsable de l'examen de ces demandes, de la reconnaissance du statut de réfugié et ultimement, de l'octroi de la résidence permanente à ces personnes;

- au regard des questions statutaires, le Canada est seul responsable d'établir et d'appliquer les normes relatives aux questions de santé, de sécurité et de criminalité. Il est également le seul à octroyer le statut de résident permanent;
- au regard des personnes sollicitant une autorisation temporaire de séjour, l'accord préalable du Québec est requis pour l'admission sur son territoire :
  - ✓ des travailleurs temporaires assujettis à la preuve de rareté de main-d'œuvre,
  - ✓ de la plupart des étudiants étrangers et
  - ✓ de toutes les personnes souhaitant être admises pour recevoir des traitements médicaux;
- au regard des procédures administratives, afin de garantir la fluidité, la cohérence et l'harmonisation des processus, les deux administrations entretiennent des communications régulières, par le biais d'instances officielles (comité mixte et comité d'application) ou *ad hoc*.

En matière d'intégration, l'Accord reconnaît au Québec la responsabilité exclusive pour tous les immigrants de toutes les catégories. Lors de la conclusion de l'Accord, les autorités fédérales se sont engagées à se retirer d'une série de programmes jusque-là financés par elles et à verser au Québec une compensation financière lui permettant de prendre la relève en ces matières. Si cette responsabilité semble très large, couvrant notamment le premier accueil, l'aide à l'établissement, la formation linguistique et l'aide à l'intégration en emploi, elle n'est pas vraiment contraignante pour les autorités fédérales car celles-ci conservent la responsabilité exclusive des conditions d'attribution de la citoyenneté et des services qui y sont liés, ainsi que celle des programmes liés au multiculturalisme. D'ailleurs, la frontière entre ces derniers programmes et les mesures d'intégration n'est pas toujours très claire.

Pendant que l'Accord de 1991 était négocié, le Gouvernement du Québec préparait un Énoncé de politique en matière d'immigration et d'intégration (Québec, Ministère des Communautés culturelles et de l'Immigration 1990c). Cet Énoncé, dont l'élaboration a été amorcée dès 1986, alors que s'ouvrait une ronde majeure de négociations constitutionnelles entre le gouvernement central et les provinces, a été adopté quatre ans plus tard, en 1990, en dépit de l'échec de cette tentative de changements constitutionnels.

En adoptant cet Énoncé, le Gouvernement du Québec a assigné à sa politique d'immigration quatre grands objectifs, à savoir que l'immigration doit contribuer :

- au redressement démographique (le nombre des nouveaux arrivants accueillis doit être suffisamment élevé pour fournir un apport significatif à la croissance démographique),

- à la pérennité de son caractère français (l'intégration doit se faire en français),
- à sa prospérité économique (la contribution des immigrants au développement économique doit être favorisée),
- à son ouverture sur le monde (l'accueil d'immigrants d'horizons divers doit contribuer à dynamiser la société au plan socioculturel et faciliter le développement de liens avec les pays d'origine de ceux-ci).

Près de vingt ans plus tard, cet Énoncé constitue toujours la référence essentielle de la politique du Québec en la matière, comme en témoigne le document de consultation publié par le ministère lors de la dernière commission parlementaire, tenue à l'automne 2007, sur la planification de l'immigration pour la période 2008–2010 (Québec, Ministère de l'Immigration et des Communautés culturelles 2007).

4. QUELQUES PRÉCISIONS MÉTHODOLOGIQUES

Avant de passer en revue l'évolution des flux d'immigration internationale au Québec et de leur gestion, il importe d'apporter certaines précisions méthodologiques. Celles-ci devraient s'avérer particulièrement utiles aux lecteurs qui ne sont pas familiers avec le mode nord-américain de gestion des statistiques migratoires, pas plus qu'avec les particularités québécoises et canadiennes en ce domaine. En effet, dans plusieurs pays, le statut juridique de ceux qu'on appelle les étrangers a peu de choses en commun avec ce qu'on connaît en Amérique du Nord, et la façon de les comptabiliser dans les données démographiques est également différente.

Au Québec, tout comme au Canada dans son ensemble et aux États-Unis, la mesure la plus fréquemment utilisée pour rendre compte du flux migratoire international est celle relative aux personnes qui, au cours d'une période donnée, sont admises au pays à titre de résidents permanents. Au Canada, il s'agit d'un statut qui leur confère le droit de résider, de travailler et de circuler sur l'ensemble du territoire sans autre formalité, et ce, tant qu'elles conservent leur lieu de résidence principal[3] au pays. Après quelques années seulement de présence au pays, ce statut donne en outre accès à la citoyenneté, à des conditions relativement peu exigeantes. Cet indicateur inclut :

- les ressortissants étrangers à qui ce statut a été octroyé au moment de leur entrée physique au pays, après avoir obtenu leur visa à cet effet dans une mission diplomatique canadienne à l'étranger, dans l'une ou l'autre catégorie (regroupement familial, travailleurs sélectionnés en fonction de leur potentiel d'insertion en emploi, gens d'affaires ou réfugiés);
- les demandeurs d'asile déjà présents au pays, dont le statut de réfugié a été reconnu, qui ont accompli les démarches formelles de demande de résidence permanente et à qui ce statut a été octroyé;

• les personnes admises initialement pour un séjour temporaire – étudiants, travailleurs temporaires, visiteurs – qui, pour des raisons particulières (familiales, humanitaires ou économiques) ont obtenu la résidence permanente sans avoir à effectuer les démarches de l'étranger, comme le requiert normalement la procédure légale.

Cet indicateur a naturellement ses limites. Par exemple, il ne témoigne pas des personnes en séjour temporaire, même pour une période prolongée, ni des demandeurs d'asile en attente d'une réponse à leur requête, ni, bien sûr, des personnes en situation irrégulière (demandeurs d'asile déboutés, ressortissants étrangers non documentés, ayant outrepassé leur période de séjour autorisé ou violé les conditions qui y étaient liées).

Comme il s'agit d'une mesure des entrées, cet indicateur ne tient pas compte des sorties : immigrants qui repartent pour l'étranger ou, dans le cas du Québec, pour une autre région du Canada.

En dépit de ces limites, cet indicateur de flux s'avère, à moyen et long terme, le plus pertinent lorsqu'il s'agit de témoigner, de manière prospective, de l'impact de l'immigration sur la composition de la population. Cela tient au fait qu'il englobe, à terme, les ressortissants étrangers admis initialement avec un statut temporaire ou provisoire (les demandeurs d'asile) et qui deviennent résidents permanents, et qu'il exclut justement ces mêmes temporaires lorsque leur séjour ne devient jamais permanent.

À plus long terme, finalement, les recensements quinquennaux, qui distinguent les « immigrants » (personnes généralement nées à l'étranger[4]), les « natifs » (personnes généralement nées au pays[5]) et les « résidents non-permanents » (étrangers en séjour temporaire pour études ou travail), permettent de rendre compte de l'ampleur et de la nature de la contribution de l'immigration à la composition de la population dans son ensemble, tout en fournissant également, par déduction, mais en tenant aussi compte des décès et d'un certain sous-dénombrement, une approximation des mouvements de sorties.

En résumé, les données relatives aux admissions permanentes sont considérées comme adéquates pour témoigner de l'ampleur et de la nature réelle des flux susceptibles d'avoir un impact tangible, à terme, sur la composition de la population. Les données censitaires, par la suite, viennent préciser ce portrait.

À ces deux types de données utilisées depuis très longtemps et dont la crédibilité est universellement reconnue peut s'ajouter un autre type qui est d'utilisation plus récente et parfois encore contesté. Il s'agit de la mesure de la présence par le biais de jumelages administratifs. Régulièrement, en effet, le ministère de l'Immigration et des Communautés culturelles du Québec procède à un jumelage des données d'admissions avec les données du fichier de l'Assurance-maladie, permettant ainsi d'évaluer dans quelle mesure les immigrants admis y résident toujours après quelques années. L'un des avantages de cet exercice est de permettre de prendre la mesure du phénomène en fonction de certaines des caractéristiques des immigrants qui ne sont pas disponibles dans les autres fichiers, comme la catégorie d'immigration, la connaissance du français et de l'anglais au moment de l'admission, et la région de résidence la plus récente.[6]

Par ailleurs, il importe de souligner l'importance du concept de résident permanent octroyé aux ressortissants étrangers admis comme immigrants. Il ne s'agit pas seulement d'une étiquette juridique, assimilable au statut temporaire ou provisoire, assujetti à l'obligation de renouvellement périodique, qu'on accorde aux « étrangers » dans nombre de pays où les assises juridiques de l'immigration sont très différentes. Il s'agit bien davantage d'un statut de « futur citoyen » : les droits et les privilèges qui y sont associés sont très près de ceux qui sont reconnus aux citoyens, natifs ou naturalisés. À tel point que la Charte canadienne des droits et libertés de la personne y fait spécifiquement référence. Il a même été démontré que sa seule obtention a un effet significatif sur l'accès à l'emploi, même pour des personnes déjà légalement présentes depuis longtemps sur le territoire et autorisées à travailler sans restriction (Renaud et Gingras 1998).

Les statistiques relatives à l'immigration permanente, tant au Québec qu'au Canada, sont très souvent ventilées en fonction de ce qu'on appelle les « catégories d'immigration ». Il s'agit des grandes composantes du mouvement : regroupement familial, immigration économique (qui comprend les travailleurs et les gens d'affaires) et immigration humanitaire (réfugiés et personnes en situation semblable, ce qui comprend les réfugiés sélectionnés à l'étranger et les demandeurs d'asile reconnus réfugiés au pays même et devenus ensuite résidents permanents). Dans les statistiques, ces catégories incluent les personnes à charge qui accompagnent les requérants principaux lors de leur migration. C'est ainsi qu'on va retrouver de jeunes enfants et des conjoints « au foyer » inscrits dans les données relatives aux travailleurs et aux gens d'affaires. Au sens strict, ne font l'objet d'une sélection formelle que les seuls requérants principaux de la catégorie des travailleurs et des gens d'affaires. Ce n'est qu'une proportion relativement faible de l'ensemble du mouvement qui peut ainsi être qualifiée de « sélectionnée » en vertu de la grille. Pour ce qui est des réfugiés sélectionnés à l'étranger, leur sélection est faite sur la base de critères élargis où le besoin de protection joue un rôle au moins aussi important que les caractéristiques socio-économiques.

Une fois admis au pays comme résidents permanents, toutefois, tous les immigrants, sélectionnés ou non, sans égard à la catégorie dont ils font partie, jouissent des mêmes droits.

Il est indispensable de tenir compte de toutes ces nuances pour interpréter correctement les statistiques relatives à l'immigration permanente au Québec et au Canada. Il faut également, dans la mesure du possible, faire état de certaines mesures spéciales qui viennent parfois, au fil du temps, gonfler plus ou moins artificiellement l'une ou l'autre composante du mouvement. Ce fut le cas, entre autres, pour les deux programmes de régularisation des demandeurs d'asile, en 1986–1987 et en 1990–1991 et pour le programme mis en place pour permettre aux Haïtiens en situation illégale d'obtenir la résidence permanente au début des années 1980. Dans les statistiques, une forte proportion de ces personnes sont classées dans la catégorie des travailleurs. Il est parfois possible de les isoler en recourant à certains recoupements, mais cela est assez complexe et requiert une connaissance intime des subtilités des données administratives.

5. L'ÉVOLUTION DU MOUVEMENT, DE SA GESTION ET DE SES COMPOSANTES

Il va sans dire qu'avant la conclusion des premières ententes fédérales-provinciales en matière d'immigration, au début des années 1970, l'impact des politiques québécoises sur la composition des flux est resté pratiquement nul. C'est pourquoi nous ne ferons que survoler très rapidement cette période pour nous concentrer sur les dernières décennies.

5.1. Le mouvement avant l'intervention du Québec

Durant la majeure partie du XIXe siècle, les immigrants admis au Québec et au Canada étaient, dans leur très grande majorité, des personnes d'origine britannique : Anglais, Écossais, Irlandais et Gallois, auxquels on peut ajouter quelques mercenaires allemands qui faisaient partie des troupes britanniques postées en Amérique. À la fin du siècle, on a assisté à une première diversification des flux, avec l'arrivée d'Asiatiques et d'Européens de l'Est. Ce phénomène a été assez rapidement suivi par l'adoption de diverses mesures visant à restreindre l'admission au pays aux seuls immigrants d'origine européenne, britannique de préférence.

Interrompu par la grande dépression des années 1930 et par la Seconde Guerre mondiale, le mouvement a repris de l'ampleur à la fin des années 1940, mais toujours on privilégiait l'immigration européenne. Ce n'est qu'au milieu des années 1960 que le Canada a abandonné la notion de ce qu'il appelait pudiquement ses « préférences géographiques ». Il a alors adopté un système de points conçu pour évaluer objectivement les candidats en fonction de caractéristiques socio-économiques universelles, susceptibles de faciliter le succès de leur établissement. Il faudra ensuite quelques années pour que ce système produise un mouvement davantage diversifié, composé d'immigrants d'origines moins exclusivement européennes.

Par ailleurs, jusqu'à la Première Guerre mondiale, le principal objectif économique poursuivi par la politique d'immigration était de mettre en valeur le potentiel agricole du pays, notamment celui des terres de l'Ouest. Cet objectif est demeuré dans les textes jusqu'aux années 1950, mais dans la pratique, l'immigration a constitué un facteur d'urbanisation du pays dès les années 1920 au moins.

Pour estimer, ne serait-ce que grossièrement, l'impact de l'intervention québécoise sur le mouvement d'immigration, on peut, dans un premier temps, mettre en parallèle certaines caractéristiques de la population immigrée résidant au Québec et au Canada lors du dernier recensement ayant précédé le début de cette intervention, celui de 1971, avec celles qu'on a observées lors du recensement le plus récent, réalisé en 2006. On pourra ensuite voir plus en détail comment les changements survenus dans la composition du mouvement ont pu être à l'origine de ces différences.

Au regard de la composition ethnoculturelle de la population, on constate le résultat de la politique poursuivie par le gouvernement fédéral depuis le début du XXᵉ siècle en observant les données du recensement de 1971 relativement aux principaux pays de naissance de la population immigrée (tableaux 1 à 4). À cette date, la liste des dix principaux pays de naissance des immigrants était constituée de neuf pays européens et des États-Unis. En outre, huit de ces dix principaux pays de naissance étaient les mêmes au Québec et au Canada. Seule la présence de la France au quatrième rang de la liste québécoise faisait timidement apparaître le caractère distinct du Québec en ce domaine.

TABLEAU 1
Population née à l'étranger* recensée au Québec en 1971 selon les 10 principaux pays de naissance

Rang	Pays de naissance	n	%
1	Italie	90.375	19,3
2	Royaume-Uni	65.605	14,0
3	États-Unis	46.480	9,9
4	France	33.315	7,1
5	Grèce	26.315	5,6
6	Pologne	22.290	4,8
7	Allemagne	20.625	4,4
8	URSS	17.065	3,6
9	Portugal	12.110	2,6
10	Hongrie	11.015	2,3
	Total, 10 pays	345.195	73,6
	Autres pays	123.735	26,4
	Total	468.930	100,0

* Inclut les personnes nées à l'étranger qui sont citoyens canadiens de naissance.
Source : Recensement du Canada 1971, compilation spéciale MICC (Québec, 1993).

TABLEAU 2
Population immigrée recensée au Québec en 2006 selon les 10 principaux pays de naissance

Rang	Pays de naissance	n	%
1	Italie	65.550	7,7
2	France	59.210	7,0
3	Haïti	56.755	6,7
4	Chine	39.190	4,6
5	Liban	34.875	4,1
6	Maroc	33.560	3,9
7	Algérie	29.510	3,5
8	Roumanie	26.950	3,2
9	États-Unis	26.575	3,1
10	Viet Nam	24.445	2,9
	Total, 10 pays	396.620	46,6
	Autres pays	454.940	53,4
	Total	851.560	100,0

Source : Statistique Canada, Recensement de 2006, 97-557-XCB2006007.

TABLEAU 3
Population née à l'étranger* recensée au Canada en 1971 selon les 10 principaux pays de naissance

Rang	Pays de naissance	n	%
1	Royaume-Uni	933.045	28,3
2	Italie	385.760	11,7
3	États-Unis	309.640	9,4
4	Allemagne	211.060	6,4
5	URSS	160.125	4,9
6	Pologne	160.035	4,9
7	Pays-Bas	133.525	4,1
8	Grèce	78.780	2,4
9	Yougoslavie	78.285	2,4
10	Portugal	71.540	2,2
	Total, 10 pays	2.512.795	76,5
	Autres pays	773.735	23,5
	Total	3.295.530	100,0

* Inclut les personnes nées à l'étranger qui sont citoyens canadiens de naissance.
Source : Recensement du Canada 1971 (cité dans Québec, 1994).

Si on met de nouveau en parallèle les dix principaux pays de naissance des immigrants résidant au Québec et au Canada au recensement de 2006, on observe que des changements importants sont survenus. Une large diversification s'est produite, tant au Québec qu'au Canada. Les dix premiers pays de naissance ne totalisent plus que la moitié environ

TABLEAU 4
Population immigrée recensée au Canada en 2006 selon les 10 principaux pays de naissance

Rang	Pays de naissance	n	%
1	Royaume-Uni	579.620	9,4
2	Chine	466.940	7,5
3	Inde	443.690	7,2
4	Philippines	303.195	4,9
5	Italie	296.850	4,8
6	États-Unis	250.535	4,0
7	Hong Kong	215.430	3,5
8	Allemagne	171.410	2,8
9	Pologne	170.495	2,8
10	Viet Nam	160.170	2,6
	Total, 10 pays	3.058.335	49,4
	Autres pays	3.128.615	50,6
	Total	6.186.950	100,0

Source : Statistique Canada, Recensement de 2006, 97-557-XCB2006007.

de la population immigrée totale, alors qu'ils en comptaient pour près des trois quarts en 1971. Des pays non-européens s'inscrivent désormais dans ces deux listes : la Chine, l'Inde, les Philippines, Hong-Kong et le Vietnam pour le Canada, Haïti, la Chine, le Liban, le Maroc, l'Algérie et le Vietnam pour le Québec. Et surtout, on observe maintenant beaucoup plus de différences, au regard des pays de naissance, entre les immigrants résidant au Québec et ceux résidant au Canada : il n'y a plus que quatre pays qui soient communs aux deux listes (Italie, Chine, États-Unis et Vietnam), tandis qu'on compte maintenant sept pays, sur les dix principaux de la liste québécoise, qui peuvent être qualifiés, en tout ou en partie, de « bassins francophones » : la France, Haïti, le Liban, le Maroc, l'Algérie, la Roumanie et le Vietnam. Seul le Vietnam, sans doute le moins francophone des sept, est aussi présent sur la liste des dix principaux pays d'origine des immigrants résidant au Canada.

Un changement important est aussi observable au regard de la connaissance du français et de l'anglais (voir tableaux 5 et 6). Au recensement de 1971, à peine un peu plus de la moitié des immigrants résidant au Québec ont déclaré connaître suffisamment le français pour soutenir une conversation. En 2006, cette proportion était passée à plus des trois quarts. Pour ce qui est de la connaissance de l'anglais, la proportion de ceux qui ont déclaré pouvoir converser dans cette langue a diminué, passant de tout près des trois quarts en 1971 à un peu plus des deux tiers en 2006.

Quand on sait le temps qu'il faut pour que des changements dans la composition du mouvement affectent significativement la composition des stocks, force est de reconnaître que l'évolution observée est remarquable.[7] Dans quelle mesure est-elle reliée aux changements survenus en matière de politique et de répartition des rôles au cours du dernier tiers de siècle? C'est ce que nous allons maintenant explorer en parallèle avec l'évolution des flux d'immigration de 1970 à 2007.

TABLEAU 5
Population née à l'étranger* recensée au Québec en 1971 selon la connaissance du français et de l'anglais

Connaissance linguistique	n	%
Français seulement	82.770	17,7
Anglais et français	164.820	35,1
Connaissant le français	*247.590*	*52,8*
Anglais seulement	184.230	39,3
Connaissant l'anglais	*349.050*	*74,4*
Ni l'anglais ni le français	37.105	7,9
Total	468.925	100,0

* Inclut les personnes nées à l'étranger qui sont citoyens canadiens de naissance.
Source : Rencensement du Canada 1971 (cité dans Québec 1990a).

TABLEAU 6
Population immigrée recensée au Québec en 2006 selon la connaissance du français et de l'anglais

Connaissance linguistique	n	%
Français seulement	232.290	27,3
Anglais et français	428.105	50,3
Connaissant le français	*660.395*	*77,6*
Anglais seulement	148.760	17,5
Connaissant l'anglais	*576.865*	*67,7*
Ni l'anglais ni le français	42.400	5,0
Total	851.560	100,0

Source : Statistique Canada, Recensement de 2006, 97-557-XCB2006021.

5.2. La gestion québécoise du mouvement depuis 1978

C'est par l'entente conclue avec les autorités fédérales en 1978 que le Québec a acquis l'essentiel de sa marge de manœuvre en matière de gestion des flux. À cet égard, l'Accord de 1991 est surtout venu consolider ces acquis et leur conférer un caractère quasi-permanent.[8]

Précisons d'abord qu'en 1978, il ne pouvait être question, pour le Québec, dans le but d'infléchir la composition ethnoculturelle du mouvement lui étant destiné, de recourir, à sa manière, à des « préférences géographiques » comme le Canada l'avait fait pendant des décennies pour s'assurer d'une immigration massivement européenne et britannique. Cela faisait plus de dix ans que des modalités universelles de gestion du mouvement étaient en vigueur au niveau fédéral, et c'est dans ce cadre que les interventions québécoises devaient s'inscrire :

- L'immigration familiale était limitée à certains liens de parenté bien définis et, de par sa nature même, largement induite par la composition des flux antérieurs, qu'ils soient de nature économique ou autre.
- L'immigration humanitaire, officiellement reconnue depuis peu (avec l'entrée en vigueur, en 1978, de la Loi adoptée en 1976), était réduite à un faible volume et concentrée à l'étranger.
- L'immigration économique était filtrée au moyen d'une grille de sélection composée d'un ensemble de critères agencés de manière à ne retenir que les candidats présentant un profil prometteur au regard de leur projet d'établissement. Les principaux critères de cette grille étaient l'âge, la scolarité, l'expérience et la préparation professionnelle, l'emploi (demande dans la profession projetée ou emploi réservé), la connaissance du français et de l'anglais ainsi que, le cas échéant, le lien de parenté avec un résidant du Canada et les perspectives générales d'emploi dans la région de destination. Initialement, la grille constituait un tout et seul le total du pointage devait mesurer le potentiel du candidat à s'établir avec succès. Les faiblesses affichées à l'un ou l'autre critère pouvaient être compensées par des résultats supérieurs obtenus pour les autres critères. Aucun n'était éliminatoire. Très tôt, toutefois, le facteur emploi est devenu déterminant. Dès 1974, l'absence de demande dans la profession a signifié un rejet automatique des candidatures ne faisant pas l'objet d'une offre formelle d'emploi ayant été soumise à une preuve de rareté de main-d'œuvre.

Ainsi donc, en 1978, lorsque le Québec a conçu et mis en œuvre sa propre grille de sélection des immigrants de la composante économique, il a maintenu le caractère éliminatoire du facteur emploi. La différence majeure d'avec la grille utilisée par le fédéral s'est manifestée par un poids relatif bien plus grand accordé au facteur linguistique. En outre, contrairement à la grille canadienne où la connaissance de l'une ou l'autre langue permettait l'obtention d'un nombre égal de points, les deux langues étaient traitées différemment. Dans la grille québécoise, les points attribués à la connaissance du français dépassaient de beaucoup ceux accordés à la connaissance de l'anglais.[9] Le facteur emploi, quant à lui, était désormais traité en fonction de la seule situation prévalant au

Québec et non plus de celle de l'ensemble du Canada : une liste distincte de professions en demande fut élaborée et les vérifications relatives à la rareté de main-d'œuvre, dans les cas des offres formelles d'emploi, se limitaient désormais au seul territoire québécois.

La mise en œuvre des modalités d'intervention proprement québécoises, rendues possibles grâce à l'Entente de 1978 s'est faite dans un contexte qui a, de toute évidence, bousculé quelque peu les plans qu'auraient pu avoir, à l'époque, les autorités en place. Les retombées de l'instauration de ces nouvelles responsabilités ont tout probablement été largement marquées par la situation politique internationale et par l'évolution de la conjoncture économique qui ont marqué la toute fin de la décennie 1970 et la première moitié de la décennie suivante.

Au plan politique, la victoire militaire des communistes en Indochine et l'exode qui en est résulté (mouvement des boat people) sont venus gonfler, dès 1979, les admissions dans la toute nouvelle catégorie des réfugiés.[10] Parmi ceux qui se pressaient dans les nombreux camps érigés en Thaïlande et ailleurs en Asie, le Québec a privilégié ceux qui maîtrisaient déjà le français et ceux qui avaient des parents au Québec. Il a même financé des cours de français dans certains de ces camps en vue de faciliter l'éventuelle intégration linguistique de ceux qu'il s'apprêtait à accueillir.

Par la suite, au début des années 1980, les bouleversements politiques survenus, notamment en Iran, au Bangladesh, au Sri Lanka et dans certains pays d'Amérique latine ont provoqué une croissance sans précédent du nombre de demandeurs d'asile se présentant aux aéroports du Canada et tout particulièrement à celui de Montréal. Il a fallu une décennie complète et deux programmes majeurs de régularisation (1986–1987 et 1991–1992) avant que ce mouvement soit, sinon contrôlé, du moins géré selon des modalités légales et administratives claires et constantes.

Au plan économique, par ailleurs, la très sévère récession du début des années 1980 a contraint les autorités à limiter les admissions dans la composante économique. Non seulement le facteur « demande dans la profession » a-t-il conservé son caractère éliminatoire mais encore la liste de ces « professions en demande » a-t-elle été réduite, pour un temps, à quelques titres seulement. Du côté fédéral, elle a même été ramenée à rien pendant quelque temps.

Au cours de la deuxième moitié des années 1980, tant du côté fédéral que du côté québécois, les autorités ont ré-ouvert quelque peu les portes à la composante économique. Les listes de professions en demande se sont allongées et, du côté québécois, le recours au pouvoir dérogatoire a été étendu, parfois encouragé et, notamment dans le cas de ce qu'on a appelé les offres d'emploi attestées,[11] encadré et normalisé administrativement.

Les autorités québécoises ont finalement fait preuve d'une volonté significative d'ouverture à l'immigration économique avec l'adoption et la mise en place d'une nouvelle grille de sélection en 1996. Avec cette nouvelle grille, il n'était plus nécessaire d'avoir une profession en demande ou une offre d'emploi formelle (validée ou attestée) pour être sélectionné. Les candidats présentant un ensemble de caractéristiques favorables au regard, notamment, de l'âge, de la scolarité et des connaissances linguistiques pouvaient être sélectionnés sans offre d'emploi formelle ni profession en demande. La mise en place de cette nouvelle grille a engendré une croissance importante du mouvement d'immigration destiné au Québec, et surtout, une augmentation du nombre et de la proportion des immigrants de la catégorie des travailleurs et, par ricochet, une croissance correspondante du nombre de ceux qui connaissent le français. Les autorités fédérales ont mis en place des modalités un peu comparables au début des années 2000.

Depuis 1996, la grille québécoise applicable à la catégorie des travailleurs a subi diverses modifications, parfois mineures, parfois plus importantes, mais pour l'essentiel, l'esprit qui l'anime est demeuré le même. Le changement le plus important a été fait en 2006, alors que la notion de profession en demande a été remplacée par celle de domaine de formation. Plutôt que d'attribuer des points au seul regard de la rareté estimée de main-d'œuvre dans une profession donnée, on en attribue pour le domaine de formation, en tenant compte non seulement de la rareté estimée de personnes ayant complété cette formation au Québec, mais également des difficultés qui peuvent exister pour une personne formée à l'étranger d'obtenir le droit, à l'intérieur de délais raisonnables, de pratiquer dans ce domaine. En outre, l'orientation retenue par cette méthode est de privilégier davantage les candidatures de techniciens et d'ouvriers spécialisés.

L'impact de cette nouveauté ne peut pas encore être mesuré, parce qu'en raison des délais de traitement, particulièrement longs dans certains pays, les candidats sélectionnés en vertu de la version la plus récente de la grille commencent à peine à apparaître dans les données sur les admissions.

On ne peut terminer ce rapide survol de la gestion québécoise du mouvement sans mentionner l'autre catégorie de la composante économique : les gens d'affaires. Cette catégorie ne comprenait à l'origine que les entrepreneurs et les travailleurs autonomes, immigrants dont la demande était évaluée sur la base de projets d'affaires dans lesquels leur rôle devait être celui de maître d'œuvre ou de partenaire. À la fin des années 1980, le Québec a pris l'initiative de créer un programme particulier pour les investisseurs passifs. Ce programme permet à un candidat d'être sélectionné en retour d'un investissement de quelques centaines de milliers de dollars pendant cinq ans, sans intérêt. Modeste au départ, ce programme est rapidement devenu le plus important volet de la catégorie des gens d'affaires, dépassant de loin celui des entrepreneurs et des travailleurs autonomes. Par contre, l'impact de ce programme sur le mouvement réel d'immigration et, à terme, sur la composition de la population, est relativement faible. En effet, le taux de présence au Québec des immigrants sélectionnés dans le cadre de ce programme est en général très faible.

Il s'agit là d'une particularité des modalités fédérales-provinciales en immigration : le Québec sélectionne, sur la base d'un investissement réalisé au Québec, une proportion très élevée des candidatures d'investisseurs voulant immigrer au Canada mais en pratique, la majorité d'entre eux s'installent dans les autres provinces, notamment en Ontario et en Colombie-Britannique. Jusqu'à présent, aucune tentative sérieuse n'a été faite, ni par le Québec, ni par le fédéral, pour corriger ce qui pourrait sembler à plusieurs comme une anomalie. Cela fait dire à certains que ce programme a davantage trait aux finances qu'à l'immigration.

5.3. Évolution du mouvement récent

Une observation détaillée de l'évolution du mouvement et surtout de ses principales caractéristiques permettra de mieux saisir la nature des changements survenus au cours des dernières décennies et comment on peut en conclure que l'intervention distincte du Québec dans sa gestion a pu être à l'origine, en grande partie, de ces changements. Cette illustration, à l'aide de données et de quelques graphiques, procédera en deux temps. En premier lieu, ce sera l'évolution du mouvement global, de 1970 à 2007,[12] qui sera présentée et en second lieu, l'évolution de la composante sur laquelle la capacité d'intervention du Québec est la plus significative : les requérants principaux de la catégorie des travailleurs, c'est-à-dire ceux dont la sélection est effectuée formellement au moyen d'une grille de critères censée mesurer leur potentiel de succès en matière d'établissement.

5.4. Évolution du volume global

La courbe de tendance qui apparaît au graphique 1a montre bien qu'en dépit de variations annuelles marquées, la tendance générale de l'immigration destinée au Québec entre 1970 et 2007 a été à la hausse. Entre 1970 et 1978, année de signature de la première entente accordant au Québec un rôle significatif dans la gestion du mouvement, 23 500 immigrants ont été admis en moyenne annuellement. Depuis 1991, année de signature de l'entente la plus récente, cette moyenne a été de plus 37 500. Depuis le début du siècle (2000 à 2007), c'est en moyenne 40 500 immigrants qui ont été accueillis annuellement. Cette tendance à la hausse étant également observable pour l'immigration se destinant ailleurs au Canada, la part de l'immigration québécoise dans l'ensemble de l'immigration canadienne, quant à elle, affiche plutôt une certaine stabilité (graphique 1b).

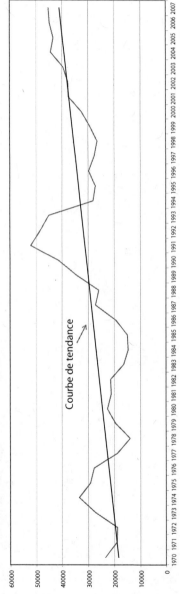

GRAPHIQUE 1a : Immigrants admis au Québec, 1970–2007*

Courbe de tendance

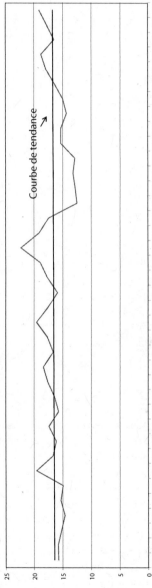

GRAPHIQUE 1b : Immigration au Québec en % de l'immigration au Canada, 1970–2007*

Courbe de tendance

*Données préliminaires pour 2007.

Source : Ministère de l'Immigration et des Communautés culturelles du Québec, Direction de la recherche et de l'analyse prospective.

5.5. Évolution des caractéristiques ethnoculturelles

En 1970, les États-Unis, le Royaume-Uni, la Grèce, l'Italie et le Portugal figuraient encore parmi les 10 premiers pays de naissance des immigrants admis. Vingt ans plus tard, ils ont été remplacés par des pays d'Asie et d'Afrique, tendance qui s'est poursuivie jusqu'à présent, comme le montrent les données du tableau 7, ci-dessous.

TABLEAU 7
Principaux pays de naissance des immigrants admis au Québec annuellement (1970, 1990, 2007)*

1970		1990		2007	
États-Unis	2210	Liban	8541	Maroc	3612
France	2198	Haïti	2087	France	3467
Grèce	1944	Viet Nam	1718	Algérie	3414
Italie	1711	France	1536	Colombie	2542
Royaume-Uni	1697	Hong Kong	1517	Chine	2471
Portugal	1371	Syrie	1357	Roumanie	1827
Haïti	915	Maroc	1342	Liban	1826
Trinité-et-Tobago	774	Chine	1287	Mexique	1304
Égypte	715	Égypte	1233	Haïti	1293
10 premiers pays	13535		20618		21756
10 premiers pays en %	57,7		49,8		48,1
Total tous pays	23457		41389		45221

*Données préliminaires pour 2007.
Source : Ministère de l'Immigration et des Communautés culturelles, Direction de la recherche et de l'analyse prospective.

Pendant la même période, les admissions de personnes ayant comme langues maternelles l'arabe, le français, l'espagnol et les langues chinoises ont pris une importance grandissante. Par contre, alors que plus de 10 pour cent des immigrants admis en 1980 avaient l'anglais comme langue maternelle, en 2007, cette proportion n'atteignait pas 4 pour cent. Au graphique 2, on voit comment les connaissances linguistiques des immigrants ont évolué, en particulier depuis la fin des années 1990 : le nombre des immigrants connaissant le français et surtout ceux connaissant à la fois le français et l'anglais a augmenté considérablement, tandis que le nombre de ceux ne connaissant que l'anglais ou aucune des deux langues est resté plus stable. En proportion du mouvement global, la part des immigrants admis connaissant le français, incluant ceux connaissant aussi l'anglais, a atteint, en 2007, plus de 60 pour cent du total. En 1970, cette part dépassait à peine 30 pour cent.

GRAPHIQUE 2
Répartition des immigrants admis au Québec selon leur connaissance du français et de l'anglais, 1970–2007*

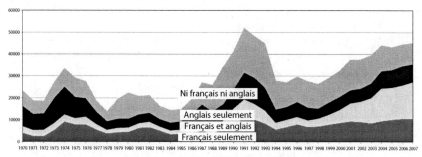

Années d'admission

* Données préliminaires pour 2007.

Source : Ministère de l'Immigration et des Communautés culturelles du Québec, Direction de la recherche et de l'analyse prospective.

5.6. *Évolution des caractéristiques socio-économiques*

Ce sont les groupes d'âge très actifs (25-34 ans et 35-44 ans) qui ont connu la croissance la plus importante. Pris ensemble, en 2007, ces deux groupes d'âge comptaient pour 58 pour cent des admissions, alors qu'en 1970, ils ne comptaient que pour 42 pour cent du total. Les dernières décennies ont également été caractérisées par une hausse remarquable du niveau de scolarité des immigrants admis. Cette hausse a été presque constante sur toute la période. Jusqu'en 1981, les immigrants admis n'ayant pas fréquenté l'école au-delà du niveau secondaire (entre 0 et 11 ans de scolarité) représentaient annuellement environ 60 pour cent des admis de 15 ans et plus. Par la suite, cette proportion a diminué de façon régulière et n'atteignait plus que 18 pour cent en 2007. La proportion de ceux qui avaient une scolarité supérieure à 11 années a, en revanche, beaucoup augmenté, particulièrement ceux ayant poursuivi des études au-delà du premier cycle universitaire (17 années ou plus). Entre 1970 et 1994, la part relative de ce dernier groupe a oscillé entre 6 pour cent et 14 pour cent, mais à partir de 1995, il s'est élevé rapidement pour atteindre 34 pour cent en 2007.

Pour ce qui est des professions projetées par les immigrants admis, l'évolution la plus remarquable, c'est l'importance prise, ces dernières années, par les sciences naturelles et appliquées. Entre 1973 et 1990, la part prise par ces groupes professionnels a varié entre 8 pour cent et 15 pour cent,[13] mais depuis 1995, cette même part a oscillé entre 26 pour cent et 39 pour cent. En revanche, le secteur primaire et le secteur des métiers, transport et machinerie, qui atteignaient, certaines années, jusqu'au quart du total, pendant la décennie 1980, n'en représentent plus qu'à peine 4 pour cent en 2007.

Finalement, caractéristique majeure lorsqu'il s'agit de témoigner de l'impact de la gestion sur le mouvement d'immigration, l'évolution de la répartition par catégorie nous apprend, au graphique 3, que c'est la composante économique, et au sein de celle-ci, la catégorie des travailleurs qui, sur l'ensemble de la période, a connu la croissance la plus importante, particulièrement ces dernières années. Cette croissance récente est d'autant plus remarquable qu'elle n'inclut aucune donnée générée par des régularisations massives, comme ce fut le cas souvent dans le passé.[14] En 1992, année qui a suivi celle de la signature de l'Accord Canada-Québec, la part de la catégorie des travailleurs dans le mouvement global atteignait 25 pour cent. Dix ans après l'Accord, en 2001, elle comptait pour 46 pour cent de ce même total. En 2007, elle atteignait plus de 56 pour cent, niveau le plus élevé de toute la période observée.

GRAPHIQUE 3
Répartition des immigrants admis au Québec selon la catégorie, 1970–2007*

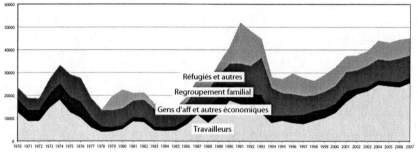

Années d'admission

*Données préliminaires pour 2007.
Source : Ministère de l'Immigration et des Communautés culturelles du Québec, Direction de la recherche et de l'analyse prospective.

Comme, d'une part, cette catégorie est celle sur laquelle la marge de manœuvre de l'État québécois est la plus large et que, d'autre part, c'est celle qui a connu la plus forte croissance des dernières années, on s'attardera maintenant à examiner plus en détail l'évolution de cette composante spécifique du mouvement. Plus précisément, ce sont les caractéristiques des requérants principaux de cette catégorie qui seront observées, car il s'agit des seuls immigrants qui sont formellement sélectionnés, c'est-à-dire que leurs caractéristiques socio-économiques sont évaluées en fonction des critères de la grille prévue à cet effet.

5.7. Évolution du profil des immigrants formellement sélectionnés[15]

En examinant l'évolution des caractéristiques des requérants principaux de la catégorie des travailleurs, on peut facilement constater que ce sont les changements survenus au sein de ce groupe particulier d'immigrants qui ont provoqué les modifications constatées précédemment au sein du mouvement dans son ensemble. En effet, on peut voir que toutes les tendances observées au sein du mouvement global sont non seulement présentes dans cette catégorie spécifique, mais elles y sont de manière beaucoup plus affirmée. Ainsi, entre 1980 et 2007 (graphique 4), le nombre total de ces immigrants est passé de 2 700 à 13 500, soit une hausse de 400 pour cent, alors que la hausse du mouvement global, quant à elle, au cours de la même période, a plutôt été de 100 pour cent (de 22 600 à 45 200).

GRAPHIQUE 4
Requérants principaux de la catégorie des travailleurs admis au Québec, 1980–2007*

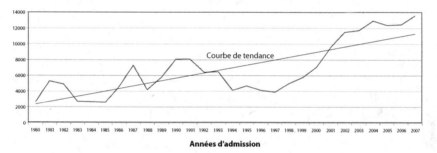

Années d'admission

*Données préliminaires pour 2007.

Source : Ministère de l'Immigration et des Communautés culturelles du Québec, Direction de la recherche et de l'analyse prospective.

Et il en va de même pour toutes les caractéristiques observables. La très forte poussée de certaines langues maternelles y est mise en évidence : le nombre d'immigrants de cette catégorie ayant l'arabe comme langue maternelle a connu, pendant cette période, une croissance de plus 1 200 pour cent (de 275 à 3 600). Pour l'espagnol, la croissance a été de plus de 830 pour cent (155 à 1 460) et pour le français, de près de 400 pour cent (650 à 3 230). Au sein du mouvement global, la poussée de ces langues maternelles a certes été forte, mais jamais dans des proportions aussi fulgurantes : 800 pour cent pour l'arabe, 500 pour cent pour l'espagnol et 150 pour cent pour le français. On constate un phénomène identique pour la connaissance du français : alors qu'au sein du mouvement global, la croissance de ceux qui connaissent le français (incluant ceux qui connaissent aussi l'anglais) a été de près de 320 pour cent (de 6530 à 27 300), chez les requérants principaux de la catégorie des travailleurs, cette hausse a été de plus de 785 pour cent (1 380 à 12 225) (graphique 5).

GRAPHIQUE 5
Réquérants principaux de la catégorie des travailleurs admis au Québec, selon leur connaissance du français et de l'anglais, 1980–2007*

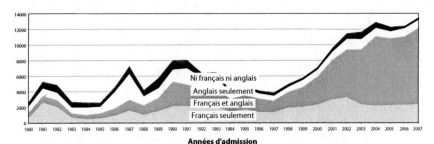

Années d'admission

*Données préliminaires pour 2007.
Source : Ministère de l'Immigration et des Communautés culturelles du Québec, Direction de la recherche et de l'analyse prospective.

Un phénomène tout à fait comparable est également observable si on examine l'évolution des caractéristiques socio-économiques de cette catégorie :

- Au regard de l'âge, cette catégorie est maintenant presque uniquement constituée de personnes appartenant aux 25-34 ans et aux 35-44 ans, les deux groupes d'âge les plus actifs;
- Au regard de la scolarité, on ne trouve presque plus de requérants principaux de la catégorie des travailleurs qui n'ont pas complété leurs études secondaires. Il y en a même assez peu qui ont moins de 14 ans de scolarité. La plupart (93 pour cent) ont poursuivi des études postsecondaires ou universitaires.
- Au regard des professions projetées, le secteur « sciences naturelles et appliquées » a vu ses effectifs croître à des niveaux très élevés, passant de 470 admissions en 1980 à 4 300 en 2007, soit une augmentation de plus de 800 pour cent.

6. ÉVOLUTION DE LA « PRÉSENCE »

Traditionnellement, on sait qu'une forte proportion des immigrants admis initialement au Québec ne s'y établissait pas à demeure. Après seulement quelques mois ou quelques années, ils migraient de nouveau vers une autre province du Canada, vers les États-Unis ou vers un autre pays (Québec, Ministère des Communautés culturelles et de l'Immigration 1990c). Qu'en est-il maintenant?

Les données les plus précises à cet égard nous proviennent de jumelages effectués entre les fichiers des admissions permanentes et le fichier de l'assurance-maladie du Québec. Ce dernier fichier constitue la banque de données la plus exhaustive de l'ensemble de la population du Québec. En outre, grâce à ces jumelages, on peut observer l'évolution de ce qu'on appelle le taux de présence en fonction des caractéristiques connues au moment de l'admission.

Ainsi, on constate (graphiques 6 et 7) que le taux de présence, cinq ans après leur admission, des immigrants accueillis depuis 1991, année de signature de l'Accord Canada-Québec, est demeuré relativement stable, autour de 80 pour cent. De surcroît, si on examine l'évolution de ce taux en fonction de la catégorie et de la connaissance du français et de l'anglais au moment de l'admission, on constate que l'accent mis par les autorités québécoises, sur la connaissance du français et sur la sélection de travailleurs a produit des résultats très favorables : les immigrants maîtrisant le français au moment de leur admission et les immigrants sélectionnés comme travailleurs sont ceux qui affichent, cinq ans après leur admission, les meilleurs taux de présence.

GRAPHIQUE 6
Évolution du taux de présence des immigrants au Québec, cinq ans après leur admission selon certaines catégories, 1981–2002

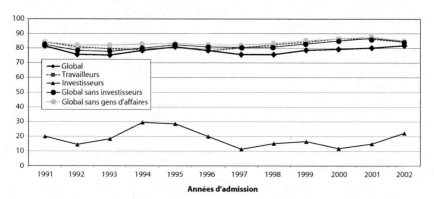

Source : Ministère de l'Immigration et des Communautés culturelles du Québec, Direction de la recherche et de l'analyse prospective.

GRAPHIQUE 7
Évolution du taux de présence des immigrants au Québec, cinq ans après leur admission selon la connaissance du français et de l'anglais, 1991–2002

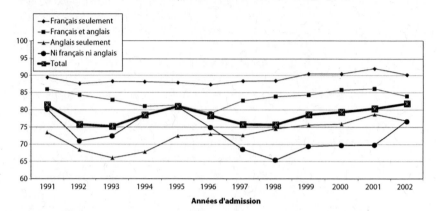

Source : Ministère de l'Immigration et des Communautés culturelles du Québec, Direction de la recherche et de l'analyse prospective.

7. CONCLUSION ET DISCUSSION

Au terme de cet exposé sommaire sur ce qu'ont été plus de trois décennies d'intervention du gouvernement québécois dans la gestion de l'immigration internationale à destination de son territoire, que devrait-on retenir et à quels enjeux sont confrontées les autorités québécoises en cette matière?

Force est d'abord de constater que l'intervention québécoise a eu des effets déterminants sur l'évolution du flux migratoire, et ce, en dépit des limites posées à cette intervention, limites fixées par le cadre constitutionnel et juridico-administratif mais limites aussi liées à la nature même des mouvements migratoires et aux facteurs qui les animent. Ainsi, les caractéristiques ethnoculturelles et socioéconomiques des immigrants admis correspondent désormais beaucoup mieux que par le passé aux intérêts de la majorité francophone du Québec. Pour ce faire, il a fallu du temps, il a fallu que la conjoncture s'y prête et il a fallu surtout que cela s'appuie sur un plan plus vaste visant à donner à la majorité démographique et linguistique du Québec les outils nécessaires à son développement et à sa pérennité.

Certaines préoccupations persistent néanmoins et de nouvelles ont émergé :

- Même si, parmi les immigrants qui arrivent chaque année, la proportion de ceux qui parlent français ou qui viennent de pays de la

Francophonie est plus élevée qu'elle ne l'a jamais été, même si la connaissance du français au sein de la population immigrée dans son ensemble est désormais plus répandue que la connaissance de l'anglais et même si les transferts linguistiques,[16] en particulier au sein des cohortes récentes, favorisent largement le français, l'inquiétude relative à la prépondérance du français demeure vive en certains milieux. Leurs appréhensions s'appuient notamment sur le fait que le poids relatif des francophones de langue maternelle au sein de la population totale du Québec a affiché une légère baisse lors du dernier recensement (2006). Cette baisse est largement attribuable aux forts volumes d'immigration des premières années du XXIe siècle, composés majoritairement de personnes de langues maternelles tierces. Toutefois, comme la majorité d'entre elles connaissent déjà le français et que leurs enfants sont scolarisés en français, tout indique qu'à terme, elles ou leurs enfants contribueront vraisemblablement à grossir les rangs de la majorité francophone, contrairement aux cohortes anciennes qui sont allées grossir les rangs de la minorité anglophone.

Mais la question linguistique n'épuise pas la problématique de l'immigration au Québec, tant s'en faut. D'autres aspects constituent autant, sinon plus, des objets de préoccupations. Qu'il suffise d'en mentionner quelques-uns :

- Au regard de la gestion de l'immigration liée à l'emploi (catégorie des travailleurs), au moins deux approches sont possibles : doit-on privilégier la micro-gestion, c'est-à-dire l'arrimage très étroit de la sélection des candidats avec les besoins immédiats des employeurs? C'est le point de vue que certains d'entre eux défendent, faisant valoir que le profil des immigrants admis est souvent trop loin de leurs besoins réels de main-d'œuvre.[17] Doit-on plutôt privilégier la macro-gestion, c'est-à-dire une sélection orientée vers les besoins de moyen et long terme, faisant le pari que des immigrants aux caractéristiques avantageuses (jeunes, hautement scolarisés, bilingues) sauront mieux s'adapter, à terme, aux exigences d'une économie du savoir? Ces deux approches peuvent être complémentaires mais on constate qu'elles sont parfois mises en opposition.
- Au regard des processus administratifs, la gestion de l'offre d'immigration pose différents défis : comment concilier le principe de l'universalité des critères avec, d'un côté, une offre parfois pléthorique dans certains pays en développement où la proportion de personnes susceptibles de satisfaire aux critères, au sein de la population totale, est relativement faible, avec, d'un autre côté, une offre parfois anémique dans des pays développés où cette proportion est au contraire élevée? Comment, par ailleurs, identifier rapidement et

traiter prioritairement, parmi les milliers de demandes en souffrance, celles qui sont les plus susceptibles d'obtenir les meilleurs résultats à la grille de sélection et, de ce fait, du moins en théorie, sont le mieux en mesure de répondre aux besoins pressants du marché du travail québécois? Comment raccourcir les délais pour ces candidatures, le tout en conservant un processus équitable pour tous les candidats?

• Au regard de l'intégration économique, il y a lieu d'être préoccupés. Même si, globalement, le processus fonctionne toujours et même si la situation des nouveaux arrivants s'améliore généralement avec le temps, ce processus est plus lent qu'il ne l'était autrefois, en particulier pour les personnes appartenant à certaines minorités visibles. De surcroît, cette situation est plus marquée au Québec qu'ailleurs au Canada. Plusieurs hypothèses explicatives ont été avancées. L'une des moins fréquemment invoquées mais peut-être la plus plausible tient au fait que l'expérience de la société québécoise francophone en matière d'accueil et d'intégration des immigrants est encore nouvelle. Elle n'a peut-être pas encore acquis à cet égard les comportements et les réflexes qui sont ceux du reste du Canda où l'immigration fait partie, depuis toujours, du tissu social intrinsèque et de l'expérience historique dans presque toutes les régions.[18] D'ailleurs, les communautés d'immigrants qui se sont implantées au Québec depuis que celui-ci intervient en ce domaine sont elles aussi assez nouvelles. Pour cette raison, elles sont moins bien établies, sont moins riches et ne sont pas en mesure d'offrir aux nouveaux arrivants le même soutien que les communautés plus anciennes pouvaient donner à l'époque où tout se passait surtout en anglais.

• Au regard de l'enjeu démographico-économique, c'est-à-dire de la décision de recourir à l'immigration pour contrer les effets économiques défavorables du vieillissement démographique, devrait-on se demander si les pénuries majeures de main-d'œuvre, appréhendées en raison du départ prochain à la retraite de la génération du *baby-boom*, vont réellement se concrétiser? Les développements technologiques et la hausse de la productivité qui s'ensuivra ne contribueront-ils pas, dans une large mesure, à atténuer les effets de ces départs à la retraite, rendant ainsi les besoins de nouvelle main-d'œuvre moins aigus, voire à peine plus marqués que ce qu'on connaît déjà? L'immigration constituera-t-elle une réponse adéquate à cet éventuel problème? L'équation n'est pas aussi évidente qu'elle puisse le paraître à première vue. Les compétences recherchées par le Québec seront susceptibles de l'être aussi par nombre d'autres pays développés. La concurrence risque donc d'être vive et les résultats plus modestes, surtout si certains pays d'Europe occidentale, géographiquement plus près des bassins potentiels d'immigrants francophones (Maghreb, Europe de l'Est) concrétisent leurs projets actuellement à l'étude d'introduire dans leur législation la notion de « résidents permanents » pour les immigrants. Ce concept, faut-il le préciser, constitue un avantage comparatif important pour le Québec dans sa quête de candidats à l'immigration qualifiés.

Une chose enfin semble évidente; le succès, relatif mais indéniable, qu'a connu l'intervention québécoise pour infléchir la composition du mouvement d'immigration dans le sens des intérêts de la majorité, tient en grande partie à deux choses : d'une part, la frontière linguistique virtuelle qui existe entre le Québec et le reste du Canada a un effet déterminant sur la composition du mouvement et sur les taux de présence et, d'autre part, la Francophonie internationale a constitué et continuera de constituer, pour le Québec, son bassin d'immigration le plus important et le plus fertile.

NOTES

1(a). La recherche nécessaire à la rédaction du présent texte a été effectuée en 2008, en vue d'une présentation au Forum tenu à Barcelone en octobre de la même année, portant sur la gestion de l'immigration et de la diversité au Québec et au Canada. Les chiffres cités relatifs à conjoncture la plus récente ne sont donc plus tout à fait à jour. Toutefois, les enjeux et les grandes tendances demeurent fort semblables.

Il importe néanmoins de préciser que les volumes globaux d'admissions permanentes ont continué de croître pour atteindre près de 54 000 en 2010. Ils se sont stabilisés en 2011 avec près de 52 000. Il en va de même pour la proportion des admis connaissant le français (65 pour cent en 2010, 63 pour cent en 2011).

Au regard des politiques et de leur mise en oeuvre, on note une volonté d'arrimer plus étroitement la sélection aux besoins à plus court terme du marché du travail, ainsi qu'un recours plus important aux permis de travail temporaires, ce qui ne va pas sans susciter des inquiétudes dans certains milieux.

1(b). La majeure partie des données utilisées dans ce texte proviennent soit de compilations spéciales effectuées par la Direction de la recherche et de l'analyse prospective du ministère de l'Immigration et des Communautés culturelles du Québec, soit de documents publiés par ce dernier. Toutefois, les modalités de présentation de ces données, ainsi que l'interprétation qui en est faite n'engagent que la seule responsabilité de l'auteur. L'auteur tient par ailleurs à remercier ses anciens collègues de ce même ministère pour leur apport indispensable à la production du présent document : Pierre Baillargeon et Nicole Turcotte pour les données, Claire Benjamin, Magdalena Planeta, Chakib Benzakour, Louis-René Gagnon et Franck Hounzangbé pour leur relecture attentive et leurs précieux commentaires.

2.   « Aubain » est un archaïsme utilisé dans le texte de la Constitution de 1867, signifiant « étranger ».

3.   Ce qui est mesuré par une proportion minimale de temps passé au pays par rapport à une période de référence.

4.   Cette notion censitaire d'« immigrants » englobe toutes les personnes qui possèdent ou ont possédé, avant d'avoir la citoyenneté, le statut de « résidents

permanents », y compris les personnes nées au Canada qui ont dû obtenir la résidence permanente.

5. Les citoyens canadiens par filiation (nés à l'étranger de parents canadiens), pour leur part, sont inclus parmi les « natifs ».

6. On pourrait également mentionner la Banque longitudinale de données sur les immigrants au Canada (BDIM), une base de données qui est le fruit d'un jumelage entre les données d'immigration et les données fiscales. Elle permet, dans une certaine mesure, de témoigner des migrations secondaires, survenues à l'intérieur du Canada après l'octroi de la résidence permanente.

7. Certes, les migrations interprovinciales expliquent en bonne partie les changements survenus dans les caractéristiques linguistiques de la population immigrée présente au Québec : on sait que les personnes unilingues anglaises, natives ou immigrées, sont celles qui ont affiché la plus forte propension à quitter le Québec pour les autres provinces dans les années 1970 et 1980. Toutefois, les autres caractéristiques n'auraient pas changé autant et surtout, elles ne se seraient pas éloignées de celles de la population immigrée du Canada si le mouvement lui-même ne s'était pas distingué de plus en plus du mouvement canadien.

8. L'Accord de 1991 n'a pas de limite de temps car pour être modifié ou abrogé, le consentement des deux parties est requis.

9. Plus tard, la grille fédérale a aussi été modifiée afin de donner davantage de points aux candidats ne connaissant que l'anglais sans pénaliser ceux ne connaissant que le français, le tout afin de préserver le principe de l'égalité des deux langues au niveau fédéral. Plutôt que d'accorder un nombre égal de points aux deux langues, on en donne un nombre significatif pour l'une, qu'il s'agisse de l'anglais ou du français et on en ajoute quelques-uns seulement pour la connaissance de l'autre. En pratique, comme la connaissance de l'anglais est beaucoup plus répandue que celle du français parmi les candidats potentiels dans le monde, c'est la connaissance de cette langue qui se trouve à être privilégiée dans la composition du mouvement se destinant ailleurs au Canada.

10. Catégorie créée par la Loi de 1976. Elle n'existait pas auparavant.

11. Il s'agissait d'offres d'emploi dont l'authenticité devait être validée par les autorités mais qui n'avaient pas à faire l'objet d'une preuve de rareté de main-d'œuvre. Les candidats qui en bénéficiaient devaient toutefois présenter un profil plus avantageux que ceux dont l'emploi avait été soumis à la preuve de rareté de main-d'œuvre.

12. Selon la disponibilité des données, cette plage chronologique pourra varier.

13. Ces pourcentages sont calculés à partir des seuls immigrants qui se destinent au marché du travail et dont la profession projetée était connue au moment de la sélection.

14. De tels programmes, mis en œuvre en 1973, 1980–1981, 1986–1987 et 1990–1991, ont eu pour effet de grossir, pour les années en question et pour les années subséquentes, les données relatives aux travailleurs. De plus, avant 1978, la catégorie des réfugiés n'existant pas, ces derniers étaient bien souvent comptabilisés avec les travailleurs.

15. L'évolution de cette composante particulière ne sera observée qu'à partir de 1980, première année pour laquelle il a été possible d'obtenir des données qui lui soient spécifiques.

16. Il s'agit de l'abandon de la langue maternelle au profit du français ou de l'anglais comme langue parlée à la maison.

17. Notamment dans les mémoires et les témoignages présentés à la Commission parlementaire sur la planification de l'immigration pour la période 2008–2010, tenue à l'automne 2007 (Québec, Assemblée Nationale, Commission de la culture 2007).

18. À l'exception peut-être des provinces de l'Atlantique dont le peuplement est presque aussi homogène et ancien qu'il l'est dans le Québec francophone.

RÉFÉRENCES

Cornell, P.G., J. Hamelin, F. Ouellet et M. Trudel. 1968. *Canada : unité et diversité*. Montréal : Holt, Rinehart et Winston. 578 p.

Harvey, F. 1987. La question de l'immigration au Québec : genèse historique. Dans F. Harvey *et al.*, *Le Québec français et l'école à clientèle pluriethnique : contribution à une réflexion*, 1-57. Conseil de la langue française, N° 29. Québec : Éditeur officiel du Québec. En ligne : http://www.cslf.gouv.qc.ca/bibliotheque-virtuelle/publication-html/?tx_iggcpplus_pi4[file]=publications%2Fpubd129%2Fd129-1.html#2.

Hawkins, F. 1988. *Canada and Immigration: Public Policy and Public Concern*, 2e éd. Kingston et Montréal : Institute of Public Administration of Canada. 476 p.

Lacoursière, J., J. Provencher et D. Vaugeois. 2001. *Canada-Québec : synthèse historique 1534–2000*. Sillery : Septentrion. 591 p.

Pinsonneault, G. 2004. *Synthèse des communications présentées dans le cadre de l'atelier portant sur « Les États fédérés et la gestion de l'immigration et de l'intégration : le Québec, modèle ou exception »*. 9e Conférence internationale Metropolis, Genève, septembre. 15 p. En ligne : http://international.metropolis.net/events/9th_conf_geneva_04/html/en/workshop_g.html.

Pinsonneault, G. 2005. L'évolution de la composition du mouvement d'immigration au Québec au cours des dernières décennies. *Santé, Société et Solidarité, Revue de l'observatoire franco-québécois de la santé et de la solidarité* 1 : 49-65.

Québec. 1991. Accord Canada-Québec relatif à l'immigration et l'admission temporaire des aubains. Brochure en ligne : http://www.micc.gouv.qc.ca/publications/fr/divers/Accord-canada-quebec-immigration-francais.pdf.

Québec, Assemblée Nationale, Commission de la culture. 2007. *Mémoires déposés lors de la consultation générale sur le document de consultation intitulé « La planification de l'immigration au Québec pour la période 2008–2010 »*. En ligne : http://www.assnat.qc.ca/fra/38legislature1/commissions/cc/depot-immigration.html.

Québec, Conseil des Communautés culturelles et de l'Immigration. 1994. *Statistiques démographie, immigration et communautés culturelles au Québec depuis 1871*. Montréal. 109 p.

Québec, Ministère des Affaires internationales, de l'Immigration et des Communautés culturelles. 1993. *Population immigrée recensée au Québec en 1991 : caractéristiques générales*. 34 p.

Québec, Ministère des Communautés culturelles et de l'Immigration. 1990a. *Caractéristiques linguistiques de la population immigrée recensée au Québec en 1986*. 85 p.

Québec, Ministère des Communautés culturelles et de l'Immigration. 1990b. *Le mouvement d'immigration d'hier à aujourd'hui*. 85 p. (annexe de l'Énoncé de politique).

Québec, Ministère des Communautés culturelles et de l'Immigration. 1990c. *Au Québec pour bâtir ensemble, Énoncé de politique en matière d'immigration et d'intégration.* 88 p.

Québec, Ministère de l'Immigration et des Communautés culturelles. 2007. *Consultation 2008–2010, La Planification de l'immigration au Québec pour la période 2008–2010.* (document de consultation). xi+68 p.

Renaud, J. et L. Gingras. 1998. *Les trois premières années au Québec des requérants du statut de réfugié régularisés.* Québec : Publications du Québec. 135 p.

Renaud, J., L. Gingras, S. Vachon, C. Blaser, J.F. Godin et B. Gagné. 2001. *Ils sont maintenant d'ici! Les dix premières années au Québec des immigrants admis en 1989.* Québec : Publications du Québec. 197 p.

Wade, M. 1966. *Les Canadiens français de 1760 à nos jours,* Tome 1 : *1760–1914.* Ottawa : Cercle du Livre de France. 685 p.

PART III

IMMIGRATION AND THE LABOUR MARKET

CHAPTER 6

Integrating Immigrants into the Canadian Labour Market: Findings from *Public Policy Forum* Research and Activities[1]

YVES POISSON, *Former Vice President, Public Policy Forum, Ottawa, Canada*

INTRODUCTION

In recent years, Canada has generally received upwards of 230,000 immigrants per year, or about 0.8 percent of its total population (Citizenship and Immigration Canada, *Facts and Figures*; and Statistics Canada's population estimates). There is broad, if not deep, support for immigration among Canadians, with a general consensus on the importance of immigration to the economy—particularly in the context of an aging population. Thus, no political party is openly advocating reducing the annual intake of permanent residents. Nevertheless, the successful integration of new Canadians into the Canadian labour market and society at large is proving increasingly difficult. Indicators of integration are showing deterioration when compared to outcomes for previous cohorts of immigrants. There is a need, very difficult to achieve, to reform the system.

Using key messages from research, conferences, and seminars conducted by the Public Policy Forum[2] over recent years, this chapter will

Managing Immigration and Diversity in Canada: A Transatlantic Dialogue in the New Age of Migration,
ed. D. Rodríguez-García. Montreal and Kingston: Queen's Policy Studies Series, McGill-Queen's University Press.

briefly highlight the main trends of immigration and integration in Canada. It will outline the extent and scope of immigration in Canada, possible reform, and current challenges to the system. The chapter concludes by looking at the current state of the immigration system, drawing questions and considerations regarding the future of immigration in Canada.

A Nation of Immigrants

Today, Canada is well recognized as a nation of immigrants. Aside from Australia and Israel, Canada has received more immigrants per capita since 1945 than any other country in the world. With the exception of only the 1930s and 1940s, Canada has admitted over 1 million immigrants per decade over the course of the 20th century (CIC, *Facts and Figures 2007*). The 1990s saw a significant increase, with over 2 million immigrants entering Canada in that decade. Since 2000, the annual intake of immigrants has usually been between 200,000 and 250,000, with over 2 million new immigrants by 2010 (see Figure 1, based on 2007 data). It should be noted that this number does not include foreign temporary workers, of which there were more than 200,000 at the end of 2007 (ibid.).

FIGURE 1
Number of Immigrants per Decade

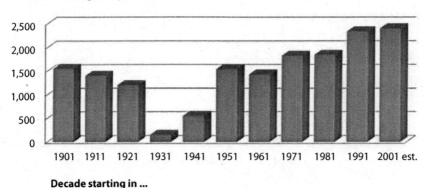

Decade starting in ...

Note: Numbers are in millions, where 2,500 = 2.5 million.
Source: Citizenship and Immigration Canada, *Facts and Figures 2007*.

The result of this planned nation-building through immigration is reflected in Canada's percentage of foreign-born residents. Although Canada has not reached the heights of the early 20th century, in 2005, the percentage of foreign-born residents in Canada was 19.2 percent (see Figure 2). This is one of the highest ratios among OECD (Organisation for Economic Co-operation and Development) countries, after only Australia (24.6 percent), and is significantly higher than in countries such as Germany and the United States, both at around 13 percent (CIC 2007). The proportion of immigrants in the workforce is even higher—over 20 percent—which points to the important role of immigration in labour force growth, in the context of an aging population. As of 2008, 75 percent of Canada's workforce growth came from immigration, and this was expected to rise to 100 percent by the end of 2010 (Competition Policy Review Panel 2008).

FIGURE 2
Foreign-born As Percentage (%) of Population

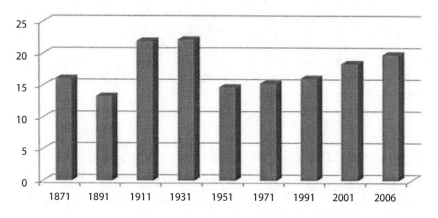

Source: Statistics Canada, censuses of population (1871 to 2006).

Over the past 30 years, there has been a drastic change in the source countries of immigrants to Canada. Prior to 1970, an overwhelming amount of foreign workers came from Europe; since then, there has been a marked shift to Asian countries. The top five source countries in 2006 were China, India, the Philippines, Pakistan, and the United States (CIC, *Facts and Figures 2007*) (see Figure 3). The result is that Canada has an increasing number of visible minorities—75 percent of recent immigrants (arriving between 2001 and 2006) were visible minorities, up from 55 percent in 1981 (Chui et al. 2008). According to the 2006 census, visible minorities accounted for 16.2 percent of Canada's total population that year. Statistics Canada projects that by 2017—Canada's 150th anniversary—fully one-fifth (20 percent) of Canadians will be visible minorities. Rough estimates suggest that 75 percent of immigrants settle in Canada's three largest cities, making immigration in Canada an intensely urban phenomenon; and so, too, are the challenges and opportunities associated with integrating new Canadians into the labour market and society at large.

FIGURE 3
Source Countries of Immigrants to Canada

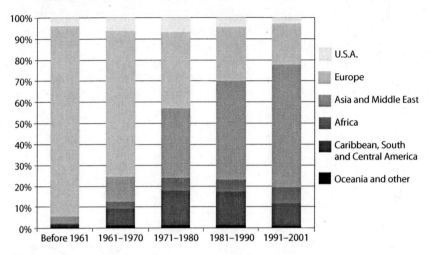

Source: Statistics Canada, censuses of population (until 2001).

Canadian Immigration Policy as "Nation-Building"

> The policy of the government is to foster the growth of the population of Canada by the encouragement of immigration. The government will seek ... to ensure the careful selection and permanent settlement of such numbers of immigrants as can advantageously be absorbed in our national economy. (Mackenzie King, 1947)

As the above quote from former prime minister Mackenzie King indicates, immigration in Canada has long been about "nation-building." This suggests that there has been a healthy streak of self-interest in Canada's immigration policies from the start. Over time, however, the nation-building and economic goals of Canadian immigration policy have been supplemented with humanitarian goals. Today, immigration policy in Canada has three explicit goals: humanitarian (refugees, displaced persons); family reunification; and economic benefit.

In recent years, the economic agenda has dominated discussion about immigration in Canada. The result is that Canada has been placing increasing emphasis on the practical benefits of recruiting skilled migrants, as opposed to the altruistic emphasis of reunifying families or providing a haven for refugees. As a result, according to data available for 2007, 55 percent of immigrants were admitted on an economic basis. It should be noted that only 17 percent were selected based on the "famous"

Canadian point system, with another 35 percent being either the spouse or dependants of the principal applicant (CIC, *Facts and Figures 2007*). In addition, another 3 percent were admitted as live-in caregivers (and their dependants) who had applied for permanent residence after two years of working in this field. Family reunification represented 28 percent; and refugees, displaced persons, and asylum seekers, admitted on humanitarian grounds, represented 12 percent (ibid.).

Canada's federal immigration legislation—the *Immigration and Refugee Protection Act* (IRPA)—was revised in 2002 to emphasize "human capital," rather than prioritizing specific occupations or labour market needs. The objective of the IRPA is to bring to Canada well-trained and flexible individuals who can adapt quickly to rapidly changing labour market conditions. Immigrants in the Economic Class are selected based on their education, official language abilities, work experience, age, arranged employment, and adaptability. The consequence is that high proportions have a university education. However, the system excludes skilled trade workers, who are quite in demand in many places. As such, some commentators suggest that Canada's refugee and immigration policies should be seen as completely distinct: The first has humanitarian and social justice aims; the second has an economic agenda. The debate of reform continues, as there is an ongoing sense of crisis within the system, associated with a huge backlog of applicants, a mismatch between immigrant skills and labour market needs, and poor performance related to employment and income. These challenges have prompted the current government to try to reform the system. Recent strategies and reform will be discussed later in the chapter.

Attitudes Towards Immigration

Given Canada's history of extensive immigration and the proportion of its foreign-born population, the government has on occasion struggled with the public perception that foreigners have abused Canada's immigration system and that restrictions are desirable (Fortin and Lowen 2005). Nevertheless, statistics show that Canadians' attitudes toward immigration are mostly positive. One survey, conducted in June 2008 by pollster Nik Nanos, revealed a broad consensus around the importance of immigration to Canada: 72.6 percent think that immigration is important or somewhat important to the future of the country (Nanos 2008). The survey also suggests, however, that Canadians' attitudes are driven in part by self-interest. For example, 85 percent of respondents agreed that immigration is important to help improve and renew Canada's workforce. At 85 percent, there is also widespread support of family reunification. Robin Sears notes, "It is the price of getting the best immigrants, and it encourages the ones we really want to stay" (Sears 2008, 39). In comparison, "being a refugee" does not appear to be as compelling a justification for Canadians to support immigration: Just 68.7 percent thought it was important. Nanos sums up these numbers by suggesting that Canadians want immigrants to "contribute" something to the country.

It is worth pointing out that in this poll, support for immigration in Quebec is lower than it is in the rest of Canada. While other provinces have had their own issues with the integration of immigrants—the Sharia law controversy in Ontario, for example—only in Quebec has the notion of "reasonable accommodation" been the subject of sustained public debate for a period of time, importantly in 2007 (Bouchard-Taylor Commission Report 2008). However, it is important to note that immigration is not an issue raised and debated during electoral campaigns, as was evident in the federal election of October 2008 and the provincial one in Quebec in December 2008. In other words, all political parties, whether at the federal or provincial level, have very similar views.

IMMIGRATION IN CANADA: IN CRISIS?

Challenges Facing the Immigration Program

Canada's immigration program faces at least three kinds of challenges.

One is the way that the backlog of applications has to be processed. In April 2008, this backlog had reached more than 925,000 applicants, of which 570,000 were in the "skilled worker" category. Those applications have to be processed by date of receipt within each broad category mentioned earlier (CIC 2007). In fact, contrary to an entrenched belief, Canada is not "selecting" its immigrants. It is only applying points on a "first in, first out" basis. There is no guarantee that the country will get what it needs to meet labour market needs. The Quebec system is different, but no assessment of the results of its approach has been carried out yet.

The federal minister is implementing changes that allow priority processing (House of Commons, Bill C-50, which became law in June 2008). It should be understood that the number of applicants being admitted each year is determined by the Annual Plan tabled by the minister. The most recent plans have called for the admission of between 240,000 and 265,000 new permanent residents. There is not much debate about these numbers, and politicians have said in the past that the yearly total objective should be to admit 300,000 or roughly 1 percent of the Canadian population. The Conservative government of Brian Mulroney set this target in the early 1990s. It was not questioned by the following Liberal government of Jean Chrétien. The objective, however, was never met.

The second challenge, considering that resources are finite, is the processing times for immigrants, which had increased by 20 percent by 2007, with times for skilled workers seeing the biggest increases (CIC, backlog date 2007). The contrast with Australia is stark: Information released in 2008 showed that the Canadian average for processing Economic Class visa applications was 33 months; in Australia, it was 6½ months (Hawthorne 2008; Panetta 2008; Stevenson 2008).

Third, there is a lack of connection between applicants' skills and labour market needs. A high proportion of immigrants have university degrees in engineering and computer sciences. Having a university degree gives more points when applications are reviewed. However, under the human capital approach, the field of study and where the degree has been obtained are only assessed to identify the number of equivalent years of schooling that the candidate will receive. Increasingly, stakeholders and policy-makers are asking themselves if this is appropriate. We will see later that this lack of responsiveness has led to ways of bringing a significant number of people to Canada through other mechanisms.

The Performance of Recent Immigrant Cohorts

In addition to problems with the immigration "system," there are also well-documented challenges associated with the "performance" of recent immigrants in Canada. For example, the 2006 census confirmed that recent immigrants to Canada face difficulty integrating into the labour market, even though between the years of 2001 and 2006, they were more likely than the Canadian-born population to have a university education: In 2006, the national unemployment rate for these immigrants was 11.5 percent, more than double the rate of 4.9 percent for the Canadian-born population (Zietsma 2007). Not surprisingly, given this fact, the incidence of low income among recent immigrants has increased. In 1980, 24.6 percent of recent immigrants were below the "low-income cut-off"; in 2000, the proportion had grown to 35.8 percent (Statistics Canada 2008). And according to research by the United Way of Greater Toronto, a growing proportion of economically marginalized recent immigrants in that city are settling in neighbourhoods of concentrated poverty—with negative implications across a range of important social outcomes, including literacy, educational attainment, and employment (United Way of Greater Toronto 2004).

When they do find work, evidence suggests that recent immigrants face growing challenges. For example, whereas in 1980 a new Canadian could realistically look forward to earnings on par with other Canadians within ten years, that is no longer the case (Statistics Canada 2008). In fact, the gap between Canadian-born and immigrants' earnings is widening. Census data from 2006 show that immigrant men on average earned only 63 cents for each dollar earned by those born in Canada; women made only 56 cents (see Figure 4) (ibid.).

FIGURE 4
Immigrant Men's Earnings As a Percentage (%) of the Canadian-born

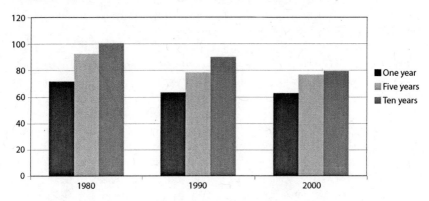

Source: Statistics Canada, censuses of population (1981, 1991, and 2001).

The earnings disparity is reflected in the phenomenon of "negative mismatching": That is, when immigrants do find work, they are more likely than Canadian-born workers to work in jobs requiring a level of education below what they have. In fact, 60 percent of immigrants with a university degree experience education-employment *negative mismatching*, whereas in 2005, Canadian workers with an identical level of education had a *negative mismatch rate* of 36 percent (HRSDC 2008).

Barriers to Integration

Commonly cited barriers to employment for recent immigrants include lack of Canadian work experience, lack of recognition of foreign credentials, and language barriers. But other factors could be added to this list: the impact of the business cycle, the concentration of immigrants in the three largest Canadian cities, and discrimination affecting certain visible minority groups. Professor Lesleyanne Hawthorne emphasizes the importance of language skills in her recent paper comparing the economic fortunes of economic migrants to Canada and Australia (Hawthorne 2008). Australia's recent immigrant outcomes have dramatically improved, thanks to a greater focus on the "core employability factors" of skill, age, and English language ability. The issue of foreign credential recognition has also received quite a bit of attention in recent years. Many jurisdictions in Canada are struggling with this issue. However, it is complicated, and there are valid reasons why foreign credentials are not recognized. The business cycle is another factor—for example, the bursting of the "technology bubble" in 2001 hit recent immigrants hard, as they were more likely than people born in Canada to have degrees in computer sciences or engineering.

Immigrants tend to settle in large cities like Toronto and Vancouver and to neglect smaller centres/provinces where jobs may be available. Finally, though hard to prove, the fact that recent immigrants' declining fortunes coincide with a growing proportion of visible minorities suggests that discrimination may also be a factor. In fact, recent Statistics Canada data based on the 2006 census show that certain immigrants are doing better than others, as well as their second and third generations, and that their ethnic/cultural background likely matters. "Chinese and Japanese surpass all other groups of newcomers, including whites, while for blacks and other groups, there is little or no economic mobility across generations" (Statistics Canada 2008).

IN SEARCH OF SOLUTIONS

The current government has introduced changes to Canada's immigration policy in budgets of recent years. The pressure started to grow when employers and their representatives could get the human resources that were needed but realized that the normal flow of "economic migrants" would not meet their needs, especially in the construction trades and in service jobs. The new measures are the following:

Significant Increase of Temporary Workers: Canadian employers, particularly in regions of the country where the economy is booming—for example, Alberta—put pressure on the federal government to allow in more temporary workers, for a wide array of jobs, including jobs in the oil and gas sector, and in the service and clerical sectors. In effect, the number of temporary workers in Alberta grew from 13,200 in 2004 to more than 38,000 at the end of 2007 (CIC, *Facts and Figures 2008*).

An unremarked side effect of the challenges facing the immigration system has been a significant increase in the number of temporary foreign workers (TFWs) in recent years. While the amount of TFWs should rise and fall with the business cycle, the overall good economic conditions in Canada have led to a constant increase during the past decade or so: from 77,500 in 1998, to 96,000 in 2001, to 126,000 in 2004, to more than 200,000 in 2007. The increase is coming mostly from lower-skilled occupations (see Figure 5). This is consistent with developments in the United States, where, according to the Migration Policy Institute, "employers have increasingly come to rely on the temporary migration system to gain access to the foreign workers they need because it is a faster, more efficient route with more predictable outcomes than the permanent system" (Batalova 2006, 5).

FIGURE 5
Temporary Foreign Workers by Occupational Skill Level, 1999–2008

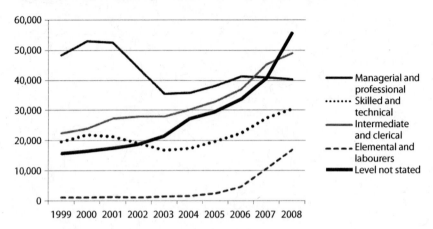

Source: Citizenship and Immigration Canada, *Facts and Figures 2008*.

The top source countries for TFWs in Canada are the United States, Mexico, France, the Philippines, Australia, and the United Kingdom. When compared to the main source countries of permanent residents, it is clear that there is a significant difference between source countries for permanent residents (mostly from Asia) and for temporary workers—most of whom come from English-speaking countries.

Expansion of the Provincial Nominee Program (PNP): Provinces also reacted. All provinces now are "nominating" candidates who are fast-tracked by Citizenship and Immigration Canada (CIC). Some 17,000 immigrants were admitted under the PNP in 2007, as compared to 6,000 in 2004 (CIC, *Facts and Figures 2007*). Less-skilled workers are admissible under the program, as long as they are nominated by a province.

Creation of the Canadian Experience Class: In September 2008, the government formally introduced the Canadian Experience Class, a new class of economic immigrants that can apply from within Canada. Temporary foreign workers with at least two years of full-time skilled work experience in Canada or foreign graduates from a Canadian post-secondary institution with at least one year of full-time skilled work experience in Canada are admissible. The actual impact of this change is still unknown.

Power Given to the Minister to Determine Who Will Be Processed: Until the recent amendments to the *Immigration and Refugee Protection Act* (IRPA), approved in April 2008, applications in the largest backlog—federal skilled workers—had to be processed in the order in which they were received, regardless of whether the applicants' skills or professions would enable them to find a job in Canada. CIC will now have greater flexibility in processing certain categories of applications; ministerial instructions will identify which categories will be prioritized for processing. A list of 38 of priority occupations was approved initially, subsequently reduced to 29 occupations.

It is clear that these measures over time could substantially change the composition of skilled immigration to Canada. Taking into account the fixed, and even decreasing, resources for processing applications, those admitted under the *federal* Economic Class will decrease, as those in other subcategories are increasing.[3]

WHAT HAS THE PUBLIC POLICY FORUM LEARNED?

In recent years, the Public Policy Forum (PPF) has conducted a series of research and dialogue projects on immigration. Through these projects, the PPF has made a number of key findings, which will be detailed below, regarding reforming the immigration selection system; foreign credential recognition; the role of employers; and engaging local communities.

Selection As a Key to Integration

Some researchers and practitioners are concerned that the immigration system may not be attracting immigrants with the right skills to meet labour market needs. The practical outcome of the 2002 IRPA reforms was that thousands of university-educated immigrants have settled in Canada's big three cities, in labour markets that may not necessarily accommodate them, at least in terms of matching education with jobs. The effect of the 2002 reforms was thus to create unrealistic expectations for immigrants, and to overvalue education at the expense of skilled trades.

This was one of the key messages from a 2006 PPF conference in Toronto entitled "Integrating Immigrants: Building Partnerships that Work." Participants at our event made three broad suggestions in reaction to this situation.

First, *modify the selection system for the Economic Class* to better reflect the labour market needs of receiving communities. Employers can play an important role by being involved in discussions with federal officials on immigrant selection criteria and numbers, helping the government develop a better understanding of labour market needs in destination communities.

Second, *the improvement of pre-migration language screening and skill certification is key.* Equivalent credentials and language skills are critical for immigrants to integrate successfully into the labour market. Many participants agreed that if economic immigrants are to be chosen based on these criteria, the equivalency of their credentials and level of language attainment should be assessed prior to immigration. As mentioned earlier, Australia has adopted this approach with success. In fact, immigration services prior to arrival—in general—should be improved, particularly with respect to employment opportunities, the benefits of living in smaller centres, and as a "reality check" to reduce misconceptions.

Third, *develop the foreign students program and build a link from it to permanent residency.* With the introduction of the Canadian Experience Class, the federal government has moved in this direction. The idea of this admission class is to attract the best and brightest to Canadian universities and to offer these people the opportunity to stay on as permanent residents; at least the United Kingdom and Australia are already doing this. This measure is bringing a large number of post-secondary students to Australia, and it will likely lead to increases in Canada, where tuition fees are low compared to those in the United States. This approach offers a route to citizenship for newcomers who are already integrating into Canadian society. It would also help "regionalize" immigration, as foreign students study across the country, not just in Toronto.

Foreign Credential Recognition

Foreign credential recognition—that is, the verifying that foreign education diplomas are equivalent to Canadian standards—has become a major barrier to immigrants trying to obtain work in Canada in their field of study. The current situation is characterized by a mismatch between excess supply of skilled immigrants and excess demand in some sectors—the taxi driver with a Ph.D. has become a cliché in Canada. Foreign credential recognition is seen as an important part of the solution to this mismatch—that is, "if only employers would recognize skills and experience earned abroad."

Yet, the situation is more complex than that. First, there is a wide variety of occupations, both regulated and unregulated, with varying approaches to credentialization and certification. Second, there is a large and complex group of stakeholders that are implicated in foreign credential recognition, including provincial governments, regulatory bodies, assessment agencies, employers, and post-secondary institutions. Third, Canada's federal structure means that credentials recognized in one province may not be recognized in another. Provinces have taken steps toward full interprovincial labour mobility, but this has proven to be a long and arduous process. Fourth, as mentioned previously, prospective immigrants need more pre-arrival resources with respect to labour market information, the realities of life in Canada, and language and credential assessment. This raises challenges in achieving the right balance between promoting Canada as a destination and preparing immigrants for life in Canada.

Finally, there is the reality that not all credentials are in fact equivalent. This reality shows the importance of pre-arrival resources that clearly spell out the requirements of various professions. It is well documented that credentials and work experience are discounted by employers and other actors. Canadian training and standards may be different than in the country where the individual was trained. It remains that not all universities have the same academic standards. While this is a quite imperfect measure, QS (Quacquarelli Symonds), a global career and education network, identifies only ten universities from China (including Hong Kong) and two from India as among the top 200 universities in the world. These numbers can be compared to 54 from the United States and 29 from the United Kingdom (Quacquarelli Symonds 2008).

Bridging programs have been shown to be useful to help close the educational gap. Some professions require some Canadian work experience before you can be licensed. This is not always a superficial requirement. Engineers Canada, for example, wants foreign-trained engineers to understand how Canada's unique climate affects their work (Public Policy Forum 2008). Connecting programs, such as apprenticeships and internships, can help bridge that gap by providing Canadian work experience.

The Role of Employers

Another finding that emerged from Public Policy Forum (PPF) research is the need to engage employers on these issues. In 2004, the PPF conducted a survey among employers about their experiences with recent immigrants. The survey revealed that while employers have a positive attitude toward immigration, they also tend to overlook immigrants in human resources planning, do not hire them at the level for which they were trained, and face challenges integrating immigrants into the workforce. Canadian work experience is by far the biggest constraint: Fifty percent of respondents said that experience in Canada was required, or that foreign experience was not considered equivalent, particularly in the public sector. Language skills were also cited as a factor. On the basis of these findings, the Forum came up with some recommendations and tested them with focus groups and at a conference.

Although previously mentioned in the context of reforming the selection system, an important awareness that came out in our discussions was *the need to engage employers in receiving communities* (Greater Toronto Area, Greater Vancouver Area, Island of Montreal) in discussions on immigration selection and numbers.

There is a need to build *awareness among employers* through better human resources information for employers on the foreign skills, training, and experience of recent immigrants in their communities, to help employers strategically take advantage of immigrants' skill sets in their communities. A secondary purpose would be that information on employer requests would help identify current and future labour market needs. Also, employers in smaller centres should be included in "regionalization" strategies. This would help to encourage immigrants to settle outside of Montreal, Toronto, and Vancouver—and given demographic trends, attracting immigrants will be important for future regional economic development.

It is necessary to *support workplace training and development*, through government-funded work placements, internships, mentoring, and occupation-specific language training. A good example would be "Career Bridge," an initiative of the Toronto Region Immigrant Employment Council (TRIEC), a multi-stakeholder group initially funded by the Ontario Ministry of Training, Colleges and Universities. Career Bridge provides work experience for immigrants through subsidized paid internships.

Engaging Communities

Although immigration policy is often nationally driven, newcomers work, access services, and interact with Canadians at the local level. More than 70 percent of immigrants settle in Canada's three largest cities, with Montreal at 11.8 percent, Toronto at 43.3 percent, and Vancouver at 17.7 percent (Canadian Labour and Business Centre 2004). As a result of demographic trends, smaller centres are at risk of experiencing population decline and labour shortages. It is therefore important that immigration policy be designed to encourage immigration to smaller centres.

At the PPF conference on the role of employers, participants highlighted the importance of community-level work in coordinating local stakeholders on immigration-related issues. With the vast majority of immigrants settling in Canada's three largest cities, much of the integration of immigrants in Canada happens in the communities of Toronto, Vancouver, and Montreal. Add to this the number of players involved—from federal, provincial, and municipal governments; non-profit organizations; community groups; and businesses—and you have a complex web of stakeholders operating at the local level.

Accordingly, in 2005, the PPF invited representatives from 26 communities to exchange information on local-level initiatives that seek to integrate immigrants into the labour market and into society in general. In this forum, the PPF heard a number of key messages:

- The first was the *importance of governance*. Successful integration of immigrants requires multi-*stakeholder coordination at the local level*. This includes the coordination across levels of government and between government departments of integration services and programs—all of which play out in communities.

- Secondly, local *realities should inform federal and provincial frameworks.* This means that local communities should be involved in shaping these policy frameworks—as already mentioned in the case of employers being involved in discussions around immigrant selection and the number to be received.
- Finally, as is often the case, it comes down to *funding.* Coordinating locally based multi-stakeholder efforts to integrate recent immigrants costs money. Government funding of non-profit organizations is focused on "project funding," however, which ignores the cost of supporting engagement efforts and coordination more generally.

Employment Assistance, Occupation-Specific Language Training, and Bridging Programs

A number of programs funded by the federal government and by provincial governments are available to recent newcomers. They range from basic language training to occupation-specific language training, where immigrants learn the specific vocabulary needed for their profession or area of work.

Various forms of employment assistance programs also exist, ranging from advice as to how to find a job, to resumé writing, to job search seminars, to internships of varied duration. Career Bridge is one of these programs that is having good success. Certain people need specialized advice. For example, professionals in health care and other technical professions have access in Toronto to an office operated by the Government of Ontario that will help them understand the maze of accessing professions in Ontario.

Bridging programs are essentially formal training programs that operate alongside other programs whose goals are to better integrate immigrants within the Canadian workforce. These other programs include those that provide information pre-arrival, those that provide information post-arrival, and those that offer assessment of foreign-acquired skills and credentials. Bridging programs assume that there is a training or work experience gap that has been properly assessed. Although such programs can be an important tool for allowing skilled immigrants to exercise their profession more quickly and for providing useful integration mechanisms, a number of problems exist concerning their availability by profession and location, as well as their continued funding and accessibility to participants. Bridging programs are still in their infancy, and better coordination is needed among provinces and with the federal government. Policy changes should be considered with respect to ensuring their continued funding and providing student aid. The PPF has published a report on bridging programs (see PPF January 2008).

CONCLUSION

It is important to note that in comparison to many countries, Canada has a positive story to tell on immigration. Canadians have an overall positive attitude towards immigration, which is reflected in polling numbers. This has also translated into Canada's political culture. Canadian political parties seem to understand the significance of immigration in Canada, showing no sign of decreasing the current immigration numbers. What seems to differ from party to party is a polarization of focus; the Left's focus is more on social justice, while the Right's is more on skilled labour.

Nevertheless, as Canada undergoes significant changes with its immigration system, and as integration problems become more and more evident, the direction of future immigration to Canada is not as easy as it seemed some years ago. Skilled immigrants and international students are very mobile resources; and Canada's open-door approach has created enormous expectations that are impossible to fill. Does keeping a very large number of applicants forever make sense? Why are too many recent immigrants poor? How should Canada deal with the integration challenges related to second-generation visible minority populations? What are the longer-term consequences of the significant increase in temporary workers? How can labour market needs be taken into account in a way that is not subject to continued variation and sudden economic fluctuations? Should yearly levels for the Economic Class be adjusted to economic conditions, such as the unemployment rate?

Relative success in integrating immigrants has been because of policies and the positive attitude of a large majority of Canadians. For sure, the large number of jobs created by the Canadian economy and our flexible labour legislation have been an important contributing factor. But as Canada may be entering a recession, this paradigm will not work anymore, and things can turn from bad to worse.

This leaves many avenues open to explore. Canada, in my view, must look at how to involve communities and cities in the planning of the number of immigrants to admit and the funding level of integration programs. This can be accomplished through the creation of local immigration advisory committees. Canada must increase co-operation with provinces and define medium-term labour market needs, based on a set of economic and demographic projections. There is a need to review foreign credentials prior to an immigrant's arrival, as well as language capacity, and to properly inform applicants of the immigration process. Canada must also look at expanding employment assistance and bridging programs.

NOTES

1. The views expressed in this chapter are those of the author alone.
2. The Public Policy Forum, established in 1987, is an independent, not-for-profit organization aimed at improving the quality of government in Canada through better dialogue between the public, private, and voluntary sectors (www.ppforum.ca). The Forum's members, drawn from business, federal and provincial governments, the voluntary sector, and organized labour, share a belief that an efficient and effective public service is important in ensuring Canada's competitiveness abroad and quality of life at home. The research program of the Forum provides a neutral base to inform collective decision-making. By promoting more information sharing and greater links between governments and other sectors, the Forum helps to ensure that public policy in Canada is dynamic, coordinated, and responsive to future challenges and opportunities.
3. Economic Class includes the following subcategories (all divided into principal applicant, and spouse and dependants): (a) skilled workers; (b) provincial nominees; (c) live-in caregivers; and (d) entrepreneurs, investors, and self-employed. As the total remains the same, and (b) and (c) are increasing, (a) will decrease; (d) remains stable.

REFERENCES

Batalova, J. 2006. *The Growing Connection Between Temporary and Permanent Immigration Systems.* No. 14, January. Washington, DC: Independent Task Force on Immigration and America's Future, Migration Policy Institute.

Bouchard, G., and C. Taylor. Commission de Consultation sur les pratiques d'accommodement reliées aux différences culturelles, Québec. 2008. *Building the Future: A Time for Reconciliation.* Report. Quebec: Gouvernement du Québec.

Canadian Labour and Business Centre (CLBC). 2004. *CLBC Handbook: Immigration and Skills Shortages.* Ottawa: CLBC. At http://www.clbc.ca/files/Reports/Immigration_Handbook.pdf.

Chui, T., K. Tran, and H. Maheux. 2008. *Ethnic Origin and Visible Minorities, 2006 Census.* Statistics Canada. At http://www12.statcan.gc.ca/english/census06/analysis/ethnicorigin/pdf/97-562-xie2006001.pdf.

Citizenship and Immigration Canada (CIC). Various years. *Statistics.* At http://www.cic.gc.ca/english/resources/statistics/index.asp.

Competition Policy Review Panel. 2008. *Compete to Win.* Final Report, June. Ottawa: Government of Canada.

Fortin, J., and P. Loewen. 2004. Asymmetrical Opinion Structures and Attitudes Toward Immigration in Canada. Paper presented at the annual meeting of the American Political Science Association, Hilton Chicago and the Palmer House Hilton, Chicago, IL, 2 September. At http://www.allacademic.com/meta/p59782_index.html.

Hawthorne, L. 2008. The Impact of Economic Selection Policy on Labour Market Outcomes for Degree-Qualified Migrants in Canada and Australia. *IRPP Choices* 14 (5), May. Montreal: Institute for Research on Public Policy (IRPP). At http://www.irpp.org/choices/archive/vol14no5.pdf.

Hiebert, D. 2006. Skilled Immigration in Canada: Context, Patterns, and Outcomes. In *Evaluation of the General Skilled Migration Categories*, eds. B. Birrell et al., 175-216. Canberra, Australia: Commonwealth of Australia. At http://www. pieronline.org/_Upload/Files/2006512103325_GSMReport.pdf.

Human Resources and Social Development Canada (HRSDC). 2008. Do Recent Immigrants Find Tailor-made Jobs in Canada? Unpublished report.

Nanos, N. 2008. Nation Building Through Immigration: Workforce Skills Comes Out on Top. *Policy Options*, June, 30-32. Montreal: Institute for Research on Public Policy (IRPP). At http://www.irpp.org/po/archive/jun08/nanos.pdf.

Panetta, A. 2008. Immigration wait-time surge angers Liberals. *Toronto Star*, 11 February.

Quacquarelli Symonds. 2008. QS Top Universities: Top 100 Universities in THE—QS World University Rankings. At http://www.topuniversities.com/index.php?id=758.

Sears, R.V. 2008. Canada: If You Build It, People Will Come. *Policy Options*, June, 38-44. Montreal: Institute for Research on Public Policy (IRPP). At http://www. irpp.org/po/archive/jun08/sears.pdf.

Statistics Canada. 2008. *Earnings and Incomes of Canadians Over the Past Quarter Century, 2006 Census: Findings*. 5 May. Statistics Canada. At http://www12. statcan.ca/english/census06/analysis/income/index.cfm.

Stevenson, M., ed. 2008. Good for Canada? We certainly hope so. *Maclean's*, 2 April, p. 2.

United Way of Greater Toronto. 2004. *Poverty by Postal Code: The Geography of Neighbourhood Poverty, 1981–2001*.

Zietsma, D. 2007. *The Canadian Immigrant Labour Market in 2006: First Results from Canada's Labour Force Survey*. Statistics Canada, Labour Statistics Division. At http://www.statcan.gc.ca/pub/71-606-x/71-606-x2007001-eng.htm.

Public Policy Forum (PPF) Reports on Immigration

(All of these reports can be downloaded free of charge from www.ppforum.ca.)

Bringing Employers into the Immigration Debate—Survey and Conference (November 2004)

Engaging Local Communities in Immigration Matters (June 2005)

Building Our Cities; Recognizing the Importance of Immigration (November 2005)

Integrating Immigrants, Building Partnerships That Work (March 2006)

Prosperity, Diversity and Citizenship (April 2006)

Comparing Approaches to Recognizing the Skills and Credentials of Foreign-Trained Workers (April 2007)

Improving Bridging Programs (January 2008)

Canada and the EU: Prospects for a Closer Economic Partnership (June 2008)

Labour Mobility Between Canada and the European Union: Current State and Future Prospects (May 2008)

From Integration to Participation (November 2008)

CHAPTER 7

The Economic Integration of Immigrants in Canada and the Quebec Difference

JACK JEDWAB, *Executive Director, Association for Canadian Studies (ACS, Montreal) and International Association for the Study of Canada (IASC)*

INTRODUCTION

Over the past decade, several studies have pointed to a declining labour market and the declining financial performance of recent immigrants to Canada. While the difference in immigrant/non-immigrant earnings generally diminishes over time, it is increasingly held that more recent waves of immigrants are encountering greater difficulties, as reflected in a widening of the income gap. Given these conditions, questions have increasingly been raised about whether the earnings of the more recent immigrant cohorts will ever "catch up" to those of their Canadian-born counterparts (Frenette and Morissette 2003). Moreover, since the early 1980s, the share of recent immigrants with low income has increased markedly despite rising levels of educational attainment among this group (Heisz and McLeod 2004; Picot et al. 2007).

Several explanations have been offered as to why the presumed gap is currently wider than it has been previously. Economic and/or cultural arguments are often advanced to account for the gap. The matter has moved to the centre of debate about the levels of immigration in the

Managing Immigration and Diversity in Canada: A Transatlantic Dialogue in the New Age of Migration, ed. D. Rodríguez-García. Montreal and Kingston: Queen's Policy Studies Series, McGill-Queen's University Press.

country, with a small minority of Canadians arguing that the gap suggests a need to rethink the number and/or source countries of immigrants. As there seem to be no credible political leaders that argue for reducing the number of immigrants, debate in the country centres to a far greater extent around the matter of immigrant integration (although even this issue was not picked up by the political leadership and had no resonance with voters in the 2008 federal election campaign).

To properly assess the phenomenon of immigrant labour market integration, ideally both quantitative and qualitative analysis should be conducted. By confining assessment of immigrant integration to empirical measure, there is a risk of providing an incomplete view of the process. In effect, the expectations of the immigrant and of the host society merit consideration when evaluating integration. Often, the notion of integration presumes that the burden for adaptation rests almost entirely upon the immigrant. This idea underestimates the importance of societal norms and the structures in place to facilitate the integration process. Moreover, where the entire burden for integration is placed upon the immigrant, the presence of societal discrimination is overlooked.

Those measuring the economic condition of immigrants generally employ such traditional benchmarks as "earnings/income" and "rates of employment" and proceed to make comparisons both between the immigrant and the non-immigrant and amongst immigrants themselves based on their length of residence in Canada. Observers correctly note that meaningful comparisons can be a challenge when focusing on the respective condition of immigrants and non-immigrants, as a variety of factors need consideration when drawing conclusions. Economic performance of immigrants may be influenced by such things as age at immigration, knowledge of official languages, share of foreign education, domestic work experience, and place of birth.

Some analysts have argued that in addition to the comparison between the foreign-born and those born in the country, the conditions of the immigrant in the new country should be compared with their situation in the country of origin. Workers with weak employment or earnings situations in their country of origin may find that job and income security in their new country represent progress, thus contributing to a heightened degree of life satisfaction. This may be the case even if their job situation does not fully correspond to their skills. This is where the issue of the "standards" established for successful integration enters the debate and invites the question of how the qualitative dimension of the immigrant experience gets taken into account.

For the most part, Canada's immigration policy is selective, and there is considerable focus on recruiting skilled immigrants that are regarded as best able to adjust to evolving economic circumstances. During the 1990s, much attention was directed at attracting immigrants with specific skills that matched the needs of the Canadian labour market. But changes in market requirements meant that the skills that seemed needed at one point in time did not correspond to changed conditions. Hence, at the beginning of the 21st century, Canada modified its selection criteria so as to accord more weight to the educational attainment of entrants. The short-term benefits of the strategy may not appear obvious to some observers, as there is considerable evidence that the income gaps between more recent waves of immigrants and the Canadian-born segment of the population are wider when compared to the situation of earlier waves of immigrants. On the other hand, Canada's human capital, as measured by the overall educational attainment level of the population, has increased substantially with the influx of highly educated immigrants.

That which follows will focus on the condition of recent immigrants in Canada and look at whether economic integration in the country can be deemed a success. Such traditional measures as gaps in employment and earnings between immigrants and non-immigrants will be included in assessing the nation's record in that area. When considering the issue of economic integration, special attention will be directed at those Canadians that identify as visible minorities. Thereafter, the qualitative aspect of immigrant integration will be considered through analysis of opinion surveys on perceived quality of life. Finally, this chapter will conclude with a focus on the province of Quebec and its challenge in addressing immigrant integration.

IMMIGRANT SELECTION PROCESS

Canada's immigration policy has been guided by three goals: to promote a strong economy across Canada, to reunite families, and to meet the country's international commitments and humanitarian tradition with regard to refugee claimants. These goals are reflected in the three principal categories for admission as a permanent resident to the country, notably Economic Class immigrants, Family Class immigrants, and Refugees. People admitted through the economic category include principal applicants (skilled workers, business immigrants, provincial/ territorial nominees, and live-in caregivers) and their accompanying spouses or dependants.

As observed in Table 1, whereas the number of permanent residents was nearly twice that of temporary workers in 2003, the substantial rise in temporary foreign workers since that year has seen this gap narrow quite substantially.

Declines in the number of immigrants occurred in every category between 2006 and 2007. The percentage of economic immigrants increased slightly between 2006 and 2007 despite a decline in real numbers of about 6 percent. The percentage of the Family Class remained the same in 2006 and 2007 (though there was a real decrease of approximately 5 percent). It was the percentage of refugees that fell from 12.9 percent to 11.8 percent, and this was accompanied by a 14 percent decrease in the numbers.

TABLE 1
Respective Stock of Temporary Foreign Workers and Permanent Residents in Canada, 2003–2007

	2003	2004	2005	2006	2007
Permanent Residents	221,349	235,823	262,240	251,643	236,758
Temporary Foreign Workers	110,476	126,031	141,743	162,046	201,057
Difference	110,837	109,729	120,497	89,597	35,001
% Difference	100%	85%	90%	55%	17.5%

Source: Citizenship and Immigration Canada, *Facts and Figures 2007*.

The 2006 census results revealed that the number of university degree holders has indeed grown substantially since 2001. In fact, Canada ranked sixth among all OECD (Organisation for Economic Co-operation and Development) countries in terms of the proportion of the adults aged 25 to 64 who had a university degree. One of the major demographic factors contributing to the rising level of university-educated Canadians has been the arrival of immigrants that, on average, are far more likely to possess university degrees than earlier immigrants or than the Canadian-born population. Census results for 2006 reveal that over half (51 percent) of recent immigrants, those who immigrated to Canada between 2001 and 2006, had a university degree. This was more than twice the proportion of degree holders among the Canadian-born population (20 percent) and also much higher than the proportion of degree holders among immigrants who arrived before 2001 (28 percent). By contrast, the percentage of the foreign-born population in the United States aged 25 and over with a bachelor's degree or more education (27.3 percent) was not statistically different from that of the native-born population (Larsen 2004).

The proportion of recent immigrant male earners with a university degree increased from 24.5 percent in 1980 to 58.2 percent in 2005. For Canadian-born male earners, the corresponding percentages were 14.1 percent and 19.9 percent, respectively. The educational attainment of recent immigrant women also rose much faster than that of their Canadian-born counterparts.

As Canada receives the vast majority of its immigration from outside Europe—that is, persons identifying predominantly as visible minorities—there is a growing gap between the educational level of Canada's visible minorities and that of the non-visible or white population. This difference is illustrated in Table 2 below. Since the visible minority population is younger on average than the overall population, focused attention has been given here to the group that is between the ages of 35 and 44 with a university certificate, diploma, or degree. As illustrated below, the immigrants aged 35 to 44 possess a considerably greater share of university degree holders than their non-immigrant counterparts. There are also vast differences across the groups. By far, the biggest gaps are between foreign- and Canadian-born of Korean background, white immigrants (those immigrants predominantly from Europe or the United States) versus whites born in Canada, as well as between foreign-born and Canadian-born Arab groups. In the case of Southeast Asian and Asian Canadians, the foreign-born are less likely than the Canadian-born to have a university degree.

TABLE 2
Percentage of Immigrants and Non-immigrants with a University Degree or Equivalent, Ages 35 to 44, by Visible Minority Identification, 2006

	Total %	Immigrants %	Non-immigrants %	Difference %
Total population	29.7	44.5	24.4	20.1
Total visible minority population	47.0	47.0	38.6	8.4
South Asian	47.4	47.3	51.7	−4.4
Filipino	58.6	58.3	53.5	4.8
Korean	74.7	74.6	58.0	16.6
Chinese	58.4	58.7	55.1	3.6
Japanese	48.5	47.5	46.5	1.0
West Asian	47.8	47.8	43.4	4.4
Arab	51.6	52.4	38.2	16.0
Southeast Asian	22.0	21.2	35.5	−14.3
Black	30.1	30.2	28.4	1.8
Latin American	33.0	32.6	25.6	7.0
Not a visible minority	25.9	39.7	24.1	15.6

Source: Statistics Canada, Census of Canada (2006).

As observed in Table 2, there is a difference of more than 20 percentage points in the share of university degree holders amongst visible minorities versus the white population. It is the group that identify themselves as Korean that has the highest level of university degree holders, at nearly 75 percent! Filipino and Chinese follow in second and third spot, at approximately 58 percent. The Southeast Asian and white populations are the least likely to possess a university degree.

There are also important differences in the rates of unemployment between the Canadian- and foreign-born populations, as well as between immigrant groups, with similar levels of educational attainment. Further, as seen in Table 3, the time of arrival of immigrants clearly plays an important role in the rate of unemployment of both the most educated segment of the white and visible minority foreign population. Amongst university degree holders, it is the Arab population followed by the Southeast Asian, West Asian, Black, and Latin American populations that arrived between 2001 and 2006 that possess the highest rates of unemployment.

TABLE 3
Rate of Unemployment by Percentage (%) for Non-immigrants and Immigrants, by Time of Arrival, by Visible Minority Identification, Ages 35 to 44, with a University Degree or Equivalent, 2006

	University Certificate, Diploma, or Degree	Non-immigrants	Immigrants	Before 1991	1991 to 1995	1996 to 2000	2001 to 2006
Total population	4.1	2.6	6.6	3.3	4.2	5.9	11.4
Total visible minority population	7.0	3.1	7.3	3.8	4.8	6.4	11.6
Chinese	6.5	2.7	6.9	3.1	4.1	6.2	11.1
South Asian	6.4	3.2	6.6	3.8	4.6	5.9	9.9
Black	8.1	3.7	8.9	5.3	7.3	7.8	15.1
Filipino	3.9	2.6	4.2	2.7	3.4	4.1	5.2
Latin American	10.1	5.1	10.0	5.6	4.6	6.5	15.0
Southeast Asian	5.0	–	5.3	2.1	6.2	7.2	15.9
Arab	13.5	1.3	14.1	4.6	6.7	11.4	23.9
West Asian	9.6	7.4	9.5	6.5	4.5	7.2	15.4
Korean	8.6	5.9	8.9	4.7	9.6	6.7	12.5
Not a visible minority	3.0	2.6	5.2	2.6	3.1	4.7	10.9

Source: Statistics Canada, Census of Canada (2006).

It is generally contended that educational attainment reduces unemployment. Yet data from the 2006 census of Canada suggest that educational attainment does not improve employment prospects across all groups of immigrants. It does, however, appear to make an important difference in the Black, Southeast Asian, and Korean groups.

TABLE 4
Rate of Unemployment by Percentage (%) for Non-immigrants and Immigrants, by Visible Minority Identification, Ages 35 to 44, by Level of Educational Attainment, 2006

	Total	No Certificate, Diploma, or Degree	High School Certificate or Equivalent	Apprenticeship or Trades Certificate or Diploma	University Certificate or Diploma below Bachelor	University Certificate, Diploma, or Degree
Total population	6.4	7.9	6.4	6.1	6.7	6.6
Total visible minority population	7.2	9.0	7.3	6.9	7.1	7.3
Chinese	7.0	6.8	7.4	6.0	8.1	6.9
South Asian	6.5	8.2	7.1	5.3	5.8	6.6
Black	8.8	13.6	9.2	9.0	9.4	8.9
Filipino	3.9	4.9	4.4	2.8	3.3	4.2
Latin American	8.3	9.6	8.0	6.2	8.9	10.0
Southeast Asian	6.7	8.8	7.0	6.0	5.2	5.3
Arab	13.5	15.5	9.2	13.4	15.5	14.1
West Asian	8.7	12.6	8.7	7.5	6.5	9.5
Korean	7.9	15.4	5.5	8.9	6.6	8.9
Not a visible minority	5.0	5.6	4.8	5.1	5.6	5.2

Source: Statistics Canada, Census of Canada (2006).

Clearly, the above data suggest that recent immigrants and certain groups are especially vulnerable to situations of unemployment despite their degree of educational attainment. However, at least insofar as immigrant status is concerned, the employment gaps do appear to narrow over time. It is unlikely that simply securing a job is the principal challenge for a new immigrant; rather, the difficulty is often with finding employment that is consistent with one's skills and that meets aspirations. Issues of underemployment need to be considered when establishing a barometer or benchmark for immigrant integration.

As the unemployment rate in Canada declined across the period 1991 to 2006, so too was there an improvement in the employment situation of Canada's visible minorities. But the broad decrease in unemployment rates does not mean that disparities in levels of employment between various groups have diminished. It is the gaps in rates of unemployment between various groups of immigrants, on the one hand, and between immigrants and the Canadian-born, on the other, that is often considered an important test of the success of integration. In Table 5 below, the rates of unemployment are provided for immigrants resident in Toronto (the city with Canada's largest number and share of immigrants) in the five years prior to the census being conducted. There has been much said about the greater challenges encountered by recent immigrants in securing employment relative to previous groups in their first five years of settlement. Nonetheless, the 2006 census results do not offer evidence in support of this observation. Although the difference is not substantial, immigrants had a lower rate of unemployment over the five years from 2001 to 2006 than those who in 2001 had settled over the five years prior. This applied to nearly all groups, with the exception of the Filipino, Southeast Asian, and Korean groups (Arab and West Asian groups were combined in the previous census).

TABLE 5
Rate of Unemployment by Percentage (%) Amongst Immigrants, According to Visible Minority Identification, Ages 35 to 44, with a University Degree, That Entered Country Within the Five Years Prior to the Census, and Resident in Toronto, 1991–2006

Toronto, 35 to 44 Years	2006	2001	1996	1991
Total population	9.7	11.4	15.3	11.2
Total visible minority population	10.0	11.2	15.8	10.6
Chinese	11.2	12.6	15.5	7.8
South Asian	9.7	10.7	18.3	11.0
Black	11.6	11.1	19.7	9.9
Filipino	4.8	4.5	8.9	7.7
Latin American	10.8	9.4	14.4	13.5
Southeast Asian	12.8	11.5	17.4	19.0
Arab	16.1	14.8	23.6	20.2
Korean	12.2	13.3	7.1	6.7
All others	8.7	12.1	14.5	12.8

Source: Statistics Canada, Census of Canada (2006).

Policy-makers have also taken an increasing interest in the condition of the Canadian-born visible minority population to determine whether the children and grandchildren of visible minority immigrants are attaining economic parity with other Canadians. Some wrongly describe this as a debate about integration, when it is better labelled as a discussion of whether, as a society, the social conditions reflect principles of fairness and equal opportunity. But in order to properly assess the disparities in the levels of unemployment between white and visible minority populations, on the one hand, and between the various groups identifying as visible minorities, on the other, it would be important to consider such things as immigrant status, age, level of education, and gender. Some of the disparities in employment have been documented above by focusing on education, immigrant status, and controlling for age. In the next section, the focus will be upon differences in income.

IMMIGRANT INCOME AND ECONOMIC INTEGRATION

Income gaps are a possible outcome when the type of employment secured by immigrants is not consistent with their background or skills. Successful economic integration should be associated with income and employment parity between immigrants and non-immigrants with similar characteristics. A Statistics Canada analysis from the 2006 census on the earnings and incomes of Canadians over the past quarter century notes that as recent immigrants (those arriving between 2000 and 2004) integrate into the Canadian labour market, they initially confront difficulties finding full-time, full-year employment as well as locating jobs that pay relatively high wages (Statistics Canada 2008b). Between 1980 and 2005, the earnings gap between recent immigrants and the Canadian-born worker widened significantly. In 1980, recent male immigrants with employment income earned 85 cents for each dollar received by Canadian-born males. By 2005, the same ratio dropped to 63 cents. The corresponding figures for recent immigrant women were 85 cents and 56 cents, respectively. The gap

TABLE 6
Median Earnings in Canada (C$) for the Canadian-born Population,
the Overall Immigrant Population, and Recent Immigrants (2001–2005)

Canada	Canadian-born		Immigrant Population		Recent Immigrants (2001–2005)	
	With University Degree	Without University Degree	With University Degree	Without University Degree	With University Degree	Without University Degree
1995	$48,805	$30,526	$40,394	$27,115	$24,368	$18,347
2000	$50,668	$33,101	$40,343	$29,142	$30,222	$20,840
2005	$51,656	$32,499	$36,451	$27,698	$24,636	$18,572

Source: Statistics Canada (2008b).

widened despite a rise in the educational attainment of recent immigrant earners as compared to the Canadian-born during this 25-year period. The gap in median earnings between recent immigrant men and women and their Canadian-born counterparts widened both for individuals with a university degree and for those without a university degree.

Explaining the Gaps

It appears that those who entered the labour market in the mid-1980s generally experienced lower levels of earnings instability in the initial years of their work experience in Canada than those who entered the labour market in the mid-1990s. The results seem to support the prevailing view that the economic fortunes of immigrants in Canada in recent years have declined in wages (Statistics Canada 2008b).

While the income gaps have indeed widened, the central question is whether, as assumed by some observers, this is a function of a problem of immigrant integration. Analysts at Statistics Canada have proposed a number of explanations for the recent widening in the immigrant/non-immigrant income gap. One of the reasons offered relates to the needs of the market in a given period and the extent to which the skills possessed by economic immigrants matched those needs. For example, the decline in employment in the information and communication technologies (ICT) sector between 2000 and 2005 had an important impact on the earnings of recent immigrants. This occurred because of the important share of immigrants trained in such professions. Statistics Canada notes that in 2005, nearly one in ten recent immigrant men with a university diploma possessed a degree in computer sciences, while four in ten had a degree in engineering. The corresponding proportions among their Canadian-born counterparts were 4.3 percent and 13.3 percent only. Between 2000 and 2005, median earnings fell 29.2 percent among recent immigrant men who had a degree in computer sciences. They fell 20.0 percent among those with a degree in engineering. However, the decline was only 10.7 percent among those with degrees in other fields of study, and only 5.7 percent among those without degrees. In contrast, median earnings fell only 5.3 percent among Canadian-born men who had a degree in computer sciences. Furthermore, they rose slightly among those with a degree in engineering, those with degrees in other fields of study, and those without a university degree.

The earnings gap between recent immigrants and Canadian-born workers was larger among individuals with a university degree than among their less educated counterparts. In 2005, recent immigrant men with a university degree earned only 48 cents for each dollar received by Canadian-born male university graduates. In contrast, recent immigrant men without a university degree earned 61 cents for each dollar received by their Canadian-born counterparts. Similar patterns were observed among recent immigrant women.

Larger earnings disparities were present among university graduates, where many recent immigrants with a degree were employed in low-skilled occupations. For instance, in 2005, 29.8 percent of recent immigrant male university graduates worked in occupations normally requiring no more than a high school education. This was more than twice the 11.5 percent rate among their Canadian-born counterparts. Similarly, recent immigrant women with a university degree were more likely to work in low-skilled occupations than their Canadian-born counterparts.

In 2005, median earnings of recent immigrant male university graduates aged 25 to 54 were 24 percent higher than those of their counterparts without a university degree. The corresponding proportion among Canadian-born individuals was 55.5 percent, more than twice as high. As a result, recent immigrants with a university degree had lower median earnings than Canadian-born individuals of comparable age with no university degree. Thus, recent immigrant men with a degree had median earnings of C$30,332, about 24.6 percent below the level of Canadian-born men without a university degree.

TABLE 7
Earnings Gaps in Percentage Between Immigrants and Non-immigrants in Canada with and/or Without a University Degree for the Years 1995, 2000, and 2005

With a University Degree/Born in Canada Versus Born Outside of Canada			Without a University Degree/Born in Canada Versus Born Outside of Canada		
1995	2000	2005	1995	2000	2005
–17.5%	–20.5%	–29.5%	–11.0%	–12.5%	–15.0%

Source: Statistics Canada (2008b).

Though the economy improved over the late 1990s through to 2006, most analysts acknowledge that there was a widening of the gap in income between the wealthier and poorer segments of the Canadian population. One of the principal disparities to which Canadian census data draw attention is the widening gap in earnings between immigrants and non-immigrants, and, notably, those respectively holding university degrees. Indeed, between 2000 and 2005, the median earnings of immigrants holding a university degree dropped by approximately 10 percent nationally. Hence, it appears safe to conclude that there was a decline in the dollar value of a university degree. It is worth noting that there are important regional variations in income gaps between immigrants and non-immigrants. The 2006 census reveals an approximate 10 percent difference in employment income between immigrant and non-immigrant full-time workers in Canada aged 25 to 44. As observed below in Table 8, the income gap widened between immigrants and non-immigrants in 2000 and 2005. At just over 40 percent, the gap was widest in Toronto and Calgary and lowest in Halifax and Ottawa.

TABLE 8
Average Employment Income in Canada and Selected Cities, in Constant Dollars (C$), for Immigrants and Non-immigrants with a University Degree Between the Ages of 25 and 54 That Worked Full Year, Full Time in 2000 and 2005

	Year	Total	Non-immigrants	Immigrants
Canada	2000	$64,807	$66,224	$59,642
	2005	$65,296	$68,104	$57,996
Halifax	2000	$56,378	$56,472	$55,343
	2005	$56,693	$56,843	$56,712
Montreal	2000	$61,654	$63,377	$53,651
	2005	$61,286	$64,374	$50,704
Ottawa	2000	$72,869	$73,540	$70,807
	2005	$71,138	$72,441	$67,450
Toronto	2000	$73,659	$81,876	$61,447
	2005	$72,838	$84,983	$59,581
Hamilton	2000	$67,168	$68,612	$60,700
	2005	$68,415	$70,518	$60,621
Winnipeg	2000	$56,312	$57,677	$49,768
	2005	$56,983	$58,990	$49,570
Calgary	2000	$76,225	$79,240	$64,090
	2005	$81,364	$88,316	$64,081
Edmonton	2000	$59,930	$62,014	$52,659
	2005	$63,821	$66,862	$55,875
Vancouver	2000	$63,366	$68,329	$55,485
	2005	$61,544	$67,592	$54,526

Source: Statistics Canada, Census of Canada (2006).

Some observers attribute the inequality of immigrant earnings to the degree of official-language knowledge, to place of birth, and to foreign education. There is some evidence that the effect of a foreign education on earnings inequality is gradually increasing as immigrants adjust to the labour market in their new country. When it comes to rates of unemployment, it appears from the table below (see Table 9) that earning a degree abroad does not have an impact on persons born in Canada, and, in fact, in the case of immigrants, with the exception of those arriving prior to 1991, those earning a university degree outside of Canada have a lower rate of unemployment than those who earned one within the country.

TABLE 9
Rate of Unemployment by Percentage (%) for Non-immigrants and Immigrants Between the Ages of 35 and 44, by Time of Arrival, with University Certificate, That Earned Degree Either Inside or Outside of Canada

2006 Census, University Degree, 35 to 44 Years of Age	Inside Canada	Outside Canada
Total	2.9	7.2
Non-immigrants	2.6	2.6
Immigrants	4.5	7.8
Before 1991	3.1	4.1
1991 to 2000	5.8	5.2
1991 to 1995	4.7	4.0
1996 to 2000	6.9	5.7
2001 to 2006	13.1	11.3

Source: Statistics Canada, Census of Canada (2006).

Yet Further Explaining the Gaps

A study amongst new immigrants, prepared for Human Resources and Social Development Canada (Phoenix Strategic Perspectives 2008), revealed that the two challenges that stood out for them most in terms of working in Canada were the requirement for prior Canadian work experience and foreign credential recognition, including, notably, the inability to work in one's field.

Other challenges frequently mentioned by the immigrants surveyed included accepting that one will probably begin life in Canada at a lower level than expected, how to go about looking for work, and establishing a network of contacts. Immigrant service providers, also interviewed for the survey, tended to mention similar concerns when describing the principal challenges that immigrants would encounter upon arrival. The service providers also stressed the need for immigrants to know what jobs were in demand in Canada and said that too frequently, information was not sought in the country of origin about work in Canada.

With regard to this issue, some service providers observed that many new immigrants tend to think of Canada and North America in general as lands of abundant opportunity, where there will be no problem finding work and improving one's quality of life. This view tended to diminish the need to better prepare for conditions in Canada. Immigration briefings prior to one's departure for Canada may further contribute to the optimism, as some were left with the impression that their skills and expertise were required. Many participants said that newcomers should not expect that after arriving in Canada, they will quickly or easily find the type of job they want or for which they were trained. Some added that newcomers should focus their efforts on simply getting a job, if only to acquire Canadian experience, and then direct their efforts on improving their employment prospects. Service providers also pointed to the need to make the immigrant better aware of the barriers that will be faced by professionals seeking to enter their professions in Canada. Amongst the principal challenges to be confronted were the potentially lengthy processes to have skills and credentials recognized, the costs that this entails, and the hesitation of some employers to hire persons trained outside Canada.

Immigrant Expectations

Important insight into the process of integration is offered from assessments made by immigrants around their adjustment to life in Canada. It was observed previously in this chapter that immigrants have identified concerns about the economic circumstances they encountered in Canada. A Longitudinal Survey of Immigrants to Canada (LSIC) provides valuable insights into how newly arrived immigrants adjust over time to living in Canada. Schellenberg and Maheux (2007) analyze immigrants' perspectives on their first four years (2001–2005) in Canada. Amongst other things, the two analysts focus on the extent to which the expectations of immigrants are being met in the country. About two in three recent immigrants reported a fairly positive congruence between their expectations of life in Canada and their experiences here after four years. Looking at the three categories of immigrants—economic (which would include the most educated segment of new arrivals), family, and refugees—Schellenberg and Maheux point to gaps in the respondents' reported expectations and experiences. Some 64 percent of economic immigrants felt that their expectations had been met, while this was the case for 70 percent of family immigrants and refugees.

Despite the uneven economic condition of some immigrants, most do not appear dissatisfied with their decision to settle in the country. The LSIC reveals that some 72 percent would make the same decision to come to Canada. This was based on the question being put to the immigrants two out of three times over their four years in the country. When the question was put to the immigrants for a third time in the fourth year of settlement, a further 12 percent, previously uncertain, expressed no regret about their decision. Overall, therefore, some 84 percent of immigrants said they would make the same decision to come to Canada (that includes 80 percent of economic immigrants, 88 percent of immigrants in the Family Class, and 93 percent of refugees).

TABLE 10
New Immigrants' Perspectives on Whether They Would Make the Same Decision to Come to Canada Again (Percentage)

	Total	Economic	Family	Refugees
Said yes 3 of 3 times	72%	67%	79%	87%
Said yes in year 4, but no/don't know at least once before	12%	13%	9%	6%

Source: Statistics Canada, Longitudinal Survey of Immigrants to Canada (2005).

When immigrants were asked what they disliked most about life in Canada, some 17 percent said that it was the lack of employment opportunities, and another 11 percent said that it was the high taxes. Economic immigrants were somewhat more likely than Family Class immigrants and refugees to mention these factors. Among economic immigrants, 84 percent said their quality of life was better in Canada than in their country of origin—this outcome, despite the fact that about one-third (35 percent) of economic immigrants said that their level of material well-being was better than it had been prior to arrival, while about one-third said that it was about the same (31 percent), and about one-third said that it was worse (34 percent). In contrast, Family Class immigrants and refugees had more favourable assessments of their material well-being, with 58 percent and 69 percent, respectively, saying that their situation in Canada (after two years) was better than it had been before immigrating there.

Finally, the small proportion of immigrants who said they planned to leave Canada (3 percent) were asked about their reasons for doing so. The most frequently cited responses were the desire to be close to family and friends (37 percent) and the desire to return to their home country (25 percent). About one-third of those planning to leave (32 percent) cited employment-related reasons, including better job opportunities, pay, working conditions, or business climate elsewhere.

IMMIGRATION: THE QUEBEC DIFFERENCE

Generalizations about immigration policy in Canada often fail to take into consideration the particular responsibility that the province of Quebec has when it comes to immigrant selection and integration. As the only province in the country whose majority population is French-speaking, Quebec is committed to preserving this distinct characteristic and thus has a particular interest and concern when it comes to those persons who choose to permanently settle there. Beginning in the late 1970s, the Government of Quebec has negotiated two agreements with the Government of Canada. The first (the 1977 Cullen-Couture Agreement) gave the province specific powers when it comes to the selection of immigrants in all categories, with the exception of refugees. The second agreement (the 1991 McDougall-Gagnon-Tremblay Agreement, also known as the Canada-Quebec Accord) saw the transfer of funds for the reception and settlement of new immigrants from the Government of Canada to the Government of Quebec. Whereas immigrant selection at the federal level favours economic background, education levels, and official-language knowledge, Quebec's selection process stresses the same characteristics but provides additional recognition for an immigrant's knowledge of the French language.

Since the agreements were enacted, the immigration policies of the province of Quebec for all political parties have pursued the same course and from year to year have successfully increased the percentage of immigrants with French language knowledge. In 2007, some six in ten immigrants to Quebec reported knowledge of French, which was up from 40 percent in 1998. It is worth noting, however, that the increase is largely attributable to the rise in the number of immigrants that know both English and French upon arrival, which soared from 13 percent to 36 percent over the 1998 to 2007 period. Since 18 percent of the immigrants arriving in Quebec in 2007 knew only English upon arrival, and not French, one might also point out that in adding this number with the percentage corresponding to newcomers who had knowledge of both official languages (36 percent), the result is that in 2008, some 55 percent of new immigrants to Quebec possessed knowledge of English. The net result of Quebec's immigrant selection pattern is likely a rise in the level of English-French bilingualism in the population of Montreal—the province's largest city, where nine in ten of the province's immigrants settle. It can be noted that knowledge of official languages upon arrival is also the object of increasing importance in immigrant selection elsewhere in Canada. Whereas in 2002, some 46 percent of immigrants to Canada had reported knowledge of neither English nor French upon arrival, that figure dropped to 30 percent in 2007.

As observed below in Table 11, a majority of Quebecers agree that their province is best suited to select immigrants and to assume responsibility for their integration, and most also agree that the province is best suited to foster intercultural contacts.

Majorities in the other provinces of Canada believe that the federal government is best suited to assume authority for immigrant selection (70 percent), immigrant integration (55 percent), and the fostering of intercultural contacts (51 percent).

But Quebec's assuming of authority over the selection and integration of immigrants has not meant that their entry into the workplace has been less of a challenge. Indeed, if the criterion for effective integration is measured by rates of unemployment, in the case of Quebec, outcomes have proven equally, if not more, complex than they have for other major immigrant-receiving parts of Canada (Brousseau-Pouliot 2008). According to a study

TABLE 11
Which Level of Government (Federal, Provincial, or Municipal) Do You Think Is Best Suited to Address the Following?

QUEBEC	Federal	Provincial	Municipal	Don't Know
Selecting immigrants	41.5%	50.9%	1.4%	6.2%
Immigrant integration	26.5%	57.1%	10.1%	6.2%
Fostering intercultural contacts	29.4%	45.2%	17.0%	8.4%

Source: Jedwab (2008). The analysis is based on a survey, conducted in February 2008, commissioned by the Association for Canadian Studies from the firm Leger Marketing.

conducted by respected Quebec economist Pierre Fortin, immigrants to Quebec that arrived between 2001 and 2006 have encountered greater difficulty securing employment than their counterparts who settled in the province of Ontario. Amongst the visible minorities (Arab, African, South Asian, Chinese, etc.), the gap in the rate of unemployment for immigrants compared to non-immigrants is reported in the study as 16 percent in Quebec and 6 percent in Ontario. As regards immigrants who do not identify as visible minorities, the study states that the gap is 11 percent in Quebec, compared with 4 percent in Ontario. Fortin concludes that "...the economic situation of immigrants in Quebec is far more difficult compared to the conditions they face in other provinces" and adds that Quebec does a poor job in integrating its immigrants when compared to Ontario (cited in Brousseau-Pouliot 2008). Still, it would be difficult to demonstrate that the responsibility for the disparity in employment is entirely a function of provincial government policy.

The Government of Quebec maintains, however, that the situation of immigrants is improving and that in 2007, the unemployment rate amongst immigrants fell from 12 percent to 10.2 percent. Immigrants that arrived in Quebec in the few years prior to 2009 fared even better, as their rate of unemployment declined from 13.4 percent to 10.7 percent, according to figures issued by Quebec's Employment Bureau. While the economic crisis in late 2008 to 2009 had a negative effect on economic conditions for the overall Quebec population, and unemployment rates increased once again, the Government of Quebec reports that the numbers are going down again, with a decline in the unemployment rate amongst immigrants from 13.7 percent in 2009 to 12.5 percent in 2010, and with immigrants occupying over 50 percent of all of the jobs created in 2010 (Gouvernement du Québec 2011).

In recent years, the Government of Quebec has aimed to increase the numbers of immigrants settling in Quebec from 40,000 to 50,000 annually in order to fill the number of jobs that will become available in the years ahead. But some observers worry that before increasing (or continuing to increase) the numbers of immigrants, it is imperative to understand why established immigrants are encountering such difficulty in entering the labour market. The chief economist for the Desjardins Bank, Yves St-Maurice, believes that "...for immigrants with medical certification to come here to work at Tim Hortons [a restaurant chain] makes no sense" (cited in Brousseau-Pouliot 2008). How widespread such situations are is unclear. However, concerns over immigrant underemployment persist in Quebec, as they do elsewhere in Canada. While nearly one in two Quebec immigrants has a university degree, according to the Government of Quebec's Employment Bureau, most of the workers the province will require in the years ahead are in the service sector, and some observers maintain that Quebec will generate a sufficient number of university degree holders to fill employment needs that require such educational background. The chief economist of the Laurentian Bank, Carlos Leitao, believes that the number of immigrants to Quebec should be increased, not so much in order to respond to labour shortages, but rather to stress humanitarian considerations. He contends that for addressing labour shortages, the principal solution is training programs (Brousseau-Pouliot 2008).

CONCLUSION

Economic data point to growing income gaps encountered by recent waves of immigrants to Canada. The findings have become the object of whether policies directed at immigrant integration are functioning effectively in the country. Underlying the data are issues of recognition of foreign education and skills; the region of the country in which the immigrant resides; and, as observed in this chapter, the visible minority identification of the immigrant. While analysts in Canada have devoted considerable effort to documenting the gaps in employment and income, they have been less successful in determining what causes the disparities. Moreover, there is some question as to the amount of time required on the part of immigrants to achieve conditions consistent with the broader population. The comparisons that suggest that recent waves of immigrants are underperforming relative to previous waves over five-year cycles may not be allowing sufficient time allotments to make meaningful conclusions. It is worth noting that there are regional variations in the disparities. It is interesting to observe that in spite of the weaker economic performances of the recent wave of immigrants, the degree of satisfaction on the part of newcomers with life in Canada remains relatively strong, even if there is also a body of evidence that suggests that for many, expectations have not been met. The relationship between immigrant expectation and economic performance in Canada merits further examination to help Canada identify the way in which it chooses to modify policy in the area of immigration.

REFERENCES

Brousseau-Pouliot, V. 2008. Intégration difficile des immigrés au marché du travail. *La Presse*, 21 November.

Citizenship and Immigration Canada. 2008. *Facts and Figures 2007*. At http://www.cic.gc.ca/english/pdf/pub/facts2007.pdf (accessed 2 November 2011).

Frenette, M., and R. Morissette. 2003. *Will They Ever Converge? Earnings of Immigrant and Canadian-born Workers over the Last Two Decades*. Analytical Studies Research Paper Series, Catalogue no. 11F0019MIE, No. 215. Ottawa: Statistics Canada.

Gouvernement du Québec. 2011. *Québec Immigration Planning for the Period 2012–2015: Summary*. Ministère de l'Immigration et des Communautés culturelles, Gouvernment du Québec. At http://www.micc.gouv.qc.ca/publications/en/planification/planning-levels-summary-20122015.pdf.

Heisz, A., and L. McLeod. 2004. *Trends and Conditions in Census Metropolitan Areas—Low Income in CMAs*. Catalogue no. 89-613-MWE, No. 010. Ottawa: Statistics Canada.

Human Resources and Social Development Canada. 2008. *Canadian Attitudes Toward Labour Market Issues: Survey of Canadian Opinion*. Prepared by Environics Research Group (February).

Human Resources and Social Development Canada. 2008. *Guide to Working in Canada Study*. Ottawa: Prepared by Phoenix Strategic Perspectives Inc. (March).

Jedwab, J. 2008. *Managing Cultural Diversity: Quebec Differs Significantly from ROC on Provincial Responsibilities*. Association for Canadian Studies. 11 April.

Larsen, L.J. 2004. The Foreign-Born Population in the United States: 2003. *Current Population Reports*. U.S. Department of Commerce, Economics and Statistics Administration, U.S. Census Bureau (August).

Picot, G., F. Hou, and S. Coulombe. 2007. *Chronic Low Income and Low-income Dynamics Among Recent Immigrants*. Analytical Studies Research Paper Series, Catalogue no. 11F0019MIE, No. 294. Ottawa: Statistics Canada.

Schellenberg, G., and H. Maheux. 2007. Immigrants' Perspectives on Their First Four Years in Canada: Highlights from Three Waves of the Longitudinal Survey of Immigrants to Canada. *Canadian Social Trends*, April. Ottawa: Statistics Canada.

Statistics Canada. 2005. Longitudinal Survey of Immigrants to Canada.

Statistics Canada. 2006. Census of Canada.

Statistics Canada. 2008a. Analytical Studies—Research Paper Series. Catalogue no. 11F0019M, No. 309. Ottawa: Statistics Canada.

Statistics Canada. 2008b. *Earnings and Incomes of Canadians Over the Past Quarter Century, 2006 Census*. Catalogue no. 97-563. Ottawa: Statistics Canada.

PART IV

CITIZENSHIP, SETTLEMENT, AND SOCIO-CULTURAL INTEGRATION

CHAPTER 8

The Place of Immigrants: Citizenship, Settlement, and Socio-cultural Integration in Canada

Myer Siemiatycki, *Professor of Politics and Public Administration, Ryerson University*

INTRODUCTION

The intersection of opposites has—for 400 years—made immigration a defining characteristic of Canada. This is a country large in territory but limited in population. From the time of the European colonization of Canada in the early 1600s, governing officials have always viewed immigration as a necessary means to their ends. Throughout Canada's history, immigration has been an instrument for achieving state objectives. Over time, these have included domination over Aboriginal peoples, maintaining supremacy over rival European-power imperial claims, preserving Canadian territory from fears of American takeover, promoting national economic development, and meeting labour market shortages and an aging population demographic resulting from low domestic fertility rates.

Canada's approach to immigration, therefore, has largely been driven by national self-interest. First, as a colony of France, then a colony of

Managing Immigration and Diversity in Canada: A Transatlantic Dialogue in the New Age of Migration, ed. D. Rodríguez-García. Montreal and Kingston: Queen's Policy Studies Series, McGill-Queen's University Press.

Britain, and since 1867, as an autonomous federal state, Canada has relied on immigrants to fulfill pressing national purposes. In the process, Canada has become one of the world's most diverse societies. The globalization of Canada's population was highlighted in the recent Canadian census of 2006. Of the country's total 31.6 million people, almost one in five—19.8 percent—were foreign-born, coming from over 200 different countries of origin. Significantly, 2006 was the first time in Canadian history that more of Canada's immigrants were born in Asia (40.8 percent) than in Europe (36.8 percent). Africa's share of recent immigrants has also been rising steadily. Canada therefore now stands among the world's most diverse multiracial, multi-religious, multi-ethnic, and multilingual countries (Chui, Tran, and Maheux 2007).

Canada is rightly classified as a "classic country of immigration," whose population has grown through successive waves of migration. Integrating immigrants has been a recurring challenge and test for Canadian society. Is immigrant integration an exercise in social inclusion or social exclusion? This chapter examines this question in four broad sections. First, I identify three different models of immigrant selection that Canada has followed since 1867. Second, I review key policy and institutional influences on immigrant integration today. Third, I discuss successes in Canada's approach to immigrant integration. Fourth, I analyze some failings in Canada's experience of immigrant integration.

A number of key themes emerge through this discussion. First is a reminder that a country and society can dramatically change its orientation to immigrants and foreigners. We will see that Canada has evolved from a narrow to a pluralistic definition of *who* can be a Canadian. Second, the Canadian experience reminds us that public policies and institutions are the main factors that influence immigrant integration. The place of immigrants in a country is most importantly determined by what place the receiving state and society assigns to newcomers. The Canadian experience further illustrates that a heterogeneous population can establish a strong sense of national identity and belonging.

Before continuing, brief mention should be made regarding terminology and some limitations of this chapter's scope. Immigrant integration is about newcomers becoming full and equal members of the country they have moved to. "Integration," as Papademitriou has written, "is the process through which, over time, newcomers and hosts form an integral whole" (2003, 1). This chapter contains minimal reference to the economic dimension of immigrant integration, nor to the specific experiences of immigrants in the province of Quebec. Other chapters in this volume address these topics. Instead, the focus here is on immigrant selection, settlement, citizenship, and socio-cultural integration in Canada. This is a canvas certainly broad enough to illustrate the place of immigrants in Canada.

I. THE CHANGING MODEL OF IMMIGRANT INTEGRATION IN CANADA

Canada is a young country, but a society whose origins reach long into the past. Archaeologists contend that Canada's Aboriginal population migrated from Asia across frozen lands sometime during the Ice Age between 12,000 to 40,000 years ago (Ray 1996). Significantly, Canada's Aboriginal people do not regard themselves as immigrants—but rather as First Nations, present since creation. As the First Nations Hall exhibit in the Canadian Museum of Civilization describes Aboriginal origins in Canada, "We are not the first immigrants; we are the native inhabitants of the land. We have been here since before the world took its present form." Aboriginal Canadians understand themselves to be part of the world's creation. A folk tale of the Mi'kmaq aboriginal people declares, "I have lived here since the world began. I have my grandmother, she was here when the world was made..." (Ray 1996, VII). Not all Canadians, therefore, insert themselves into the celebrated narrative of Canada as a nation of immigrants.

By the time of the first permanent European settlement on Canadian soil 400 years ago, Canada's Aboriginal population was estimated to be about 500,000 (Ray 1996). The encounter of Europeans and Aboriginals represents Canada's first experience of immigrant integration into a previously established society. What ensued was not a model of equitable, harmonious integration. Instead, European imperialism would subjugate and marginalize Aboriginals. War and disease killed many Aboriginals. Eurocentric superiority and assimilation unleashed devastating assaults on Aboriginal culture. Canada's founding European peoples—the French and the English—left a legacy not of immigrant integration, but of immigrant imperialism and domination over a host population. The burden of this past continues to weigh heavily on Canada's 1.1 million Aboriginal population.

The more recent record of immigrant integration in Canada demonstrates that societies and countries can dramatically change their attitudes and policies towards immigration. Since Canada's establishment as a country in 1867, we can identify three different "models" or approaches to immigration and diversity in Canada. In summary form, they are—

- 1867–1960s: Building a White, British, Christian Canada
- 1960s–2000: Building a Multicultural Canada with Global Human Capital
- 2000–   : "Creating the World's Most Flexible Workforce" in a Securitized State

These three periods have involved radically different approaches to immigration in Canada.

Building a White, British, Christian Canada: 1867–1960s

Canada is now widely regarded as a welcoming, pluralistic destination of global migration. This is, in fact, a relatively recent development. "In fact," notes the leading text on Canadian immigration policy, "for most of its history, Canada's immigration practices have been racist and exclusionary" (Kelley and Trebilcock 1998, 442). For Canada's "first century" (1867–1967), the country enforced a highly restrictive and discriminatory approach to immigrant selection. Canada pursued a fixed formula of desirable and undesirable immigrants with race, nationality, and religion as the chief distinguishing divide between wanted and unwanted immigrants to Canada.

Until the 1960s, Canada adopted a series of measures to prevent or limit the migration of Blacks, Asians, and Jews into Canada. Conversely, the most preferred immigrants were newcomers from Britain, Western Europe, and Northern Europe. For 100 years, there was an overwhelming consensus in Canada supporting this rigid distinction of which immigrants were wanted in Canada. Political leaders representing different parties, different ideologies, and different regions of the country all expressed similar views. The intensity of their convictions, moreover, was unmistakable and worthy of note.

Canada's first prime minister, Conservative leader John A. Macdonald, spoke in Canada's Parliament during the 1880s of his commitment to "preventing a permanent settlement in this country of Mongolian or Chinese immigrants"; he justified this exclusion on the grounds that the Chinese immigrant to Canada "has no British instincts or British feelings or aspirations" (Kelley and Trebilcock 1998, 95, 97). In 1904, Quebec intellectual and political leader Henri Bourassa declared, "Canada should not be a land of refuge for the scum of all nations" (cited in Brown 1996, 14). Five years later, J.S. Woodsworth—a Methodist reverend and, notably, the future leader of Canadian social democracy, from Winnipeg in Western Canada—asserted, "Non-assimilable elements are clearly detrimental to our highest national development, and hence should be vigorously excluded" (cited in Day 2000, 134).

The belief that immigration to Canada should be limited to white, Christian, and, preferably, British newcomers was reasserted in 1947 by Canada's longest serving prime minister, Liberal Party leader Mackenzie King. In announcing that Canada would again reopen its doors to immigrants after the end of World War II, Prime Minister King, nonetheless, made it clear that not all wishing to enter the country would be welcomed: "The people of Canada do not wish, as a result of mass immigration, to make a fundamental alteration in the character of our population ... Any considerable Oriental immigration would ... be certain to give rise to social and economic problems" (Kelley and Trebilcock 1998, 312).

It is striking, therefore, that *after* waging five years of war against Hitler's racist Nazi regime, Canada reaffirmed its own discriminatory racist immigration policies. Why were such views so strongly held in Canada? And for so long? The reasons run deep. The colonial legacy of the British empire was important for English Canada (outside Quebec). Until later in the 20th century, Canada imagined itself to be a country and society attached to British identity and ties. Immigration was intended to attract other Britons, or those who were regarded as readily able to assimilate to a British norm. As for Quebec, its francophone majority was concerned that mass migration could dilute the French, Catholic character of its distinct minority society in Anglo, Protestant North America. And for more than half of the 20th century, Social Darwinism and eugenics held significant currency across Canada. Canadians did believe in racial essentialism, a hierarchy of races, and the incompatibility of racial mixing.

Because of exclusionary admissions policies, therefore, immigrant admissions to Canada were regulated and restricted according to geographic and racial criteria. Before 1960, 90 percent of all immigrants to Canada came from Europe and only 3 percent from Asia, the world's most populous continent (Knowles 2007). This was about to change.

Building a Multicultural Canada with Global Human Capital: 1960s–2000

Canada's approach to immigration changed dramatically in the 1960s and early 1970s. This involved historic changes in the approach to immigrant selection and integration. Both are reviewed in this section.

In 1962, for the first time, race and nationality were dropped as criteria for immigrant selection. By 1967, a point system was introduced to screen the selection of immigrants applying to enter Canada. The point system measured prospective immigrants according to their human capital by ranking applicants according to criteria such as age, education, training, occupational experience, knowledge of English or French, relatives in Canada, and prior offers of employment in Canada.

The point system revolutionized Canadian immigration. Human capital replaced identity (race, nationality, and religion) as the basis of immigrant selection. A host of factors explain this shift in Canadian immigration policy. As a number of authors explain, both principled and pragmatic influences played a part in this transition (Troper 1993; Kelley and Trebilcock 1998; Knowles 2007). Beginning in the late 1940s, an anti-racist human rights discourse developed through such diverse influences as the United Nations, a rising awareness of the racist underpinnings of the Holocaust, and the moral claims required of the West during the Cold War. Overtly racist policies were now regarded as unjustifiable discrimination. It helped, too, that they now compromised Canada's economic interests. By the 1960s, emigration was declining from the traditional immigrant-sending countries of Europe. Canada needed to look farther afield to meet its labour market immigration needs. Additionally, in the decolonized world of the 1960s, racist immigration policies were now an impediment to Canada's international trade interests in Asia, the Caribbean, and Africa.

Racist immigration policies were no longer compatible with Canada's values or economic interests. Yet some observers believe that the point system replaced one form of immigration discrimination (based on race/ nationality) with another (based on human capital). In the provocative formulation of Luis Aguilar, Canada shifted from selecting newcomers on the basis of racial eugenics to screening them based on social eugenics (Aguilar 2006, 206). This involved a new definition of desirable immigrants as "the best and brightest" from their homeland, bringing high levels of education and skills to the Canadian labour market.

Soon after the point system was adopted, Canada formalized its commitment to three distinct categories of immigrant admissions. These are the Economic Class, based largely on the point system; the Family Class, based on family sponsorship and reunification; and the Refugee Class, based on providing asylum under Canada's international obligations. These continue to be the three categories under which Canada admits immigrants. For the past two decades, Canada has maintained high annual immigrant admission numbers—typically ranging between 225,000 and 250,000 newcomers per year. Generally speaking, the distribution of these admissions by immigrant category has been 60 percent admitted in the Economic Class, 30 percent admitted in the Family Class, and 10 percent admitted under the Refugee Class.

As noted earlier, immigration to Canada has been truly globalized under this regime of immigrant selection. Asia has dominated the ranks of sending countries, with large numbers also arriving from the Middle East, Africa, and Eastern Europe. Accordingly, the majority of immigrants to Canada in recent decades have been non-white. "Visible minority" is the official term for Canada's non-white, non-Aboriginal population. From 1981 to the 2006 census, the visible minority share of the total Canadian population quadrupled from 4.7 percent to 16.2 percent. And from 2001 to 2006, visible minorities accounted for 75 percent of all immigrants to Canada (Fenlon 2008).

Changes to newcomer selection criteria were not the only innovations in Canadian immigration policy in the last third of the 20th century. In 1971, Canada's Prime Minister Pierre Trudeau announced that Canada would follow a policy of multiculturalism—the first country in the world to do so. This would be an important policy companion to the point system. While the latter opened Canada to newcomers from around the world, multiculturalism meant that immigrants would no longer be expected to assimilate to a British standard of identity. Multiculturalism stretched

Canada's redefinition of itself to officially recognize that Canadians come in all races, religions, and ethnicities. As we will see in a fuller discussion of multiculturalism to come, this has significantly reframed the terms of immigrant integration in Canada.

"Creating the World's Most Flexible Workforce" in a Securitized State: 2000–

The new millennium has brought a new orientation to immigrant selection and integration in Canada. The recent period has seen neo-liberalism and anti-terrorism gain heightened government support. Both have made immigrants more vulnerable in Canada.

Neo-liberalism became ascendant in the later decades of the 20th century as "the dominant political and ideological form of capitalist globalization" (Brenner, Peck, and Theodore 2005, 2). As Katharyne Mitchell succinctly defines it, neo-liberalism is "an ideology of world market domination" (2004, 12). Specifically, it entails giving markets and capital pre-eminence as allocators of resources and influences on public decisions. This has manifested itself in a more fervently market-oriented approach to immigration admissions to Canada.

This was evident in Canada's adoption of its new current immigration act in 2001, the *Immigration and Refugee Protection Act*. At the time, Prime Minister Jean Chrétien proclaimed the new act's goal: "to allow the immediate needs of employers to be met faster; to attract people who are skilled and on the move and to encourage them to make Canada their destination of choice" (cited in Abu-Laban and Gabriel 2002, 80). Under the more recent Conservative government of Prime Minister Stephen Harper, Canada has become even more explicit about using immigration policy to meet employer needs in a changing global economy. Soon after taking office in 2006, the government introduced a national economic plan titled *Advantage Canada: Building a Strong Economy for Canadians*. The plan aimed to "gain a global competitive advantage" for Canada in five key areas, including "creating the world's most flexible workforce" (Department of Finance Canada 2006, 6). In its 2008 Budget, the government declared that Canada is committed to establishing a "'just-in-time' competitive immigration system" that expeditiously delivers migrants to jobs where they are needed (Department of Finance Canada 2008).

A rising reliance on temporary migration has been Canada's policy of choice in establishing its more market-oriented approach to immigration. In 2007, Canada admitted 165,198 temporary foreign workers (typically on two-year work visas). Significantly, this total is higher than the 131,248 permanent immigrants admitted in 2007 as Economic Class newcomers under the point system (Citizenship and Immigration Canada 2008). In other words, Canada now relies more on "guest worker" temporary migration than on permanently selected immigrants to fill its labour market needs. Already, there are many concerns over the exploitation of these workers through low pay and dangerous working conditions (Flecker 2008).

Temporary labour migration is now the fastest-growing stream of newcomer admissions into Canada. The temporary admissions in 2007 represented a 60 percent increase over the number admitted just four years earlier. Canada's shift to temporary migration represents a major change in the country's philosophy of migration. As we will discuss below, migration to Canada has traditionally been connected to nation-building, since immigrants are eligible to become citizens after three years of residency. Now, however, migration is increasingly about admitting a temporary, disposable workforce to meet employers' short-term needs.

Renewed security measures and attitudes adopted following the terrorist attacks of 11 September 2001 have further isolated some immigrant communities in Canada. A discourse of immigrants as unassimilable, or worse—as a threat to security—became more prevalent after the Islamist attacks on New York. Canada, like other countries, adopted more punitive border control and domestic security measures. As in other countries, sometimes these measures violated civil liberties and portrayed certain immigrant communities as threats to security. As legal authority Audrey Macklin has stated, "While many look to the criminal law to protect us from the enemy within, I urge us to attend to the law's role in producing the alien within" (Macklin 2001). The result has been an "othering" of immigrant and minority communities that Canada has not experienced since it dropped race and nationality as criteria of immigrant selection in the 1960s. Muslims and Arabs, in particular, have faced the brunt of suspicion and adverse treatment. As Sami Aoun notes, "[t]he average Canadian has become more reticent and more suspicious of things coming from the Arab and Muslim community" (2008, 116).

To sum up this section, it is evident that Canada's approach to immigration and integration has not been static. From 1867 to the 1960s, Canada's model was to keep non-whites out of Canada and to require newcomers to assimilate into the dominant Anglo culture of the country. From the 1960s to 2000, Canada's priority was attracting immigrants with high human capital, promoting multiculturalism, and encouraging immigrants to become citizens in a shared nation-building project. Since 2000, neo-liberal and anti-terrorism measures have created impediments to the integration of some migrants and their communities.

II. KEY INFLUENCES ON IMMIGRANT INTEGRATION IN CANADA TODAY

Immigrant integration does not occur in a vacuum. Rather, it is the result of intersecting patterns, policies, and practices of receiving states. What then are the chief contextual factors that influence the nature of immigrant integration in Canada today? This section discusses six factors that shape the integration of newcomers. These are immigrant settlement patterns; immigrant settlement programs; Canada's multiculturalism policy; human rights protection; Canada's citizenship policy; and inclusive public institutions. Together, they create a framework for integration in a globally interconnected world.

Immigrant Settlement Patterns and Programs in Canada

Immigrants are not randomly distributed across Canada. Quite the opposite, they are spatially highly concentrated. This is dramatically evident from provincial and urban settlement patterns. As noted earlier, according to Canada's recent census of 2006, immigrants accounted for 19.8 percent of the country's population. (Canada defines an immigrant as a foreign-born person with permanent residency rights in the country. This means that temporary and illegal migrants in the country are not counted among Canada's immigrants.) The 2006 census confirmed the overwhelming preference of immigrants for specific locations. Provincially, Ontario has by far the country's largest share of immigrants with 54.9 percent of the national total. Considerably further behind are British Columbia (18.1 percent), Quebec (13.8 percent), Alberta (8.5 percent), and Manitoba (2.4 percent), while the remaining five provinces of Newfoundland, Prince Edward Island, Nova Scotia, New Brunswick, and Saskatchewan each are home to less than 1 percent of Canada's immigrant population (Chui et al. 2007).

Immigrants to Canada are particularly drawn to its largest cities. In 2006, 94.9 percent of Canada's immigrants lived in a metropolitan area. Very few immigrants live in small-town or rural areas. Still more striking is the fact that almost two-thirds of all immigrants live in one of Canada's three largest urban centres: Toronto (37.5 percent), Vancouver (13.4 percent), and Montreal (12 percent) (Chui et al. 2007). The result is that immigrants comprise extraordinarily high proportions of the total population of some Canadian cities. The greatest concentrations are found in the Toronto and Vancouver urban areas. The Canadian municipality with the highest proportion of immigrants in 2006 was the Vancouver suburb of Richmond, with 57.4 percent of its population foreign-born. In another nearby suburb, Burnaby, 50.8 percent of residents were immigrants. And in the City of Vancouver itself, immigrants accounted for 45.6 percent of the total population. In 2006, the City of Toronto reached the "tipping point," with 49.9 percent of its population foreign-born. At the same time, three of its suburban municipalities were majority immigrant cities—Richmond Hill (57.4 percent), Markham (56.5 percent), and Mississauga (51.6 percent). Immigrant integration, therefore, is overwhelmingly a process playing out in Canada's largest cities and their surrounding suburbs (Chui et al. 2007). Unlike the pattern in European urban areas such as Paris, suburbs of Canadian cities typically attract affluent, home-owning immigrants.

Immigrant Settlement Services

Governments in Canada play an important role in providing settlement services to newcomer immigrants. "Unlike other immigrant nations, like the United States," Lynch and Simon note, "Canada takes an extensive and active role in facilitating the integration of its immigrants…" (2003, 68). As Bloemraad also notes, this sets Canada apart from the United States, where a laissez-faire approach to newcomer integration prevails. In the Canadian context, government-funded settlement services reflect a more interventionist welfare-state orientation (Bloemraad 2006).

The delivery of these programs reflects the complexities of intergovernmental relations in Canada. Constitutionally, immigration is a shared responsibility between the federal and provincial governments in Canada. Through formal federal-provincial agreements, both levels of government coordinate the provision of settlement services to promote newcomer integration. The actual delivery of these programs is typically contracted by governments to non-profit immigrant service agencies. Foremost are programs that teach Canada's official languages—English or French—and that provide a range of support services, such as information and referrals, translation, counselling, employment, and housing assistance, etc. The agencies providing these services are located across Canada's big cities and often are staffed by earlier immigrants who have experienced the challenges of migration and integration. In 2005, for instance, a total of 238 immigrant settlement agencies operated in the Toronto area alone. These organizations not only build newcomer skills and resources, but they signal to immigrants that the Government of Canada is committed to their integration.

Canada's Multiculturalism Policy

Canada, in 1971, became the first country to officially adopt a policy of multiculturalism. Ever since, multiculturalism has been a key element of both Canada's self-definition and its image in the world. This policy's impact on immigrant integration has been profound. The paradox of Canadian multiculturalism is that a policy with limited tangible substance has accomplished so much. Canada's approach to multiculturalism provides few specific guarantees to diverse communities and little direct funding support. And yet, it has transformed the place of immigrants and minorities in Canada. As numerous scholars have observed, multiculturalism has succeeded symbolically in creating a new narrative and self-definition of Canada as a society that values diversity and identities of difference (Kymlicka 1998; Triadafilopoulos 2006; Adams 2007).

Several factors—both principled and pragmatic—prompted then prime minister Pierre Trudeau to declare Canada the world's first multicultural state in 1971. Multiculturalism commended itself to Prime Minister Trudeau as a single initiative that could achieve multiple goals: (1) acknowledge the increasing ethno-racial diversity of Canada ushered in by postwar migration and the 1960s adoption of the point system; (2) reconstruct Canada's self-understanding as a country of many cultures, rather than two founding nations (French and English), thereby minimizing the distinctive claim of Quebecois nationalism and separatism; and (3) consolidate election support for Trudeau's Liberal Party in immigrant and minority communities.

In his parliamentary address, Prime Minister Trudeau expressed the essence of multiculturalism by stating that in Canada "there is no official culture, nor does any ethnic group take precedence over any other. No citizen or group of citizens is other than Canadian, and all should be treated fairly" (Trudeau 1971). Interestingly, in explaining the implications of the policy, the prime minister emphasized the government's commitment to promoting full participation of immigrants and minorities in Canadian society.

Will Kymlicka is correct in declaring that Canada's multiculturalism policy amounts to "renegotiating the terms of integration" in Canada. "Adopting multiculturalism," he notes, "is a way for Canadians to say that never again will we view Canada as a 'white' country…; never again will we view Canada as a 'British' country" (Kymlicka 1998, 57). The effect, as Irene Bloemraad observes, is that multiculturalism "makes room for others," and thereby "makes Canadianism possible" (Bloemraad 2006, 153). By stretching the definition of *what* and *who* a Canadian is, multiculturalism has fostered a warmer welcome for immigrant integration. Canada has signalled that being Canadian and retaining ancestral homeland culture are not incompatible. Interestingly too, as Biles, Burstein, and Frideres remind us, multiculturalism's redefinition of Canada means that immigrant integration is "a 'two-way street', where both immigrants and current citizens are expected to adapt to each other, to ensure positive outcomes for everyone in the social, cultural, economic, and political spheres" (Biles et al. 2008, 4).

However, Canada's approach to multiculturalism does not confer an absolute right to practise homeland traditions in Canada. Multicultural claims must be consistent with Canadian laws and must be balanced against other rights. Thus, a recent request by some Muslims in the province of Ontario to have Sharia law accepted as a basis of voluntary family dispute arbitration, (much as orthodox Jews and evangelical Christians could base dispute resolution on their religious laws), was rejected. And to establish uniformity, Ontario abolished all religious options for such dispute resolution (Boyd 2007).

Canadians now demonstrate a high degree of support for multicultural-ism—perhaps because it has generally succeeded in both promoting and placing limits on diversity. In 2003, 85 percent of Canadians surveyed agreed that multiculturalism was important to Canadian identity; and 81 percent believed that multiculturalism has made a positive contribu-tion to Canadian identity (Adams 2007, 20). Three-quarters of Canadians agreed with this statement: "Other cultures have a lot to teach us. Contact with them is enriching for us" (ibid., 38). These positive attitudes towards multiculturalism also help to explain why Canadians consistently express the most favourable attitude towards immigration in surveys done across many different countries. A 2006 international survey found that 75 percent of Canadians believe that, on balance, immigrants have a posi-tive impact on their country. In Australia, the country with the second highest positive outlook, only 54 percent held the same view; and in Spain, this view was supported by 45 percent of respondents (ibid., 13). Canada's multiculturalism policy promotes acceptance of diversity and immigration.

Human Rights Protection

Canada has a variety of laws and policies that prohibit discrimination and racism. Instruments such as the *Charter of Rights and Freedoms*, hate crime legislation, and human rights codes all make it illegal to discriminate based on factors such as ethnicity, race, religion, and immigrant status. These are important state policies that declare racism and discrimination to be unacceptable in Canada.

Canadian Citizenship Policy

Citizenship policy in Canada is another key instrument promoting im-migrant integration in Canada. Yet the formal status of Canadian citizen-ship only came into being in 1947. Until then, Canadians held the status of British subjects. The *Citizenship Act* of 1947, for the first time, created a distinct *Canadian* citizenship. Today, Canada has one of the world's most permissive regimes of citizenship acquisition for immigrants. After spending three years in the country, immigrants are eligible to apply for Canadian citizenship. To acquire Canadian citizenship, immigrants must (a) pay an application fee; (b) demonstrate an adequate knowledge of English or French; (c) write a test demonstrating a basic knowledge of Canada's history, geography, and government; and (d) take an oath of allegiance to Canada. Since 1977, Canada has also permitted its citizens to hold citizenship in another country.

In this respect, immigration to Canada is fundamentally about nation-building. This is reflected in the name of the government department responsible for immigration in Canada: It is called "Citizenship and

Immigration Canada." Immigrants to Canada are encouraged and expected to become Canadian citizens. Immigrants are regarded as "Canadians-in-the-making," who will soon have the same nationality and rights as native-born Canadians. As we will see further below, the great majority of immigrants do become Canadian citizens.

Inclusive Public Institutions

The final important influence on immigrant integration is Canada's pattern of inclusive public institutions. In some countries, immigrant and native-born residents can live largely separated, even segregated, lives. This is less likely in Canada, thanks to a range of public institutions that are committed to social inclusion in their daily practice. This stems from a universalistic ethos of public services and institutions in Canada.

Canada's medicare system provides universal health care services to all immigrants and citizens in the country. Hospitals and doctors' offices are places where patients of diverse culture, race, religion, and birthplace typically share a room, along with their medical concerns. In this way, health care institutions become sites of immigrant integration, where newcomers have the same rights—and share space with!—the native-born.

Other institutions have also significantly contributed to immigrants' sense of belonging in Canada. Schools, colleges, and universities have been proactive in making themselves accessible and responsive to diverse communities. Compared to other Western countries, Canada has a minimal tradition of private schooling. The vast majority of students are in public schools, colleges, and universities. In Canada, students of diverse backgrounds learn side by side. And educational institutions have a range of policies that reflect a multicultural orientation that values differences of identity. These include heritage language, religious accommodation, and settlement worker programs in elementary and secondary schools; and a commitment to equitable access and learning opportunities in colleges and universities. As we will soon see below, some of the most impressive indicators of successful integration for immigrants are found in their educational experiences.

Libraries are another noteworthy example of Canadian public institutions reaching out to immigrants. As one study declared, Canadian libraries provide "many of the resources, both electronic and print, that immigrants value as they search for jobs, acquire language skills, find out about their new communities and their new country, and retain links to their cultures" (Frisken and Wallace 2000, 303). Canada has an extensive network of public libraries, typically administered and funded at the municipal level.

The Toronto Public Library (TPL) is a prime example. With 99 branches across the city, the TPL has the highest annual circulation of any library system in North America. Moreover, foreign-born residents are more frequent users of the TPL than Canadian-born residents of Toronto. As a recent study of the TPL concluded, "With its presence in many neighbourhoods and large investments in programming and services for newcomers, the library plays an important role in the lives of recent immigrants to Toronto" (Quirke 2007, 157). Examples of immigrant-aimed services include multilingual library guides and collections, English as a Second Language classes, Canadian citizenship test preparation classes, immigrant settlement workers in libraries, and advice for newcomer parents on how best to help children with school homework. In this manner, libraries and many other public institutions convey to immigrants that Canada is where they are welcomed and belong.

III. SUCCESSES OF IMMIGRANT INTEGRATION IN CANADA

Scholars of migration are in agreement that there is no consensus over how best to measure immigrant integration. Thus, James Lynch and Rita Simon state, "[w]hile it is universally recognized that it is beneficial to include immigrants in the host society, there is much less consensus over what this means..." (2003, 252). In their pioneering study, *Immigration the World Over*, Lynch and Simon compare immigrant integration across seven different countries—Australia, Canada, France, Germany, Great Britain, Japan, and the United States. The authors assess these countries' records against six dimensions of newcomer integration: labour force participation, host country language acquisition, naturalization (citizenship acquisition), educational achievement, intermarriage, and religion. They conclude, based on these criteria, that Canada has the strongest record of immigrant integration. "In every respect," Lynch and Simon state, "immigrants in Canada appear to be integrated both culturally and structurally into Canadian society" (2003, 259).

While Canada clearly has recorded significant accomplishments in immigrant integration, its record is not unblemished. The balance of this chapter, then, examines the successes and failures of immigrant integration in Canada today. Our focus is on the place of immigrants in Canada's socio-cultural landscape. Particular attention is devoted to dynamics and data related to such criteria as civic participation, belonging, racism and discrimination, language acquisition, intermarriage, educational achievement, and cultural recognition. In this third section of the chapter, I identify major successes of immigrant integration in Canada. The fourth and final section addresses shortcomings in immigrant integration. The balance sheet, it will be shown, clearly lies in Canada's favour.

Naturalization and Belonging

Naturalization is a key dimension of immigrant integration. It is the process by which immigrants become citizens and, therefore, full members of the country they have moved to. Canada has the highest per capita rate of naturalization in the world (Bird 2005). Significantly, immigrants in Canada have a far higher rate of naturalization than immigrants in the United States. In 2001, 72 percent of all immigrants in Canada had become Canadian citizens. This was almost double the naturalization rate in the United States, where in 2004, only 38 percent of all immigrants had become U.S. citizens (Bloemraad 2006, 2, 26). It should be noted that the "real" rate of naturalization in Canada is actually higher than stated above, since a more accurate statistic would measure the number of naturalized immigrants relative to the total number *eligible* for citizenship rather than the total number of immigrants living in the country. Recall that immigrants require three years' residency before applying for Canadian citizenship. The 2006 census revealed that 85.1 percent of eligible immigrants had naturalized and become Canadian citizens (Chui et al. 2007).

This indicates that immigrants want to be Canadian. This is so even though there are relatively few differences between the rights of immigrants and citizens in Canada. There are not great tangible inducements to naturalize in Canada. In their status of permanent residents, immigrants have the same health, educational, social program, and legal rights as native-born Canadian citizens. Becoming a citizen adds the right to vote, to hold elected office, to carry a passport, and to work for the national government. These are not insignificant benefits, but nor are they the prime motivation for immigrants to naturalize. Scholars agree that it is *state* policy and practice in Canada that best explain the high rate of immigrant naturalization here (Lynch and Simon 2003; Bloemraad 2006; Triadafilopoulos 2006). In Canada, government promotion of immigration, funding of newcomer services, recognition of multiculturalism, and encouragement of citizenship all encourage immigrants to identify themselves with Canada. As Triadafilos Triadafilopoulos observes, the Canadian experience "suggests that state policies can be quite effective in facilitating immigrant integration and solidarity" (2006, 80).

Political Participation

Electoral politics is clearly a significant indicator of immigrant integration. In Western liberal democracies, elections are the mechanism by which state leaders and policies are selected. Whether immigrants vote and get elected to public office says a great deal about their integration or marginalization. The record in Canada reflects both successes and shortcomings. Here we discuss the achievements, while deficiencies will be addressed in the next section on failures of integration.

As Michael Adams notes, "Canada has the highest proportion of foreign-born legislators in the world" (2007, 69). In 2007, 13 percent of the elected seats in Canada's Parliament were held by naturalized immigrants born abroad. The comparable rate of immigrant representation among elected officials in other countries was 11 percent in Australia, 7.5 percent in Great Britain, 6.2 percent in France, and 2 percent in the United States House of Representatives. Not only does Canada lead in the percentage of available positions held by immigrants, but it has an even more commanding pre-eminence when comparing this ratio of immigrant seats held to the percentage of immigrants living in the country.

This suggests that Canada's political system is more open to immigrants than in other countries. There are a variety of reasons for immigrant electoral successes in Canada. These include Canada's high rate of immigrant naturalization, which converts most immigrants into voters; the residential concentration of some immigrant communities, creating a large "ethnic voting bloc" for immigrant candidates; Canada's multicultural orientation, which extends legitimacy to all identities as representatives of Canada; Canada's strong orientation of public and newcomer services, which gives immigrants a stake in Canadian government policy; the extensive institutional network of immigrant and ethnic organizations, which generates political leaders and support from within newcomer communities; and the self-interest of political parties, which recognize they must have immigrant candidates to reflect the diversity of Canada's population. As we will see further below, however, Canada's political system also has its deficiencies in integrating immigrants and minorities.

Charitable Giving and Volunteering

Donating money or time to a Canadian institution or cause is an indicator of attachment, commitment, and integration. Research shows that immigrants are generous in both charitable giving and volunteering. Indeed, a survey by the Canadian Centre for Philanthropy in 2000 found that immigrants were more likely than native-born Canadians to donate (82 percent, compared with 78 percent) and were more generous in giving (annual donations totalling C$313, compared with C$259). With respect to volunteering, while immigrants contributed significantly, they participated less than the native-born. Survey results found that 21 percent of immigrants had volunteered in the previous year, contributing 144 total hours, compared with 27 percent of native-born Canadians, contributing 162 hours. Interestingly, however, the survey also found that while immigrants engage in minimal volunteering during their early years in Canada, those in the country longer than 20 years engaged in more volunteering than the native-born (Canadian Centre for Philanthropy 2000). Immigrants in Canada, then, have a strong record of voluntarily donating time and money to their new country.

Language Acquisition

Acquiring the host country's language may be regarded as a virtual precondition for immigrant integration. Being able to speak, read, and write in the mother tongue(s) of the receiving society opens opportunities of employment, friendship, and information, all of which connect immigrants to their new country. In their comparative study of immigrant integration in different countries, Lynch and Simon observe, "The language ability of immigrants in Canada is very high" (2003, 257). In Canada, they note, less than 4 percent of immigrants were reported not to have conversational ability in one of the country's official languages, English and French. The comparable rate in other countries was 9 percent in Australia, 23 percent in the United States, and 39 percent in Great Britain. The prevalence of English and French among immigrants in Canada is not happenstance, but the result of government policy. The point system rewards immigrant applicants who speak an official language of Canada. And Quebec's control over immigrant selection to the province allows it to favour francophone immigrants.

Intermarriage

Intermarriage is the most personal indicator of integration in a diverse society. Again, Canada ranks high on this criterion. Lynch and Simon report that as of 1996, 18 percent of all marriages in Canada were between a foreign- and native-born person. In the United States, such unions accounted for only 5 percent of all marriages (Lynch and Simon 2003, 257). Mixed race marriages have also increased dramatically. From 1991 to 2006, the number of biracial marriages climbed by 50 percent (Adams 2007; Barrera 2008). And predictably, biracial marriages are most prevalent among younger Canadians in our largest cities. While such marriages accounted for just over 3 percent of all Canadian marriages as of 2001, 13 percent of all marriages involving Vancouver residents in their twenties were biracial unions. Toronto had a rate of 11 percent; and Montreal, 6 percent. Clearly, hybridity is on the rise in Canada's population. In the 2006 census, 41 percent of Canadians reported that they belonged to more than one ethnic ancestry. Canadian families are becoming increasingly multi-ethnic and multiracial, like the country itself.

Cultural Recognition

A significant dimension of immigrant integration is whether newcomers can become cultural icons of their new society. Let us look for evidence in the realm of both high and popular culture.

Canada is currently living its literary "golden age." Canadian novelists have established global reputations and audiences for their fiction.

Among the leading authors of Canadian fiction are Ondaatje, Vassanji, Mistry, Selvadurai, Mootoo, Lam, Choy, Sakamoto, Hage, Skvorecky, Ricci, Bezmogis, Clarke, Cooper, and Brand. Most are non-white immigrants, including the final three, each of Caribbean origin. Since 1994, the Giller Prize has been awarded annually for the best Canadian novel. Seven times over its 18-year history, the Giller Prize has been awarded to a non-white author—all were immigrants except two. Canadian fiction today is very much the literature of diaspora and homeland, and immigrant writers are its finest voices. Their stories are recognized to be Canada's stories.

In Canada, hockey may be the closest thing to a "national religion." Perhaps the best-known Canadians are hockey players. The National Hockey League, the sport's major competitive league, has six teams in Canada. These are located in Montreal, Ottawa, Toronto, Calgary, Edmonton, and Vancouver. Each hockey team has one captain, selected to be the team's leader in play and in the community. In 2008, four of the Canadian teams had a foreign-born captain; another team was captained by a Canadian-born black player. This suggests that Canadians are comfortable with non-whites and foreign-born as their heroes. In literary fiction and in sporting arenas, the foreign-born have reached the highest ranks in Canada.

Educational Performance

Seeking a better future for their children is how most newcomers to Canada typically explain their decision to migrate. The educational performance of immigrant children is a major determinant of their future prospects. Lynch and Simon observe that in Canada "[t]he educational attainment of immigrants is higher than that of the native population" (2003, 256). There is considerable empirical evidence to support this claim.

To begin with, adult immigrants themselves are better educated than the Canadian-born population they are joining. A Statistics Canada study reported that in 2007, 37 percent of all immigrants aged 25 to 54 held a university degree. This compared with just 22 percent for Canadian-born in the same age group. And the more recently the immigrants arrived, the better educated they were. Thus, 50 percent of all immigrants who entered Canada from 2002 to 2007 held a university degree (Statistics Canada 2008a). Again, this elevated educational background is not a random occurrence, but a reflection of the human capital priorities of the point system.

The children of immigrants typically achieve higher levels of education in Canada than their native-born cohorts. Indeed, a Statistics Canada study found that some immigrant children educated in Canada were more than twice as likely to have a university degree than the native-born! Based on data from 2002, Statistics Canada reported that 65 percent of young adults aged 25 to 34 born to immigrant parents from China and

India had completed a Canadian university degree. The degree completion rate for children of Canadian-born in the same age bracket was only 28 percent. Immigrant children from other backgrounds were closer to or below the native-born degree completion rate. Children of Caribbean and Portuguese immigrant parents each had 33 percent university graduation rates; those of Central and South American ancestry had a 24 percent university graduation rate.

In the main, however, children of immigrants have a greater likelihood of earning a university degree in Canada than children of the native-born (Statistics Canada 2008b). Immigrant children are also winning the lion's share of Canada's most prestigious scholarships to pursue graduate studies after their first university degree. In 2008, for instance, nine of eleven Canadian recipients of Rhodes scholarships to study at Oxford in Britain were children of Canadian immigrants. "You don't have to be an immigrant to win the Rhodes," commented journalist Margaret Wente, "but it helps" (Allemang 2008, F1). So it is that in immigrant families, parental expectations and encouragement produce high-achieving children.

The relation between student identity and school achievement has also been studied at the high school level. Canada's largest school board, in Toronto, reported that children from some immigrant communities where the household mother tongue was not English had *lower* school dropout rates than children from English-speaking homes. The 2006 study found that for students beginning high school in the year 2000, there was a dropout rate of 22.9 percent for students where the home mother tongue was English. Interestingly, students coming from nine non-English mother tongue households had *lower* dropout rates, including Urdu at 19.5 percent, Tamil at 16.9 percent, and Chinese at 12 percent. Across the Toronto school system as a whole, the high school dropout rate was 21 percent (Brown 2006).

On the other hand, students from nine other mother tongue languages had considerably *higher* high school dropout rates than the system average or English language group. These included Portuguese at 42.5 percent, Spanish at 39.1 percent, and Somali at 36.7 percent. The study also found that 40 percent of students whose parents migrated from the English-speaking Caribbean had dropped out of high school (Brown 2006). These disadvantaged statistics remind us that immigrant integration in Canada is not always, nor entirely, a success story.

IV. FAILINGS OF IMMIGRANT INTEGRATION IN CANADA

As the previous section demonstrates, there are many strong indicators of successful immigrant integration in Canada. However, the record is far from perfect. Some immigrants also continue to face disappointments and marginalization in Canada. This section identifies the major shortcomings in immigrant integration in Canada.

Economic Performance

While other chapters in this book discuss the economic status of immigrants in Canada, in the context of integration, it is impossible to entirely ignore the subject here. There is increasing evidence of deteriorating economic well-being among immigrants in Canada. The situation is especially problematic for immigrant arrivals over the past ten years, three-quarters of whom are non-white.

This trend of worsening immigrant economic performance is, of course, surprising since recent immigrants are the best-educated newcomers Canada has ever attracted. Despite their high human capital, many immigrants languish in unemployment or in marginalized jobs requiring little education (Weeks 2008). And yet these immigrants were selected for admission to Canada precisely because of their university education and high human capital. This squandering of human capital and dashing of immigrant aspirations is Canada's biggest failing in immigrant integration.

Reflecting on the paradox of highly educated immigrants faring poorly in Canada's economy, Triadafilopoulos perceptively observes, "It is precisely where the state has not played an active role in facilitating integration that we see the greatest problems" (2006, 91). As we saw earlier, Canada's promotion of immigrant naturalization, of multiculturalism, and of accessible public institutions creates a context for successful socio-cultural integration of newcomers. But in the current neo-liberal environment, the economic well-being of immigrants is largely left to market forces to determine. Too often for immigrants, this has translated into a host of insurmountable barriers, such as lack of credential recognition and professional accreditation, an absence of networks to secure employment, job competition from Canadian-educated graduates, and discrimination in hiring.

The result for many immigrants has been precarious employment in poorly paid jobs at the low end of the labour market. Thus, a recent study found that 40 percent of university-educated females and 24 percent of university-educated males who immigrated to Canada in the last five years were employed in jobs requiring little education, such as clerks, cashiers, salespeople, and taxi and truck drivers (Statistics Canada 2008c). The economic difficulties immigrants face can jeopardize other dimensions of integration, such as their ability to afford appropriate housing or costly university education for their children, or to maintain their physical and psychological health.

Political Participation

Earlier we noted that Canada has a more successful record than other countries in electing foreign-born citizens to government positions.

However, the political arena also has marginalized immigrants and non-whites, in particular. Indeed, a recent book on the subject concludes that Canadian politics suffer from an "identity representation gap" (Andrew et al. 2008, 257). So while Canada can boast the highest rate of immigrants elected to its national legislature, the 13 percent share of seats held by immigrants in 2007 was still significantly below the 19.8 percent of Canada's population who were foreign-born in 2006. The representation of non-whites in Canadian government is even worse. In 2006, non-whites accounted for almost 15 percent of Canada's population but held only 7 percent of elected seats in the national Parliament (Black 2008). In Canada's largest cities, where most immigrants live, non-whites have been especially under-represented among politicians elected to represent the city in municipal, provincial, and national government. In order for non-whites to have the same share of elected positions as they comprise of the urban population, Montreal would need to elect more than six times the number of visible minorities it did in 2005 (Simard 2008); Toronto, four times as many (Siemiatycki 2008); and Vancouver, more than twice as many (Bloemraad 2008). This is not an equitable pattern of immigrant integration.

Another dimension of immigrant political marginalization recently gaining attention is the lack of municipal voting rights for non-citizen immigrants (Siemiatycki 2006; Siemiatycki 2007). Over 40 countries permit immigrants who have not naturalized to vote in municipal elections in the city where they live. Since immigrants pay municipal taxes and depend on local services, these countries regard municipal voting as a way of giving all immigrants a voice in the community where they live. Canada's cities, as we have seen, have extraordinarily high rates of foreign-born residents. And while most immigrants to Canada have naturalized as Canadian citizens, the number who have not is large. For instance, just before the municipal election in 2006, the City of Toronto dropped 246,924 names from its Voters List because they were not Canadian citizens (Essensa 2007).

This amounted to one in every seven Toronto voters on the list. Across Canada, according to the 2006 census, one in every 17 residents is not a citizen, and most of these foreign-born residents live in large cities. Non-citizen residents of Canada come in several categories. First, there are permanent residents waiting to fulfill the three-year residency requirement for naturalization. Second, there are the 15 percent of immigrants eligible for citizenship who choose not to naturalize. These first two groupings account for most of Canada's non-citizen residents. In the final two categories are temporary and non-status migrants, who are ineligible for citizenship. In Toronto, a campaign titled "I Vote Toronto" is under way to secure municipal voting rights for non-citizen immigrants.

Racism and Discrimination

Finally, it must be noted, significant numbers of non-whites in Canada report experiencing discrimination in Canada. This is despite the fact that Canada has laws and policies prohibiting discrimination. Statistics Canada, through its Ethnic Diversity Survey, asked Canadians about their experiences of discrimination (Statistics Canada 2003). Overall, 7 percent of Canadians reported that they had sometimes or often faced discrimination because of their ethnocultural characteristics (e.g., ethnicity, race, religion, skin colour, accent) over the previous five years. For whites, this response rate was 5 percent; but for non-whites, it was 20 percent. And among non-whites, 32 percent of Blacks reported being discriminated against sometimes or often, along with 21 percent of South Asians and 18 percent of Chinese. Additionally, 17 percent of Blacks, 13 percent of South Asians, and 15 percent of Chinese stated they had faced discrimination in Canada as a rare occurrence. If we combine all those who reported *any* experience of discrimination in Canada, it amounts to 49 percent of Black respondents, 34 percent of South Asians, and 33 percent of Chinese. The survey also found that 11 percent of visible minorities feared becoming the victim of a hate crime in Canada. Another survey conducted between the end of 2006 and early 2007 found that 66 percent of Canadian Muslims were concerned about discrimination and 30 percent were very concerned (Adams 2007). Clearly, these adverse experiences and fears of discrimination remind us that Canada has not perfected its approach to immigrant integration.

CONCLUSION

Canada today is widely regarded as a model of successful immigrant integration. The country does indeed have a strong record of equitable immigrant inclusion. Particularly impressive is that Canada has achieved this after a lengthy history of racist and discriminatory treatment of immigrants. Canada has consciously come to define itself as an *immigrant nation*, "a country that accepts, even encourages, immigration to the point where immigrants figure prominently in the population, the culture, and the mythology of that nation" (Lynch and Simon 2003, 209). Tolerance, multiculturalism, and migration origins (from all parts of the globe) are now highly valued by Canadians.

Irene Bloemraad has written that immigrant integration is especially influenced by "the degree of material and symbolic public support offered to newcomer communities." She contends that "government ideologies, policies, and programs influence immigrant citizenship" (2006, 102, 246). In the last half of the 20th century, Canada adopted a set of measures that became a formula for successful immigrant integration. These included (1) making Canadian citizenship readily available to immigrants;

(2) removing identity restrictions (e.g., race, ethnicity, nationality, religion) as criteria for immigrant admission; (3) adopting multiculturalism as a pluralistic definition of Canadian identity; (4) passing a series of laws prohibiting racism and discrimination; and (5) promoting access and equity as characteristics of Canada's public institutions and services.

Recent years have seen the erosion of these "pillars of integration" in Canada. Increasing numbers of temporary foreign workers are admitted to Canada to fill labour market needs. They typically are ineligible for either permanent residency or Canadian citizenship. Neo-liberalism has discredited the role of government, promoting instead the virtues of market forces. And multiculturalism is on the defensive, criticized in other countries and even in its Canadian "homeland" as antithetical to liberal democratic values. Yet the Canadian experience should stand as evidence that immigration serves newcomers and the receiving society best when it is framed by ideologies, policies, and programs of shared citizenship, valuing diversity, and tangible settlement support.

REFERENCES

Abu-Laban, Y., and C. Gabriel. 2003. *Selling Diversity: Immigration, Multiculturalism, Employment Equity and Globalization.* Peterborough: Broadview Press.

Adams, M. 2007. *Unlikely Utopia: The Surprising Triumph of Canadian Pluralism.* Toronto: Viking.

Aguilar, L. 2006. The New "In-Between" Peoples: Southern-European Transnationalism. In *Transnational Identities and Practices in Canada,* eds. V. Satzewich and L. Wong, 202-215. Vancouver: UBC Press.

Allemang, J. 2008. A fork in the Rhodes. *Globe and Mail,* 29 November.

Andrew, C., J. Biles, M. Siemiatycki, and E. Tolley. 2008. *Electing a Diverse Canada.* Vancouver: UBC Press.

Aoun, S. 2008. Muslim Communities: The Pitfalls of Decision-Making in Canadian Foreign Policy. In *The World in Canada: Diaspora, Demography, Domestic Politics,* eds. D. Carment and D. Bercuson, 109-122. Montreal & Kingston: McGill-Queen's University Press.

Barrera, J. 2008. Highlights from Statistics Canada's 2006 Census. Canwest News Service, 2 April. At http://www.canada.com/globaltv/national/story.html?id=b8f21525-cb3d-4b1c-b236-4f6af1196c96.

Biles, J., M. Burstein, and J. Frideres. 2008. *Immigration and Integration in Canada in the Twenty-first Century.* Montreal & Kingston: McGill-Queen's University Press.

Bird, K. 2005. Guess Who's Running for Office? *Canadian Issues/Thèmes canadiens.* Summer, 80-83.

Black, J. 2008. Ethnoracial Minorities in the 38th Parliament: Patterns of Change and Continuity. In *Electing a Diverse Canada,* eds. C. Andrew et al., 229-254. Vancouver: UBC Press.

Bloemraad, I. 2006. *Becoming A Citizen.* Berkeley: University of California Press.

Bloemraad, I. 2008. Diversity and Elected Officials in the City of Vancouver. In *Electing a Diverse Canada,* eds. C. Andrew et al., 46-69. Vancouver: UBC Press.

Boyd, M. 2007. Religion-Based Alternative Dispute Resolution: A Challenge to Multiculturalism. In *Belonging: Diversity, Recognition and Shared Citizenship in Canada*, eds. K. Banting, T.J. Courchene, and F.L. Seidle, 465-473. Montreal: Institute for Research on Public Policy.

Brenner, N., J. Peck, and N. Theodore. 2005. Neoliberal Urbanism: Cities and the Rule of Markets. Demologos Working Paper. Department of Geography: University of Wisconsin–Madison.

Brown, L. 2006. Dropout, failure rates linked to language. *Toronto Star*, 23 June.

Brown, R.C. 1996. Full Partnership in the Fortunes and Future of the Nation. In *Ethnicity and Citizenship: The Canadian Case*, eds. J. Laponce and W. Safran, 9-25. London: Frank Cass.

Canadian Centre for Philanthropy. 2000. The Giving and Volunteering of New Canadians. At http://www.frameworkfoundation.ca/pdf/File_3.10%20G&V%20(New_Canadians).pdf (accessed 26 December 2008).

Centre for Research and Information on Canada. 2004. *Portraits of Canada 2004*. 4 November. At www.cric.ca.

Chui, T., K. Tran, and H. Maheux. 2007. *Immigration in Canada: A Portrait of the Foreign-born Population, 2006 Census*. Ottawa: Statistics Canada.

Citizenship and Immigration Canada. 2007. *Facts and Figures 2007: Immigration Overview*. Ottawa: Statistics Canada.

Day, R. 2000. *Multiculturalism and the History of Canadian Diversity*. Toronto: University of Toronto Press.

Department of Finance Canada. 2006. *Advantage Canada: Building a Strong Economy for Canadians*. Ottawa: Government of Canada.

Department of Finance Canada. 2008. *Budget 2008: Responsible Leadership*. Ottawa: Government of Canada.

Essensa, G. 2007. Personal Correspondence. 5 February.

Fenlon, B. 2008. Canada's visible minorities top 5 million. *Globe and Mail*, 2 April.

Flecker, K. 2008. Building "The World's Most Flexible Workforce": The Harper government's "double-doubling" of the Foreign Worker Program. *OCASI Newsletter*, Spring, 6-8.

Frisken, F., and M. Wallace. 2000. The Response of the Municipal Public Service to the Challenge of Immigrant Settlement. Ottawa: Citizenship and Immigration Canada.

Kelley, N., and M. Trebilcock. 1998. *The Making of the Mosaic: A History of Canadian Immigration Policy*. Toronto: University of Toronto Press.

Knowles, V. 2007. *Strangers at Our Gates: Canadian Immigration and Immigration Policy, 1540–2006*. Hamilton: Dundurn Press.

Kymlicka, W. 1998. *Finding Our Way: Rethinking Ethnocultural Relations in Canada*. Don Mills, Ontario: Oxford University Press.

Lynch, J., and R. Simon. 2003. *Immigration the World Over: Statutes, Policies, and Practices*. Lanham: Rowman and Littlefield Publishers.

Macklin, A. 2001. Borderline Security. In *The Security of Freedom: Essays on Canada's Anti-Terrorism Bill*, eds. R. Daniels et al., 383-404. Toronto: University of Toronto Press.

Mitchell, K. 2004. *Crossing The Neoliberal Line: Pacific Rim Migration and the Metropolis*. Philadelphia: Temple University Press.

Omidvar, R., and T. Richmond. 2003. Immigrant Settlement and Social Inclusion in Canada. Working Paper. Toronto: Laidlaw Foundation.

Papademetrious, D. 2003. Policy Considerations for Immigrant Integration. *Migration Information Source*, 1 October.

Quirke, L. 2007. More Than Books: Examining the Settlement Services of the Toronto and Windsor Public Libraries. *Our Diverse Cities: Ontario* (Fall): 156-60.

Ray, A. 1996. *I Have Lived Here Since The World Began*. Toronto: Lester Publishing Ltd.

Siemiatycki, M. 2006. The Municipal Franchise and Social Inclusion in Toronto: Policy and Practice. Working Paper. Toronto: Inclusive Cities Canada.

Siemiatycki, M. 2007. Invisible City: Immigrants Without Voting Rights in Urban Ontario. *Our Diverse Cities: Ontario* (Fall): 166-68.

Siemiatycki, M. 2008. Reputation and Representation. Reaching for Political Inclusion in Toronto. In *Electing a Diverse Canada*, eds. C. Andrew et al., 23-45. Vancouver: UBC Press.

Simard, C. 2008. Political Representation of Minorities in the City of Montreal: Dream or Reality? In *Electing a Diverse Canada*, eds. C. Andrew et al., 70-91. Vancouver: UBC Press.

Statistics Canada. 2003. *Ethnic Diversity Survey: Portrait of a Multicultural Society.* Ottawa: Statistics Canada.

Statistics Canada. 2008a. *The Daily.* 18 July.

Statistics Canada. 2008b. *The Daily.* 22 September.

Statistics Canada. 2008c. *The Daily.* 22 December.

Triadafilopoulos, T. 2006. A Model for Europe? An Appraisal of Canadian Integration Policies. In *Politische Steurung von Integrationsprozessen*, eds. S. Baringhorst, U. Hunger, and K. Scholnwalder, 79-94. Wiesbaden: VS Verlag.

Troper, H. 1993. Canada's Immigration Policy Since 1945. *International Journal* 48 (2):255-81.

Trudeau, P. 1971. Speech in Parliament, 8 October. At http://www.northernblue.ca/canchan/cantext/speech2/1971ptmu.html (accessed 20 December 2008).

Weeks, C. 2008. Established immigrants increasingly stuck in low-education jobs, study finds. *Globe and Mail*, 23 December.

CHAPTER 9

Relations ethniques et crise des « accommodements raisonnables » au Québec

MARYSE POTVIN, *Professeure, Département d'Éducation et Formation spécialisées, Université du Québec à Montréal*

INTRODUCTION

La société québécoise a été marquée de 2006 à 2008 par une crise sociale et médiatique dite des « accommodements raisonnables » (AR),[1] un concept juridique propre au Canada et qui découle de la jurisprudence de la Cour suprême en matière de discrimination indirecte et de droits de la personne. Le débat sur les « accommodements raisonnables » a commencé son ascension et sa cristallisation à partir de mars 2006, lors du jugement de la Cour suprême du Canada (jugement Multani) qui autorisait, sous certaines conditions, le port du kirpan à l'école publique québécoise pour un élève sikh baptisé (Potvin 2008a).[2] En janvier-février 2007, le débat se transforme en « crise » et atteint son apogée : il « s'enlise », « sert la division sociale » et nécessite « des assises qui seront celles de la raison et des valeurs communes », affirme le Premier ministre du Québec, Jean Charest.[3] Dans un contexte de montée de l'intolérance, de discours populistes du chef de l'Action démocratique du Québec (ADQ) et de dérapages médiatiques, le Premier ministre crée dans l'urgence, le

Managing Immigration and Diversity in Canada: A Transatlantic Dialogue in the New Age of Migration,
ed. D. Rodríguez-García. Montreal and Kingston: Queen's Policy Studies Series, McGill-Queen's University Press.

8 février 2007, la *Commission de consultation sur les pratiques reliées aux différences culturelles* (Commission Bouchard-Taylor) qui constituera le plus vaste exercice de « délibérations citoyennes » autour de la définition du « Nous » de la communauté québécoise. Sa création, en plein début de campagne électorale québécoise de 2007, visait à freiner la récupération populiste (voire raciste) du débat par ses adversaires, celle-ci contribuant à banaliser et à légitimer ce type de discours dans l'opinion publique, de même qu'à accroître l'idée d'une « menace identitaire ».

Mais que s'est-il donc passé au Québec en 2006 et en 2007 dans ce débat sur lesdits « accommodements raisonnables »? Les médias ont-ils dérapé ou bien ce sont les citoyens ou les politiciens qui se sont emballés? Les médias ne font-ils que refléter les tensions et les contradictions présentes au sein de la société ou les provoquent-ils?

Ayant été impliquée dans l'analyse de cette crise par le biais d'un rapport d'expert sur le traitement médiatique et les discours d'opinion sur les « accommodements raisonnables », rédigé à la demande de la Commission Bouchard-Taylor (Potvin 2008a, 2008b), je vais résumer ici les conclusions de mon étude. Je présenterai quelques constats généraux sur le traitement événementiel et sur les discours d'opinion d'éditorialistes, de chroniqueurs, d'intellectuels et de lecteurs dans la *presse écrite québécoise,*[4] en portant une attention particulière à la présence de mécanismes d'une rhétorique populiste et racisante dans ces discours (Potvin 2000, 2004).

À travers ces discours sociaux, cette « crise » autour des AR a non seulement mis en lumière l'état des rapports ethniques et des perceptions réciproques entre les groupes au Québec mais aussi l'écart important entre le discours « normatif » (juridique et institutionnel) et les discours d'opinion, la méconnaissance du dispositif en matière d'immigration et d'égalité au sein d'une bonne partie de l'opinion publique et chez nombre de journalistes, la présence de discours populistes et néoracistes[5] souvent inconscients et, enfin, l'impact du passage récent des francophones du statut de minoritaires à majoritaires.

Dans ce débat, les discours médiatiques et les images sur les événements ont été plus au centre des expériences de la population que les événements eux-mêmes. Le langage des médias ou des personnalités publiques est devenu celui de nombreux citoyens, qui reprenaient les mêmes termes et métaphores. Nous avons cherché à mesurer, même minimalement, l'influence qu'a pu avoir la presse écrite sur la construction du débat, par l'ampleur, voire la légitimité, attribuée à ces « événements » – souvent des faits divers dévoilés comme des « enquêtes exclusives » – et par la recherche de controverses, qui ont alimenté certains sentiments (injustice, peurs, victimisation…) chez une partie du public, voire même une banalisation des discours racistes, par l'octroi d'un espace élargi à leur expression. L'analyse a montré qu'il y a eu maintien artificiel et continu du débat par les médias, provoquant un effet crescendo ayant mené à la création de la Commission Bouchard-Taylor en février 2007, par la récurrence des

« affaires » mises à la Une comme des AR, par l'amalgame de différentes problématiques (immigration, multiculturalisme et autres), par la mise en visibilité parfois excessive accordée à ces questions, et par la mise en scène des événements ou du débat dans son ensemble. Évidemment, dans un jeu de va et vient, les discours d'opinion des publics alimentent aussi celui des médias et des politiciens, au point où chacune se targue de ne rapporter (ou de ne répéter) que ce que les autres disent ou pensent.

Le rôle des médias ou des différents acteurs n'est jamais univoque, ni facile à mesurer dans le déclenchement de « crises » aussi multidimensionnelles que celle qu'a connue le Québec en 2006 et 2007. Les épisodes de crises naissent d'un « faisceau de conditions » historiques, politiques, symboliques, socio-économiques ou culturelles qui sont activées ou réactivées par différents acteurs pour créer une conjoncture propice à une cristallisation autour d'un « enjeu », objet d'un débat social intense. Les conflits internationaux, la mondialisation, les inégalités mondiales et locales, le terrorisme, l'immigration, les différences religieuses et culturelles, les enjeux identitaires et politiques propres à la dynamique Québec-Canada s'entremêlent, implicitement ou explicitement, dans ce débat public. Dans le contexte de la campagne électorale provinciale de 2007, à travers un jeu politique et médiatique de stimulation des conflits, de désignation d'adversaires et de construction d'enjeux artificiels, nombre d'observateurs ont constaté et condamné les discours populistes de certains politiciens sur la question des accommodements. Ces discours ont clairement exploité, voire légitimé les sentiments de victimisation, d'exaspération, d'injustice ou de menace au sein d'une partie de l'opinion publique.

La fragilité du statut de « majoritaire » des francophones québécois a certainement joué un grand rôle dans les craintes et sentiments de « menace » exprimés par de nombreux citoyens lors de ce débat. Par exemple : craintes de perdre les acquis récents (et fragiles) de la modernité québécoise, qui composent « l'identité collective » (ex. égalité des sexes, acquisition du français chez les immigrants, etc.); craintes quant aux capacités de la population majoritaire à se concevoir comme un NOUS inclusif et à intégrer les immigrants; craintes d'être taxés de « racistes » par le « *Rest of Canada* »[6] et par le reste du monde; bref, craintes quant à la réussite ou à l'échec du « modèle d'intégration » développé par le Québec depuis 30 ans. Ces craintes ont été particulièrement visibles dans les discours de lecteurs, mais aussi de journalistes et d'intellectuels, lorsqu'ils voulaient « abolir » la charte des droits[7] ou lorsqu'ils mettaient l'accent sur la victimisation du groupe majoritaire, qui serait menacé par les exigences de ces « intégristes religieux » imposant leur « loi », recevant des « privilèges » et multipliant leurs « demandes excessives » auxquelles la majorité se « plierait » jusqu'à en perdre son identité.

S'il est difficile de mesurer avec exactitude la responsabilité des médias dans l'alimentation de discours racistes, ou leur impact réel sur l'opinion publique, il n'en demeure pas moins qu'en décembre 2007, dans le cadre du congrès de la Fédération des journalistes du Québec, de nombreux journalistes ont fait leur *mea culpa*. Le journaliste Jean-Claude Leclerc disait, dès février 2007, que les médias avaient exagéré. Ce débat, qu'il considère comme une « psychose publique », aurait été une pure fabrication des médias, « les seuls qui ont mis cet enjeu sur la table[8] ». Avant la fin des audiences publiques de la Commission Bouchard-Taylor (décembre 2007), plusieurs journalistes ont commencé à dire qu'il ne se passait rien de concret ou de grave pour justifier un tel alarmisme, alors qu'ils avaient abondamment parlé de « crise » pendant des mois. C'est ce que soutiennent par exemple les reportages de l'*Actualité* du 1er octobre 2007, et de *La Presse* des 12–13 novembre 2007. Lysiane Gagnon, une chroniqueuse qui a elle-même contribué à mettre le feu aux poudres,[9] écrivait soudainement en novembre 2007 :

> « Que se passe-t-il concrètement dans les écoles et les hôpitaux multiculturels – là où, justement, se poserait le soi-disant problème des accommodements raisonnables? […]: de fait, il ne se passe pas grand-chose qui puisse justifier l'alarmisme médiatique et les cris d'orfraie de ceux qui voient déjà nos valeurs foulées aux pieds par l'afflux de minorités revendicatrices. Rien non plus qui puisse justifier l'existence de la commission Bouchard-Taylor. […] Quand on va sur le terrain […] on voit bien que toute cette histoire était une tempête dans un verre d'eau, et qu'il n'était nul besoin de gaspiller des millions de dollars et les précieux neurones de nos intellectuels pour enquêter sur le sujet. […] La réalité, c'est que 1) il y a très peu de demandes d'accommodements provenant de minorités religieuses; 2) ces demandes sont parfois agréées, parfois non, dans un climat de savoir-vivre. Cela se fait au jour le jour, de manière pragmatique[10]… ».

Pourtant, de nombreuses voix parmi les chercheurs et intervenants des milieux scolaires et de la santé répétaient depuis 2006 que les médias dramatisaient les situations, interprétaient abusivement certains faits (associés indûment à des AR) et qu'il fallait dénoncer et freiner le discours populiste montant. Or, la plupart des médias analysés n'ont pas rendu audibles ou visibles ces points de vue. Par exemple, une lettre et une pétition envoyées aux médias en novembre 2006, signées par Marie Mc Andrew et par 230 experts en relations ethniques et représentants d'organismes, n'ont pas été publiées; la mise sur pied du comité sur les accommodements raisonnables du ministre de l'Éducation (comité Fleury) en octobre 2006 (avant la Commission Bouchard-Taylor), puis le rapport qui en a découlé, ont à peine été couverts, de même que le débat entre 200 praticiens et chercheurs lors des « Journées d'études sur les pratiques d'accommodements en éducation », organisées en mars 2007 par les membres du comité Fleury.[11] Bref, les articles ou reportages montrant des réalités non conflictuelles, des réalités « ordinaires » de gens des milieux scolaires, de la santé et des services sociaux, qui gèrent généralement sans heurts des demandes d'accommodements au quotidien, ont été très rares dans les médias jusqu'en avril 2007.[12] Au même moment, des faits divers insignifiants faisaient la « Une » pendant des jours (Potvin 2008b), parmi lesquels plusieurs qui se sont révélés être de véritables constructions imaginaires de problèmes ou de conflits par les médias (Rioux et Bourgeoys 2008).

Pour permettre une meilleure compréhension de la crise des « Accommodements raisonnables » chez un lecteur non-Québécois, il importe de situer les rapports historiques entre les groupes majoritaires et minoritaires au Québec et au Canada – qui expliquent le sentiment de « fragilité » de la majorité francophone – de même que le concept juridique d' « accommodements raisonnables » et l'évolution du dispositif juridico-politique en matière de gestion de la diversité, d'égalité et de droits de la personne – largement mis en cause dans cette « crise ». Au Canada, la structure constitutionnelle du pays et les politiques de citoyenneté, d'immigration, d'égalité et de « gestion du pluralisme » sont interreliées historiquement et découlent des rapports de pouvoir entre les groupes. Nous aborderons finalement le rôle des médias et les discours d'opinion entendus au cours de cette « crise ».

RAPPORTS ENTRE MAJORITAIRES ET MINORITAIRES ET ÉVOLUTION DU DISPOSITIF JURIDICO-POLITIQUE

L'histoire du Canada se caractérise par des vagues successives d'établissements de populations, les Premières Nations (ou Autochtones) d'abord, suivis des colons français puis britanniques, et enfin d'une immigration de « peuplement », de plus en plus diversifiée. À partir du XVIIIe siècle, les rapports de concurrence politiques, économiques et démographiques qui vont s'établir entre colonisateurs français et anglais – qui se sont appelés les « deux peuples fondateurs » – vont déterminer l'ensemble de l'organisation sociale et de la structure politique du Canada, en minorisant d'abord les Autochtones – sous la tutelle de la *Loi sur les Indiens* de 1876, encore en vigueur[13] – puis les diverses populations immigrantes venues s'installer au Canada à partir du XIXe siècle. Ainsi, deux types de rapports majoritaires-minoritaires caractérisent ce contexte : les rapports entre « groupes nationaux » dits « fondateurs », ainsi que les rapports qu'ils entretiennent respectivement avec les nations autochtones (Amérindiens et Inuits) et avec les groupes minoritaires formés par la migration.

Le Canada constitue, depuis ses origines, un pays divisé et profondément pluraliste, non seulement sur le plan culturel – puisqu'il comporte plusieurs identités distinctes (nationales, majoritaires ou minoritaires) et plusieurs « Histoires » autoréférentielles – mais aussi structurel, puisqu'il se caractérise par un dédoublement de la structure sociale en institutions parallèles.

Après la Nouvelle France, puis la Conquête britannique de 1759, qui a mis les Anglais dans une position dominante face aux Français, le poids démographique des deux groupes de colonisateurs restera, jusqu'à la fin du XIXe siècle, un enjeu majeur dans leurs rapports de pouvoir réciproques, et dans leurs rapports avec les Amérindiens et les immigrants. Les colons britanniques ont d'abord voulu attirer des immigrants d'origine britannique (et loyalistes) pour consolider la colonisation dans une perspective d'homogénéisation et de contrôle de la population du territoire. Ils ont également accru l'esclavage des Noirs et des Amérindiens jusqu'en 1833 pour assurer le développement économique de la colonie.[14]
Les rapports de concurrence entre colonisateurs se sont traduits par des régimes politiques successifs après la Conquête, qui vont élargir ou réduire les droits juridiques, linguistiques, politico-institutionnels ou religieux des francophones et ce, jusqu'à l'Acte de l'Amérique du Nord britannique en 1867 (Loi constitutionnelle), qui fonde la Confédération canadienne autour de l'idée d'une entente entre « deux peuples fondateurs », unis politiquement mais possédant respectivement des « droits acquis » par l'histoire et garantis par la Constitution. Cette dialectique identitaire a généré la création d'un État fédéral dont les compétences et pouvoirs sont distincts de ceux des États provinciaux qui en sont membres. La Constitution prévoit une division des compétences législatives et administratives – la plupart exclusives – entre l'État fédéral et les dix provinces, celles-ci possédant leur propre gouvernement, institutions et assemblée législative.[15]

À partir des années 1960, le « nationalisme étatiste » qui s'est instauré au Québec au cours de sa « Révolution tranquille » va marquer le passage d'une vision minoritaire, ethnique et religieuse des « Canadiens-français » à une vision majoritaire, territoriale, civique et étatique de « l'identité québécoise ». Par ces changements, les rapports Canada-Québec se cristallisent davantage en identités « universalistes » concurrentes. Les échecs des référendums de 1980 et de 1995 sur la souveraineté du Québec, le rapatriement de la constitution sans l'accord du Québec (1982), puis les échecs des Accords de Meech (1990) et de Charlottetown (1992), qui visaient à octroyer un statut distinct au Québec (par rapport aux autres provinces) et à le faire entrer dans la constitution, ont renforcé le développement de deux « desseins » majoritaires, ou « deux solitudes » à la mémoire sélective, qui offrent leurs propres interprétations de l'histoire et de l'identité.

Ces rapports de pouvoir entre les groupes nationaux ont eu des répercussions sur l'immigration et l'intégration des immigrants à l'un ou l'autre des deux « peuples ». À l'instar des Autochtones, les immigrants se retrouveront souvent, au cours de l'histoire, pris « en sandwich » dans les débats et conflits qui opposent les deux « peuples fondateurs ». La dynamique des rapports entre les colonisateurs a toujours exclu les Autochtones du pouvoir politique et économique. Même si certaines dispositions de la *Charte canadienne des droits et libertés* reconnaissent un statut de minorité « nationale » aux Autochtones,[16] et même si diverses ententes leur permettent d'élargir progressivement leur autonomie gouvernementale, ces derniers ont été souvent tenus à l'écart des négociations constitutionnelles. Il en va de même des immigrants et de leurs descendants, qui seront appelés à « s'assimiler » aux deux pôles majoritaires. Les relations concurrentes et hiérarchisées entre les deux « peuples fondateurs » resteront déterminantes dans la façon de percevoir, de traiter et de « gérer » l'immigration et les minorités au fil du temps.

Les grandes vagues d'immigration européenne, qui débutent en 1816, remplissent de plus en plus un objectif « d'utilité économique » pour assurer le développement « national » canadien. Les immigrants recevront gratuitement des terres agricoles (*Plan Sifton*), vont constituer une main-d'œuvre à bon marché dans les zones industrielles ou travailler à la construction des chemins de fer, dans le cadre de la *National Policy* de John A. Macdonald.[17] La politique d'immigration de l'époque est ouvertement discriminatoire et fondée sur l'*Anglo Conformity* : les immigrants britanniques et américains étaient d'abord recherchés, suivis des Européens du Nord, alors que les Européens du Sud étaient plutôt « tolérés » et les « minorités visibles »,[18] carrément indésirables. Cette hiérarchie des « préférences », qui a conduit à l'exclusion des non-blancs ou à des mesures de recrutement sélectif et de quotas à l'endroit des Asiatiques et des Indiens au début du XXe siècle, caractérisera la politique d'immigration canadienne jusqu'en 1967. Cette année-là, le Gouvernement fédéral adopte un Règlement qui abroge toutes les dispositions préférentielles et discriminatoires fondées sur la race, la religion, la culture, la langue et l'origine nationale et les remplacent par des critères de sélection « objectifs » (niveau d'études, qualifications professionnelles, etc.) et un système d'évaluation par « points » appliqué à tous les candidats à l'immigration. Le visage du Canada va alors se diversifier. Les immigrants d'origine européenne diminuent alors que ceux du « Tiers-Monde » augmentent considérablement. Cette diversification va entraîner des changements majeurs en ce qui concerne la « gestion » de la diversité et l'application d'un système effectif de droits.

C'est aussi au cours des années 1960 que le Gouvernement fédéral met sur pied la *Commission Royale d'Enquête sur le Bilinguisme et le Biculturalisme* (1963–1970), qui va montrer la profonde stratification ethnique et sociale du Canada. Les rapports issus de cette commission ont révélé de profondes inégalités socio-économiques entre les Français, les Anglais et les minorités issues de l'immigration. Dans un contexte de fortes revendications autonomistes et indépendantistes du Québec, ce constat mènera le Gouvernement fédéral à traiter à la fois les enjeux linguistiques entre groupes nationaux et les enjeux de la polyethnicité.

Il adopte d'abord en 1969 la *Loi sur les langues officielles*, afin de donner à tout le Canada un caractère bilingue et de favoriser l'accès des francophones à tous les postes de la fonction publique fédérale. Il s'agit de ce qu'on pourrait appeler aujourd'hui le premier « programme d'action positive » canadien (*Affirmative Action*), qui va consacrer juridiquement l'existence des « individus » anglophones et francophones, donc des minorités de langues officielles dans toutes les provinces du Canada. Cette loi sera suivie d'une *Politique du Multiculturalisme* en 1971, qui reconnaît le pluralisme culturel et normatif, stipulant que le pays est formé de diverses cultures qui ont droit au respect et à l'existence dans le cadre du bilinguisme. La dimension symbolique est importante : le premier ministre Trudeau déclara : « [...] bien qu'il y ait deux langues officielles, il n'y a pas de culture officielle, et aucun groupe ethnique n'a la préséance » (Débats de la Chambre des communes, 8 octobre 1971 : 8545). Cette politique sera mal reçue au Québec car, selon certains, elle « *ramenait la culture canadienne-française au même rang que toutes les autres, tournait le dos à l'histoire canadienne et se référait à l'idée "ahistorique" d'une égalité de toutes les cultures et de toutes les communautés ethniques* » (IRPP, Meisel, Rocher et Silver 1999, 168).

On se rappellera que dans le Québec des années 1960, où se super-posaient une frontière historico-ethnique et une frontière de classes entre francophones et anglophones, les immigrants, qui aspiraient à gravir les échelons socio-économiques, tendaient à s'intégrer à la communauté anglophone. Celle-ci contrôlait alors l'économie et le marché de l'emploi à Montréal, résidait dans les beaux quartiers, jouissait d'un prestige inégalé dans le reste du Canada et possédait les institutions scolaires les plus riches et les services sociaux les plus développés pour les accueillir (Levine 1990). Pour les Canadiens français, qui se définissaient comme minoritaires, l'immigration était perçue comme une « menace » que l'État québécois ne contrôlait pas. Pour planifier son propre développement, le Québec décide alors d'intervenir sur le processus de sélection et d'inté-gration des immigrants *à la majorité francophone*. L'immigration est élevée au rang d'enjeu politique majeur, et liée à la « consolidation » nationale. Après une série d'ententes avec le gouvernement fédéral, le Québec aura la responsabilité exclusive de l'intégration des immigrants et de la sélection des immigrants « indépendants » (travailleurs qualifiés). L'immigration et l'intégration seront perçues comme des moyens de contrer le déclin démographique et linguistique des francophones en Amérique du Nord.

Mais les pouvoirs accrus du Québec en ces matières ont aussi accru son rapport de concurrence avec le Canada, comme cadres de légitimité et de loyauté des immigrants, à travers diverses stratégies d'allégeances citoyennes, d'intégration et de mobilisation politique.

Lorsque le Premier ministre Trudeau décide d'enchâsser la *Charte des droits et libertés* dans la Constitution canadienne en 1982, il vise à construire une citoyenneté et une identité canadiennes autour de valeurs « universelles » et une interprétation libérale : ce sont les individus qui sont porteurs de droits, de langues et de « cultures », les provinces sont égales entre elles et le fondement historique des deux « peuples fondateurs » est évacué (Leydet 1992). Le « patriotisme constitutionnel » que cette réforme érige va se traduire par un « patriotisme de la Charte » (*Charter Patriotism*) (Cairns 1995), qui modifie les rapports entre gouvernants et gouvernés ainsi que les modes de participation des citoyens : les citoyens se tournent davantage vers le processus judiciaire pour faire respecter leurs droits, qu'ils soient ou non contraires aux décisions de la majorité.[19]

La « citoyenneté de la Charte » a donc des effets sur la définition de la polyethnicité et de la « multinationalité » du Canada, dont les enjeux sont davantage ceux de l'autonomie gouvernementale et de l'autodétermination des groupes nationaux (Québécois et Autochtones). Car bien que la Charte repose sur le principe d'égalité des droits individuels, elle *consacre aussi le caractère multiculturel et partiellement multinational (reconnaissance des peuples autochtones) du pays*. En effet, le Multiculturalisme est enchâssé dans l'article 27 de la Charte canadienne, qui stipule que « cette Charte doit être interprétée en conformité avec la préservation et la promotion de l'héritage multiculturel des Canadiens » et que « toute interprétation de la présente Charte doit concorder avec l'objectif de promouvoir le maintien et la valorisation du patrimoine multiculturel des Canadiens », une disposition interprétative invoquée par la Cour suprême du Canada dans plusieurs arrêts. L'interprétation des articles 15 (égalité des droits) et 27 (sur le Multiculturalisme) de la Charte va mener à l'adoption de la *Loi sur le Multiculturalisme canadien* en 1988. Cette loi renforce le caractère « fondamental » et permanent de la diversité canadienne, reconnue comme une caractéristique de l'identité et du patrimoine. L'approche est soumise à une interprétation libérale : la loi indique que les identités collectives sont d'abord des attributs individuels (art. 3(1)). Codifié par la Charte, le Multiculturalisme vise donc à gérer la diversité en fonction des libertés fondamentales de l'individu tout en faisant la promotion de l'*unité* nationale, par un sentiment d'appartenance au Canada et par la participation civique.

Ainsi, le cœur du dispositif en matière d'égalité, « d'accommodements raisonnables » et de lutte contre les discriminations repose, au Canada, sur la *Charte canadienne des droits et libertés*, enchâssée dans la Constitution de 1982, et sur les législations provinciales sur les droits de la personne, lois fondamentales à caractère quasi-constitutionnel.[20] L'article 15 de la Charte (sur le droit à l'égalité) interdit la discrimination fondée sur un ensemble de motifs, mais la Cour suprême du Canada, cour de dernière instance qui entend les appels provenant de tous les tribunaux canadiens dans tous les domaines du droit (civil, administratif, pénal et constitutionnel), a donné une interprétation large à l'article 15 : la discrimination est prohibée non seulement pour les motifs énumérés, mais aussi pour tout motif « analogue », et l'ensemble des instruments provinciaux, fédéraux ou internationaux sur les droits de la personne peuvent être pris en considération pour déterminer ces motifs analogues.[21] Puisque les questions constitutionnelles peuvent être soulevées dans tout litige impliquant des particuliers, des gouvernements ou des organismes gouvernementaux, la Charte a eu une incidence majeure sur la promotion et la protection des droits de la personne, ainsi que sur la reconnaissance et l'exécution des droits de plusieurs groupes minoritaires et défavorisés. Par exemple, les droits ancestraux des Autochtones ont été largement définis par les décisions des tribunaux en raison de la difficulté, lors de discussions constitutionnelles, de les faire reconnaître par un texte juridique qui fasse consensus.

La Cour suprême a construit par sa jurisprudence un concept évolutif de la discrimination au cours des 25 dernières années, qui est passé de la discrimination directe à la discrimination indirecte (par « effet préjudiciable »), à l'obligation « d'accommodement raisonnable » lorsqu'il y a atteinte indirecte aux droits fondamentaux d'une personne, et enfin, à la discrimination systémique. Sa jurisprudence affirme que l'égalité exige plus qu'une simple concurrence égale, pour les emplois et les services par exemple (égalité des chances), mais aussi l'adoption de mesures positives pour répondre aux besoins des individus lorsque leur participation égale n'est pas assurée (égalité substantive). L'interprétation de l'égalité repose désormais sur l'idée d'égalité des chances évaluée en regard d'une analyse des résultats (ou des effets), un passage de l'égalité formelle vers l'égalité réelle ou substantive. .

La notion de discrimination par suite d'un « effet préjudiciable » (discrimination indirecte) signifie que les employeurs et les fournisseurs de services ne peuvent ignorer l'effet de leurs politiques sur leurs employés et leurs clients s'ils manifestent une inégalité de fait identifiable sur la base des motifs prohibés par la Charte. À cet égard, les arrêts *O'Malley c. Simpsons-Sears* (supra), et *Bhinder c. Chemins de fer nationaux* créent « l'obligation d'accommodement raisonnable » et en fixent les limites. Cette obligation exige une adaptation des normes, des pratiques ou des politiques institutionnelles ou organisationnelles en fonction des besoins de certaines personnes, en raison de leur handicap, religion, etc. Dans l'arrêt O'Malley, la Cour suprême du Canada a confirmé que lorsqu'une politique d'horaire d'entreprise est préjudiciable à un employé du fait de sa religion, l'employeur doit prouver qu'il s'est efforcé d'accommoder les besoins religieux de cet employé au point de causer une « contrainte excessive » à l'entreprise en termes de coûts, de santé et de sécurité.[22] Dans *Commission des droits de la personne de l'Alberta c. Central Alberta Dairy Pool*

(1990) 2 RCS 489), la Cour a décidé que l'obligation d'accommodement aux besoins particuliers d'un employé surgissait dès qu'un règlement (d'emploi) avait pour lui une conséquence préjudiciable sur ses droits fondamentaux. La Cour estime désormais que toute discrimination en matière d'emploi doit être motivée par une « exigence professionnelle justifiée », avec l'obligation de chercher un accommodement jusqu'à ce que cela crée « une contrainte excessive » pour l'employeur.

L'employeur a donc l'obligation d'assurer à ses employés plus qu'une simple égalité formelle en mettant en œuvre – sous réserve de certaines limites – des accommodements susceptibles de corriger entièrement ou partiellement les effets discriminatoires non intentionnels de diverses pratiques ou normes institutionnelles qui peuvent être, au demeurant, parfaitement justifiables sur d'autres plans. Cette obligation juridique doit porter sur l'un (ou plusieurs) des motifs de discrimination énumérés par les chartes canadienne et québécoise. Elle émane de la reconnaissance que les institutions publiques ne sont pas neutres mais qu'elles sont légitimement et historiquement marquées, par exemple, par la religion traditionnellement majoritaire, ce qui peut avoir un effet potentiellement discriminatoire sur les personnes pratiquant des religions minoritaires. Il ne s'agit donc pas d'un privilège, comme on l'a souvent et indûment entendu au cours du débat sur les AR, mais d'une exception permettant de rétablir et de garantir le droit à l'égalité d'une personne. Comme le montre l'ensemble de la jurisprudence sur l'AR, c'est précisément au nom des valeurs fondamentales qu'on peut équilibrer les droits entre eux et juger de la légitimité ou non de consentir une exemption à des normes ou à des pratiques à caractère universel.

Il s'agit d'un passage évident d'une justice procédurale (selon laquelle on ne fait pas de discrimination lorsqu'on « traite tout le monde de la même façon »)[23] à une justice distributive ou compensatoire, qui met l'accent sur une responsabilité plus grande des institutions en matière des droits et libertés de leur personnel ou de leur effectif. La justice distributive repose sur trois concepts centraux : la discrimination par effet préjudiciable, l'accommodement raisonnable et l'égalité des chances. Ce dernier concept repose sur le postulat que les institutions (scolaires ou autres) ne peuvent se contenter de traiter « tout le monde de la même façon », mais qu'elles doivent donner à certaines personnes plus de services ou des services adaptés à leurs besoins (élèves handicapés, en difficulté d'adaptation/d'apprentissage ou nouvellement arrivés).

Les notions d'effet préjudiciable et d'AR, qui ont permis d'appréhender la complexité du phénomène des discriminations, ont aussi mené au concept de « discrimination systémique », adopté et consacré par la Cour suprême, dans *Action Travail des Femmes c. Chemins de fer nationaux* (1987 1 RCS 1114). Ce concept repose sur l'idée d'une interaction (et rétroaction) entre des pratiques, des idées, des règles ou des normes en matière de recrutement, d'embauche, de promotion, etc., qui créent un effet circulaire de la discrimination pour certains groupes. La discrimination systémique combine donc la discrimination directe et indirecte.

La Cour a conclu que la discrimination systémique nécessitait des *remèdes* de nature systémique, comme l'ordonnance d'une mesure d'équité en matière d'emploi. C'est dans ce but que la Commission sur l'égalité en matière d'emploi (Commission Abella) est crée en 1983. Elle conduira à l'adoption, en 1986, de la *Loi sur l'équité en matière d'emploi*, qui opère de concert avec les législations sur les droits de la personne. Cette loi a pour but de réaliser l'égalité en milieu de travail et, à cette fin, de corriger les désavantages subis par quatre groupes historiquement victimes de discrimination en emploi : les femmes, les membres des « minorités visibles », les Autochtones et les personnes souffrant d'une incapacité physique ou mentale (handicapées). Elle oblige les entreprises sous juridiction fédérale à se doter d'un Plan d'équité, l'équivalent des « Programmes d'accès à l'égalité » appliqués au Québec et inscrits dans la Charte québécoise des droits. Outre un traitement identique des personnes, l'équité en emploi est donc associée à la nécessité d'implanter de façon proactive des programmes spéciaux comportant des objectifs numériques à atteindre en termes d'embauche, en fonction des compétences des personnes. L'objectif est d'assurer la représentation des groupes désavantagés dans le personnel des institutions ou entreprises afin qu'elle reflète leur distribution dans le bassin de main-d'œuvre disponible.

Dans le même sens, le Québec a aussi mis en œuvre un important dispositif en matière de droits de la personne et d'intégration depuis 30 ans. Il adopte d'abord la *Charte des droits et libertés de la personne* en 1975, qui pose les droits fondamentaux des citoyens comme principe inaliénable, puis la *Charte de la langue française* en 1977, qui établit des liens entre l'intégration des immigrants et la langue publique commune. Ces deux lois fondamentales marqueront le passage sociologique des francophones au statut de « groupe majoritaire », statut qui va orienter le discours normatif dominant à caractère civique, interculturel et inclusif sur l'intégration des minorités à la majorité francophone. Dans ce changement de statut, et avec l'arrivée du Parti québécois (souverainiste) au pouvoir en 1976, le discours public et normatif se dissocie des anciennes rhétoriques militantes et anticolonialistes. Il ne s'agit plus de dénoncer les « rapports d'oppression » (dont le groupe francophone se sentait historiquement victime) mais d'intégrer les minorités dans une nouvelle « société » majoritairement francophone. Le discours de « libération nationale » comme minoritaire a fait place à un discours d'affirmation nationale comme majoritaire. Le Québec développera une conception officielle de « convergence culturelle » (1978), puis passera par l'approche du « contrat moral » (1990) avec l'*Énoncé de politique en matière d'immigration et d'intégration* pour ensuite, en 2002, tendre vers un « contrat civique commun » (nettement plus « républicain » et nationaliste) qui n'a jamais abouti sous forme de politique ou de plan d'action. Dans ce processus, les groupes ethniques ont été successivement des « communautés culturelles », des « Québécois des communautés culturelles », puis des « citoyens de toutes origines » pour redevenir des communautés culturelles.

L'*Énoncé de politique en matière d'immigration et d'intégration* de 1990, remis à jour dans un Plan d'action en 2004, a posé les jalons du « modèle d'interculturalisme » québécois, qui se distingue en partie du Multiculturalisme canadien. L'Énoncé se fondait sur des choix de société ayant valeur de principes : le français langue commune de la vie publique; la pleine participation de tous les citoyens à une société démocratique; l'ouverture au pluralisme dans les limites imposées par le respect des valeurs démocratiques fondamentales; le respect de ces choix de société par les Québécois de toutes origines. Cette politique s'appuyait sur une sorte de « contrat moral » entre l'immigrant et la société québécoise et posait les premiers jalons d'une « culture publique commune », au centre du « contrat » que tous devaient respecter. Cette culture était chapeautée par *la Charte québécoise des droits et libertés de la personne*, qui protège la liberté de chacun de conserver son identité par le droit à l'égalité, et fixait les limites de la diversité en référence au cadre juridique existant, c'est-à-dire aux lois adoptées démocratiquement par l'Assemblée nationale et aux institutions démocratiques. Enfin, l'*Énoncé* privilégiait trois axes d'intervention : le développement de l'apprentissage du français; la pleine participation des immigrants et des Québécois des communautés culturelles à la vie économique, sociale, culturelle et institutionnelle; les relations intercommunautaires harmonieuses. Les actions ont pris la forme d'un plan d'action gouvernemental, de programmes d'appui à l'intégration et à la francisation et de différents services en ce sens. L'Énoncé sera suivi, au début des années 2000, par un projet de « citoyenneté québécoise », à la fois proposé au *Forum national sur la citoyenneté et l'intégration* (2000) et par la *Commission des états généraux sur la situation et l'avenir de la langue française au Québec* (2001), qui n'a pas connu de suites.

RÔLE DES MÉDIAS ET DISCOURS D'OPINION DANS LA « CRISE » DES ACCOMMODEMENTS RAISONNABLES

Dans le débat sur les AR, c'est tout ce dispositif juridico-politique et son discours normatif qui a été pointé du doigt, voire remis en question par nombre de citoyens et de journalistes. C'est d'abord le rôle des chartes canadienne et québécoise qui sera indûment présenté comme unidirectionnel, comme si celles-ci contraignaient les institutions publiques à toujours accepter les demandes des minorités, voire à leur consentir des privilèges. Ensuite, les journalistes se sont mis à « scruter » les politiques publiques sur l'immigration et l'intégration et leur application pour chercher « du conflit ». Pendant ce débat, la confusion sur le concept d'AR – sur ses objectifs et son application – a conduit certains citoyens et même des municipalités (dont Hérouxville) à demander aux gouvernements de changer les chartes, voire de les abolir et ce, au nom d'une supposée injustice à l'égard du groupe majoritaire ou de « l'état d'urgence ».[24] Si les tribunaux ont établi des balises et limites pour accommoder une personne discriminée, ces balises étaient visiblement incomprises par le public et par nombre de journalistes.

Dans notre analyse du traitement médiatique et des discours d'opinion, nous avons montré une importante participation des médias écrits à la construction du débat, nettement perceptible par certaines mises en scènes, procédés et cadrages ayant permis de mettre cet enjeu à « l'ordre du jour » politique et de créer un état de « panique morale » (*Moral Panic*) (Cohen, 1972). La plupart des médias n'ont pas fait de distinction entre, d'une part, l'accommodement raisonnable, qui est une mesure réparatrice en raison d'une discrimination et, d'autre part, l'ajustement volontaire et les ententes privées, qui ne résultent pas de la violation d'une liberté fondamentale et qui n'ont pas de caractère obligatoire. Plus de 75 pour cent des « affaires » rapportées par les médias comme des AR entre mars 2006 et avril 2007 étaient des ententes privées ou des faits divers montés en épingle par des journalistes, qui ne visaient pas forcément à « informer le public ». Certains journalistes, visiblement peu informés sur ces sujets, ont contribué à nourrir une grande confusion sur les AR. Les discours d'opinion analysés, aussi bien ceux des journalistes que des lecteurs, reposaient souvent sur une vision impressionniste ou fausse des réalités relatives à la diversité.

L'analyse démontre que plusieurs grands médias écrits ont abordé la question des AR sous l'angle d'une polarisation entre les groupes minoritaires et majoritaires (cadre conflictuel), laissant supposer au lectorat que certaines minorités jouiraient de « privilèges » et menaceraient les valeurs communes (voire le « Nous » québécois), interpellant ainsi les lecteurs du groupe majoritaire à travers une lecture victimisante des événements. La couverture événementielle (et souvent éditoriale) de certains faits anecdotiques, par les photos, les titres, les *lead*, les mini-sondages, la parole donnée principalement à tel acteur, le cadrage dramatique, la multiplication des « affaires dévoilées » dans une logique de concurrence, la surenchère dans la mise à la Une de faits divers, la « fiction » de certaines affaires, la montée en spirale du traitement de ce type « d'histoires », montrées comme des « déviances » et des comportements antisociaux ou non-conformes aux normes du groupe majoritaire (*Deviancy amplification spiral*, selon la théorie de la *Moral Panics*), l'emballement médiatique (*media hype*) et la couverture disproportionnée par rapport aux cas réels d'AR, le mimétisme des médias (écrits et électroniques), qui se relancent mutuellement et la mise en scène de « l'enjeu » dans le cadre de la campagne électorale ont contribué sans contredit à transformer le débat en « crise de société » et à exacerber les préjugés populaires envers certaines minorités, dont les demandes ont été désignées, dans plusieurs discours d'opinion, comme étant les principales responsables des diverses turbulences identitaires et économiques que vit la société québécoise.

Les données d'ensemble ont montré l'ampleur, la fréquence et la récurrence de la couverture médiatique sur les accommodements raisonnables, autant en ce qui concerne le « débat général » sur le sujet que les douze affaires spécifiques analysées en profondeur. La couverture a connu un effet crescendo, car après une courte pause, en novembre et décembre 2006, le débat est réanimé à chaque semaine par de nouvelles « affaires » et par un « activisme » médiatique.[25] On constate, en simultané et de manière continue dans tous les médias écrits et électroniques, des séries de reportages et des entrevues récurrentes. Le débat a été ponctué par de nombreuses prises de position des politiciens lors de la campagne électorale et par différents sondages qui ramenaient constamment cet « enjeu » au centre de la campagne. Plus le débat évoluait, plus il déviait : la question des accommodements s'amalgamait à un ensemble de sujets divers et de préoccupations générales (l'identité nationale, la question linguistique, l'immigration, l'intégration des immigrants), plus ou moins liés aux faits, réels ou supposés, dont il était question. Après la création de la Commission Bouchard-Taylor, les médias dévoilent encore quelques faits divers mais la tension médiatique s'atténue, pour reprendre sur le ton de l'analyse et du *Mea Culpa* au moment des audiences publiques de la Commission, à l'automne 2007.

Faits divers anecdotiques ou véritables cas d'accommodements raisonnables?

Entre mars 2006 et avril 2007, seulement 3 affaires médiatisées étaient des cas judiciarisés d'accommodements raisonnables.[26] *La Presse* et le *Journal de Montréal*, deux grands quotidiens qui se livrent une forte concurrence, ont déclenché plusieurs histoires plus ou moins fictives à partir de faits divers anecdotiques, en les mettant à la Une à des fins commerciales et en les « dévoilant » sous forme « d'enquête exclusive ». De l'installation de fenêtres givrées au YMCA du Parc à la demande de Juifs hassidiques, en passant par la lettre des conseillers municipaux d'Hérouxville et les « cabanes à sucre accommodantes », ces faits divers étaient traités de manière quasi hebdomadaire sous l'angle des AR. De mars 2006 jusqu'en avril 2007, tous les journaux analysés ont adopté un cadrage (*framing*) qui amalgamait de véritables cas d'accommodements raisonnables, au sens juridique, avec des faits divers anecdotiques qui n'en n'étaient pas (souvent des affaires privées). Entretenant la confusion, les titres des articles sur ces faits divers comportaient l'appellation (*label*) d' « Accommodements raisonnables ».

En recherchant et en amalgamant plusieurs incidents ou faits divers anecdotiques, certains médias ont procédé à la mise en récit d'un

« problème » de société. En l'inscrivant de façon aussi spectaculaire à leur ordre du jour, ils en ont fait un enjeu dont on devait débattre dans la sphère publique. Cette montée en épingle a eu une grande influence sur l'agenda public et politique de cette période. À grand coups de sondages sur le « racisme des Québécois », de mini-sondages quotidiens et d' « enquêtes exclusives », ces journaux ont mis ce « débat » à l'ordre du jour (*agenda setting*), forçant les politiciens (et les citoyens) à se prononcer sur un ensemble de questions associées, souvent indûment, aux AR. Le premier ministre Charest n'aurait d'ailleurs jamais créé la Commission sans « l'activisme médiatique » autour desdits AR, et sans la campagne électorale qui démarrait en février 2007. L'influence qu'ont les médias sur les ordres du jour des acteurs publics et politiques s'accompagne d'un certain mimétisme entre médias, créant un renforcement des ordres du jour médiatiques (*inter-media agenda*). Ce phénomène a conduit, par moment, à une certaine uniformisation des contenus et à un effet consensuel, multiplicateur et grossissant des événements.

Cadre juridique et cadre de dramatisation

La façon dont les questions ont été formulées et présentées par les journalistes, ainsi que l'importance accordée à certains points de vue, ont pu affecter la compréhension des enjeux par le public (McCombs et Shaw 1993). Par exemple, le cadre (*frame*) légal ou juridique par lequel a été abordée la majorité des faits divers a induit en erreur le public ou, du moins, a alimenté la confusion en associant indûment les aménagements ou ententes privées à des AR. Outre le « cadre légal », c'est le « cadre dramatique » qui a été le plus utilisé. Par le titrage, les images, l'interprétation conflictuelle, la course aux « nouvelles affaires » réelles ou imaginées d'AR, les médias ont élevé des événements anecdotiques au rang de crise de société. Plus que les autres, le *Journal de Montréal* (journal populaire) a, de manière répétitive, créé une mise en scène dramatique des affaires, en mettant constamment en opposition les « Québécois » de vieille souche et les « Autres », attisant ainsi un sentiment de victimisation chez le groupe majoritaire.

La couverture de certains médias tendait souvent à confirmer « ce que tout le monde semblait penser », c'est-à-dire ce qui était présumé être l'opinion majoritaire. Dans cette logique, certains médias ont autorisé l'expression de discours racisants en octroyant un droit de parole aux acteurs ayant les positionnements les plus extrêmes. La reprise de certaines perceptions populaires dans les entrevues et la large publication de lettres de lecteurs très défavorables à certaines ententes en témoignent. Les autres points de vue semblent avoir été confinés à la « spirale du silence ».[27] Les médias ont même créé des « personnalités publiques » un peu clownesques, qu'ils invitaient à répétition pour exposer leurs points de vue extrémistes. Ce fut le cas, par exemple, de la mise en spectacle du conseiller d'Hérouxville ou de l'imam Jaziri,[28] invités de manière récurrente par différents médias à se prononcer sur toutes sortes d'affaires.

L'utilisation répétée d'un cadre « dramatique » est aussi associée à la concurrence commerciale que se livrent les grandes entreprises médiatiques québécoises. La recherche de profits les a conduits à distordre la réalité et à amplifier le nombre de scoops, de conflits et d'histoires spectaculaires pour augmenter leur auditoire. Certains médias ont joué le rôle du « pompier incendiaire » (Bourdieu 1996), excitant les passions populaires en pointant du doigt les fautifs ou les déviants, pour ensuite « dénonc[er] à grands cris et condamn[er] sentencieusement l'intervention raciste de celui qu'ils ont contribué à faire » (ibid., 75).

Accommodements et campagne électorale

Ce débat a été avant tout celui des médias et des politiciens. Il a servi d'enjeu et de décor dans la mise en scène de la campagne électorale provinciale de février-mars 2007. Sollicités constamment sur les « affaires » d'accommodements, les politiciens ont en quelque sorte participé à l'entretien artificiel du débat médiatique autour de faits parfois inexistants ou inexacts (Rioux et Bourgeoys 2008): en donnant leur opinion sur des « histoires » sans vérifier la véracité des faits relatés par les journaux, ou en ne distinguant pas les anecdotes des véritables AR. Ces « affaires » étaient donc utilisées comme « critères de référence » pour juger de la compétence ou de l'incompétence des personnalités publiques.

Le gain de popularité de l'Action démocratique du Québec (ADQ) (parti populiste de droite) durant cette période a même été attribué, par nombre de journalistes, aux prises de position populistes de son chef (Mario Dumont) dans ce débat. Les prises de position de Mario Dumont ont été davantage couvertes que celles des autres politiciens. Les titres de nombreux articles ont repris, avec récurrence, les propos sensationnalistes de Mario Dumont. Le 17 novembre, le *Journal de Montréal* met une photo de Mario Dumont en page 5 avec, en gros titre, une citation de lui: « Accommodements raisonnables. On glisse dans des abus de la Charte ». En sous-titre, « Le chef de L'ADQ juge inquiétantes certaines *concessions faites aux minorités* » (sic!). Le *lead* de l'article renforce cet angle généralisant et négatif : « Les accommodements consentis aux minorités ethniques et religieuses dépassent les limites du bon sens, selon Mario Dumont ». L'article débute sur une citation de Dumont, qui joue sur la victimisation du groupe majoritaire : « Pendant qu'un jeune sikh se promène avec son poignard à l'école, la majorité québécoise ne peux plus utiliser le mot Noël… ». Dans l'article, l'enchaînement de citations de ce type oriente clairement le débat : « Qu'une majorité de citoyens défende les valeurs qui lui sont propres n'est ni une attitude raciste, ni une singularité dans le monde moderne ». La société québécoise est définie comme « généreuse » dans l'article, renforçant l'idée que les minorités reçoivent des « privilèges » et qu'en échange, ils doivent respecter « nos valeurs » : « La police n'est pas allée kidnapper personne dans le monde pour les forcer à venir au Québec », soutient Dumont. Il amalgame constamment les immigrants et les minorités religieuses. Sur la même page, un autre article titre : « Des limites à ne pas dépasser ». Il s'agit d'entrevues avec des musulmans qui disent la même chose que Mario Dumont, de manière plus nuancée. La mise en page de ces deux articles a pour effet de renforcer la position de Dumont.

Le même jour (p. 27), un autre article portant sur Mario Dumont tend à le légitimer et à renforcer certains préjugés à l'égard des minorités : « Pas commode, super Mario ». Le journaliste soutient que Dumont « s'est emparé du flambeau » et que « la politique québécoise ne peut pas se passer de super Mario pour dire les vraies affaires ». Le lendemain, 18 novembre, de nombreuses réactions du public (favorables à Dumont) sont publiées dans le journal, accompagnées de deux photos (un sikh et un Hassidim), et un article événementiel repose sur les réactions des chefs des autres partis (« Charest invite à la réflexion »).

Mario Dumont, en prétendant parler au nom de la majorité, voulait légitimer son discours populiste au sein de l'opinion publique. Cette légitimation politique a été très visible lorsqu'il a justifié l'initiative « des gens dans les municipalités » (« Hérouxville ») par le « vide de leadership » et parce que « l'intégration des immigrants a été négligée au cours des dernières années ». Il accuse constamment ses adversaires politiques de « mollesse » dans ce dossier, favorisant ainsi la « ligne dure » (« On ne peut pas défendre notre identité avec un genou à terre », *Journal de Montréal*, 19 novembre, p. 5). Ce type de légitimation a ouvert la porte à des discours qui n'auraient pas eu droit de cité un an auparavant, banalisant ainsi l'expression de l'intolérance. Comme en témoignent les nombreux extraits cités dans notre étude (Potvin 2008a et 2008b), plusieurs lecteurs réutilisaient abondamment les expressions de Mario Dumont (telles que : « mettre ses culottes », « genou à terre », « se plier aux exigences des minorités », etc.), reprises dans les titres et les *lead* de nombreux articles événementiels.

Représentation des minorités

Le traitement médiatique de certaines minorités a été, à plusieurs reprises, fort négatif et biaisé dans le *Journal de Montréal* et dans *La Presse*. Les images des communautés musulmane, juive orthodoxe et sikhe ont été, à répétition, celles des franges les plus minoritaires de ces communautés (femmes avec le niqab ou la burka, sikh baptisé portant le kirpan, juifs hassidiques, mise en spectacle récurrente de l'imam Jaziri), images qui étaient toutefois généralisées à tout un groupe par l'usage de titres globalisants, tels que : « Privilège spécial pour les Juifs ». Le dénigrement de pratiques vestimentaires et des croyances de certaines minorités religieuses a été observé à plusieurs reprises. En outre, les demandes d'aménagement issues de ces communautés étaient fréquemment abordées sous l'angle de privilèges ou « d'abus », plutôt que sous l'angle du droit à l'égalité ou d'ententes négociées. Certaines anecdotes étaient présentées comme des demandes « abusives » alors que les minorités concernées n'avaient fait aucune demande aux institutions (ce fut le cas pour ladite « directive » du Service de police de la Ville de Montréal et pour celle du Directeur général des élections concernant le niqab), où il s'agissait d'ententes privées entre un commerçant et des clients (l'Hôtel de Gatineau qui « accommode un groupe de juifs orthodoxes » dans *La Presse*, comme l'histoire des « cabanes à sucre accommodantes » dans *Le Journal de Montréal*).

Les biais négatifs ont été particulièrement observables dans la couverture d'événements impliquant des juifs hassidiques. À au moins six reprises, des « faits divers » différents ont été explicitement présentés sous l'angle de « privilèges » accordés aux Juifs en général, notamment dans le *Journal de Montréal*. Ainsi, le 17 mai 2006, ce dernier titrait : « Privilège spécial pour les Juifs. Le gouvernement Charest accommodant » (histoire du Centre de la Petite Enfance-CPE). Le 18 mai 2006, c'était : « Québec aurait bafoué la Charte » au sujet des garderies, afin de créer un bureau juif. Le 25 mai 2006, il titrait encore (p. 2) « Québec impose l'omerta à 2 CPE », avec un sous-titre négatif : « La communauté juive *favorisée* par une procédure ». Le *lead* est tout aussi stigmatisant et utilise la victimisation : « Les CPE, bousculés pour faire de la place à un bureau coordonnateur juif, ont été contraints de se taire ». Le 19 novembre (p. 9) : « CLSC[29] Lavallois. Traitement de faveur pour un Juif ». Cet article relate que la veille, un juif serait passé devant tout le monde dans une file d'attente d'un service de santé afin de ne pas manquer le Shabbat. Le 15 décembre 2006, le Journal déclenche « l'affaire » du CLSC de Ste-Thérèse de Blainville (p. 3) en titrant : « Accommodements raisonnables. Privilèges spéciaux pour les juifs ». Le sous-titre souligne que : « Les infirmières doivent *se plier* à leurs exigences pour prodiguer des soins aux patients de la communauté ». De même à la Commission scolaire de Montréal, deux articles à la Une mentionnaient que « les employés juifs et musulmans *ont droit à plus de congés…* ». On constate l'usage d'une victimisation du groupe majoritaire, de même qu'une généralisation desdites « demandes » à « tous les Juifs ». Dans plusieurs affaires, la parole est peu ou pas du tout donnée aux membres des minorités concernées.

Présence des mécanismes de la rhétorique populiste et raciste dans les discours d'opinion

Notre analyse a révélé la présence explicite et implicite de 8 mécanismes discursifs et sociocognitifs de type populiste et (néo)raciste dans la moitié de tous les textes d'opinion de notre corpus, mécanismes qui « débordent » des règles (discursives) socialement admises en matière de « rapports ethniques » au Québec (Potvin 2000, 2004, 2008a, 2008b). Ce débat a donc ouvert un large espace aux discours qui vont à l'encontre du « discours normatif » légitime et dominant (certains diraient « hégémonique ») en matière d'égalité, de droits de la personne, de pluralisme... Leur usage témoigne d'une sorte de « backlash » à l'égard du discours normatif. Ces mécanismes discursifs inversent, en quelque sorte, les valeurs inscrites dans les chartes et textes législatifs.

Sans entrer ici dans les détails théoriques, soulignons qu'un discours peut franchir différents « paliers » du racisme : lorsqu'il y a co-occurrence et passage d'un mécanisme à l'autre, le discours se cristallise et se durcit[30] :

1. *La dichotomisation négative* : la différenciation ou le marquage d'une frontière *Nous/Eux* (*In-group/Out-group*) constitue le premier niveau. Ce premier acte perceptif qu'est la catégorisation (Tajfel 1972) se présentera, dans le discours raciste, sous la double forme d'une désignation positive de soi et négative de l'Autre (Guillaumin 1972). Dans une logique raciste, il doit inclure un jugement de valeur sur l'existence d'une « frontière » Nous-Eux. Ce mécanisme repose sur un schéma d'opposition (l'Autre est extérieur au Nous) et sépare, par exemple, les vrais et les faux, les bons ou les mauvais (immigrants, musulmans, nationaux, etc.). Le Nous repose sur *la présomption de l'homogénéité du groupe* et parle d'une seule voix. C'est l'utilisation du NOUS-EUX à des fins d'exclusion de certaines composantes du NOUS qui constitue, ici, un mécanisme du discours racisant. Ce premier palier inverse le « Nous inclusif » du discours normatif.

2. *L'infériorisation* : plus que la simple négativité, l'infériorisation implique une dévalorisation des comportements, des traits culturels ou linguistiques, des croyances ou institutions de l'Autre (minoritaire, marginal, fondamentaliste, orthodoxe), et la valorisation de ceux du groupe majoritaire. La négativité de certains traits ou comportements est perçue ici comme menaçante envers l'ordre ou les valeurs dominantes (majoritaires). Ce mécanisme s'alimente du premier palier, puisqu'il se fonde sur le *comparatisme* : l'évaluation des comportements ou agissements de l'Autre s'effectue en fonction d'un Nous qui fixerait la « normalité » par rapport à la « déviance ». Ce mécanisme inverse la « valeur » d'égalité, préconisée par le discours normatif.

3. *La généralisation* de certains « traits », comportements, croyances d'un individu à tout un groupe (« ils sont tous pareils »). Ce mécanisme s'appuie généralement sur *une essentialisation* des attitudes et comportements des membres d'un groupe, qui instaure une « nature », pérennise une différence et la situe hors des rapports sociaux concrets. Ce mécanisme inverse le principe libéral « d'individuation » des droits de la personne.

4. *La victimisation* : l'accusation de l'Autre ou le désaveu du racisme (*disclaimers*). La victimisation comporte un renversement des rôles et son autojustification : c'est l'Autre qui est raciste en ne respectant pas « Nos normes »; celui qui se positionne comme victime estime qu'il doit assurer (et justifier) sa « légitime défense ».

5. *Le catastrophisme* : construction de scénarios apocalyptiques et prévision de la violence ou de la guerre, conséquemment à la « crise » actuelle et à la complexité de la situation. Il repose sur une vision pessimiste de l'avenir, un appel à la responsabilité des élus, à la fin du laxisme, à la « ligne dure » ou à la revanche. La comparaison porte également sur le passé, jugé glorieux, et le présent, vécu comme une dégénérescence, une décomposition et une incertitude.

6. *La diabolisation* : consiste à dépeindre l'adversaire comme l'incarnation du mal, à le transformer en ennemi, à le délégitimer en tant qu'acteur possédant une indépendance morale. Le trait ou comportement jugé négatif est amplifié au point de susciter la peur d'être exterminé ou violenté, d'être l'objet d'un complot démoniaque ou d'une manipulation perverse.

7. *La légitimation politique* : banalisation du discours racisant et récupération politique par certaines personnalités publiques, afin de construire un enjeu et de légitimer une situation aux yeux d'une partie de la population, qui peut y trouver l'occasion d'exprimer son exaspération.

8. *Le désir d'expulser l'Autre* : refus du rapport social ou du négociable (« Retournez chez vous »).

Le discours d'opinion des éditorialistes, chroniqueurs et intellectuels

Nous avons retracé près d'une quarantaine d'éditoriaux, chroniques ou lettres d'intellectuels (14 pour cent du corpus) qui comportaient des mécanismes de la rhétorique populiste et raciste, de manière implicite ou explicite. Par contre, tous ceux qui s'opposaient à une décision ou à une « affaire » n'ont pas fait usage de mécanismes racisants, car 47 pour cent des réactions des éditorialistes, chroniqueurs et intellectuels étaient défavorables aux AR, 29 pour cent favorables et 24 pour cent plutôt nuancées ou neutres dans l'ensemble des 5 journaux.[31]

Les « affaires » impliquant des juifs hassidiques ont suscité des discours éditoriaux beaucoup plus catégoriques, dont certains étaient empreints d'agressivité et de préjugés. La *dichotomisation négative* fut utilisée pour mettre en opposition lesdits droits et valeurs de la communauté hassidique et ceux de la majorité (définie comme « les citoyens » ou « la société »), notamment sur l'égalité des sexes, posée comme irréductible et non négociable. La *dichotomisation* combinée à l'*infériorisation* fut utilisée par certains pour montrer que les hassidim n'étaient pas adaptés au mode de vie moderne. Mais le dénigrement ou l'infériorisation de certaines pratiques vestimentaires ou croyances religieuses de minorités ciblées (musulmane, sikhe et hassidim) ont été observées à d'autres reprises : port de la burka et du niqab dans la décision du Directeur Général des élections (comparé au déguisement de Youppi, une mascotte des « Canadiens » au hockey), retour aux mœurs et coutumes des années 1950, « excès » dont feraient preuve certaines minorités dans leurs demandes... Les journalistes ont fréquemment utilisé la dérision, l'absurde et les exemples extrêmes pour dénoncer l'escalade potentielle de demandes « farfelues » des minorités, décrire les « limites » qui ont été franchies et soutenir que le multiculturalisme est sur une pente « dangereuse ». L'amalgame ou la corrélation des accommodements, réels ou supposés, avec des groupes intégristes a aussi été assez fréquent. Plusieurs ont pris clairement position pour la laïcité de l'espace public et ont associé les « accommodements » non seulement aux « immigrants », mais surtout aux « intégristes ». Une bonne dizaine a parlé de progression des intégrismes religieux dans la sphère publique et de la « mollesse » des Québécois envers les demandes de ces minorités. Ce fut, pour certains, une manière implicite d'exprimer une victimisation ou un catastrophisme.

Nous avons finalement observé la présence des mêmes mécanismes dans les textes portant sur le code de vie d'Hérouxville. Certains éditorialistes et chroniqueurs dénonçaient le caractère « raciste » du code de vie des habitants de cette municipalité en utilisant certains mécanismes de manière « inversée ». On a donc observé une *infériorisation* des gens d'Hérouxville, de leur compréhension du monde et de leur vision des « immigrants » par le cynisme et la dérision,[32] ou encore par la *dichotomisation* Québec urbain vs Québec « profond ».[33]

Le discours d'opinion des lecteurs

Plus que les journalistes, les lecteurs s'estimaient lésés, en tant que membres de la « communauté majoritaire », par des minorités qui « abuseraient » de la « mollesse » des « Québécois », ou par des juges, des politiciens ou des institutions, qui octroieraient « indûment » des privilèges à des minorités perçues comme « intégristes » ou « obscurantistes ». Le sentiment d'être menacés dans leurs valeurs et repères culturels s'exprime clairement dans le discours des lecteurs. Plusieurs transforment les juges, la Cour suprême ou la Charte en boucs émissaires. La capacité des juges à émettre des jugements qui « servent » la population est questionnée. Alors que certains plaident en faveur de l'amendement de la Charte, d'autres remettent en question son bien-fondé et son adéquation avec les réalités sociales actuelles. L'argument sécuritaire revient avec récurrence, suivi de l'exagération dans les demandes, de l'égalité entre les sexes, de la nécessité pour les immigrants de s'adapter et de la préservation des valeurs communes.

La grande majorité des lettres de lecteurs publiées étaient défavorables aux « accommodements » réels ou supposés. En excluant les 61 lettres faisant référence au code de vie d'Hérouxville – événement qui a suscité le plus de lettres favorables – on constate que 79 pour cent des lettres publiées sur les 11 autres « affaires » analysées étaient défavorables, contre 18 pour cent favorables et 5 pour cent nuancées. Si 79 pour cent des lettres étaient défavorables, 202 lettres de lecteurs (52 pour cent du corpus) comportaient des mécanismes racisants.

Les représentations dominantes de « l'Autre » dans les discours racisants témoignent d'une dichotomisation Nous-Eux importante. Par exemple, pour la quasi-totalité des lecteurs défavorables au jugement sur le port du Kirpan, parlant souvent au nom d'une majorité abstraite, le Eux renvoie aux immigrants récents et aux étrangers. À l'intérieur du Eux, l'amalgame sikh-musulman, voire islamistes-intégristes, revient fréquemment. Les événements sur la scène internationale depuis le 11 septembre 2001 et les mesures sécuristes adoptées subséquemment par le Canada et les États-Unis semblent venir cautionner une attitude de rejet ou de méfiance à l'égard des minorités religieuses ciblées dans certains discours d'opinion. La rigidité (perçue) des « préceptes » de ces communautés est souvent mise en opposition avec la « liberté » acquise de haute lutte par la population et ses mouvements sociaux (féministe, ouvrier, etc.). Certains nuancent parfois leur dichotomisation en distinguant les « bons immigrants » (qui « veulent » s'intégrer à la société en devenant « pareil à soi ») et les « mauvais » (qui demandent des accommodements, donc refuseraient selon eux les « normes communes »). Ceux qui semblent vouloir continuer à vivre « comme dans leur pays » ne feraient pas partie du Nous.

Dans une large partie de l'opinion publique, on constate un sentiment de distance et d'impuissance à l'égard des pouvoirs politique et juridique, qui prendraient des décisions désincarnées et jugées contraires à la « volonté populaire ». Ce rejet des décisions prises par des forces « supérieures » s'exprime à travers la critique de la Charte et du pouvoir des juges, dans un double mouvement contradictoire. La Charte, qui incarne l'universalisme abstrait, reconnaîtrait des droits aux individus, droits qui iraient parfois à l'encontre des choix de la « majorité ». Inversement, ces individus seraient issus de minorités religieuses, donc de communautés (particularismes) qui iraient à l'encontre de « l'universalisme ».

La Charte est également perçue, non pas comme assurant la protection des droits (égalité) en tant que valeur centrale de l'identité collective, mais comme brimant les droits des uns (majoritaires) pour privilégier les autres (minoritaires). On constate, dans certains discours d'opinion, un renversement des valeurs de la Charte à des fins de « délégitimation » et d'infériorisation de ceux qui sont définis comme « Autres ». Le respect des droits et libertés fait alors place au refus de la divergence et à l'exigence d'un « loyalisme » ou d'un conformisme social présumé consensuel. L'égalité des individus est remplacée par la conviction d'un favoritisme à l'égard de certains groupes et d'une injustice pour les autres citoyens; la flexibilité de l'identité (le « Nous inclusif », qui se définit par la négociation démocratique entre ses diverses composantes) se transforme en désir d'homogénéité. Les mécanismes discursifs s'appuient sur la conviction de parler au nom de l'universel et sur une représentation stéréotypée, voire mythique de l'accusé.

CONCLUSION

Nous avons montré dans cet article que la « crise » des AR au Québec s'est alimentée de plusieurs sources historiques et contemporaines. D'abord, elle a été produite par un ensemble de procédés, cadrages et stratégies commerciales des grands médias, qui sont loin d'avoir joué un simple rôle d' « espace public » de délibérations raisonnables entre citoyens. Les « enquêtes exclusives dévoilées » par ces journaux témoignent d'un phénomène *d'agenda setting* et de constructions d'enjeux dans le cadre de la campagne électorale. De plus, la disproportion entre les affaires médiatisées et la fréquence réelle des véritables « cas » d'accommodements (au sens juridique), de même que la disproportion entre les cas supposés « litigieux » par les médias et les aménagements « bien gérés » qui se produisent au jour le jour, ont contribué à l'édification d'un climat de tension, d'intolérance et de « crise identitaire ».

Ensuite, cette crise n'est pas un phénomène « soudain » d'exaspération à l'égard des minorités religieuses (transformées en boucs émissaires dans ce débat), mais puise dans les malaises historiques issus des rapports de concurrence avec le Canada anglais, concernant notamment l'allégeance des immigrants, tant sur le plan linguistique que symbolique. Ces malaises sont aussi liés à la fragilité du statut de majoritaire des francophones et à la perception négative du Multiculturalisme au Québec. La Réforme constitutionnelle de 1982, qui évacue l'idée des deux « peuples fondateurs », enchâsse la Charte des droits dans la Constitution, consacre le bilinguisme et le multiculturalisme du Canada autour d'un « Patriotisme constitutionnel » (Leydet 1992), a été perçue comme une « trahison » par bon nombre de nationalistes et souverainistes québécois. Ce sentiment s'est à nouveau manifesté, dans le débat sur le AR, par des discours fortement opposés à la « charte », au Multiculturalisme canadien et au « pouvoir des juges » mais en transformant les « minorités » et les « immigrants » en boucs émissaires.

Enfin, elle a été un *symptôme* de la fragilité des identités « nationales », d'une crise de légitimité politique et des transformations sociétales et économiques dans un contexte de mondialisation. Ce même type de débat a aussi eu lieu au « Canada anglais », lorsque la politique du

Multiculturalisme, mais aussi celle du « bilinguisme officiel » ont connu un important « *backlash* » après le référendum de 1995 sur la souveraineté du Québec. Les critiques à l'égard des « excès du Multiculturalisme » s'étaient multipliées : ghettoïsation des minorités, affaiblissement du tissu social, dépenses coûteuses, « culte » de l'ethnicité, etc. (Bissoondath 1994; Abu-Laban et Stasiulis 1992). Plusieurs craignaient une coexistence de communautés, non liées à un projet commun autour d'un centre identitaire ou national unificateur. Les échecs des ententes constitutionnelles avec le Québec et le Référendum de 1995 avaient créé un climat de crise nationale, alimenté par une multiplication de « dérapages racistes » à l'endroit du Québec dans les médias anglo-canadiens, et par un vaste mouvement visant la « partition » du Québec chez les défenseurs du fédéralisme canadien. Les discours racistes avaient fait place à une violence verbale suffisamment répétitive pour que le problème ne soit plus jugé secondaire et exige l'intervention du Premier ministre du Canada (Potvin 2000, 2004). Le mouvement partitionniste ressemblait donc, sur certains plans, au Code de vie d'Hérouxville, et la crise des AR, à la « psychose de l'identité nationale » post-référendaire au Canada anglais.

Dans ce débat sur les AR, les discours analysés nous renseignent donc sur l'état des frontières ethniques au Québec : victimisation du groupe majoritaire (menacé par les demandes des minoritaires qui imposeraient leur « loi »), « menace des intégrismes religieux » et « peurs de ne pouvoir intégrer les immigrants » comme société. Les divers cas, réels ou supposés, d' « accommodements » ont offert à plusieurs citoyens l'occasion de faire part de ce qui, à leurs yeux, « poserait problème » à la société québécoise. Souvent, ces « problèmes » sont impressionnistes ou imaginaires, et relèvent d'une méconnaissance du pluralisme et du dispositif public mis en œuvre au Québec. À cet égard, le « code de vie » d'Hérouxville constitue un exemple symptomatique de construction imaginaire de « l'Autre ».

Les discours racisants ont franchi différents « paliers » entre mars 2006 et avril 2007, comme si leur banalisation dans l'espace médiatique avait légitimé leur progression et leur durcissement. Un glissement important s'est opéré dans certains des discours analysés, passant d'un mécanisme à l'autre : de la frontière *Nous-Eux* (*dichotomisation négative*, l'Autre n'est pas le « Même » ou l'égal), à la *généralisation* d'un cas à tous les « immigrants » ou à tous les membres d'une minorité, et à leur amalgame (« ils sont tous pareils », « ils sont intégristes »), puis à leur *infériorisation* (« ils n'évoluent pas... »), à la *victimisation* de soi (offense et perte de pouvoir et d'identité du groupe majoritaire à cause desdits « privilèges » de certaines minorités), au *catastrophisme* (état d'urgence, ça va empirer) et à la *diabolisation* (envahissement, menace, l'autre est « inassimilable » à « nos » valeurs démocratiques d'égalité, « ils sont étranges, imprévisibles, inquiétants »), justifiant le refus du changement social ou l'évolution du droit, pour atteindre chez certains un *désir d'expulser l'autre* (« du balai » « retournez chez vous ») et une *légitimation politique* (ADQ, élus d'Hérouxville et de d'autres municipalités).

Ce débat n'a donc été ni civil, ni civique, ni inclusif. Au contraire, il a révélé, comme dans plusieurs sociétés occidentales d'ailleurs, la présence au sein du discours d'opinion d'un « néoracisme » qui définit les minoritaires non pas comme « biologiquement inférieurs » mais comme différents, inassimilables, porteurs de différences pathologiques ou irréductibles. Par des mécanismes discursifs souvent inconscients, le néoracisme entend protéger les droits de la personne, les acquis récents des luttes sociales de la modernité québécoise : l'égalité hommes-femmes, la laïcité, les droits des enfants…, tout en différenciant et infériorisant « L'Autre ». En d'autres mots, le néoracisme condamne les formes flagrantes de racisme, jugées socialement inacceptables au regard des droits de la personne, mais explique les rapports sociaux « problématiques » par les différences culturelles (inassimilables) afin de justifier la préservation des droits « acquis » par l'histoire, des valeurs démocratiques ou de l'unité nationale.

Ce que le rapport Bouchard-Taylor a principalement montré, c'est que le « modèle québécois » dit « d'interculturalisme » qui peut certes être constamment amélioré, a surtout été mal compris par la population. Un écart grandissant s'est creusé entre le discours public inclusif et pluraliste, la compréhension et la connaissance qu'en ont les citoyens et la persistance de différentes formes d'exclusion et de discriminations au sein de la vie sociale. Cet écart semble avoir créé une forme d' « aliénation » du public à l'égard du « pouvoir des juges » et une incompréhension de leurs décisions. C'est donc cet écart entre le discours normatif et le discours « populaire » qui doit être réduit, notamment par l'éducation. À cet égard, cette « crise » aura eu des effets pédagogiques, en suscitant une prise de conscience, chez les pouvoirs publics québécois, de l'urgence d'élever la question du racisme et des discriminations au rang des préoccupations civiques et du discours normatif.[34]

NOTES

1. Nous utiliserons souvent l'abréviation « AR » dans ce texte, par économie d'espace.
2. Bien que le débat ait réapparu de manière ponctuelle depuis 1985, il portait généralement sur de véritables « accommodements raisonnables », au sens juridique. Toutefois, à partir de mars 2006, après le jugement de la cour Suprême sur le port du kirpan à l'école publique québécoise, les médias ont multiplié les manchettes sur des faits divers catégorisés indûment par eux comme « des accommodements raisonnables », créant la confusion et l'intolérance au sein de l'opinion publique (Potvin 2008; Bouchard et Taylor 2008, 14-16).
3. Jean Charest, « Le débat doit se faire », Extraits de sa déclaration du 8 février, *La Presse*, 9 février 2007, p. A-1.

4. Articles publiés dans les grands quotidiens du Québec : *La Presse, Le Devoir, Le Journal de Montréal, Le Soleil et The Gazette,* du 1er mars au 30 avril 2006. Nous avons recueilli un total de 1105 articles de presse, soit 451 articles de type événementiel, 263 éditoriaux, chroniques et lettres d'intellectuels et 391 lettres de lecteurs, du 1er mars 2006 au 30 avril 2007. Nous avons divisé ces articles en deux catégories: ceux qui portaient sur les « accommodements raisonnables » en général (578 articles), et ceux qui portaient spécifiquement sur les 12 cas sélectionnés (527 articles). Nous avons analysé les articles « événementiels » et les articles d'opinion avec des catégories d'analyse différentes. Il est impossible de présenter ici chaque affaire et leur analyse détaillée (Potvin 2008a et 2008b).

5. À l'ère des droits de la personne, on parle d'un « néoracisme » plus implicite, culturaliste et fondé sur des critères de différenciation à l'apparence plus légitime en raison de son illégalité et illégitimité (Balibar 1988; Potvin 1999).

6. Les accusations de racisme venant du « Rest of Canada » à l'égard du Québec (et en particulier à l'égard du souverainisme) ont une longue histoire (Potvin 2000, 2004). Elles sont perçues comme une forme de dénigrement du cara-ctère « national » des francophones du Québec par le groupe dominant au Canada (anglophone) et une tentative de réduire les francophones au statut de « minorité comme les autres ».

7. Autant la Charte canadienne que la Charte québécoise, indûment confondues (Coutu et Bosset 2008).

8. Leclerc, Jean-Claude, « Les médias ont-ils exagéré? », *Le Devoir,* 5 février 2007, p. B6.

9. Elle affirmait, par exemple, en mai 2006 : « L'accommodement raisonnable? Bien d'accord. À condition qu'il se fasse entre gens relativement raison-nables. Or, on constate que les revendications sont presque toujours le fait d'extrémistes religieux. L'immense majorité des sikhs ne porte pas le kirpan. L'immense majorité des musulmans ne réclame pas des lieux de prières au travail ou à l'école, ni des bassins pour les ablutions. Une société doit-elle se plier aux revendications de groupes marginaux que même leurs coreli-gionnaires trouvent excessifs? ». Lysiane Gagnon, « Du Kirpan à la Charia. Tirez-vous une bûche », *La Presse,* 13 mai 2006, p. A28.

10. *La Presse,* 22 novembre 2007.

11. Ce comité sur les pratiques d'accommodements raisonnables en éducation a été mis sur pied par le ministre de l'Éducation en octobre 2006, avant la Commission Bouchard-Taylor.

12. Si la plupart des « affaires » ont été présentées comme des cas litigieux par les médias, le rapport Fleury, remis à la ministre de l'Éducation en décembre 2007, a montré dans son enquête que la grande majorité des situa-tions d'aménagement étaient « bien gérées » dans la vie quotidienne des institutions (écoles, hôpitaux). Ce rapport sera largement cité par le rapport Bouchard-Taylor, qui en arrive aux mêmes conclusions.

13. La *Loi (fédérale) sur les Indiens* de 1876, révisée en 1951, constitue un régime de tutelle des Indiens, en faisant d'eux des pupilles de l'État. Elle déter-mine à la fois le statut d'Indien, l'appartenance à la bande, la structure politique et administrative, la gestion des réserves, les exemptions de taxes et l'administration financière.

14. Le Canada a été un système esclavagiste pendant 200 ans, ce qui a longtemps été occulté. L'esclavage a été introduit chez les colons français en 1626; il obtiendra un statut quasi-légal en 1685 (adoption du *Code Noir* par la France) et sera renforcé sous le Régime britannique jusqu'à son abolition en 1833 (Trudel 1960).

15. Les provinces ont juridiction exclusive en matière de droit civil, de santé et services sociaux, d'éducation, de ressources naturelles, d'aide sociale, de fonction publique provinciale, de planification et développement du territoire, ainsi que certaines compétences partagées avec le gouvernement fédéral, comme l'immigration.

16. L'article 25 de la *Charte*. En outre l'article 35 de la *Loi constitutionnelle de 1982* stipule que « les droits existants - ancestraux ou issus de traités - des peuples autochtones du Canada sont reconnus et confirmés ». La Cour suprême a aussi été amenée à définir les droits ancestraux des Autochtones dans plusieurs arrêts.

17. La *National Policy*, adoptée en 1879, entendait favoriser l'industrialisation du Canada, réduire le départ de milliers d'ouvriers vers les États-Unis par la construction d'infrastructures (chemins de fer d'Est en Ouest, ports) et accroître les échanges économiques entre les provinces canadiennes.

18. « Minorité visible » est un terme officiel inscrit dans la *Loi sur l'équité en matière d'emploi*, adoptée en 1986. Il s'agit des « personnes autres que les Autochtones, qui ne sont pas de race blanche et qui n'ont pas la peau blanche ». Le terme constitue une catégorie statistique du recensement canadien, aux fins d'application de la loi. Selon le Dictionnaire du recensement de 2006, cette catégorie inclut les Chinois, les Sud-Asiatiques, les Noirs, les Philippins, les Latino-Américains, les Asiatiques du Sud-Est, les Arabes, les Asiatiques occidentaux, les Coréens et les Japonais.

19. Au Canada, le droit constitutionnel peut être invoqué directement par les citoyens pour mettre en cause la légalité de la loi dans le cadre de tout litige.

20. Les provinces ont leurs législations sur les droits de la personne, qui couvrent les entreprises et les organisations sous leur autorité. Au Québec, il s'agit de la *Charte québécoise des droits de la personne*, adoptée en 1975. Toutes ces législations ont un statut quasi constitutionnel et elles ont préséance sur les autres lois en cas de litige. Elles offrent aux individus une protection contre la discrimination provenant des autorités gouvernementales ou des rapports privés entre individus. Leur application relève des Commissions des droits de la personne (Potvin et Latraverse 2004).

21. Par exemple, la Charte québécoise couvre un éventail plus large de motifs que la Charte canadienne, comme la condition sociale, la grossesse, l'orientation sexuelle, l'état civil, l'opinion politique, l'âge et le harcèlement.

22. La notion de contraintes excessives est inhérente à celle d'accommodement raisonnable. Il s'agit de la limite légitime au-delà de laquelle l'obligation d'accommodement raisonnable cesse de s'imposer, que ce soit pour des raisons de coût, d'efficacité de la production, de mise en cause de la mission fondamentale de l'institution, d'effet négatif sur les droits des autres personnes et de sécurité. En milieu scolaire, un accommodement doit se référer à six éléments centraux : 1) respect de l'égalité des droits et libertés; 2) respect des programmes de formation et des régimes pédagogiques; 3) respect de la langue de scolarisation (Loi 101); 4) obligation d'assurer les services prévus

par les lois et conventions collectives; 5) sécurité des élèves et du personnel; 6) capacités normales du personnel et des autres ressources disponibles. Il est donc faux de croire que toutes les demandes d'accommodements sont acceptables : il doit y avoir un effet préjudiciable visible, qui nécessite de corriger la situation afin de garantir le droit à l'égalité d'une personne.

23. Les limites de la justice procédurale sont évidentes pour les élèves handicapés physiques, qui ne peuvent accéder comme les autres aux escaliers...

24. Le Conseil municipal d'Hérouxville, petite municipalité de 1 300 habitants, a adopté un code de vie à l'intention des immigrants potentiels en interdisant, entre autres, la lapidation, l'excision et le voile intégral. Rédigé par un conseiller municipal fort médiatisé, André Drouin, le « code de vie » suscite très rapidement des réactions. La nouvelle fait le tour du monde. Le 5 février, André Drouin demande au Premier ministre du Québec de décréter « l'état d'urgence ». Cinq villages voisins demandent aussi aux deux niveaux de gouvernement de revoir les chartes canadienne et québécoise des droits et libertés.

25. Par exemple : en février 2007, 275 articles événementiels, éditoriaux, chroniques sont publiés par ces 5 journaux seulement, en 27 jours de couverture (sur 28), dont 119 articles dans la semaine du 1er au 7 février (entre 14 articles dans *Le Soleil* jusqu'à 37 articles dans *La Presse*), et 86 articles du 8 au 14 février (26 articles dans la seule journée du 7 février). C'est une moyenne de plus de 10 articles par jour pour ces 5 quotidiens!

26. Il s'agit du jugement sur le port du Kirpan à l'école publique, de la décision de la Commission des droits de la personne (CDPDJ) sur les salles de prières à l'École de technologie supérieure et de la décision de la CDPDJ relative à l'ambulancier non-juif « expulsé » de l'hôpital juif parce qu'il refusa de manger son repas non casher dans une zone réservée à cet effet à la cafétéria de l'hôpital. Pour le détail et l'analyse de chaque cas, voir Potvin (2008b).

27. Plus une opinion semble dominer, moins ceux qui ont une opinion inverse vont vouloir intervenir dans le débat. Ce qui crée un effet d'intimidation.

28. Imam très controversé qui a été expulsé du Canada pour avoir menti lors de sa demande du statut de réfugié.

29. Centre local de services communautaires (Santé et services sociaux).

30. Si les mécanismes peuvent s'articuler et s'enchaîner en séquences successives, il peut arriver que seuls les deux premiers paliers s'articulent entre eux, sans déboucher sur des paliers supérieurs. Par contre, la diabolisation et la victimisation impliquent toujours une dichotomisation et une infériorisation de l'autre.

31. Voir Potvin (2008a et 2008b) pour les données détaillées par journal et les nombreux extraits illustrant ces mécanismes.

32. « Que les talibans se le tiennent pour dit », *La Presse*, 29 janvier 2007, p. A5: « Enfin des élus qui ont le courage de se tenir debout face aux hordes de talibans qui débarquent sur nos rivages avec leurs grosses valises pleines de traditions obscurantistes ».

33. « L'ignorance et la fracture », *Le Devoir*, 3 février 2007, p. A6.

34. En 2006, le gouvernement du Québec lançait une consultation publique (commission parlementaire) sur un projet de politique de lutte contre le racisme et la discrimination. Il avait annoncé à plusieurs reprises son intention de l'adopter en 2007. Or, il a attendu la fin du débat sur les accommodements

raisonnables et le dépôt du rapport Bouchard-Taylor avant d'adopter, 3 jours avant le déclenchement des élections de novembre 2008, une politique transformée substantiellement et intitulée : « *La diversité : une valeur ajou-tée. Politique gouvernementale pour favoriser la participation de tous à l'essor du Québec.* »

RÉFÉRENCES

Abu-Ladan, Y. et D. Stasiulis. 1992. Ethnic Pluralism under Siege: Popular and Partisan Opposition to Multiculturalism. *Canadian Public Policy* 18 (4) : 365-386.

Balibar, É. 1988. Y-a-t-il un « néo-racisme »? Dans *Race, Nation, Classe : les identités ambiguës*, dir. E. Balibar et I. Wallerstein, 27-41. Paris : La Découverte.

Bissoondath, N. 1994. *Selling Illusions: The Cult of Multiculturalism.* Toronto : Penguin Books.

Bouchard, G. et C. Taylor. 2008. *Fonder L'avenir : le temps de la réconciliation.* Rapport de la Commission de consultation sur les pratiques d'accommodement reliées aux différences culturelles. Rapport abrégé. Québec : Éditeur officiel du Québec.

Bourdieu, P. 1996. *Sur la télévision* suivi de *L'emprise du journalisme.* Paris : Raisons d'agir.

Cairns, A.C. 1995. *Reconfigurations: Canadian Citizenship and Constitutional Change.* Toronto : McClelland and Stewart.

Cohen, S. 1972. *Folk Devils and Moral Panics.* London : MacGibbon and Kee.

Guillaumin, C. 1972. *L'idéologie raciste : genèse et langage actuel.* Paris/La Haye : Mouton.

Institut de recherche en politiques publiques (IRPP) avec J. Meisel, G. Rocher et A. Silver, dir. 1999. *Si je me souviens bien/As I Recall : Regards sur l'histoire.* Montréal : McGill-Queen's University Press.

Levine, M.V., dir. 1990. *The Reconquest of Montreal: Language Policy and Social Change in a Bilingual City.* Philadelphia : Temple University Press.

Leydet, D. 1992. Patriotisme constitutionnel et identité nationale. *Philosophiques* 19 (2) : 81-92.

Mc Andrew, M. 2007. Pour un débat inclusif sur l'accommodement raisonnable. *Éthique publique* 9 (1) : 152-158.

McCombs, M. et D. Shaw. 1993. The Evolution of Agenda-Setting Research: Twenty-five Years in the Marketplace of Ideas. *Journal of Communication* 43 (2) : 58-67.

Potvin, M. 2000. Some Racist "Slips" About Quebec in English Canada between 1995 and 1998. *Canadian Ethnic Studies/Revue canadienne des études ethniques* 32 (2) : 1-26.

Potvin, M. 2008a. *Les médias écrits et les accommodements raisonnables : l'invention d'un débat : analyse du traitement médiatique et des discours d'opinion dans les grands médias (écrits) québécois sur les situations reliées aux accommodements raisonnables, du 1er mars 2006 au 30 avril 2007.* Rapport d'expert remis à Gérard Bouchard et Charles Taylor, co-présidents de la *Commission de consultation sur les pratiques d'accommodement reliées aux différences culturelles.* Montréal. 230 p. En ligne : www.accommodements.qc.ca/documentation/rapports/rapport-8-potvin-maryse.pdf.

Potvin, M. 2008b. *Crise des accommodements raisonnables. Une fiction médiatique?* Montréal : Athéna Éditions.

Potvin, M. et S. Latraverse. 2004. *Comparative Study on the Collection of Data to Measure the Extent and Impact of Discrimination in a Selection of Countries: Medis Project (Measurement of Discriminations) Final Report on Canada.* Bruxelles : European Commission, Directorate General for Employment and Social Affairs (Commission européenne, direction générale de l'emploi et des affaires sociales). En ligne : http://ec.europa.eu/employment_social/fundamental_rights/pdf/pubst/stud/canada_en.pdf.

Potvin, M., A. Morelli et L. Mettewie. 2004. Du racisme dans les rapports entre groupes nationaux au Canada et en Belgique? *Revue canadienne des études ethniques/Canadian Ethnic Studies* 36 (3) : 25-60.

Rioux, M. et P. Bourgeoys. 2008. *Enquête sur un échantillon de cas d'accommodement (1998–2007).* Rapport à la Commission Bouchard-Taylor. En ligne : www.accommodements.qc.ca/documentation/rapports/rapport-1-rioux-marc.pdf.

Tajfel, H. 1972. La catégorisation sociale. Dans *Introduction à la psychologie sociale,* dir. S. Moscovici, Tome 1, 272-302. Paris : Larousse.

Taylor, C. 1992. The Politics of Recognition. Dans *Multiculturalism and the "Politics of Recognition,"* dir. A. Guttman, 25-73. Princeton : Princeton University Press.

Trudel. M. 1960. *L'esclavage au Canada français : histoire et condition.* Québec : Presses de l'Université Laval.

Windisch, U. 1978. *Xénophobie? Logique de la pensée populaire.* Paris : L'Âge d'Homme.

PART V

LINGUISTIC POLICIES AND LINGUISTIC PLURALISM

CHAPTER 10

Multilingualism in Ontario, Canada: An Educational Perspective

ELIZABETH COELHO, *Ontario Institute for Studies in Education, University of Toronto; Former District Coordinator for English as a Second Language, Toronto District School Board*

This chapter outlines some key policies and practices in relation to education in the multilingual and multicultural context that is increasingly typical of schools in Ontario, Canada. The chapter concludes with a brief discussion of the results in terms of educational outcomes for immigrant students in Ontario.

The use of the term "immigrant" in this chapter refers to students born in other countries; however, many of the policies and practices described in the chapter also apply to students born in Canada whose first language is other than English or French, the two official languages of Canada.

THE CONTEXT

This chapter focuses on the education of immigrant children and youth and the acquisition of English as a second or additional language in English-language schools in Ontario. There is a different reality in the

Managing Immigration and Diversity in Canada: A Transatlantic Dialogue in the New Age of Migration,
ed. D. Rodríguez-García. Montreal and Kingston: Queen's Policy Studies Series, McGill-Queen's University Press.

province's French-language schools because only those students who already have a French-language background attend these schools: that is to say, students whose first language is French or who have received their education in the French language. All other newcomer students attend English-language schools, whether they have any knowledge of English or not. In Quebec, the opposite situation applies: Only those students who already have an English-language background attend English-language schools, and all others attend French-language schools.

This chapter describes some of the policies, initiatives, and programs related to the social, linguistic, and academic integration of immigrant students, as well as orientation of their parents to the new school system. Three levels of government are involved in this work:

- The federal government of Canada, the architect of immigration, has primary responsibility for the selection, admission, and resettlement of immigrant adults and families.
- The provincial government, in this case Ontario, has primary responsibility for education and for community and social services.
- At the municipal level, the district school boards, such as the Toronto District School Board, are responsible for implementing educational and social policies in local schools and communities.

Other government-funded institutions are also involved in supporting immigrant families. For example, public libraries provide key services for newcomers, including children's books and other resources in the languages of the community. As well, various levels of government collaborate with many non-governmental organizations (NGOs) that provide direct service to immigrants. Many of these organizations receive funding from the federal or provincial government. Some examples of this collaboration will be provided as the role of each level of government is explained below, beginning with the federal government's role.

THE ROLE OF THE FEDERAL GOVERNMENT

The federal government provides funding and guidelines to the provinces and to various NGOs for the provision of programs and services for recent immigrants and for the promotion of multiculturalism within a bilingual context.[1]

Citizenship and Immigration Canada

This department of the federal government not only has responsibility for the selection and admission of newcomers under various categories of admissibility, but also provides support for resettlement. A website funded by Citizenship and Immigration Canada is a communications, information, and research tool to support the work of the Canadian settlement community.[2] The department also provides funding, in collaboration with other government departments, for CERIS – The Ontario Metropolis Centre,[3] one of five research centres in Canada that are part of the International Metropolis Project.

Collaboration with NGOs

Many NGOs that provide services for newcomers were established by various groups within the immigrant community. Many of these organizations serve specific linguistic and cultural communities in their own languages, and their contribution to the integration of more recently arrived immigrants is invaluable. For example, the members and clients of the Centre for Spanish-Speaking Peoples (Centro para Gente de Habla Hispana),[4] a Toronto organization, are mainly from Latin America.

With funding from the federal government, some NGOs employ settlement workers, a job category that perhaps does not yet exist in a formal way in Catalonia, Spain. Settlement workers are social workers whose role is to help newcomers with the many tasks and problems that they have to deal with in their first few months and years after arrival. Some settlement workers are located within schools to help orient newcomer families to the school system.

Collaboration with the Provinces

The federal government also provides funding to the provincial governments for resources and services intended to help newcomers integrate, and to facilitate their employment in jobs where they can use the skills and training they bring with them. Increasingly, such information and support are available online. An Ontario website that is jointly funded by the federal government and the Government of Ontario provides many resources for recent immigrants and for the professionals that work with them, including social workers and teachers.[5] Many of the resources for newcomers can be obtained in various languages; an example is the "First Days Guide," which offers basic advice on topics such as housing, health, employment, and education.[6] The resources for professionals available on this same site provide advice on working with new immigrants, such as guidelines for career counselling and language tutoring. There are also research studies, such as "Second Language Tutoring Programs: An Inquiry into Best Practices," published in 2008, which examines language tutoring programs for immigrants settling in Canada (Luazon and Coombs 2008).

In addition, there is a site hosted by Settlement Workers in Schools, specially trained settlement workers who assist in the integration of newcomer families when parents register their children for school. This site provides a guide to the education system, which can be downloaded and distributed to parents either when they first register their children in a school or during special orientation meetings with newcomer parents. There are different versions for the French- and English-language schools and for public and Catholic schools.[7] There are also DVDs dubbed in various languages showing parents how to access local resources such as the public library, or how to become involved in their children's education.

Language Classes for Adults

About 25 percent of newcomer adults have limited knowledge of English or French, or do not have a level of proficiency adequate for their intended employment. In order to ensure that all Canadian residents speak at least one of the official languages, the federal government funds full- and part-time classes all over the country, to enable immigrants over the age of 18 to develop their communication skills for everyday situations at work, in the community, and in use of media. Funding and guidelines such as the Canadian Language Benchmarks for assessing language proficiency[8] are provided to public organizations such as district school boards, community colleges, public libraries, and NGOs as well as private (for-profit) organizations, which actually provide the classes. In many locations there are nursery services as well, so that preschool children can also begin their early learning of English or French.

▪ LINC, Language Instruction for Newcomers to Canada, provides instruction in basic language skills for everyday communication and for work in contexts where a high level of language proficiency is not required. Information about these courses is available in various languages.[9]

▪ ELT, Enhanced Language Training, is a new program offering special language training for those newcomers whose education and experience qualify them for employment in professional and highly skilled fields that demand a high level of language proficiency.[10] These programs include a practical component, such as work placements, mentoring and internships, cultural orientation to the workplace, and preparation for professional exams. This program was established about five years ago because it was evident that many immigrants were not able to find employment comparable to the work they had been doing in their own countries. Notably, new immigrants face many obstacles in addition to the language barrier. In Canada, as in most countries that receive immigrants, there are many taxi drivers, cleaners, security guards, and other service-sector workers with professional skills and qualifications who are unable to find employment in their fields. This represents a waste of human resources, as well as a devastating loss of expectations, self-esteem, and socio-economic status for skilled and professional immigrants who chose to come, and were chosen to come, specifically because there is demand for employees in their fields in Canada.

Support for Official Languages

Government policy in Canada promotes bilingualism in the two official languages within a context of multilingualism. However, most Canadians are not bilingual—at least, not in the two official languages—in spite of the federal government's support for the teaching of French in anglophone communities and the teaching of English in francophone communities. Very few students actually achieve bilingualism in English and French by the time they graduate from secondary school, especially those in English-language schools.

The federal government has quite recently established a goal to increase the percentage of students who graduate from secondary school with a working knowledge of their second official language from 24 percent in 2003 to 50 percent by 2013 (Government of Canada 2003). However, this relatively modest goal will be difficult to achieve because education is the responsibility of the provinces, and there are major differences in their approaches to the instruction of the second official language. There is evidence that across English-speaking Canada, the teaching of French is in decline (Kissau 2005). For example, the teaching of French in English-language schools is not compulsory in some provinces. Even in Ontario, where students must accumulate 700 hours of French instruction in order to graduate, the results have so far not been very positive.

Heritage Language Instruction

According to the *Canadian Multiculturalism Act* (1988), it is the policy of the Government of Canada to "facilitate the acquisition, retention and use of all languages that contribute to the multicultural heritage of Canada" (Department of Justice Canada 1985). In support of this policy, the federal government contributes funding for heritage language classes offered by schools and community groups, where students of various linguistic backgrounds study their own languages (Harrison 2000). In Toronto, thousands of students attend classes in more than 50 languages, normally outside regular school hours. There is ample evidence that maintenance and continued development of the first language provides cognitive, affective, and social benefits—indeed, immigrant students in the United Kingdom who maintain their first language do better academically than those who abandon their first language as well as those students whose first language is English (CILT 2006).

TABLE 1
Federal Legislation and Policies on Heritage Languages

1969: The Royal Commission on Bilingualism and Biculturalism recommends that languages other than English and French be incorporated into the curriculum in public elementary schools.

1971: Canada's Multiculturalism Policy provides the framework for subsidies for out-of-school heritage language programs, support for materials development, sponsorship for national heritage languages conferences, and the establishment of a national heritage language centre.

1988: The *Canadian Multiculturalism Act* guarantees the continued existence of heritage language training and states that it is the policy of the Government of Canada to "facilitate the acquisition, retention and use of all languages that contribute to the multicultural heritage of Canada."

1991: The *Canadian Heritage Languages Institute Act* provides for the establishment of a national Institute "to facilitate throughout Canada the acquisition, retention and use of heritage languages." This legislation is not yet in force.

Source: Author's compilation.

THE ROLE OF THE PROVINCIAL GOVERNMENT

The provincial government is responsible for the education of children and youth in elementary and secondary schools. In the last five years, the Ontario Ministry of Education has been paying increased attention to the needs of immigrant students and Canadian-born children whose first language is neither English nor French. Key initiatives include the development of a new policy on the education of these students, as well as the distribution of funds to support implementation of the policy, and the development of resources for teachers.

The New Policy

A new policy now in effect in Ontario directs English-language district school boards and schools to provide the support required to enable English language learners (recent immigrants and Canadian-born children in English-language schools whose first language is not English) to succeed in school (Ontario Ministry of Education 2007a). This policy was in response to community pressure as well as to a government report that was critical of the fact that the Ministry of Education had no way of knowing whether English language learners (ELLs) were achieving appropriate proficiency in English. In addition, although the ministry was providing funding to district school boards for the teaching of English as a second language (ESL), the ministry had no information on how much school boards were actually spending on ESL classes. Indeed, in the Toronto District School Board, more than half of the funding was spent on other areas (Rushowy 2007). The report also noted the lack of a centrally coordinated process to develop ongoing training programs for teachers (Office of the Auditor General of Ontario 2005).

Key components of the policy include the following requirements and expectations:

- All schools and district school boards are required to develop procedures for the reception, assessment, and orientation of newcomer students and their parents.
- There are clear requirements for the teaching of English as a second language, although models of program organization may vary depending on the context. For example, in schools with large numbers of recent immigrants, there is more likely to be an ESL teacher who works with them for part of the school day. In areas where there are few newcomer students, they are more likely to be integrated into the regular classroom for the whole day, where the classroom teacher is expected to adapt curriculum and instruction to meet their needs. There may be an itinerant ESL teacher who visits the school two or three times a week to work individually with students and to provide support to the teacher. In all cases, there is an expectation that all teachers will adapt the curriculum and their teaching methods so that ELLs can participate in classroom activities in a way that promotes their learning of English.
- ESL teachers in Ontario are required to have specialist training in addition to their regular teacher certification. There are three courses of 100 hours each, taught in faculties of education. All ESL teachers must take at least the first of these courses, while those who seek a position of responsibility, such as head of department or program consultant, must complete all three. These courses are designed and accredited by the Ontario College of Teachers, the licensing body for the teaching profession in Ontario (Ontario College of Teachers 2004).
- Schools and school boards are responsible for monitoring and documenting the progress of each ELL over a multi-year period.
- There is an expectation that all teachers will receive training to enable them to support ELLs in their own classrooms.
- School boards are required to include in their annual plans a component related to the support of ELLs and to report to the Ministry of Education on the programs and services they provide for ELLs.

Funding

The Ontario government provides funding to enable schools and school boards to implement the requirements laid out in the policy. Most of the funding is used to hire ESL teachers and to provide additional professional development for classroom teachers. School boards may also use some of the funding to provide services such as reception centres, which will be described later in this chapter, as well as services for parents, such as translation and interpretation.

There is a formula for the distribution of funds, based on two components:

- Most of the funding is distributed according to the number of students in each school district who have arrived from other countries within the last four years. However, this does not mean that all newcomers will receive support for four years, or that they may not receive support for longer. Some newcomers need little or no support, having received a good education and having learned English in their own countries, while others need more support over a longer period of time—especially those from countries where they have had limited opportunities for education.
- The second component of the funding is based on census data on the number of families within a municipality who report a home language other than English or French. This component is intended to recognize the needs of students born in Canada whose first language is other than the language of instruction.

Support for Teachers

The Ontario government has developed the following curriculum and teaching guidelines for teachers working with ELLs in various contexts:

- A resource guide for kindergarten teachers on how to teach young children who first start learning English when they begin school (Ontario Ministry of Education 2007b).
- A resource guide for elementary schools (grades 1-8) (Ontario Ministry of Education 2008a).
- A curriculum for English as a Second Language and English Literacy Development in secondary schools (grades 9-12) (Ontario Ministry of Education 2007c).
- An introductory guide for all educators on how to welcome students and parents of all backgrounds and how to incorporate linguistic and cultural diversity into the mainstream classroom (Ontario Ministry of Education 2005).
- A resource guide on the education of students who arrive from countries where they have had limited opportunities for education (Ontario Ministry of Education 2008b).
- Web-based video and support materials on how to make an asset of linguistic diversity in the classroom (Literacy and Numeracy Secretariat 2005).

- Research-based articles for teachers and school administrators (Cummins 2007).

IMPLEMENTATION AT THE MUNICIPAL LEVEL

District school boards, schools, and educators are responsible for implementing federal and provincial policies related to linguistic and cultural diversity in schools. Key initiatives at the local level include reception centres, initial assessment and orientation services, and language instruction.

1. Reception Centres

Most of the larger urban centres in Ontario have established reception centres as the point of first contact for newcomer students and Canadian-born ELLs and their parents. These reception centres are staffed with teachers and community workers with expertise in language assessment or immigrant resettlement and, in many cases, with knowledge of some of the community languages. The centres aim to provide—

- a respectful and encouraging welcome to newcomer families;
- an initial assessment of the student's educational needs;
- basic orientation to the school system.

Normally, the student spends one day, or a morning or an afternoon, in the centre before registering in the appropriate school. Teachers at the reception centre send a report to the school on the student's assessment, as well as recommendations for placement and programming.

A centralized process for initial assessment and orientation offers several advantages. For example, the concentration of staff with the necessary expertise and linguistic or cultural knowledge can be very time- and cost-effective. Also, an assessment process of several hours may be more in-depth or complete than an assessment carried out by busy teachers in the school, who may already have a full timetable.

It should be noted that newcomer reception centres in Ontario are not designed as schools or special classes for immigrant students. They may be located within a school building, but they offer only an initial assessment and basic orientation to the new school system before referring students to the most appropriate schools in their neighbourhoods. Ontario's newcomer reception centres are completely different from the *centro de acogida* model that has been proposed in Catalonia, Spain.

2. Initial Assessment

The initial assessment process is intended to provide educators and parents with a profile of the learner and his or her academic needs. A thorough and fair initial assessment, whether it is conducted at the school or at a centralized reception centre, consists of four components:

- information about prior schooling, based on documents that the students or parents may bring with them, as well as an interview in the family's first language if possible;
- an assessment of the student's level of proficiency in his or her first language, which may consist of a writing sample and an opportunity to read a text aloud;
- an assessment of the student's proficiency in the language of instruction (English), based on an oral interview and reading/writing tasks;
- an assessment of the student's background in mathematics, which, because it is less dependent on language than many other areas of the curriculum, may also be a useful indicator of general academic background.

3. Orientation to the School

Newcomer families have travelled a long way, physically and psychologically, before arriving at the new school. The parents need reassurance that their children will receive good care in this strange new environment, and the students need reassurance that there is a place for them. A well-designed orientation program can help students get off to a good start and initiate a positive relationship between the parents and the school.

If there is an ESL teacher, he or she is usually responsible for providing the initial orientation. The ESL teacher meets with the parents and the student, providing basic information about the school day, important phone numbers, the names of key teachers, etc. Often there is information available in various languages. Sometimes there is a welcome gift for the student, such as a picture dictionary or a set of pens and pencils. The teacher also provides information to the other teachers so that the student's arrival will not come as a surprise the next day.

Finally, in many schools, there are student guides who provide a guided tour, introduce newcomers to their teachers, help them with tasks such as getting a locker or a bus pass, and accompany them during lunch for the first few days. Often these guides understand the needs of newcomers, having gone through a similar experience themselves a few months or years earlier, and they may even speak the same language.

4. Language Instruction

In designing a language program for newcomer students, there may be a tendency to focus only on their need to learn the language of instruction. While this is an immediate and obvious need, it is advisable to consider at least three languages:

- The language of instruction
- Heritage languages
- Additional language(s)

Language of instruction

In multilingual communities, some or all of the children begin learning the language of instruction when they start school, or when they arrive from other countries at a later point in their educational careers. The various models of language education that have been proposed and implemented in such contexts can be broadly categorized as the bilingual education model, the immersion model, or the second-language instruction model. Each of these models has advantages and disadvantages, as outlined below. However, for practical and political reasons, instruction in English as a second language is the prevailing model of education for language minorities in Ontario's English-language schools.

Bilingual education. Children learn best in the language they know best. This is not a new concept: More than half a century ago, a UNESCO report on the use of vernacular languages in education stated that "the best medium for teaching is the mother tongue of the pupil" (UNESCO 1953). In a 2003 position paper, UNESCO reiterated that "Mother tongue instruction is essential for initial instruction and literacy and should be extended to as late a stage in education as possible ... [E]very pupil should begin his [or her] formal education in his [or her] mother tongue" (UNESCO 2003).

Bilingual education programs use two languages of instruction: the home language of the students as well as the dominant language or the usual language of instruction. Bilingual education is practical where there are large numbers of students of the same language group in a local area, as is the case in some areas of the United States. Bilingual education is also offered in some Canadian provinces. For example, in 1978, the Saskatchewan *Education Act* stated that a heritage language (mother tongue) may be used as a language of instruction 100 percent of the time in kindergarten and up to 50 percent of the time in grades 1 to 12 (Saskatchewan Education 1994). However, in areas of Ontario where bilingual education might be a practical and common sense option in some schools, the use of languages other than English and French as languages of instruction is not allowed. The Ontario *Education Act* states that the curriculum may be delivered only in French and English, the two official languages of Canada (Government of Ontario 1990). So even if all the children in an English-language school speak Urdu, and have little or no knowledge of English, they will receive instruction in English only. So far, this legislation has not been challenged in the courts.[11]

However, as the UNESCO report recognizes, it is difficult to provide bilingual classes in areas where students of a particular language group are spread over a large geographical area, or where students of many language groups attend the same school. While it may be possible to centralize programs for specific language groups in designated schools, there may be negative social consequences from separating students from those of other linguistic and cultural backgrounds.

Even where bilingual education is well established, and research studies have documented its benefits, opposing ideologies may prevail. Bilingual education has come under fire recently in some parts of the United States. Critics argue that bilingual education causes children to become dependent on their first language and may inhibit their learning of English. In 1998, California replaced bilingual education programs with one-year English-only programs, after which time most students are fully mainstreamed with little or no continued support for the acquisition of English. Similar legislation was passed in Arizona in 2000, and similar initiatives are under way in other states. The debate is often acrimonious, with language acquisition researchers pitted against organizations such as English First, which opposes the provision of services in languages other than English,[12] or U.S. English, which advocates for the declaration of English as the official language of the United States.[13]

For practical and political reasons, then, the bilingual model is not always feasible. In communities where the language of the school is a minority language, as is the case in francophone Ontario or the Basque Country in Spain, the situation is even more complex.

Lessons from immersion. The immersion model, as used for French Immersion in anglophone communities in Canada, and for Basque immersion in Spain, has been extensively studied and has proved to be very successful. In such programs, the entire curriculum and instructional methods are adapted to meet the needs of children who are learning the language of instruction, beginning in preschool or kindergarten. The success of French Immersion programs in Canada, where most of the learners are English-speaking and most instruction is delivered in French, seems to belie the principle that learning in one's first language is more effective than learning in a second language. Although most instruction is not offered in their own language, anglophone students in French Immersion do at least as well as, and often better than, their peers in monolingual English programs (Canadian Council on Learning 2007).

While there are many factors involved in the success of French Immersion, including educational background and socio-economic status of parents who choose French Immersion, a key factor is that the teachers are bilingual in English and French, are sensitive to the needs of their students as second language learners, and use second language teaching techniques to integrate language and content instruction (Genesee 1994).

This is an important lesson for teachers of students of all backgrounds who are learning the language of instruction through engagement with a curriculum delivered in that language. However, few teachers in English-language schools have been prepared through their initial training to teach in multilingual classrooms.

Another important factor is that in French Immersion programs, all the children start learning French at the same time. However, most immigrant children arrive later in their educational careers and are several years behind the other children when they start learning the language of instruction.

Finally, French Immersion programs do not deny the importance of validation, maintenance, and development of English, the first language of most of the students. On the contrary, the aim is to produce fluent bilinguals who are equally proficient in the two official languages of Canada, English and French. As well, like Spanish (*castellano*) in the Basque Country, Galicia, Catalonia, and Valencia, English is supported inside and outside the school and is not threatened as a result of participation in French Immersion programs. Most students are immersed in an English-speaking environment in the community and at home. English is usually the majority language of the local community, and it has status as an official language of the country. Moreover, students study *"Anglais"* as a subject and also receive some subject instruction in English, in order to foster the continued development of skills in English. In contrast, immigrant students in English-language schools receive scant recognition or support for their own languages in the school environment or in the wider community.

English as a second language (ESL). Ontario's ESL programs are designed for students in English-language schools whose first language is other than English. These students may be Canadian-born or newcomers from other countries. They may speak one of more than 100 languages, including several Aboriginal languages, or an English-related Creole language such as Jamaican Creole or West African Krio.

About 20 percent of Ontario's students in English-language elementary schools are English language learners (i.e., their first language is other than English). More than half were born in Canada. These children enter a new linguistic and cultural environment when they start school in Ontario. Since literacy instruction in Ontario's English-language schools is in English, these children require particular attention, consideration, and support in order to overcome the mismatch between their first language and the language of instruction.

The most common model for organizing support for English language learners (ELLs) consists of a combination of ESL classes and integration in mainstream classes. In areas of high immigration, almost every school may provide an ESL program. In school districts where English language learners are distributed thinly across the district, making it difficult to provide ESL support in each school, newcomers may be congregated in one or two designated schools.

TABLE 2
Why Not Offer Self-contained Programs?

It is sometimes suggested that self-contained ESL programs that provide an intensive full-day program for newcomers would enable them to adjust more quickly to their new academic and social environment and learn sufficient English after a year or two to join a regular class. Self-contained programs have the advantage of concentrating resources and providing an intensive language and orientation program specifically designed for newcomers. However, the disadvantages of this model outweigh the advantages. For example,

- Students may have no regular contact with their English-speaking peers; as a result, they may be denied valuable opportunities for language learning.

- It is simply not possible to learn a new language to the level required for academic success within a year or two. Newcomers will still require support from all of their teachers when they join their age peers in the regular classroom.

- Students' engagement with the regular curriculum is delayed, and many parents are justifiably anxious that their children are falling behind in the mainstream curriculum while they attend the reception program.

- Students who attend a school other than their neighbourhood school may not have a chance to make friends with whom they can socialize out of school.

Source: Author's compilation.

The ESL teacher often works with groups of students from several grade levels and/or at various levels of proficiency in English, depending on the school timetable. The amount of time that each student spends with the ESL teacher may vary, with newcomers spending a significant portion of each day in the ESL class, while others may receive only an hour or two of ESL time each week. Many secondary schools congregate English language learners in classes that combine language instruction with content from a specific subject such as Canadian Geography. In some school districts with very small numbers of English language learners distributed in a number of schools, an itinerant ESL teacher may provide resource support in several schools, meeting with each student or group of students for an hour or two each week.

The ESL class provides a low-risk setting for learners to begin speaking English, learn about their new environment, and make friends. The ESL teacher also has opportunities to assess the learners' needs and strengths and to select content and resources that are directly related to the learners' needs and backgrounds.

In the first year, students may spend most of the day in the language class, but even beginners are usually integrated into the regular class for part of the day. It is recommended that students remain in the mainstream classroom for those aspects of the program in which they can participate, such as physical education, the arts, and (in many cases) mathematics. The mainstream classroom offers opportunities for second language acquisition, social integration, and academic growth that the ESL classroom alone cannot offer. The mainstream classroom provides important opportunities for students to interact with English-speaking peers and experience the grade-level curriculum. It would be counterproductive to keep English language learners apart from the mainstream program while they learn English; a language is best acquired by using it to do something meaningful, such as learning how to play baseball, solving a mathematics word problem, creating a dramatic retelling of a story, planning a class outing, or working on a group project. A well-planned integrated model also fosters positive intercultural attitudes among all the learners.

Integration does not occur simply by giving a student a desk in the classroom. Such an approach to "integration" might more properly be termed the "sink or swim" or "submersion" approach. Without carefully planned program adaptation and support, failure is the most likely result. In the multilingual school, where the learners are at various stages of proficiency in the language of instruction, from fully proficient to beginner, it is important that all teachers support second language acquisition and social integration by adapting curriculum and assessment, so that the learning outcomes are attainable and appropriate for students at various stages of proficiency in English.

Heritage languages

Attitudes towards students' first languages have changed considerably in the last two or three decades. Once considered detrimental to children's cognitive development and social integration, first language maintenance is now recognized as an important factor in second language acquisition, and as a significant source of cultural pride and personal identity. Heritage language programs are an important component of Canada's approach to multiculturalism and are available in many school districts across Canada.

Heritage language classes are usually offered by district school boards in local schools, outside regular school hours. Many community groups also offer heritage language classes. In these classes, students develop their skills in their own language (or the language of their parents) and learn about the history, important leaders and personalities, traditions, and values of their cultural communities. As well, students of secondary school age can take courses in their own language for academic credit.

Because they are usually offered outside the regular school program, heritage language classes are often perceived to be less important than the "regular" school curriculum. Also, students may be reluctant to attend extra classes at times when they might otherwise be playing or socializing with friends. In many jurisdictions, heritage language teachers are not members of the teachers' unions or licensing bodies, are not required to have the same qualifications and do not receive the same pay as "regular" teachers, have limited job security, and may have little contact with the other teachers. Some are relatively new in Canada, and their methods of teaching, while culturally appropriate in their own countries, may be quite different from the methods the learners are exposed to in the mainstream program. As a result, they may not be regarded as "professionals" in the same way as their mainstream colleagues.

In spite of all these difficulties, parents who recognize the benefits of maintaining their children's proficiency in their home language are eager to enrol their children in heritage language classes. Heritage language programs flourish in school districts across Canada, often with little or no direct support from the school district or provincial Ministry of Education. In British Columbia, approximately 150 organizations offer heritage language classes outside the school system, attended by 30,000 learners. In Saskatchewan, 62 member organizations teach 25 languages. Forty-five languages are taught in Toronto public schools, mostly outside school hours.

Additional languages

Ontario students are required to develop some proficiency in Canada's other official language, which means that students in English-language schools must study French. There is no requirement that Ontario students study a foreign language.

Many newcomers arrive in Canada with little or no knowledge of French, whereas their age peers may have already received several years of instruction. Because learning English is such a high priority, it often seems a "common sense" approach to delay instruction in French until the newcomer has a good grasp of English. However, in most cases, it is not necessary to delay instruction in French—as long as the French teacher adapts the program for students who are new to the language.

Many English language learners are competent language learners. Their experience in learning an additional language helps them to learn new sounds, acquire vocabulary, and perceive language patterns. Also, it must be remembered that many newcomers have already learned additional languages prior to arrival in Canada. For example, many Punjabi speakers also speak Hindi; many Ukrainians know Russian; and many Cantonese speakers have learned Mandarin. For many newcomers, English is not a second, but a third or fourth, language, and French is just one more.

In general, younger newcomers benefit from placement in the French class alongside their age peers, as long as the program is adapted for them. Some secondary schools provide a beginner-level French course for newcomers, many of whom are subsequently able to continue learning French alongside their grade-level peers. However, Ontario's new policy allows some flexibility for the small minority of newcomers who may benefit from delaying instruction in French, or in exceptional cases, from exemption altogether—as long as a more appropriate program is available in its place. For example, students who arrive with significant gaps in their schooling and limited literacy development in their own language might benefit from additional time in an ESL/literacy class, while students who have clearly identified special needs might receive Special Education support instead of French instruction.

THE RESULTS

Canada is often cited as a country with much experience of immigration and with well-developed programs for the support of immigrants and the education of their children. Educational outcomes for immigrant children, as measured by the results of provincial literacy tests in Ontario, and when viewed in the aggregate, appear very positive (Coelho 2007). Key findings include the following:

- It takes an average of five or more years for both newcomer children and Canadian-born ELLs to achieve results similar to those of their age peers. The data are consistent with research from the United States (Garcia 2000).
- Tracking students beyond the five-year period shows that immigrant children eventually outperform their English-speaking Canadian-born peers. These data are consistent with the 2006 PISA report on the academic achievement of immigrant children (OECD 2006).
- Students who begin learning English later eventually do better than their younger siblings—even though they have more English to catch up on.

The Ontario assessment data seem to show that, given sufficient time, immigrant children do well in Ontario's schools. Unfortunately, the aggregate data on immigrant children do not show the great variability among children of different language backgrounds and from different immigrant communities. The fact is that while some subgroups of immigrant students do astonishingly well within their first year or two in Canada, others seem never to catch up. According to a recent study in the Toronto District School Board, students from some regions of the world, and from some language backgrounds, experience significantly more academic difficulty than others and eventually drop out in much higher numbers. For example, students from the English-speaking Caribbean, students from East Africa, and students from Latin America, as well as

Portuguese- and Spanish-speaking students (immigrant and Canadian-born), have a dropout rate of 30 to 40 percent or more, compared with about 20 percent for Canadian-born English-speaking students and about 10 percent for students from Eastern Europe and East Asia (Brown 2006).

CONCLUSION

Responding to the needs of immigrant children and the children of immigrants requires coordinated effort on the part of national and provincial governments. NGOs established by immigrant communities are an important resource, as are other institutions such as public libraries.

Schools and school districts need to be held accountable for the educational outcomes of immigrant children and the children of immigrants. This requires the tracking of student outcomes over a multi-year period.

English language learners take five or more years to catch up to their age peers in English language and literacy skills. Some achieve this in a much shorter period of time, while others take much longer. Some never do, and students from certain countries of origin or language backgrounds are at much higher risk than others. From this, we can infer that students from some linguistic communities and some groups of immigrant students are not deriving equal benefit from their schools at the present time. It is not that these students cannot learn; it is the school that has to learn how to serve them better.

NOTES

1. In Canada, the terms "bilingual" and "bilingualism," as used in official policy documents, usually refer to bilingualism in the two official languages, English and French. However, in educational contexts, these terms are more often used to refer to individuals who are proficient in any two (or more) languages. For example, students who arrive from other countries are already proficient in at least one language at an age-appropriate level when they arrive and then add English or French (or both).
2. See Integration.Net at http://integration-net.ca.
3. For more information on CERIS – The Ontario Metropolis Centre, see http://ceris.metropolis.net.
4. See the website for the Centro para Gente de Habla Hispana at http://www.spanishservices.org.
5. See Settlement.Org, Welcome to Ontario at www.settlement.org.
6. For the "First Days Guide," see http://www.settlement.org/site/FIRSTDAYS/home.asp.
7. These newcomers' guides to education in Ontario can be found on the Settlement Workers in Schools site, at www.swisontario.ca.
8. See the website for the Centre for Canadian Language Benchmarks at www.language.ca.

9. See Language Instruction for Newcomers to Canada, at www.settlement. org/sys/faqs_detail.asp?faq_id=4000331 and http://www.cic.gc.ca/english/ resources/publications/welcome/wel-03e.asp#linc.
10. See Enhanced Language Training, at www.settlement.org/sys/link_redirect. asp?doc_id=1004024.
11. Presently in Ontario, two school districts are experimenting with the use of Arabic or Mandarin alongside English in kindergarten. If the results are promising, there will probably be some pressure to change Ontario's education law in order to allow some form of bilingual schooling, at least in the early years.
12. See http://www.englishfirst.org.
13. See http://www.us-english.org.

REFERENCES

Brown, R.S. 2006. *The TDSB Grade 9 Cohort Study: A Five-Year Analysis, 2000–2005.* Toronto: Toronto District School Board. Executive summary. At www.tdsb. on.ca/wwwdocuments/about_us/external_research_application/docs/ Grade9CohortVol2Iss1.pdf.

Canadian Council on Learning. 2007. *French-Immersion Education in Canada.* At http://www.ccl-cca.ca/pdfs/LessonsInLearning/May-17-07-French-immersion.pdf (accessed 10 November 2011).

CILT, The National Centre for Languages. 2006. *Positively Plurilingual: The Contribution of Community Languages to UK Education and Society.* London, U.K.: CILT. At http://www.cilt.org.uk/community_languages.aspx (accessed 14 November 2011).

Coelho, E. 2007. How Long Does It Take? Lessons from EQAO Data on English Language Learners in Ontario Schools. *Inspire, The Journal of Literacy and Numeracy for Ontario.* At www.edu.gov.on.ca/eng/literacynumeracy/inspire/ equity/ELL_July30.html (accessed 24 August 2008).

Cummins, J. 2007. Promoting Literacy in Multilingual Contexts. *What Works? Research into Practice.* Research Monograph #4. The Literacy and Numeracy Secretariat, Ontario Ministry of Education. At www.edu.gov.on.ca/eng/ literacynumeracy/inspire/research/whatWorks.html (accessed 28 August 2008).

Department of Justice Canada. 1985. *Canadian Multiculturalism Act.* At http:// laws-lois.justice.gc.ca/eng/acts/c-18.7 (accessed 10 November 2011).

Garcia, G.N. 2000. *Lessons from Research: What Is the Length of Time It Takes Limited English Proficient Students to Acquire English and Succeed in an All-English Classroom?* Issue Brief No. 5. Washington, DC: National Clearinghouse for Bilingual Education. At http://www.eric.ed.gov/PDFS/ED450585.pdf (accessed 14 November 2011).

Genesee, F. 1994. Integrating Language and Content: Lessons from Immersion. *Educational Practice Reports, No. 11.* National Center for Research on Cultural Diversity and Second Language Learning. Washington, DC: Center for Applied Linguistics. At http://repositories.cdlib.org/crede/ncrcdslleducational/ EPR11 (accessed 24 August 2008).

Government of Canada. 2003. *The Next Act: New Momentum for Canada's Linguistic Duality. The Action Plan for Official Languages.* At http://www.cpfnb.com/articles/ActionPlan_e.pdf (accessed 11 November 2011).

Government of Ontario. 1990. *Education Act.* At www.e-laws.gov.on.ca/html/statutes/english/elaws_statutes_90e02_e.htm#BK414 (accessed 11 November 2011).

Harrison, B. 2000. Passing on the Language: Heritage Language Diversity in Canada. *Canadian Social Trends,* Autumn (No. 58): 14-19. At www.statcan.ca/bsolc/english/bsolc?catno=11-008-X20000025165 (accessed 27 August 2008).

Kissau, S. 2005. The Depreciated Status of FSL Instruction in Canada. *Canadian Journal of Educational Administration and Policy,* Issue no. 44, 1 August. At www.umanitoba.ca/publications/cjeap/articles/kissau.html (accessed 10 November 2011).

Literacy and Numeracy Secretariat. 2005. Teaching and Learning in Multilingual Ontario. At www.curriculum.org/secretariat/december7.shtml.

Luazon, C., and D. Coombs. 2008. *Second Language Tutoring Programs: An Inquiry into Best Practices.* At http://atwork.settlement.org/sys/atwork_library_print.asp?doc_id=1004592 (accessed 10 November 2011).

Office of the Auditor General of Ontario. 2005. *2005 Annual Report.* Toronto: Queen's Printer for Ontario. At www.auditor.on.ca/en/reports_2005_en.htm (accessed 28 August 2008).

Ontario College of Teachers. 2004. Additional Qualifications Course Guidelines: English As a Second Language. At http://www.oct.ca/additional_qualifications/guidelines/scheduled.aspx?lang=en-CA (accessed 10 November 2011).

Ontario Ministry of Education. 2005. *Many Roots, Many Voices: Supporting English Language Learners in Every Classroom.* At www.edu.gov.on.ca/eng/document/manyroots (accessed 11 November 2011).

Ontario Ministry of Education. 2007a. *English Language Learners/ESL and ELD Programs and Services: Policies and Procedures for Ontario Elementary and Secondary Schools, Kindergarten to Grade 12.* At www.edu.gov.on.ca/eng/document/esleldprograms/index.html (accessed 11 November 2011).

Ontario Ministry of Education. 2007b. *Supporting English Language Learners in Kindergarten: A Practical Guide for Ontario Educators.* At www.edu.gov.on.ca/eng/document/kindergarten/index.html (accessed 11 November 2011).

Ontario Ministry of Education. 2007c. *The Ontario Curriculum, Grades 9 to 12: English As a Second Language and English Literacy Development.* At www.edu.gov.on.ca/eng/curriculum/secondary/esl.html (accessed 11 November 2011).

Ontario Ministry of Education. 2008a. *Supporting English Language Learners: A Practical Guide for Ontario Educators, Grades 1 to 8.* At www.edu.gov.on.ca/eng/document/esleldprograms/guide.html (accessed 11 November 2011).

Ontario Ministry of Education. 2008b. *Supporting English Language Learners with Limited Prior Schooling: A Practical Guide for Ontario Educators, Grades 3 to 12.* At www.edu.gov.on.ca/eng/document/manyroots/schooling.html (accessed 11 November 2011).

Organisation for Economic Co-operation and Development (OECD). 2006. *Where Immigrant Students Succeed—A Comparative Review of Performance and Engagement in PISA 2003.* Paris: Programme for International Student Assessment (PISA), OECD. At www.oecd.org/dataoecd/2/38/36664934.pdf (accessed 24 August 2008).

Rushowy, K. 2007. ESL funds used to heat schools. *Toronto Star,* 13 June. At http://www.thestar.com/News/article/224604 (accessed 14 November 2011).

Saskatchewan Education. 1994. *Multicultural and Heritage Language Education Policies.* Regina, Saskatchewan: Saskatchewan Education. At https://webtest. sasked.gov.sk.ca/docs/policy/multi/index.html (accessed 11 November 2011).

United Nations Educational, Scientific and Cultural Organization (UNESCO). 1953. *The Use of Vernacular Languages in Education.* At http://unesdoc.unesco. org/images/0000/000028/002897eb.pdf (accessed 11 November 2011).

United Nations Educational, Scientific and Cultural Organization (UNESCO). 2003. *Education in a Multilingual World.* At http://unesdoc.unesco.org/ images/0012/001297/129728e.pdf (accessed 11 November 2011).

CHAPTER 11

Les services d'accueil, d'intégration scolaire et de francisation offerts aux immigrants au Québec

ZITA DE KONINCK, *Professeure titulaire,*
Département de Langues, Linguistique et Traduction,
Université Laval

L'accueil d'enfants immigrants dans un réseau scolaire de même que celui d'adultes dans le marché du travail pose un réel défi d'intégration lorsque cet accueil doit se réaliser à l'intérieur d'une société où plusieurs langues sont en présence et où une d'entre elles exerce une force d'attraction exceptionnelle. Alors qu'au début des années 1960 le Québec connaissait une chute drastique de son indice de natalité et que cet indice signifiait que sa population ne pouvait plus désormais à elle seule assurer le remplacement des générations, sa survie en tant que société était menacée. Il fallait donc intensifier le recours à l'immigration internationale pourtant déjà bien existante dans cette province d'Amérique. Pour les francophones du Québec, le poids d'une augmentation de cette immigration n'était cependant pas sans conséquence si la majorité des nouveaux arrivants persistaient à opter pour l'anglais comme langue d'usage plutôt que pour le français pourtant la langue de la majorité à cette époque, mais dont le statut était plutôt faible comparativement à celui de l'anglais. Le défi

Managing Immigration and Diversity in Canada: A Transatlantic Dialogue in the New Age of Migration,
ed. D. Rodríguez-García. Montreal and Kingston: Queen's Policy Studies Series, McGill-Queen's University Press.

qu'a voulu relever le Québec dans les années 1970 était donc celui de l'intégration des nouveaux arrivants à la population francophone. Marc V. Levine (2003, 366) parle de « véritable révolution linguistique » pour décrire les changements qui se sont opérés dans les dernières décennies dans le but d'assurer la pérennité du français. Une conjugaison de facteurs a été à l'origine de cette révolution, soit une forte mobilisation populaire et le recours à des lois linguistiques.

En 1977, le gouvernement du Québec se dotait d'une Chartre de la langue française ou Loi 101 dont l'application allait changer le visage linguistique du Québec. Lors de son dépôt à l'Assemblée nationale, la Charte était accompagnée d'un Énoncé de politique faisant état des principes sur lesquels allait s'appuyer la législation à adopter. Tel que le rapporte Rocher (2000, 275-276), le Livre blanc de la politique linguistique mise de l'avant s'appuyait sur quatre principes :

1) « Le premier principe s'attache à situer la langue d'un peuple dans le contexte global qui est le sien. »
2) « Le deuxième principe : faire du français la langue du Québec doit se réaliser dans le respect des minorités, de leurs langues et de leurs cultures. »
3) « Le Livre blanc pose comme troisième principe l'importance d'apprendre au moins une *langue seconde*. »
4) Enfin comme quatrième principe, le Livre blanc affirme que le « statut de la langue française au Québec est une question de justice sociale. »

Les aires d'application de la Loi 101 faisaient du français la langue de la législation, de la justice et de l'administration publique, la langue de l'enseignement et la langue du commerce et des affaires. Très tôt les répercussions se sont fait sentir. Bernard (2000) parle ainsi des répercussions sociales ainsi que des répercussions juridiques et politiques. D'une part, s'est vu profiler chez les francophones une « reconquête » par la langue française de son statut de « langue officielle, normale et habituelle » et, d'autre part, chez les anglophones, une reconnaissance de la nécessité d'apprendre le français se traduisant par une augmentation significative d'individus bilingues appartenant à cette communauté. Tel que le rapporte l'auteur, l'effet le plus spectaculaire de la législation sera cependant celui d'avoir complètement inversé la tendance de l'inscription des élèves allophones aux écoles de langue anglaise. En effet, d'après les chiffres du ministère de l'Éducation, avant la promulgation de la Loi 101 en 1977, la majorité des élèves allophones étaient inscrits dans les écoles anglaises. Néanmoins, cette tendance a très vite changé puisque si globalement, pour les trois ordres d'enseignement confondus, en 1978–1979, 27,3 pour cent d'élèves fréquentaient le secteur francophone du système public et 72,7 pour cent le secteur anglophone, en 1989–1990 la pyramide s'est inversée : 70,84 pour cent d'élèves allophones fréquentaient le secteur francophone et 29,16 pour cent le secteur anglophone.

TABLEAU 1
Répartition des élèves allophones dans les secteurs français et anglais du réseau public (1978–1979, 1983–1984, 1987–1988, 1989–1990)

Langue d'enseignement	Année scolaire			
	1978–1979	1983–1984	1987–1988	1989–1990
Préscolaire				
Français	57,5%	67,9%	70%	75,22%
Anglais	42,5%	32,2%	30%	24,78%
Primaire				
Français	29,4%	58,9%	70,31%	73,48%
Anglais	70,5%	41,1%	29,69%	26,52%
Secondaire				
Français	18,3%	35,8%	58,90%	67,14%
Anglais	81,6%	64,2%	41,11%	32,86%
Total				
Français	27,3%	48,7%	65,19%	70,84%
Anglais	72,7%	51,3%	34,82%	29,16%

Source : Gouvernement du Québec, Ministère de l'Éducation du Québec (MEQ). *L'École québécoise et les communautés culturelles* (1988, 56); Gouvernement du Québec, MEQ. *Le point sur les services d'accueil et de francisation de l'école publique québécoise* (1996).

Ainsi, peu à peu les rapports de force entre les groupes linguistiques se sont modifiés et les francophones en sont sortis avantagés. Désormais, le français allait occuper la place qui lui revenait dans la majorité des espaces communs soit les écoles, l'Administration publique, les transactions commerciales et les échanges sociaux du quotidien.

L'État a donc eu recours à une législation pour soutenir cette démarche d'intégration des nouveaux arrivants et c'est pour cette raison que l'on dit très souvent que l'historique des classes d'accueil est très lié à la législation en matière linguistique. Avant de se pencher sur les différents modèles de services d'accueil mis en place pour favoriser l'intégration scolaire des élèves immigrants de même que sur les services offerts aux adultes immigrants, il est souhaitable de prendre connaissance de la démarche adoptée par le Québec pour réussir un tel projet de société. Après un bref aperçu de la dimension législative de l'intervention de l'état nous prendrons connaissance de la réponse du système scolaire québécois à une présence croissante d'élèves allophones dans les écoles françaises.

Dans un article traitant des ajustements juridiques liés à la Charte de la langue française, Woehrling (2003, 290-291) résume les grandes lignes de l'évolution de la législation. Tel que les désigne l'auteur, en voici les principaux repères :

1969 : Loi 63 ayant pour but la promotion de la langue française au Québec. S'y trouve une première mention de l'objectif visant à faire du français la langue du travail et la langue prioritaire de l'affichage public. Elle rend obligatoire l'enseignement du français dans les établissements scolaires anglophones.

1974 : Loi 22, sur la langue officielle. Cette loi fait du français la langue officielle du Québec et impose l'utilisation du français dans l'affichage public. Elle oblige les entreprises ayant à traiter avec l'État à adopter des programmes de francisation et limite l'accès à l'école anglaise aux seuls enfants ayant une maîtrise suffisante de l'anglais pour être scolarisés dans cette langue.

1977 : Loi 101, Charte de la langue française. Loi qui impose l'usage exclusif du français dans l'affichage public et la publicité commerciale et qui accroît les exigences de francisation pour les entreprises ayant 50 employés et plus. L'école anglaise n'est désormais accessible qu'aux seuls enfants dont un des parents a reçu son enseignement primaire en anglais au Québec. Désormais sur le plan juridique, seule la version française des lois est considérée officielle.

Par la suite, entre 1979 et 1997, une série d'ajustements sont apportés venant invalider certains articles de la Charte notamment sur les questions de la langue officielle de la jurisprudence, de l'affichage, de la disponibilité de certains services en anglais. Néanmoins, l'accès restreint à l'école anglaise demeure quasi identique pour les groupes non francophones. Pour une revue de cette question voir Woehrling (2003, 290-291).

Pour l'école québécoise, plusieurs de ces dates sont importantes car elles ont eu des retombées fort concrètes pour les milieux éducatifs. En 1969, année de la promulgation de la *Loi pour promouvoir la langue française* (projet de loi 63) qui accordait aux parents le libre choix de la langue d'enseignement, s'ouvraient à Montréal les premières classes d'accueil. En 1973 suivait une mesure incitative, soit la création des maternelles d'accueil pour les enfants de 4 et 5 ans. Cette action relevait du *Plan de développement d'enseignement des langues* (plan DEL) dont l'objet était l'amélioration de l'enseignement du français et de l'anglais langue seconde. Aussi, au début des années 1970, époque de consolidation des services d'accueil et de francisation, le ministère de l'Éducation (MEQ) décidait de créer le *Bureau de coordination de l'accueil aux enfants immigrants* (aujourd'hui, cette instance est désignée *Direction des services aux communautés culturelles*).

En 1978, les *Programmes d'enseignement des langues d'origine* (PELO) voient le jour. Deux motifs pédagogiques sont invoqués pour offrir de tels programmes aux élèves issus des communautés culturelles les plus importantes, établies à Montréal : (1) l'amélioration des apprentissages – de toutes les matières, y compris celle de la langue seconde – qu'amènerait une plus grande connaissance de la langue d'origine; (2) la consolidation identitaire des élèves qui voient l'acceptation de leur culture par le milieu scolaire.

En 1981, le MEQ décide d'abandonner les maternelles d'accueil pour les enfants de 4 ans, mises en place depuis 1973, pour mieux cibler son intervention en procédant à l'ouverture de classes de francisation destinées à rejoindre les élèves issus de l'immigration mais nés au Québec. La raison invoquée serait le fait que ces élèves nécessitent moins d'ajustements au milieu socioculturel que constitue l'école, comparativement aux élèves nés à l'étranger. Aussi le Ministère procède à la mise en place des *Mesures spéciales d'accueil et de francisation* en région destinées à offrir des mesures de soutien linguistique individualisées ou en sous-groupes là où le nombre ne permet pas l'ouverture de classes spécialement dédiées à des élèves issus de l'immigration.

Après avoir reconnu les classes du PELO comme contributoires à la formation académique des élèves appartenant à des communautés culturelles, en 1985 le MEQ accorde également des unités pour la sanction des études aux élèves ayant suivi des cours dans le cadre des *Programmes des langues ethniques* (PLE). Ces derniers programmes ont été développés par les communautés culturelles en ayant fait la demande et sont offerts par ces dernières.

En 1988, le MEQ fait le point sur les Services d'accueil et de francisation. Après un certain nombre de constats, le Ministère décide d'accorder un appui financier spécial aux Commissions scolaires ayant des effectifs fortement multiethniques. En effet, les milieux à forte concentration ethnique ont eu l'occasion de faire entendre leur voix et de solliciter une aide particulière pour réussir le défi de l'intégration. Il est alors décidé de procéder à une mise en place de services de soutien linguistique destinés aux élèves ayant intégré le secteur régulier de la formation et de mettre sur pied des activités d'aide pédagogique en français destinées aux élèves non francophones inscrits en classes ordinaires.

En 1996, le MEQ fait de nouveau le point. À la suite de ce dernier examen, le Ministère réunit les diverses mesures de soutien dans un programme unique : le *Programme d'accueil et de soutien à l'apprentissage du français* (PASAF) qui vient confirmer l'autonomie et la pleine responsabilité des commissions scolaires dans l'organisation des services. L'année suivante, soit en 1997, un projet de politique voit le jour : *Une école d'avenir : Intégration scolaire et éducation interculturelle : Projet de politique*. Le MEQ avait longtemps hésité à prendre position sur ces questions. Les motifs invoqués s'appuyaient principalement sur le fait que la majorité des immigrants se trouvaient à Montréal et que, pour cette raison, il ne pouvait pas y avoir de projet de politique qui soit acceptable aux yeux de tous et qui puisse s'appliquer à l'ensemble de la province. Il s'agit donc d'une décision importante. Pour cette raison, depuis 1997, une diversification de modèles de soutien à l'apprentissage du français a vu le jour (voir Armand 2005 pour une synthèse).

Voici, en résumé, ces différents modèles :

TABLEAU 2
Modèles de soutien à l'apprentissage du français

Modèle	Description du modèle
Classe d'accueil fermée	Les élèves suivent tous leurs cours en classe d'accueil.
Classe d'accueil fermée avec aide à l'intégration	Les élèves suivent tous leurs cours en classe d'accueil, et bénéficient aussi d'aide à l'intégration de la part d'une personne ressource (en mathématique, en français, en compétences d'ordre intellectuel, etc.).
Intégration partielle	Les élèves suivent des cours en classe d'accueil et assistent aussi à des cours avec les élèves du régulier.
Intégration totale avec soutien à l'apprentissage du français	Les élèves suivent tous leurs cours avec les élèves du régulier et bénéficient de soutien à l'apprentissage du français.
Intégration totale sans soutien à l'apprentissage du français	Les élèves suivent tous leurs cours avec les élèves du régulier.
Autre modèle	Tout autre modèle ne correspondant à aucun des modèles ci-dessus.

Source : compilation de l'auteur.

La responsabilité des services de soutien à l'apprentissage du français incombe à la *Direction des services aux communautés culturelles* (DSCC) du ministère de l'Éducation, du Loisir et des Sports (MELS). Un des changements fondamentaux intervenus à la suite de cet examen de 1996 est le fait que désormais le droit à des services de soutien à l'apprentissage du français est inscrit dans la *Loi sur l'instruction publique*. À cet effet, consulter le site suivant : http://www2.publicationsduquebec.gouv.qc.ca/dynamicSearch/telecharge.php?type=2&file=/I_13_3/I13_3.html.

Par ailleurs, est mis en place un système d'attribution des services généreux en soi s'il trouve une application adaptée au milieu. Pour comprendre le mode de fonctionnement de l'attribution des allocations liées aux services de soutien à l'apprentissage du français, voir le *Guide de gestion des allocations relatives aux services aux élèves des communautés culturelles 2006–2007* à la page 10 (http://www.mels.gouv.qc.ca/dscc/pdf/GuideGestionAlloc_CS2006-2007.pdf).

En 2003, préoccupé par la présence de plus en plus importante d'élèves sous-scolarisés et par les interrogations soulevées par les enseignants, le MEQ avance des solutions d'intervention auprès des élèves sous-scolarisés. Il propose un certain nombre de documents à cet effet :

Ministère de l'Éducation du Québec (1996). *Travailler au développement des habiletés de littératie des élèves en les initiant à la culture de l'écrit.* Québec, Direction des services aux communautés culturelles.

Ministère de l'Éducation du Québec (2003). *Outils diagnostique pour les élèves immigrants en situation de grand retard scolaire.* Québec, Direction des services aux communautés culturelles.

Ministère de l'Éducation du Québec (2003). *Plan d'intervention auprès des élèves immigrants nouvellement arrivés en situation de grand retard scolaire.* Trousse pédagogique. Québec, Direction des services aux communautés culturelles.

En résumé, quels sont les effectifs touchés par ces différentes mesures de soutien à l'apprentissage du français? De 1980 à 1995, entre 13 000 et 14 000 élèves par année. On observe une légère baisse due à la diminution du niveau d'immigration, stabilisation autour de 15 000. Néanmoins, une tendance à une légère augmentation se manifeste après 2000. À titre d'exemple : 13 132 élèves en 1998–1999; 15 729 en 2002–2003; 17 485 en 2007–2008. Par ailleurs, sur l'île de Montréal, 237 langues différentes sont parlées.

Maintenant que nous nous sommes donnés une vue d'ensemble de la façon dont ont été mis en place les services d'accueil destinés aux élèves issus de l'immigration, nous nous attarderons à la dimension pédagogique de ces services. Dans son projet de politique : *Une école d'avenir : Intégration scolaire et éducation interculturelle de 1997,* le MEQ énonce clairement dans son deuxième chapitre, la nécessité d'assurer un soutien à une plus grande maîtrise du français auprès des élèves immigrants. L'école devient alors le principal responsable de l'intégration linguistique de ces élèves de même que de leur mise à niveau scolaire. Dorénavant, les élèves du primaire auront droit à deux années de soutien à l'apprentissage du français et ceux du secondaire à trois années. Malgré cette prolongation des services, le défi est de taille lorsque l'on prend en compte la spécificité de la clientèle scolaire fréquentant des classes d'accueil. Rappelons brièvement les caractéristiques de cette clientèle. Les élèves des classes d'accueil sont le plus souvent regroupés par cycles (réunissant des élèves de 3 années scolaires); on trouvera cependant malgré tout à l'intérieur d'un même groupe-classe une grande hétérogénéité due à plusieurs facteurs. Nous tenterons ici d'en dégager les incidences sur le plan de l'activité pédagogique.

a) des groupes multi-âges :

Le développement psychologique intellectuel et social des élèves diffère selon l'âge et l'expérience de chacun. Dans une classe régulière, dite homogène, il est déjà difficile de prévoir des activités d'apprentissage qui savent répondre aux intérêts de tous.

Comme les regroupements multi-âges sont une des réalités des classes d'accueil, l'enseignant doit constamment tenir compte de cette variable dans le choix des activités ou, encore, du matériel pédagogique à proposer aux élèves.

Par ailleurs, l'âge constitue un facteur important dans le développement des habiletés langagières notamment en ce qui a trait à la compétence à communiquer. Il peut donc y avoir un écart important entre des élèves de 12 à 16 ans sur ce plan.

Enfin, on peut avoir l'impression que des élèves identifiés comme de parfaits débutants sont tous sur le même pied au départ. Il convient cependant de ne pas négliger de prendre en ligne de compte le niveau d'expérience de l'élève qui influencera sans cesse son rythme d'apprentissage, ou tout au moins sa façon d'aborder les connaissances nouvelles.

b) des groupes multi-niveaux :

En classe d'accueil, on trouve fréquemment regroupés des élèves de plusieurs niveaux. Il arrive même que l'on puisse traiter la notion de "niveau" sous des angles différents. Ainsi, on peut parler de niveau en termes de compétence à communiquer à l'oral et à l'écrit, ou bien en termes de scolarisation.

Ceci implique pour l'enseignant une planification des activités d'apprentissage susceptible de tenir compte de ces écarts et, plus concrètement, une adaptation de ces activités faisant varier le niveau de complexité des contenus de même que celui des tâches à exécuter.

Il importe également de rappeler que certains élèves peuvent présenter de sérieux retards scolaires correspondant à plusieurs années de scolarisation et ainsi être considérés comme sous-scolarisés.

c) des groupes en constante mobilité :

Une autre dimension caractérise la clientèle des classes d'accueil : la mobilité des élèves. L'inscription en classe d'accueil s'effectuant tout au long de l'année, de nouveaux élèves arrivent dans une classe à tout moment.

Par ailleurs, les élèves ayant réalisé des progrès rapides peuvent quitter la classe d'accueil pour intégrer une classe ordinaire avant la fin de leur stage de dix mois.

Enfin, pour faciliter leur intégration scolaire, ils peuvent suivre certains cours disciplinaires en se joignant à des groupes réguliers, et ce, à des heures différentes déterminées par leur niveau scolaire d'intégration ou par l'organisation de l'école.

Cette brève description des principales caractéristiques du milieu des classes d'accueil nous permet de conclure que le défi pédagogique qui consiste principalement à créer des conditions favorables à une intégration des apprentissages langagiers et multidisciplinaires est de taille.

Pour nous donner une bonne idée de ce que cela veut dire en termes d'organisation scolaire, nous allons examiner comment fonctionne une classe d'une école secondaire qui pratique un *Modèle d'intégration partielle*. Les élèves sont d'abord placés dans une classe d'accueil pendant environ trois semaines pour y recevoir un enseignement intensif de français. Puis, tout en demeurant associés à cette classe de départ, ils sont progressivement intégrés dans des classes ordinaires pour y suivre un certain nombre de matières scolaires et ceci en fonction de leur âge et de leurs antécédents académiques. Les élèves peuvent demeurer associés à leur classe d'accueil pendant deux ans tout en fréquentant de plus en plus la classe ordinaire avec des élèves de leur âge et de leur niveau académique. En d'autres mots, l'élève n'est pas placé en situation de submersion; bien au contraire, il est accompagné pendant toute cette période d'accommodation. Il importe ici de signaler qu'un élève du secondaire a droit à trois ans de mesures de soutien à l'apprentissage du français. Du côté des enseignants, un tel modèle exige énormément d'ouverture d'esprit et de souplesse, et requiert de procéder à des préparations de classe multiples pour s'ajuster à la mobilité des élèves.

Les choix pédagogiques liés à un tel modèle mènent à une *Pédagogie de projet*, se caractérisant par une suite d'activités qui s'enchaînent les unes aux autres et qui aboutissent à des réalisations concrètes créant ainsi les conditions propices à l'apparition de situations de communication réelles, spontanées et variées.

Cette pédagogie permet de développer chez l'élève un savoir-faire où l'usage de la langue est fonctionnellement lié à des activités réelles qui se déroulent dans la classe, dans l'école ou même à l'extérieur, et elle fournit les moyens concrets d'enchaîner et d'intégrer des activités d'oral, de lecture et d'écriture qui favorisent le renforcement réciproque des habiletés langagières.

Elle permet d'aborder un même contenu linguistique de différentes façons, sans perdre le fil conducteur, et propose une variété de modes d'apprentissage permettant ainsi une meilleure participation des élèves. Par ailleurs, elle permet d'initier l'élève à divers modes de travail en classe : le travail individuel, le travail en dyade, le travail en sous-groupe ou encore le travail en grand groupe. Enfin, l'accent est mis sur l'apprentissage coopératif.

Cette pédagogie de projet est encore aujourd'hui celle qui prévaut, notamment parce qu'elle permet de travailler les dimensions linguistiques de la nouvelle langue à acquérir et l'initiation en français aux différentes disciplines scolaires, favorisant ainsi la préparation des élèves à une intégration à la classe ordinaire.

Par ailleurs, il importe de souligner que sur le plan pédagogique, à partir de 1973, le MEQ aura soutenu les efforts du milieu par la production de nombreux documents ou d'ateliers de perfectionnement destinés aux principaux intervenants travaillant auprès de la clientèle allophone. Pensons notamment aux Programmes cadres, aux Programmes de français, aux Guides pédagogiques, aux Guides d'évaluation pour le français, aux Épreuves sommatives pour le français, aux *Guide d'initiation à la vie québécoise* (1983), *À la découverte des nouveaux mondes* (1984), au *Guide pour l'élimination des stéréotypes discriminatoires dans le matériel didactique* (1988), aux Sessions d'éducation interculturelle (1987–1995), au Module de formation : *La prise en compte de la diversité culturelle et religieuse en milieu scolaire* (1995). Pour une liste des documents récents, voir aussi les publications des Services aux communautés culturelles du MEQ (http://www.meq. gouv.qc.ca/publications/menu-pub-ped-2.htm#com-cult).

De tout ceci nous pouvons saisir que l'État a joué un rôle primordial dans l'accueil des enfants issus de l'immigration dans le système scolaire francophone. Il est aussi vrai que les milieux recevant cette clientèle ont pris localement de nombreuses initiatives. Malheureusement, nous ne pouvons pas dans le cadre de cet article faire part du détail de ces dernières.

En ce qui concerne les adultes, les interventions de l'État ont aussi été importantes et le sont toujours.

Tout d'abord, nous situerons la création du ministère de l'Immigration et des Centres d'orientation et de formation des immigrants suivie de l'ouverture des Carrefours d'intégration. Ensuite, nous nous attarderons sur quelques tableaux traçant le portrait de l'immigration au Québec afin de saisir la variété des sources d'immigration. Finalement, nous décrirons ce qui est offert au Québec en termes de cours : cours à temps plein, à temps partiel, sur mesure. Pour conclure, nous nous interrogeons sur les enjeux liés à la francisation des adultes immigrants et sur les défis à venir.

En 1968, on assiste à la création du ministère de l'Immigration. Le contexte est celui dont nous avons fait mention plus tôt, soit le problème de dénatalité auquel fait face le Québec dans les années 1960. La création de ce Ministère permet au Québec d'élaborer ses propres politiques d'accueil des immigrants et de veiller à l'élaboration de mesures favorisant l'arrivée d'immigrants francophones.

Une des premières mesures de ce Ministère aura été celle de la création des *Centres d'orientation et de formation des immigrants* (COFI). Ces centres offraient 30 semaines de cours de français aux immigrants. Ils seront fermés en l'an 2000 par le Parti Québécois au pouvoir pour être remplacés par des *Carrefours d'intégration* qui viseront à ce que les immigrants puissent mieux s'intégrer en les dirigeant vers des institutions d'enseignement déjà existantes : commissions scolaires (secteurs adultes) cégeps, universités et organismes communautaires.

Avant d'aborder la question des cours offerts à ces populations, il importe de signaler qu'un des principaux défis auquel fait face le Québec relativement à ses immigrants est la diversité des sources d'immigration et de leur provenance. Les désignations suivantes correspondent aux différentes sources d'immigration telles que catégorisées au Québec : immigration économique, regroupement familial, réfugiés et autres. Le Québec reçoit des immigrants de toutes les régions d'Afrique, des Amériques, de toutes les régions d'Asie et de l'Europe. En consultant un document produit par la Direction de la recherche et de l'analyse prospective du ministère de l'Immigration et des Communautés culturelles et, plus précisément le Tableau 3a de la page 23, intitulé *Population immigrante admise au Québec de 1997 à 2006 et présente en 2008 selon la catégorie, par année d'admission* (cf. annexe 1) ainsi que le Tableau 4 de la page 25, intitulé *Présence en 2008 des immigrants admis au Québec de 1997 à 2006, et présente en 2008 selon le continent ou la région de dernière résidence, par catégorie* (cf. annexe 2), il est possible de se donner une idée de cette variété que ce soit en termes de sources d'immigration ou de provenance. La lecture de ces tableaux nous permet d'envisager le défi posé pour réaliser une intégration harmonieuse de populations fort diversifiées sur les plans linguistique et culturel.

En examinant le Tableau 10, tiré de la page 31 du même document et intitulé *Population immigrante admise au Québec de 1997 à 2006 et présente en 2008 selon la région de résidence, par période d'immigration* (cf. annexe 3), nous sommes amenés à constater qu'au cours de la dernière décennie la façon dont les immigrants se répartissent sur le territoire est visiblement constante, avec les conséquences qui en découlent. Pour pousser un peu plus loin la réflexion dans ce sens, il est aussi intéressant d'examiner le Tableau 11, tiré de la page 32 du même document, qui nous donne un aperçu de la façon dont la population immigrante s'est installée et s'installe présentement au Québec, mais cette fois en tenant compte des différentes catégories établies. Dans ce tableau, intitulé *Population immigrante admise au Québec de 1997 à 2006 et présente en 2008 selon la région de résidence, par catégorie* (cf. annexe 4), on trouve les totaux d'immigration hors de la Région métropolitaine de Montréal, dans la Région métropolitaine de Montréal et selon un regroupement non déterminé et ceci en fonction de chaque source d'immigration. Il est clair que la concentration la plus importante se trouve dans la région métropolitaine et que certaines sources d'immigration sont plus importantes que d'autres. Si nous examinons ces tableaux dans la perspective d'offrir des cours de français pour faciliter l'intégration des immigrants, en termes de défi, l'offre de services peut être facilitée par les nombres en présence dans la métropole et complexifiée par la dispersion en région éloignée où l'on trouve le plus souvent de très petits groupes de citoyens issus de l'immigration.

Pour ces différentes populations, nous pouvons maintenant nous interroger sur ce qui est offert au Québec en termes de cours. La réponse est la suivante : cours intensifs à temps plein, cours à temps partiel, cours spécialisés, et accès à un Centre d'auto-apprentissage. Il faut ici comprendre qu'il aura fallu au fil des ans modifier l'offre de cours; d'une part, pour mieux tenir compte de la variété des sources d'immigration et, d'autre part, des besoins qu'ont ces immigrants de s'insérer le plus rapidement possible dans le milieu du travail.

Les cours intensifs à temps plein constituent la première mesure offerte aux nouveaux arrivants. Au départ, les futurs étudiants doivent se soumettre à une évaluation de leur compétence en français. Une mesure est donc prise par un évaluateur du MICC. Trois habiletés font l'objet d'une évaluation : l'interaction orale, la compréhension écrite et la production écrite. Par la suite, les étudiants sont alors répartis en fonction de trois niveaux : Débutant, Intermédiaire et Intermédiaire avancé.

Pour faciliter l'accès à ces cours et permettre aux immigrants de les suivre jusqu'à la fin, une aide financière est déterminée selon le statut d'immigration, le nombre d'enfants à charge, et l'aide du gouvernement déjà octroyée. Trois formes d'aide sont disponibles : allocation de participation (115$ ou 30$ par semaine); allocation de frais de garde (maximum de 25$ par jour); allocation de trajet ou de transport.

Même si au départ les cours étaient offerts dans des établissements destinés uniquement à ces clientèles, depuis l'an 2000 les lieux de formation sont désormais des institutions d'enseignement publiques qui accueillent différentes populations scolaires adultes du Québec. Ce sont donc dans les Cégeps, les Universités, les Organismes communautaires et les Commissions scolaires que les adultes immigrants suivent des cours de francisation. Ils sont dirigés vers l'une ou l'autre de ces institutions en fonction de leur âge et de leur niveau de scolarisation. Ainsi, peu à peu le Québec a reconnu l'importance de placer ces immigrants dans des milieux éducatifs où ils seraient amenés à côtoyer des locuteurs natifs et de la pertinence de tenir compte de la formation académique antérieure que ces immigrants avaient reçue dans leur pays d'origine.

Par exemple, pour un débutant, la durée, la fréquence et le calendrier suivi sont les suivants : 3 cours de 11 semaines, à raison de 6 heures par jour, 5 jours par semaine. 20 heures d'enseignement sont assurées par un enseignant et 10 heures d'activités de soutien à l'apprentissage sont prises en charge par un moniteur.

Il importe également de souligner qu'un *Programme spécial pour les adultes peu scolarisés* (ces derniers pouvant également être désignés *adultes ayant peu ou pas fréquenté un établissement d'enseignement*) a vu le jour. Selon cette formule, visant à rejoindre cette clientèle moins scolarisée, 20 heures d'enseignement sont assumées par un enseignant alors que 5 heures de soutien à l'apprentissage le sont par un moniteur.

Sur le plan pédagogique, au fil des années différentes approches pédagogiques ont été retenues en fonction des courants en didactique des langues secondes ou étrangères. Cependant, depuis les années 1980, c'est peu à peu l'approche communicative qui a été privilégiée et les étudiants sont évalués en fonction d'habiletés langagières développées dans le cadre de cette approche. Des évaluations sont menées tout au long du parcours.

En ce qui a trait aux cours à temps partiel, le stagiaire peut être soumis à un test le jour des inscriptions pour déterminer sa compétence de départ. Il reçoit une aide financière de 7$ par jour pour les frais de garde. Les lieux de formation sont les mêmes que ceux des cours à temps plein. La durée, la fréquence et le calendrier retenu sont les suivants : 11 semaines pendant les sessions d'automne et d'hiver, 7 semaines pendant la session d'été. Les cours sont offerts le matin, l'après-midi, le soir et la fin de semaine pour permettre à la personne d'avoir un horaire qui correspond à ses besoins de travailleur. Le nombre d'heures de cours peut varier de 4 heures à 12 heures selon le niveau de classement.

En ce qui a trait aux cours spécialisés et aux centres d'auto apprentissage, l'offre prend la forme de cours à temps plein et de cours à temps partiel pour besoins spécifiques : (1) Français écrit, (2) Communication orale, (3) Français écrit et réalités du travail. Ces cours sont parfois dispensés en milieu de travail, ce qui permet d'élargir le bassin d'immigrants s'inscrivant à la francisation.

Le Centre d'auto-apprentissage du français (CAF) de Montréal s'adresse aux travailleurs. Les cours qui y sont offerts le sont en fonction de deux volets : Laboratoires informatiques ou Ateliers de formation sur des thèmes professionnels.

Malgré une offre de cours assez diversifiée et un soutien réel pour faciliter l'accès à ces cours de même que leur poursuite, les principaux enjeux demeurent les suivants : (a) la fréquentation des cours puisque certains immigrants préfèrent ne pas attendre pour s'insérer dans le milieu de travail; (b) la fréquentation des cours : homme et/ou femme d'un même foyer puisqu'à l'intérieur d'un ménage c'est l'un ou l'autre des individus qui aura accès au cours, la nécessité de travailler constituant souvent un obstacle à une fréquentation des deux personnes; (c) la durée de la fréquentation aussi conditionnée par des raisons économiques ou d'insertion sur le marché du travail faisant en sorte qu'il y a une grande fluctuation dans la persévérance jusqu'aux niveaux de compétence les plus élevés; (d) les défis interculturels posés par la mixité des groupes en présence dans les cours; (e) le défi soulevé par la présence d'apprenants peu alphabétisés ou peu scolarisés qui requièrent le recours à des approches d'enseignement très spécialisées.

Pour conclure, que retenir de ce survol des choix effectués par le Québec pour répondre aux besoins de formation des élèves issus de l'immigration ainsi qu'à ceux des adultes immigrants en processus d'insertion au marché de travail ? D'abord, il est primordial de constater qu'en ayant recours à une législation linguistique visant à circonscrire le rôle du français dans la société et à orienter les enfants issus de l'immigration vers les écoles françaises, l'État québécois a assuré le développement du français comme langue commune. Aussi, en mettant en place des services de soutien à l'apprentissage du français et en s'assurant que les modèles mis en place soient constamment révisés, le MEQ a pu constamment veiller à ce que les mesures se diversifient en fonction des milieux. Du côté des adultes, un long chemin a été parcouru pour tenir compte de la variété des sources d'immigration et de la provenance des immigrants. Un soutien financier et la prise en compte des besoins des familles a permis de faciliter l'accès aux services de francisation et d'intégration. Au fil des années, une variété de programmes ont vu le jour, de mieux en mieux adaptés aux réalités du marché de travail. Pour l'avenir, vigilance et innovation devront être au rendez-vous pour que le projet de société francophone continue de prendre forme.

RÉFÉRENCES

Armand, F. 2005. Les élèves immigrants nouvellement arrivés et l'école québécoise. *Santé, société et solidarité* 4 (1) : 141-152.

Bernard, A. 2003. Les répercussions sociales et politiques de la Loi 101. Dans *Le français au Québec : 400 ans d'histoire et de vie*, dir. M. Plourde avec H. Duval et P. Georgeault, 292-300. Montréal : Fides/Conseil supérieur de la langue française.

Levine, M.V. 2003. L'usage du français, langue commune. Dans *Le français au Québec : 400 ans d'histoire et de vie*, dir. M. Plourde avec H. Duval et P. Georgeault, 366-378. Montréal : Fides/Conseil supérieur de la langue française.

Québec, Ministère de l'Immigration et des Communautés culturelles. 2008. *Présence en 2008 des immigrants admis au Québec de 1997 à 2006*. Québec : Ministère de l'Immigration et des Communautés culturelles, Direction de la recherche et de l'analyse prospective. 32 p.

Rocher, G. 2003. La politique et la loi linguistiques du Québec en 1977. Dans *Le français au Québec : 400 ans d'histoire et de vie*, dir. M. Plourde avec H. Duval et P. Georgeault, 273-284. Montréal : Fides/Conseil supérieur de la langue française.

Woehrling, J. 2003. La Charte de la langue française : les ajustements juridiques. Dans *Le français au Québec : 400 ans d'histoire et de vie*, dir. M. Plourde avec H. Duval et P. Georgeault, 285-291. Montréal : Fides/Conseil supérieur de la langue française.

ANNEXE 1 : TABLEAU 3A
(extrait du document *Présence en 2008 des immigrants admis au Québec de 1997 à 2006*, p. 23, 2008)

Tableau 3a
Population immigrante admise au Québec de 1997 à 2006 et présente en 2008 selon la catégorie, par année d'admission

Catégorie	1997	1998	1999	2000	2001	2002	2003	2004	2005	2006	Total
Immigration économique											
Travailleurs qualifiés	5 722	7 013	8 058	10 182	14 193	16 788	17 572	20 054	19 615	18 932	138 129
Parents aidés	285	291	327	354	488	514	713	389	225	169	3 755
Gens d'affaires, total	805	923	943	827	1 184	849	868	948	913	971	9 231
• Entrepreneurs	513	462	502	407	484	314	237	273	231	236	3 659
• Travailleurs autonomes	103	178	149	147	203	158	196	161	120	148	1 563
• Investisseurs	189	283	292	273	497	377	435	514	562	587	4 009
Aides familiaux	346	299	357	241	199	170	293	338	361	552	3 156
Autres[1]	434	281	137	57	9	7	10	19	20	24	998
Total	7 592	8 807	9 822	11 661	16 073	18 328	19 456	21 748	21 134	20 648	155 269
Regroupement familial											
Époux, conjoints, partenaires	4 648	3 826	4 519	4 990	5 318	4 794	5 635	5 938	5 885	6 314	51 867
Enfants	736	592	629	572	639	551	523	425	416	412	5 495
Adoption internationale	663	876	761	687	688	722	795	667	495	389	6 743
Parents ou grands-parents	955	732	732	855	1 039	920	979	662	521	820	8 215
Autres parents	21	23	27	20	18	27	241	557	606	932	2 472
Total	7 023	6 049	6 668	7 124	7 702	7 014	8 173	8 249	7 923	8 867	74 792
Réfugiés et personnes en situation semblable											
Réfugiés pris en charge par l'État	1 395	1 295	1 506	1 817	1 828	1 362	1 905	1 726	1 711	1 658	16 203
Réfugiés parrainés	191	149	98	182	276	227	292	251	192	493	2 351
Réfugiés reconnus sur place	3 158	2 334	3 392	3 356	3 107	2 807	2 382	3 198	3 442	3 069	30 245
Membres de la famille d'un réfugié[2]	1 106	911	869	1 214	985	1 008	761	1 359	1 083	1 199	10 495
Autres réfugiés	1	6	8	1	22	15	13	-	-	-	66
Total	5 851	4 695	5 873	6 570	6 218	5 419	5 353	6 534	6 428	6 419	59 360
Autres immigrants[3]	91	39	50	36	14	10	203	708	666	1 040	2 857
Total	20 557	19 590	22 413	25 391	30 007	30 771	33 185	37 239	36 151	36 974	292 278

1 Immigrants visés par une mesure de renvoi, retraités et candidats des provinces.
2 Membres de la famille d'un réfugié reconnu sur place.
3 Demandeurs non reconnus du statut de réfugié et cas d'ordre humanitaire.

Source : Ministère de l'Immigration et des Communautés culturelles, Direction de la recherche et de l'analyse prospective.

ANNEXE 2 : TABLEAU 4

(extrait du document *Présence en 2008 des immigrants admis au Québec de 1997 à 2006*, p. 25, 2008)

Tableau 4
Population immigrante admise au Québec de 1997 à 2006 et présente en 2008 selon le continent ou la région de dernière résidence, par catégorie

Continent ou région de dernière résidence	Immigration économique			Regroupement familial			Réfugiés			Autres immigrants			Total		
	Imm.[1]	Prés.[2]	%	Imm.	Prés.	%	Imm.	Prés.	%	Imm.	Prés.	%	Imm.	Prés.	%
Afrique															
Afrique occidentale	3 017	2 504	83,0	2 584	2 278	88,2	2 776	2 479	89,3	111	101	91,0	8 488	7 362	86,7
Afrique orientale	1 707	1 341	78,6	862	719	83,4	4 518	3 903	86,4	105	88	83,8	7 192	6 051	84,1
Afrique du Nord	42 733	39 150	91,6	9 834	9 020	91,7	3 569	3 254	91,2	636	616	96,9	56 772	52 040	91,7
Afrique centrale	1 473	1 237	84,0	1 638	1 483	90,5	6 846	6 088	88,9	254	227	89,4	10 211	9 035	88,5
Afrique méridionale	118	47	39,8	83	60	72,3	51	44	86,3	1	1	100,0	253	152	60,1
Total	49 048	44 279	90,3	15 001	13 560	90,4	17 760	15 768	88,8	1 107	1 033	93,3	82 916	74 640	90,0
Amérique															
Amérique du Nord	2 118	1 292	61,0	3 453	2 696	78,1	354	311	87,9	54	44	81,5	5 979	4 343	72,6
Amérique centrale	3 210	2 541	79,2	3 006	2 720	90,5	3 051	2 826	92,6	155	142	91,6	9 422	8 229	87,3
Amérique du Sud	11 499	9 542	83,0	4 924	4 364	88,6	10 707	9 991	93,3	307	281	91,5	27 437	24 178	88,1
Antilles	5 849	5 318	90,9	12 168	11 303	92,9	2 189	1 991	91,0	304	276	90,8	20 510	18 888	92,1
Total	22 676	18 693	82,4	23 551	21 083	89,5	16 301	15 119	92,7	820	743	90,6	63 348	55 638	87,8
Asie															
Moyen-Orient	16 574	12 763	77,0	4 837	4 141	85,6	2 447	2 007	82,0	157	136	86,6	24 015	19 047	79,3
Asie occ. et centrale	4 049	2 837	70,1	2 436	2 131	87,5	7 677	6 776	88,3	80	67	83,8	14 242	11 811	82,9
Asie orientale	31 306	13 518	43,2	9 531	8 301	87,1	292	261	89,4	37	28	75,7	41 166	22 108	53,7
Asie méridionale	4 257	2 311	54,3	10 522	8 786	83,5	16 691	12 214	73,2	724	590	81,5	32 194	23 901	74,2
Asie du Sud-Est	4 356	3 611	82,9	5 746	5 226	91,0	427	370	86,7	72	54	75,0	10 601	9 261	87,4
Total	60 542	35 040	57,9	33 072	28 585	86,4	27 534	21 628	78,6	1 070	875	81,8	122 218	86 128	70,5
Europe															
Europe occ. et sept.	41 719	31 894	76,4	5 996	4 896	81,7	509	388	76,2	57	50	87,7	48 281	37 228	77,1
Europe orientale	27 575	23 228	84,2	5 375	4 765	88,7	2 445	2 075	84,9	132	105	79,5	35 527	30 173	84,9
Europe méridionale	1 743	1 392	79,9	1 699	1 428	84,0	5 901	4 093	69,4	51	43	84,3	9 394	6 956	74,0
Total	71 037	56 514	79,6	13 070	11 089	84,8	8 855	6 556	74,0	240	198	82,5	93 202	74 357	79,8
Océanie et autres pays	954	743	77,9	573	475	82,9	338	289	85,5	11	8	72,7	1 876	1 515	80,8
Total	204 257	155 269	76,0	85 267	74 792	87,7	70 788	59 360	83,9	3 248	2 857	88,0	363 560	292 278	80,4

1 Imm. : Immigrants
2 Prés. : Présents
Source : Ministère de l'Immigration et des Communautés culturelles, Direction de la recherche et de l'analyse prospective.

ANNEXE 3 : TABLEAU 10
(extrait du document *Présence en 2008 des immigrants admis au Québec de 1997 à 2006*, p. 31, 2008)

Tableau 10
Population immigrante admise au Québec de 1997 à 2006 et présente en 2008 selon la région de résidence, par période d'immigration

Région de résidence	1997-2001		2002-2006		Total, 1997-2006	
	n	%	n	%	n	%
Régions hors de la Région métropolitaine de Montréal (RMM)						
Bas-Saint-Laurent	273	0,2	451	0,3	724	0,2
Saguenay–Lac-Saint-Jean	422	0,4	613	0,4	1 035	0,4
Capitale-Nationale	4 738	4,0	7 158	4,1	11 896	4,1
Mauricie	527	0,4	1 234	0,7	1 761	0,6
Estrie	2 134	1,8	3 455	2,0	5 589	1,9
Outaouais	3 249	2,8	3 964	2,3	7 213	2,5
Abitibi-Témiscamingue	160	0,1	224	0,1	384	0,1
Côte-Nord	113	0,1	142	0,1	255	0,1
Nord-du-Québec	71	0,1	80	0,0	151	0,1
Gaspésie–Îles-de-la-Madeleine	100	0,1	107	0,1	207	0,1
Chaudière-Appalaches	629	0,5	834	0,5	1 463	0,5
Lanaudière	1 868	1,6	2 032	1,2	3 900	1,3
Laurentides	2 697	2,3	3 093	1,8	5 790	2,0
Montérégie Est[1]	2 511	2,1	3 189	1,8	5 700	2,0
Montérégie Ouest[1]	2 469	2,1	2 560	1,5	5 029	1,7
Centre-du-Québec	643	0,5	1 242	0,7	1 885	0,6
Total, régions hors de la RMM	22 604	19,2	30 378	17,4	52 982	18,1
Région métropolitaine de Montréal (RMM)						
Montréal	72 419	61,4	119 010	68,3	191 429	65,5
Laval	9 214	7,8	10 256	5,9	19 470	6,7
Longueuil (agglomération)[1]	7 599	6,4	10 590	6,1	18 189	6,2
Total, RMM	89 232	75,6	139 856	80,2	229 088	78,4
Non déterminée	6 122	5,2	4 086	2,3	10 208	3,5
Total	117 958	100,0	174 320	100,0	292 278	100,0

1 Territoire de la Conférence régionale des élus.

Source : Ministère de l'Immigration et des Communautés culturelles, Direction de la recherche et de l'analyse prospective.

ANNEXE 4 : TABLEAU 11
(extrait du document *Présence en 2008 des immigrants admis au Québec de 1997 à 2006,*
p. 32, 2008)

Tableau 11
**Population immigrante admise au Québec de 1997 à 2006 et présente en 2008
selon la région de résidence, par catégorie**

Région de résidence	Immigration économique		Regroupement familial		Réfugiés		Autres immigrants		Total	
	n	%	n	%	n	%	n	%	n	%
Régions hors de la Région métropolitaine de Montréal (RMM)										
Bas-Saint-Laurent	260	0,2	366	0,5	98	0,2	-	-	724	0,2
Saguenay–Lac-Saint-Jean	290	0,2	498	0,7	246	0,4	1	0,0	1 035	0,4
Capitale-Nationale	6 034	3,9	2 592	3,5	3 240	5,5	30	1,1	11 896	4,1
Mauricie	781	0,5	459	0,6	519	0,9	2	0,1	1 761	0,6
Estrie	2 113	1,4	876	1,2	2 564	4,3	36	1,3	5 589	1,9
Outaouais	2 970	1,9	1 754	2,3	2 434	4,1	55	1,9	7 213	2,5
Abitibi-Témiscamingue	166	0,1	201	0,3	17	0,0	-	-	384	0,1
Côte-Nord	118	0,1	132	0,2	5	0,0	-	-	255	0,1
Nord-du-Québec	56	0,0	90	0,1	4	0,0	1	0,0	151	0,1
Gaspésie–Îles-de-la-Madeleine	79	0,1	119	0,2	9	0,0	-	-	207	0,1
Chaudière-Appalaches	657	0,4	682	0,9	114	0,2	10	0,4	1 463	0,5
Lanaudière	1 768	1,1	1 381	1,8	704	1,2	47	1,6	3 900	1,3
Laurentides	3 295	2,1	1 791	2,4	692	1,2	12	0,4	5 790	2,0
Montérégie Est[1]	2 341	1,5	1 901	2,5	1 438	2,4	20	0,7	5 700	2,0
Montérégie Ouest[1]	2 734	1,8	1 641	2,2	608	1,0	46	1,6	5 029	1,7
Centre-du-Québec	453	0,3	434	0,6	993	1,7	5	0,2	1 885	0,6
Total, régions hors de la RMM	24 115	15,5	14 917	19,9	13 685	23,1	265	9,3	52 982	18,1
Région métropolitaine de Montréal (RMM)										
Montréal	105 968	68,2	48 160	64,4	35 071	59,1	2 230	78,1	191 429	65,5
Laval	10 383	6,7	5 537	7,4	3 380	5,7	170	6,0	19 470	6,7
Longueuil (agglomération)[1]	10 463	6,7	4 248	5,7	3 348	5,6	130	4,6	18 189	6,2
Total, RMM	126 814	81,7	57 945	77,5	41 799	70,4	2 530	88,6	229 088	78,4
Non déterminée	4 340	2,8	1 930	2,6	3 876	6,5	62	2,2	10 208	3,5
Total	155 269	100,0	74 792	100,0	59 360	100,0	2 857	100,0	292 278	100,0

1 Territoire de la Conférence régionale des élus.

Source : Ministère de l'Immigration et des Communautés culturelles, Direction de la recherche et de l'analyse prospective.

PART VI

PARTNERSHIPS AND
KNOWLEDGE TRANSFER
BETWEEN GOVERNMENT,
UNIVERSITIES, AND CIVIL
SOCIETY: THE METROPOLIS
CENTRES

CHAPTER 12

The International Metropolis Project: A Model Worth Emulating?[1]

JOHN BILES,[2] *Special Adviser to the Director General of Integration at Citizenship and Immigration Canada; Former Director of Partnerships and Knowledge Transfer, International Metropolis Project*

HISTORY

Metropolis was first conceived of in 1992/93 when the then Director General of Strategic Planning, Research and Analysis at Citizenship and Immigration Canada, Meyer Burstein, and Demetrios Papademetriou, then at the Department of Labor in the United States, and their Australian counterpart discussed how they could move beyond the rigid exchange of data at the annual OECD SOPEMI meetings[3] to a more thematic and comparative approach to analyzing key migration issues. *Lesson one: Committees can be productive spaces for developing relationships.*

At the same time, program review within the Government of Canada had pared back government expenditures and reduced the size of the federal public service by 45,000 people. Often, the first areas to be cut were research programs. The result was a government where evidence-based decision-making became a challenge (Fellegi 1996). Citizenship and

Managing Immigration and Diversity in Canada: A Transatlantic Dialogue in the New Age of Migration, ed. D. Rodríguez-García. Montreal and Kingston: Queen's Policy Studies Series, McGill-Queen's University Press.

Immigration Canada (CIC) had also just been created as a stand-alone department, with elements pulled together from the former departments of Employment and Immigration Canada, Foreign Affairs Canada, and Multiculturalism and Citizenship Canada. Its research capacity was confined to a very small number of individuals with a tiny operating budget in a group entitled "Strategic Policy, Planning and Research."[4] Leveraging resources from across departments and across sectors thus became much more appealing. *Lesson two: Leveraging funds is critical.*

With the idea developed, Meyer Burstein created a proposal, persuaded his American colleague of the merits of the initiative, and then set about creating the Canadian component of the project. He met with the Social Sciences and Humanities Research Council of Canada (SSHRC) to explore the possibility of a strategic joint initiative. SSHRC agreed to participate, if 50 percent of the funds were provided by federal departments. Meyer met with his Deputy Minister (Peter Harder), and the project was cleared to launch with an agreement in place between SSHRC and CIC. *Lesson three: Multi-level leadership matters.*

Basic parameters needed to be adjusted, including the scope of the enterprise (what topics should be developed and, therefore, which federal departments and agencies should be approached), under what circumstances would academic researchers feel insulated enough against the vagaries of a fast-changing and mercurial policy environment, and what structures would be needed to make things work. Funding also had to be lined up so that CIC, as the lead federal partner, could build a coalition to provide the 50 percent of funds required to launch a Strategic Joint Initiative with SSHRC. Meyer Burstein met with other Directors General across the Government of Canada and created the Interdepartmental Committee, which continues to be a vital governance structure for the project today.

A call for proposals was issued, and as the name of the project (Metropolis) suggests, the intent was to create three Centres of Excellence in Canada's largest immigrant-receiving cities (Toronto, Montreal, and Vancouver). However, in the process, a unitary proposal from a consortium of universities located in the Prairie provinces of Manitoba, Saskatchewan, and Alberta was deemed stronger than two competing proposals submitted by the two large universities based in Vancouver. *Lesson four: Partnerships matter.*

It was inconceivable that the Government of Canada could launch a project without a Centre in Vancouver, the location where an enormous number of new immigrants were settling. Consequently, the Deputy Minister of CIC decided to fund a fourth Centre based in Vancouver provided that the two competing consortia would marry and work collaboratively.[5] *Lesson five: Politics matter.* (Note that this was illustrated even more directly when a fifth Centre was created in Atlantic Canada in 2002).

At the same time as the Canadian portions of the project were taking shape, Meyer Burstein and Demetrios Papademetriou set about recruiting international members to their cause. First, John Nieuwenhuysen, who was then a research director of the Australian Bureau of Immigration, Multicultural and Population Research and had been involved in initial discussions, was persuaded to join the formal enterprise. The North American duo then took a road trip throughout Europe, persuading their colleagues from the OECD SOPEMI meetings to join the international network.

The European Commission sponsored two meetings in Brussels to bring the interested parties together, and the International Steering Committee was created. The fruits of their labour were amply displayed at the First International Metropolis Conference, held in Milan, Italy, in November 1996. Of critical importance, the lavish event was attended by a range of ministers, including those from the two key Canadian ministries—then Minister of Citizenship and Immigration Canada Sergio Marchi and then Secretary of State for Multiculturalism Hedy Fry. The stage was set, and the annual international conferences were established and continue until today.[6] A bilateral agreement was signed between the Government of Canada and the Government of Italy in advance of the conference, committing them to working with one another. A similar Memorandum of Understanding was also signed with Israel.

The initial two international conferences were spent principally in plenary sessions, with follow-up working sessions. This format was not deemed an overwhelming success, and beginning with the Third International Metropolis Conference, held in Zichron Yaacov, Israel, in 1998, a highly decentralized format was launched, whereby workshop proposals on tightly focused topics were submitted for adjudication, while the plenary topics were developed by the International Steering Committee. Largely speaking, this format continues to this day. *Lesson six: Immigration and diversity is a broad field, and general discussions do not lead to productive outcomes.*

The annual Canadian National Metropolis Conference began four months after the first international conference.[7] Once again, the two main Canadian ministers were present: the Minister of Citizenship and Immigration Canada, Lucienne Robillard, and the Secretary of State for Multiculturalism, Hedy Fry. Ministerial presence remains very visible, and often several ministers jockey for the opportunity to speak at these events.

Absolutely essential to the success of these enterprises has been their predictability (they are annual events, scheduled years in advance), their geographic location (both conferences are held in different locations annually), their structure (plenary sessions on issues of broad-based interest; workshops on tightly focused topics), and their insistence on the mixture of participants drawn from different levels of government, community/local partners, and researchers.

Predictability matters, as people and organizations begin to plan to attend. As a result, the costs diminish since many people attend under their own steam. At least three years into the future need to be made public so that researchers can build travel and registration costs into their research grant applications; non-governmental partners can build expenses into their contribution agreements; and policy-makers can build a necessary case to be able to attend. This is especially important today during an economic downturn. *Lesson seven: Predictability matters.*

The idea of the conferences as a movable feast, both nationally and internationally, is important. Obviously, costs of participation decline dramatically when travel and accommodation are removed from the equation. Reduced registration fees for non-governmental organizations (NGOs) and graduate students go some distance to promoting access, but geographic proximity is even better at levelling the playing field. In addition, a far greater number of policy-makers from all three levels of government are more likely to be able to attend when the conferences are held in their backyard. *Lesson eight: Home-field advantage facilitates participation.*

As I mentioned earlier, the structure of the conferences also matters. If people's names are not in the program, many of them will not receive the necessary authority or funding to travel. More substantively, immigration and diversity is a vast field, and it is simply not possible to make headway if the only venues are the necessarily general plenary sessions of most conferences. Instead, key research, topical issues, or new and interesting ideas are featured in the plenary sessions, and then nearly 100 highly focused workshops allow experts from the different sectors to get into the detail necessary to tackle complex issues. This decentralized approach is also a great way to ensure that many issues are aired, and not just those that are predominant in public discourse at the time. Often, emerging issues are telegraphed through workshops long before they become major societal preoccupations. *Lesson nine: Autocracy in the selection of "important" topics to discuss leads to myopia.*

Finally, the mixture of individuals from different orders of government, from across the academic spectrum, and from non-governmental and other local partners greatly enhances how grounded the discussions at these conferences are able to be. It ensures that all of the implicated players are involved in discussions and that no sandbox issues are able to control who is at the table and what they are going to discuss. To take a concrete example, when Metropolis was launched, provincial governments were not very active on immigration issues. Although they are now much more actively engaged, CIC decided not to formally involve them in Phase III of Metropolis. Nevertheless, the provinces are vital players in the integration of newcomers to Canada, and the Metropolis conferences are one key way that they are able to network with other players in the immigration field (Biles 2008; Clippingdale 2009; Biles et al. 2011). *Lesson ten: There is no monopoly on knowledge.*

Of course, Metropolis is more than two large annual conferences. Yet the import of these events to create the Metropolis network and to keep it productive should not be underestimated. There is, of course, other key infrastructure that undergirds the project. This infrastructure has evolved over the three five-year funding phases of the project (Phase I, 1997–2002; Phase II, 2002–2007; Phase III, 2007–2012) as federal interests have evolved, lessons have been learned, and the partnership has matured.

STRUCTURE

One of the most unique features of Metropolis is its structure: the broad brush strokes of which include five university-based research Centres; a project Secretariat based within CIC; and a range of governance structures that connect both the federal funders to the project and the international partners, the latter of which are connected through the International Steering Committee. There is also a bifurcated international Secretariat, half of which is co-located with the Canadian Secretariat and the other half of which is presently based at the University of Amsterdam.[8]

Hands down, the most unique element of the Metropolis Project is the Secretariat. Other strategic joint initiatives of SSHRC have simply sought to set the parameters of research at the outset and then to sever the direct link with policy-makers. In the case of Metropolis, the Secretariat, a small group of individuals who are technically employees of CIC, also has an accountability structure that includes all of the funders via two major interdepartmental committees (the Interdepartmental Committee and the National Metropolis Committee). The Secretariat, or the Metropolis Project Team, as this group has also been known over time, acts as the principal liaison between the university-based Centres and the federal partners. As such, the Secretariat was the first group of knowledge brokers to emerge within the network (in Phase III, this role has been more widely expanded to include researchers occupying the roles of Centre Directors,[9] Domain Leaders,[10] and Priority Leaders,[11] as well as federal representatives that sit on the Interdepartmental Committee). *Lesson eleven: A dedicated team is essential to act as knowledge brokers and to maintain linkages over time.*

The governance structures have evolved over time. In this chapter, because of space restraints, I will simply speak to the current structures (see Appendix 1 for greater detail). Initially, these structures were simply viewed as a means to manage the project. As a result, the meetings of the major components—the Interdepartmental Committee and the International Steering Committee—were rather staid affairs operating in a very transactional manner.

The Interdepartmental Committee (IDC) was the first of the two main committees to evolve from strictly a management forum to one that sought to make productive use of the space to build relationships and to transfer knowledge. From the commencement of Phase II of the Canadian portion of the project, this committee was organized around thematic topics for discussion, and researchers from the Centres were invited to present on these topics. Naturally, the committee retained the transactional update components and management elements, but half of its meeting sessions were now given over to the presentation of research findings and to discussion with policy-makers.[12]

In Phase III, the IDC has further evolved, with considerable emphasis placed on transferring knowledge but also on discussion of the most effective means to do so. Critically, the role of IDC members has evolved over time from that of passive recipients of information to active producers and consumers of information, as well as to their latest role as knowledge brokers. In the Memorandum of Understanding that structured the project in Phase II, a section on the role of these individuals was added (Metropolis 2002). This was significantly enhanced in Phase III, and the 2007 Memorandum of Understanding delineates responsibilities much more clearly. In addition, the Phase III Logic Model, which appears later in this chapter, explains what the project seeks to accomplish and now recognizes the responsibility of these individuals (Metropolis 2007). *Lesson twelve: Clearly defined roles for all players are necessary.*

In addition to the evolution of this structure over time, the continuity brought by the chair of this committee has been critical. Only three people ever chaired the committee during the ascendant years of the project[13]: founding Director General Meyer Burstein; current Executive Head Howard Duncan; and myself, the Director of Partnerships and Knowledge Transfer.[14] The quarterly meetings attract roughly 40 participants from more than a dozen federal departments and agencies. Among these individuals turnover is extremely high: Often 50 percent change positions every year. *Lesson thirteen: Continuity of leadership matters.*

This stability is not limited to simply the IDC; it has been equally important at the international level for the International Steering Committee and at the Centres. I will not go into detail here about the Centres since both Anneke Rummens and Annick Germain have contributed chapters to this publication that explain the evolution of two of the Metropolis university-based Centres. Both authors have been connected to Metropolis for as long as I have, and in Annick Germain's case, even longer. This continuity among academic leadership has also proven important to build, maintain, and deepen relationships among policy-makers and researchers. In particular, the trust that has been established among the long-standing Centre leadership and the Secretariat has enabled Metropolis to evolve, especially during the difficult period leading up to the renewal of the project for Phase III, which will be discussed later. *Lesson fourteen: Trust is slow to develop, but vital to success.*

It is also important to note that while each Centre had a unique structure at the outset of the project, over time, some convergence has taken place, and best practices have been generalized across the Centres. That said, each remains unique in many ways, thus creating five Centres of innovative practices. *Lesson fifteen: Innovations should be nurtured, evaluated, and generalized when appropriate.*

For the International Steering Committee, the initial co-chairs, Meyer Burstein and Demetrios Papademetriou, are still involved as Emeritus co-Chairs, and the subsequent co-chairs, Howard Duncan and Rinus Penninx, were involved almost since the outset of the project.[15] In addition, many of the same members of the committee are still present, albeit with different institutional affiliations.

One new piece of infrastructure that has been added in this third phase of the project is the National Metropolis Committee (NMC). This body is the only national-level governance structure that brings together all of the major players in the project: Each major federal funder is represented by a Director General; each Centre is represented by a Director; the Secretariat has two representatives; two civil society members and six Priority Leaders have been added.[16] The position of Priority Leader is a new position in this phase of the project. As is the case with the NMC itself, the jury is still out on whether or not this new infrastructure will be successful. In broad brush strokes, the idea behind the Priority Leader positions is to try to encourage work across the Centres, not just within them. After a decade, a persistent critique levelled by the federal funders was that while the Centres were doing great work, it was primarily of benefit to the local partners and did not necessarily speak to the federal policy concerns. Whatever we may think of this critique, it nevertheless needed to be addressed, and a requirement for both infrastructure and money to be allocated to this problem was a non-negotiable condition for the funders to renew the project for a third time. *Lesson sixteen: Resources (both human and financial) need to be aligned with priorities.*

The manner in which Phase III of Metropolis was developed by CIC was cause for considerable dissatisfaction among most of the partners, including the other federal funding organizations and the universities where the Centres are based. This was especially noticeable as it was in stark contrast to the process pursued for the renewal between Phases I and II of Metropolis, which was far more collegial. It was not entirely clear that the Metropolis Project would survive this departure in operating protocols: It has, but some of the hard-earned trust has been weakened among the partners. *Lesson seventeen: Partners must be valued and treated accordingly.*

Happily, the robust nature of the Metropolis network meant that the key players remained committed to the enterprise, and, indeed, a number of new funders joined the coalition. The numerous evaluations that were undertaken as part of CIC's decision-making process concluded that Metropolis was a success and that further emphasis needed to be placed on knowledge transfer—particularly from the Centres to the federal partners (Clippingdale 2006; SSHRC 2006; CIC 2006; PWGSC 2009[17]). Critically, it was also acknowledged that this responsibility lay in equal parts with the Centres, the Secretariat, and, for the first time, with the federal partners themselves. While many felt that the level of evaluation was excessive, if not punitive,[18] the result has been an unmatched level of data on how a social science research project can forge linkages with policy. I will draw upon this in the section on achievements and outcomes below. *Lesson eighteen: Evaluation data are vital to achieving success.*

FUNDING

Metropolis is a modestly funded enterprise that pools resources from a broad number of institutions. Generally, there are three kinds of funds associated with the project: core funding of the research Centres, core funding of the Secretariat, and project-based funding.

Core Funding: Centres

The first two kinds of funding provide the basic infrastructure that ensures that Metropolis exists. Core funding for the research Centres is contributed by a broad federal partnership that has been largely stable over the last 12 years, while the funding for the basic operations of the Secretariat is provided by CIC. It is important to note that in Phase I of the project, the Centres each received approximately C$340,000[19]/year; this edged up somewhat to $340,739/year in Phase II and declined to $307,000/year in Phase III. All funds come from pre-existing programs within the federal partnering organizations. In the absence of Metropolis, these funds would be deployed to different objectives within each organization. Using the Bank of Canada's inflation calculator, inflation would have stipulated a 25.7 percent increase in prices, yet core funding for the Centres has declined by approximately 10 percent, thus leaving them with 35 percent less purchasing power today than at the outset of the project.

There are, however, some important considerations to bear in mind. First, university partners have increasingly contributed resources to the Centres in terms of course release time for Centre leadership, administrative support, space, and even direct financial support in some cases. The result is that the Centres have more capacity now than they did at the outset, a trend that will likely need to be continued in the future if the present emphasis on knowledge transfer remains important. In addition, this support means that universities are more important partners now than they have been in the past. This has not been formally recognized to date, in part because these contributions have been too nebulous to track. The Centres were working to change this prior to negotiations beginning for Phase IV of the project.[20]

Second, over time, a shift has occurred away from the principal focus on generating research and towards an emphasis on knowledge transfer; the result has been an increase in funding for knowledge transfer activities. Most notably, in Phase III, approximately $175,000/year has been retained for knowledge transfer activities directed by the National Metropolis Committee. While the explicit focus of Phase III is on knowledge transfer to the federal partners, provincial and municipal partners are increasingly important as well. During Phase III, relationships with these partners have been left with the Centres without any allocation of resources to enable them to organize knowledge transfer activities for these partners similar to those the Secretariat pursues for the federal partners. This is clearly a shortcoming that needs to be addressed in the future if these other orders of government are deemed important target audiences for Metropolis (Clippingdale 2009).[21]

Third, because it was recognized that the dispersal of research funds by the five Centres through their own granting processes was not creating structural encouragement of national-level studies, in Phase III, $125,000/year has been set aside for a National Research Competition. The questions addressed by this research are selected by the National Metropolis Committee and must be national in scope and address a policy interest.

These two centralized funds have actually increased the total expenditures on the Metropolis network, albeit at the supra-Centre level. Importantly, these centralized funds have begun to align resources with the objective of encouraging cross-Centre linkages. Taken with the core funding for the Centres, these two funds actually represent an annual increase of 13 percent in core funding for the Metropolis Project as a whole in comparison to the last three years of Phase II.[22]

Core Funding: Secretariat

The role of the Metropolis Secretariat has expanded over the life course of Metropolis as the principal locus of knowledge brokering. This labour-intensive activity has seen the skeletal Secretariat of 1997, which relied on a small number of loaned bodies, grow to 12 full-time staff today. In concrete terms, the Secretariat had a budget of $689,000 in 1997/98, which broke down into a one-off allocation of $80,000 for operations, $321,000 for salaries, and $288,000 for regular operations. By the 2008/09 fiscal year, this had increased to a total budget of $1,331,700: $909,000 going to salaries and $422,000 to operations. In total, this amounts to a 93 percent increase, with the vast majority of that funding going to salaries, as the size of the Secretariat had expanded to keep pace with its knowledge-brokering roles.[23]

Project-Based Funding

There are three main forms of project-based funding that flow into Metropolis. The first are the, usually though not exclusively, additional research grants that are leveraged by the modest investment in research at the Centres. These funds often exceed triple the value of the initial grant. However, there is an animated debate about how these funds should be counted—does a seed grant of a few thousand dollars that allows a researcher to develop a network of colleagues and to conduct a pilot project, which in turn helps to firm up a really large research grant application to one of the research funding councils, count as a multiplier of the initial grant? The preponderance of opinion is inclined to count the leveraging of funds, and after more than a decade of watching the Metropolis network grow, I am very much of the opinion that the seed funding is important, but that the networking opportunities are even more valuable. With the exception of those scholars who were firmly established prior to the launch of the project, the vast majority have definitely benefited from participation, and it is regularly the small projects that act as stepping stones to further work.

The second pool of project-based funding is activities that the Secretariat lines up each year—usually, though not exclusively, focused on knowledge transfer to the federal partners. This source of funding usually doubles the core operational budget of the Secretariat. These additional resources are provided by a wide array of federal partners and are targeted at extracting value from Metropolis for those partners. A number of partners either sign annual or multi-year agreements for targeted activities.

A third pool of funds is created by partners other than the federal funders. A most notable instance in Phase III is the $100,000/year invested by the Government of British Columbia in the British Columbia Metropolis Centre. In this way, other sources, including provincial and municipal governments, non-governmental/local partners, and universities, often contribute to either research projects or knowledge transfer activities, like the annual national conferences. For example, the 11th National Metropolis Conference in Calgary had a total estimated budget of around $800,000. Less than half of that was covered by registration (steep discounts for graduate students and NGOs greatly diminish the impact of registration fees on revenues), so the rest was contributed by the federal partners and the three Prairie provinces, as well as by a number of Alberta municipalities and universities. As these conferences are the main face-to-face gathering of the network, investment in them is of critical importance. *Lesson nineteen: The right balance between core investment in infrastructure to instill confidence in the longevity of the enterprise and targeted investment to provide policy steering must be maintained.*

MANDATE

As mentioned in the introduction of this chapter, the mandate and scope of the project have evolved over time. Initially, the mandate was focused on promoting, coordinating, conducting, and communicating multidisciplinary research in the areas of immigration and integration (Dubois and Watson 1998, 3).

By Phase II, this mandate had evolved somewhat to include "immigration, integration, *and diversity.*" I am particularly proud of this development because I can say that I was instrumental in broadening this scope. For five years, I was shared between CIC and the Department of Canadian Heritage (which meant walking across the bridge at lunch each day because one department was based on each side of the Ottawa River). I worked for the multiculturalism program at Canadian Heritage, one of the most important funders of the Metropolis Project, and this federal partner wanted to see the scope expand to explore both immigrants and ethnic/racial/religious/linguistic minorities. While Canadian Heritage was not the largest funder, its strategy to ship a person to the Secretariat half time served the department well. To this day, it remains true that those federal partners most engaged in the project are those that reap the largest reward. *Lesson twenty: Engagement matters.*

Throughout the lifespan of the project, there have always been three principal foci for the project: volume, focus, and utilization of research. All have been present in the three phases of the project, yet it would be fair to generalize and suggest that the first phase of the project emphasized volume; the second concentrated on focusing the research on priority areas for policy; and the third phase has a decided focus on utilization.

In some ways, Metropolis has evolved from its origins as a research enterprise to a network on immigration and diversity that does research. Research is still central, but it is now viewed as a critical component of the spectrum of knowledge transfer.

If we imagine Metropolis, as the Logic Model for Phase III of the project suggests, as a network dedicated to the spectrum of knowledge transfer in the area of immigration and diversity, we can look at measures for each of the five areas: research, training, research capacity/networks, knowledge facilitation, and knowledge uptake. It seems fair, therefore, to evaluate whether or not we have made headway on these five fronts over the last 15 years.

FIGURE 1
Metropolis Phase III Logic Model (2008)

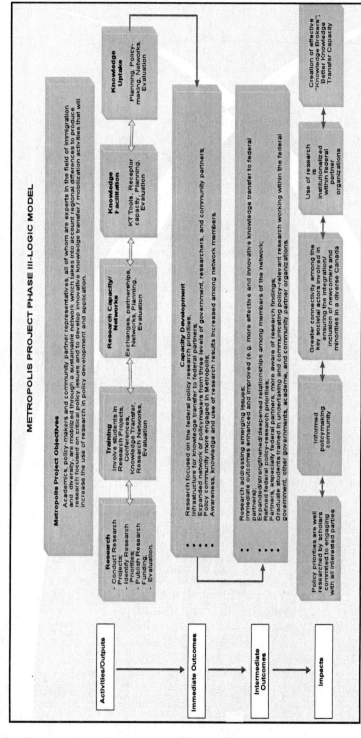

Source: Metropolis (2008a).

ACHIEVEMENTS/OUTCOMES

Research

Metropolis was designed to increase both the volume of research on immigration and the number of researchers engaged in this field. There can be no doubt that Metropolis is an unusually productive research network. To take a concrete example, in the first four years of Phase II of the project, the Metropolis Centres produced 44 books, 86 chapters; 306 popular articles, 274 peer-reviewed articles; 120 working papers; and 760 presentations. This output compares with that of the highly regarded Canadian Policy Research Networks, Inc., which produced 140 research reports, 11 presentations, and 92 summaries (but received 25 percent more funding than Metropolis in the same period) (HRSDC 2005).

Using another metric, if we just use the annual reports prepared by the Centres for SSHRC, the number of affiliated researchers increased from 333 in 2002 to 461 in 2008. The absolute growth would be far larger except that the Ontario Centre does not report all affiliates in its annual report because the nearly 20 universities in Ontario simply have too many scholars working in these areas.[24] Instead, it reports solely those affiliates actively engaged with the Centre in that calendar year. The number of researchers and graduate students attending the Metropolis conferences has also increased significantly since the outset of the project: nine students and 86 researchers at the national conference in 1996; 124 students and 198 researchers at the 2008 conference.

The increase in research on immigration was even noted by policy-makers. An internal review of Metropolis conducted by CIC noted that 82 percent of those interviewed felt that the amount of research conducted on immigration and integration issues had increased, and 89 percent believed that Metropolis had contributed to this (CIC 2007).

One of the most persistent critiques of Metropolis has been the extent to which the research is "policy relevant." Over the three phases, this perennial issue has been tackled in a number of ways. In Phase I, the Centres were simply required to conduct research within broad "domains of research." Annually, individual policy-makers were invited to speak at Centre-based research retreats to articulate their research priorities. This approach resulted in the communication of numerous, very uneven, often idiosyncratic priorities that were seldom reflective of organizational priorities, let alone cross-government priorities.

In Phase II, the domain structure was continued, but this time, 11 federal policy-research priorities were identified, and at least 50 percent of research funds at the Centres had to be expended in these areas. The result was a move towards a more all-of-government approach and synergies across government departments. This tighter focus was further promoted by the cross-cutting issues addressed by the previously described Interdepartmental Committee.

By Phase III, the 11 priorities were deemed too numerous, and it was clear that the uneven domain structure across the Centres was itself a systemic barrier to collaborative work across Centres. Accordingly, the domain structure was redefined for the first time since 1996, and six policy-research priorities were identified by federal funders and replaced the original domain structure.

TABLE 1
Metropolis Policy Priorities

Phase I and II Domains	Phase III Six Priorities/Domains
Social	Citizenship and Social, Cultural, and Civic Integration
Citizenship and Culture	
Citizenship and Political	
Social and Cultural	
Economic	Economic and Labour Market Integration
Education	Family, Children, and Youth
Health	Interspersed among all priority areas
Housing and Neighbourhoods	Housing and Neighbourhoods
	Justice, Policing, and Security
	Welcoming Communities: The Role of Host Communities in Attracting, Integrating, and Retaining Newcomers and Minorities

Source: Author's compilation (2008).

It was felt that this change, which would ensure uniformity across Centres (every priority area now had to be a domain at a minimum of three Centres), would encourage cross-Centre comparative work. At the same time, the creation of the Priority Leader position would facilitate a focus on the priorities. It should be noted that each Centre, to allow for local specificity, could nominate to maintain one "elective" domain—something that three of the five Centres opted to do.[25]

Apart from a macro effort to ensure the connections between Centre research and broad cross-cutting federal priorities, a number of reviews and evaluations have surveyed a wide swathe of policy-makers to ask them about their perceptions of the research's relevance. In the CIC Internal Review, 59 percent of those surveyed were satisfied that Metropolis research was relevant (18 percent were not; and 15 percent did not know). The most satisfied were regions, research officers, and those who had been in the department between two to five years. Those who were least satisfied were senior managers and those who had been in the department for more than five years—coincidentally, the two groups least likely to use research on a regular basis (CIC 1997). For senior management, most of this kind of work is undertaken by their analysts, and for long-time employees, it is unlikely that external experts are going to have more knowledge than those who work on immigration full-time.

The use of Metropolis research offers another vantage point. In the summative evaluation of knowledge transfer in Phase II, 46 percent of the total time that policy-makers indicated they spent reading or reviewing materials or attending research dissemination events was Metropolis related; 17 percent indicated that 100 percent of their time on these activities was spent on Metropolis (PWGSC 2009, 24).

Despite this evolution and fine tuning, it is interesting to note that the "major lacunae and emerging themes" that sociologist Morton Weinfeld identified—when he wrote a synthetic overview of the seven literature reviews that had been commissioned at the outset of Metropolis—remain central questions for examination today (Weinfeld 1997). In a manner, this fact indicates a strength of Metropolis. If there are no projects completed to help with urgent policy questions of the day, face-to-face interactions like the Metropolis Conversations can at least be arranged to get informed people together for a discussion about emergent issues and possible policy options. On the other hand, most issues are cyclical, and Metropolis can work to ensure that a knowledge base underpins issues that we know will re-emerge as priorities. In Table 2, I indicate issues flagged back in 1996 and recent publications or activities that Metropolis has undertaken at the request of our policy colleagues, thus indicating these issues' continuing/reoccurring salience to policy debates.

The similarities in key areas requiring research over more than a decade and the emergence of a large volume of recent material speak to the longitudinal nature of research. The fruits of investing in Metropolis should become ever more apparent as research is completed and the knowledge landscape of many complex immigration and diversity issues becomes more nuanced.

During the renewal of Metropolis for Phase III, the question was asked, What would happen if funding was eliminated? Would research continue in this area? Our answer was that some certainly would, especially that which was already in the pipeline, but that much of the effort currently focused on immigration and diversity topics would dissipate and fairly rapidly drift to related, but better funded areas of research. We must be careful that elimination of funding does not diminish research output. For example, when the Department of Canadian Heritage eliminated direct support for ethnic studies, many of the researchers who had worked in that area migrated to Metropolis and took a more immigration-centred focus than the ethnic focus they had previously explored.

TABLE 2
Research Gaps

Lacunae Identified by Weinfeld in 1996	Metropolis Publications/Activities Requested by Federal Partners
The need for more research on the urban setting and on immigrant integration in Canada	*Our Diverse Cities* magazines (2004–)
The need for comparative work: There has been little systematic intercity comparative research within Canada.	Annual National Research Competition since 2007 Revised workshop format at national conferences (e.g., requirement for cross-Centre representation) since 2007
The approach to immigrant integration should grapple with the issue of benchmarking.	Biles, Burstein, and Frideres, *Immigration and Integration in Canada in the Twenty-first Century* (2008).
The role of immigrant families	*Canadian Issues* magazine on the theme of "Immigration and the Family" (2006) Family, Children, and Youth as a priority since 2007
The relative importance of the "second generation"	*Canadian Diversity* magazine issue on the theme of the "Experiences of Second Generation Canadians" (2008)
The absence of research on political integration	Andrew, Biles, Siemiatycki, and Tolley (eds.), *Electing a Diverse Canada: The Representation of Immigrants, Minorities, and Women* (2008).
There is a glaring lack of scientific research on many aspects of the linkage of immigration and crime, on the one hand, and the justice system, on the other.	Policing, Justice, and Security as a priority since 2007
Housing conditions	*Canadian Issues* magazine on "Housing and Homelessness" (2009)
There is a need for continuing research on impacts on language knowledge and use in Canada.	Priority Seminar on Language Acquisition (October 2009)
The importance of exploring the "nested" nature of integration and important organizations in the process, like churches and mainstream voluntary associations	Biles, Burstein, Frideres, Tolley, and Vineberg (eds.), *Integration and Inclusion Across Canada* (2011).

Source: Author's compilation (2008).

Training

Much of the hope expressed by the senior official who asked the question above is tied up with the numbers of graduate students and young scholars who have adopted immigration and diversity as their research focus. The belief underpinning the question is clearly that once people embark on a research trajectory, they will stay with it for the duration of their careers. I do not believe that this is the case in the 21st century. I increasingly see scholars move among topics depending upon a variety of factors, not least of which are available funding and, in some cases, a desire to make a societal difference. That said, to some extent, of course, the senior official was correct, and many of these new scholars will continue to have an interest in these issues.

How many people are we speaking about? In 2005 to 2006, 259 graduate students were involved in Centre research and activities (internships, research projects, seminars, workshops), as compared to 104 in 2001.

New programs have also begun to emerge in this field. For example, the SSHRC Mid-term Review Committee highlighted the new Master's Program on Immigration and Settlement Studies at Ryerson University as an excellent example of a new training initiative facilitated by the Metropolis Project. More recently, the University of Western Ontario has launched a graduate program in Migration and Ethnic Relations (Esses, Beajot, and Dodson 2007). Little more proof could be needed that immigration and diversity studies have arrived as a bona fide field of academic inquiry.

Finally, prior to the national conference, there is now a pre-conference training day for graduate students that provides opportunities to learn about policy, data access and utilization, and other skills. At the 10th National Metropolis Conference in 2008, 85 graduate students registered for this event.

Research Capacity/Networks

As I mentioned at the outset, as Metropolis has evolved, the network itself has become increasingly valued, rather than simply the research that flows from the project. This belief is shared by all three sectors (government, research, and community) involved in the project. In part, this value can be measured by the actual members of the network. There are over 8,000 subscribers to the Metropolis database: One-third are government employees; one-third, academics; and one-third, NGOs/local partners. Despite the high turnover in government, the number of network subscribers has stayed approximately the same for the duration of Phase II and Phase III.[26]

The various evaluations have also drawn some conclusions about the network. For example, according to the academic peer reviewers on the

SSHRC Mid-term Review Committee, "The networks that the Metropolis Project have created over time are the strongest contribution flowing from Metropolis funding." The committee goes on to note that the key value-added element of the Metropolis Secretariat is the support for networks, and the report states that these networks have helped establish a culture of collaboration among the diverse actors interested or involved in immigration issues: "The Centres have built trust among all levels of government and NGOs and have become a valuable source, for them, of new research knowledge" (SSHRC 2006).

As for the policy-makers, in the CIC Internal Review of Metropolis, 63 percent of survey respondents indicated that one of the three most important functions of Metropolis is to connect policy-makers, researchers, and other partners working on immigration and diversity, including other federal departments. One interviewee stated, "It [Metropolis] puts immigration on the agenda of every department in town—HRSDC, Status of Women, etc. Multiple departments are on board. It's collectively forcing people to take ownership of a broad societal issue. CIC used to be antagonistic towards service providers for immigrants, but now, after years of dialogue, the sides respect each other more. Now we have an environment where all partners can discuss issues" (CIC 2006).

A scan of NGO involvement with Metropolis concluded that "the Metropolis initiative is seen by NGO representatives as making a significant contribution to the field of immigration by increasing the knowledge available to policy-makers and the public regarding immigration issues. ... The enhanced networks created by Metropolis bring new people into contact with immigrant settlement agencies, ensuring a broader presentation of relevant issues" (Legault et al. 2006).

The conferences are an interesting exercise, as they really combine volume, focus, and utilization of research, and, of course, they are probably the best indicator of the vitality of the Metropolis network.

The First International Metropolis Conference, held in Milan, Italy, in 1996, attracted 300 participants from 20 countries and four international organizations. The 12th International Metropolis Conference, held in Melbourne, Australia, in 2007, attracted 700 delegates from 30 countries. This was considerably smaller in size than the recent norm because of its location and the relative expense of travelling to Australia. For example, the previous year's conference in Lisbon, Portugal, involved 995 participants from 43 countries—in short, triple the gross size and double the number of countries involved since the first international conference.

To use another metric, when the tightly focused workshops were introduced at the Third International Metropolis Conference in Israel in 1998, 16 workshops were organized. By the 13th Conference in Bonn, Germany, in 2008, this number had swollen to more than 90.

Growth at the national level has been even more astounding. The First National Metropolis Conference, held in Edmonton, Alberta, in 1997, attracted roughly 200 participants from across Canada and a number of international delegates. The 10th National Conference, held in Halifax, Nova Scotia, in April 2008, attracted 925 participants and included 99 workshops and round tables. In short, it was five times the size of the first event. The national distribution of participants was extraordinary. There was far more representation from all provinces than at the outset of Metropolis. This growth has been sustained, with 970 participants at the 13th National Conference, held in Vancouver in March 2011.

TABLE 3
National Metropolis Conferences—Number of Participants

Province of Participants	1st National Conference (Edmonton), # of Canadian Participants	4th National Metropolis Conference (Toronto), # of Canadian Participants	10th National Metropolis Conference (Halifax), # of Canadian Participants
British Columbia	15	23	80
Alberta	71	37	70
Saskatchewan	15	10	10
Manitoba	10	13	28
Ontario	55	212	313
Quebec	12	44	120
New Brunswick	1	1	73
Prince Edward Island	0	0	14
Nova Scotia	1	1	173
Newfoundland and Labrador	0	0	28

Source: Table compiled by author from administrative data (2008).

Also worthy of note is the distribution of policy-makers, researchers, students/post-docs, and NGOs/local partners. The numbers and percentages of total participants have increased massively for both students and NGOs/local partners. No doubt, this reflects, to some extent, the accessibility initiatives that have been put in place since that period, including reduced registration fees for these two groups and direct subsidies—dispersed through the five Centres—provided by the Department of Canadian Heritage and by the Integration Branch of CIC. At the same time, it is quite likely that as the format of these events has shifted to be more inclusive and accessible, there is more interest from NGOs and local partners in particular.

Absolute numbers of academic researchers and government officials have also increased, although both have decreased as a percentage of the total number of participants. The largest observable drop is the 17 percent decline in the representation of professors at the conference. In part, and based on anecdotal experience, this could simply be a reporting error (with reduced registration fees available for NGOs, many professors have selected to register wearing another of their "hats," thereby qualifying for reduced rates). More troubling is a concern raised by some senior scholars that the nature of the conferences has shifted away from a formal academic venue and that the insistence on plenary formats that appeal to a broad cross-section of societal members, rather than a preference for more academic-style presentations, plus the structural requirement that all workshops be multi-sectoral in nature, turns away some senior scholars. It is hard to say if this is the case, but it is an issue that is being closely monitored.

The bottom line is that Metropolis conferences are *not* standard academic conferences, and, in fact, the roughly one-third, one-third, one-third mixture of researchers (professors and students), policy-makers, and NGOs/local partners/other partners is what we strive to accomplish.

TABLE 4
National Metropolis Conferences—Type of Participants

Type of Participant	1st National Metropolis Conference, # of Canadian Participants (% of total participants)	4th National Metropolis Conference, # of Canadian Participants (% of total participants)	10th National Metropolis Conference, # of Canadian Participants (% of total participants)
Students/post-doctoral fellows	9 (5%)	38 (9%)	124 (13%)
Academic researchers	86 (46%)	162 (38%)	198 (21%)
NGOs/local partners	25 (13%)	65 (15%)	218 (24%)
Government	59 (32%)	143 (34%)	304 (33%)
Other	7 (4%)	18 (4%)	81 (9%)
TOTAL	**186**	**426**	**925**

Source: Table compiled by author from administrative data (2008).

Knowledge transfer has always been a critical element of Metropolis, but in this funding period, it has been given a more central role. In addition to annual knowledge transfer plans developed for each of the six policy-research priorities, each federal funder develops an internal knowledge transfer plan to ensure that their department/agency derives maximum benefit from the research and activities of the Metropolis network.

The Logic Model for Phase III of Metropolis divides knowledge transfer into knowledge facilitation and knowledge uptake. The division is premised upon the belief that the Centres and the Secretariat can lead policy-makers to water, but cannot force them to drink.

Knowledge Facilitation

Facilitation includes conducting research on policy questions and packaging it in a manner that facilitates utilization. Traditionally, this is one of the more difficult areas for the social sciences to record. Happily, Metropolis is large enough and has been running for long enough that a number of quantitative studies have been undertaken to provide some evidence of what works. The CIC Internal Review only yielded general impressions, as it did not, for the most part, ask about specific knowledge transfer products. That said, 90 percent of CIC web survey respondents using Centre products felt that Centre workshops, publications, the National Conference, and research projects were useful. Only a few people indicated any dissatisfaction with Metropolis products (CIC 2006).

Metropolis largely divides its knowledge transfer activities into three areas: face-to-face interactions, publications, and web-based/electronic communication. I will briefly describe findings in each of these areas below.

i) Face-to-face interactions

For the development of trust and collaborative partnerships, there can be no replacement for face-to-face interactions. Metropolis organizes these on a variety of scales, from the 800- to 1,000-person annual national and international Metropolis conferences, to the smaller Brown Bag presentations, or to the closed-door high-level Metropolis Conversations.

The Summative Evaluation of Phase II of Metropolis included a survey of employees at Citizenship and Immigration Canada, Canada Mortgage and Housing Corporation, Canadian Heritage, and Human Resources and Skills Development Canada (the four largest funders of Phase II). This evaluation asked specific questions about various Metropolis knowledge transfer activities, and I will describe the results here.

Of those surveyed, 42.7 percent had been to a national or international Metropolis conference; 25.2 percent had attended a Centre-based workshop; 11.7 percent had been to a Centre-based research retreat; and 29.2 percent had participated in a Metropolis Conversation. Of those who had attended these face-to-face interactions, 84.6 percent of those who attended the conferences found them to be useful; 76.2 percent of those who participated in a Metropolis Conversation found it to be useful; 75.4 percent found the Centre workshops to be useful; while just 53.1 percent found the Centre-based retreats to be useful (PWGSC 2009).

Clearly, the Centre retreats were the least valued of the face-to-face interactions by the federal policy-makers. As a result, the focus of these events has been adjusted accordingly, and the emphasis on encouraging federal partners to attend these events has been downplayed with the introduction of Ottawa-based Brown Bag Seminars that bring researchers to Ottawa to present to federal partners. Initial results after the first year of these events were entirely positive (nearly 400 policy-makers attended, and the event evaluations were extremely positive).[27]

One surprisingly successful face-to-face interaction has been the Interdepartmental Committee (IDC) meetings, described in the previous section on Structure. Nearly 500 officials from 27 federal departments attended IDC meetings over Phase II of the project. Interest remained high at the outset of Phase III and only decreased once the decision to sunset the project had become widely known.

ii) Publications

Reaching a wide range of network members drawn from universities, governments, and local partners, with different knowledge levels and needs, requires a richly diversified publication strategy. Accordingly, Metropolis publishes edited volumes on key policy topics both nationally and featuring international comparisons. For similar expert audiences, special issues of academic journals and the Metropolis-produced *Journal of International Migration and Integration* (JIMI) are focused on key policy issues. In the Summative Evaluation, 35.8 percent of the policy-makers surveyed had used JIMI, and of those people, 79.6 percent had found it useful (PWGSC 2009). Of those surveyed, 24.8 percent had made use of other special issues of journals, and of those people, 69.1 percent had found them to be useful.

For audiences looking for quick primers on a given topic or for a wide range of perspectives, Metropolis partners with the Association for Canadian Studies to produce special editions of their magazines, *Canadian Issues/Thèmes canadiens* and *Canadian Diversity/Diversité canadienne*. Themes for these magazines are selected by the Secretariat based on discussions with federal partners on policy areas of cross-cutting interest. Generally, the *Canadian Issues/Thèmes canadiens* magazines focus on a domestic immigration and/or diversity topic, while the *Canadian Diversity/Diversité canadienne* magazines focus on international comparisons.[28] For municipal officials or those interested in how immigration and diversity play out in Canadian communities, Metropolis publishes *Our Diverse Cities*, another magazine-style publication. According to the survey results, 45.3 percent had read *Our Diverse Cities*; 42 percent had read *Canadian Issues*; and 44.5 percent had read *Canadian Diversity*. Of those who had read them, 81.6 percent, 82.6 percent, and 78.7 percent, respectively, had found them useful. *Our Diverse Cities* and select editions of *Canadian Issues* and *Canadian Diversity* are also available on the Metropolis website. By December 2011, the first seven editions of *Our Diverse Cities* had been downloaded 643,000 times in English and 248,000 times in French.[29] The

Canadian Diversity on "Experiences of the Second Generation" had been downloaded 85,800 times; "Citizenship: Values and Responsibilities" had been downloaded more than 46,000 times; and "Immigration and the Intersections of Diversity" had been downloaded 22,000 times. The *Canadian Issues* magazine on "Immigration and Diversity in Francophone and Minority Communities" had been downloaded 30,000 times in both English and French.

The magazines are also an important means for policy-makers to get material out in the public domain: Fifteen ministers have been interviewed for Metropolis magazines; and during Phase II, 63 policy-makers, including 14 from CIC, contributed articles to magazines on policy considerations or on activities of their programs.

The *Metropolis World Bulletin* is the annual newsletter of the International Metropolis Project. It has begun to evolve from a strictly reporting publication to one that includes articles organized around a theme.[30] The last three thematic issues ("Our Diverse Cities" in 2005; "Diasporas and Transnationalism" in 2006; and "Social Cohesion" in 2007) have each been downloaded around 17,000 times.

In addition, working papers and research summaries of specific projects funded by the Centres are widely disseminated via the suite of Metropolis websites (www.Metropolis.net). These websites are visited by millions of stakeholders annually, and the working papers are downloaded thousands of times. Of surveyed policy-makers, 60.6 percent had made use of the working papers, and 90.4 percent of those who had consulted these documents had found them to be useful (PWGSC 2009).

iii) Web-based/electronic communication

Like all research networks, Metropolis is increasingly utilizing web-based communications. In 2005 to 2006, there were 1,770,968 visits to the Metropolis websites, with an average of 16 hits per visit. In 2005, there were 1,539,491 downloads from the Metropolis websites.[31] To put this in perspective, the most recent statistics produced by the Canadian Policy Research Network show that there were 599,062 downloads from its website in 2003 (HRSDC 2005).

Every week, a featured piece of research is showcased—rotating among the six priority areas—on the Metropolis web network. Every sixth week, an electronic bulletin titled *The Bridge* is sent to all 8,000 members of the Metropolis network to draw their attention to these features and to other new materials posted on the Metropolis website.

A new initiative is an "Ask the Experts" section, which includes short opinions by knowledgeable researchers. In 2008, two were piloted, one on the "reasonable accommodation" debate in Quebec, and one on earnings disparities between newcomers and the Canadian-born. Between them, these resources were accessed 3,074 times. Subsequently, two more, on extremism and multiculturalism and on the English riots of 2011, have been added.

Other electronic knowledge transfer activities include a partnership with the Canada School of the Public Service to webcast Armchair Discussions with researchers who are drawn from the Metropolis Centres. As well, there are various means to capture plenary presentations from the national and international conferences. *Lesson twenty-one: Strategic alliances with various organizations are critical to reaching key potential audiences. These alliances must be structured around mutual benefit.*

Knowledge Uptake

If knowledge facilitation is difficult to measure in the social sciences in general, knowledge uptake within a policy environment is next to impossible to measure. In particular, the challenges include the extraordinary range of sources that are used in the development of policy, the numbers of iterations of documents written by committees, and the absence of references or bibliographies in most of that work.

Despite this challenge, both the CIC Internal Review of Metropolis and the Summative Evaluation sought to capture some of this information. For example, in the Internal Review, 39 percent of those polled claimed that Metropolis had influenced the way that CIC thinks about, does, or uses immigration research (importantly, 58 percent could not assess the question). Senior managers, research staff, those working at national headquarters, and those who had been with the department longest were the most likely to think this was true. Particular examples that were described where Metropolis research informed policy were foreign credential recognition, immigrant youth, experiences of refugees, the importance of family ties and education vis-à-vis migration and secondary migration, and the skilled worker selection system (CIC 2006).

In the Summative Evaluation, 43 percent of the federal policy-makers polled indicated that Metropolis had informed policy decisions. However, when just those who actually work on policy were separated out, 79 percent of them had made use of Metropolis in policy work. This difference indicates the critical importance of whom one is aiming at with knowledge transfer products.

This knowledge has led to significant changes in Phase III of the project. For the first decade, no specific audiences were identified, although senior management, research officers, and policy analysts were implicitly the principal targets. When the CIC Internal Review was conducted at the close of Phase II, the net was cast far broader. Whatever the motivation for this move, the result has been a significant broadening of the scope of Metropolis' target audience for Phase III. For example, a typology of all CIC staff has been developed, and specific knowledge transfer products and activities are being developed to more effectively reach those audiences (see Appendix 2). All of the other federal partners have also been asked annually to identify whom they consider the core audience for Metropolis to be within their organizations.

At the same time, there is some disagreement among the federal funding partners whether the only audience of importance is federal policy-makers. It seems increasingly likely that, at a minimum, provincial officials, and possibly municipal officials, will become core target audiences, and this may be extended further to community/local partners and, of course, to researchers themselves. But those are discussions for the future... *Lesson twenty-two: Identify your target audience(s) in advance, and tailor knowledge transfer approaches to them.*

CONCLUSIONS

Many lessons can be learned from the Metropolis experience of developing and refining a policy-research network. However, a few key ideas should guide the thinking of anyone interested in developing a similar initiative.

First, trust builds over time, and nothing can rush this process. It is developed by doing things together, treating each other with respect, and pursuing mutually beneficial goals together.

Second, clearly delineating roles, responsibilities, and expectations is critical to the success of a network. Wishful thinking rather than pragmatism (e.g., that researchers will be able to make as sharply honed policy recommendations as policy-makers will be able to do) is a recipe for unhappiness and failure.

Third, aligning resources with priorities is essential. Enough financial support needs to be implicated long term to attract people to the network and to maintain it over time, but retaining resources for strategic purposes allows necessary flexibility to respond to quick-changing policy priorities.

Fourth, infrastructure and resources need to be deployed to thicken relationships across the network and to maintain the flow of communication among partners. This is especially critical with policy-makers, who have high turnover rates—only an organization like the Secretariat can reforge broken links when network members change positions. The Secretariat is an essential network spanner that can bridge differences across sectors and identify areas of horizontal interest.

Finally, evaluation of the efficacy of activities and knowledge transfer needs to be built in from the outset of the project. Leaving these evaluations to moments of existential crisis weakens the network's ability to adjust in a timely manner and risks damaging relationships upon which the enterprise depends.

NOTES

1. This chapter was originally drafted in the fall of 2008. Where possible, material has been updated in the fall of 2011, immediately prior to publication. Sincere thanks are due to Justin Cavacciuti for information on activities after fall 2009, when the author left the Secretariat after more than 12 years of working in many capacities, including as Director of Partnerships and Knowledge Transfer.

2. The opinions expressed in this chapter are those of the author and do not necessarily reflect those of the Metropolis Project, Citizenship and Immigration Canada, or the Government of Canada.

3. SOPEMI is the yearly report on Migration, Immigrants and Policy for the Continuous Reporting System on Migration of the OECD (Organisation for Economic Co-operation and Development).

4. While it is hard to disaggregate the actual budget for this branch from the corporate services line of the Main Estimates, it is worth noting that today these three areas are all their own branches, thus implying that they have expanded considerably (Government of Canada 1997). Some research suggests that in 1995/96, six FTEs (full-time equivalents) and a budget of C$600,000 were assigned to internal research and data development, and by 2010/11, this had grown to 67 FTEs and a budget of C$7.4 million (Biles 2011).

5. Note that this was the point at which the original agreement of 50 percent of funding from SSHRC and 50 percent from the federal departments and agencies was changed to a much less clear formula—SSHRC has never contributed the originally agreed upon 50 percent of funding.

6. Copenhagen 1997; Israel 1998; Washington, DC, 1999; Vancouver 2000; Rotterdam 2001; Oslo 2002; Vienna 2003; Geneva 2004; Toronto 2005; Lisbon 2006; Melbourne 2007; Bonn 2008; Copenhagen 2009; the Hague 2010; the Azores 2011; and China 2012 (cancelled in March 2012).

7. Edmonton 1997, Montreal 1998, Vancouver 1999, Toronto 2000, Ottawa 2001, Edmonton 2003, Montreal 2004, Vancouver 2006, Toronto 2007, Halifax 2008, Calgary 2009, Montreal 2010, Vancouver 2011, and Toronto 2012.

8. The European half of the International Secretariat has been based in a number of locations, including Belgium, the Netherlands, and Italy. Unlike the Canadian half, which is co-located with a group specifically tasked with running Metropolis, the international portion of the Secretariat is usually co-located with a European policy-research network that works on similar issues: There are no Metropolis Centres outside of Canada.

9. Centre Directors are the primary leaders and representatives of the Metropolis Centres of Excellence (see Metropolis 2007, 10).

10. Domain Leaders are tasked with coordinating research efforts of researchers within each Centre (see Metropolis 2007, 14).

11. Priority Leaders are academic researchers tasked with coordinating work on their policy-research priority area across the entire National Project, as well as creating and maintaining connections with the federal funders most interested in their priority area (see Metropolis 2007, 12).

12. 2002: Phase II of Metropolis (October), Social Capital (December);
2003: Regionalization (March), Public Space (June), Poverty (September), Security and Justice (December);

2004: Language (March), Residential Concentration (July), Housing and Homelessness (October);

2005: Economic Integration (February); Social, Cultural, and Political Integration (March); Role of Cities (October); Role of Provinces (November);

2006: Temporary Migrants (January), Family (March), Knowledge Transfer (May), Knowledge Utilization (September);

2007: Phase III Launch (September); Policing, Justice, and Security (December);

2008: Economic and Labour Market Integration (February); Welcoming Communities (April); Family, Children, and Youth (September); Citizenship and Social, Cultural, and Political Integration (December);

2009: Housing and Neighbourhoods (February); Policing, Justice, and Security (April); Economics and Labour Market Integration (September); and Welcoming Communities (December).

2010–2012: These meetings occurred only sporadically after December 2009 owing to a combination of change in key personnel at the Secretariat and then the acknowledgement by the partners that the project had been sunset by CIC. For example, only two very transactional abridged meetings were held in 2010.

13. While the life cycle of Metropolis will be 15 years, a notable sharp decline was perceived following the departure of key Secretariat personnel and, subsequently, CIC's decision to sunset the project, so 12 to 13 years is a better time period for the purpose of evaluating the success of the initiative, as the last few years have been marked by declining investment of time and resources in the management of the project by all federal partners.

14. A fourth chair, Julie Boyer, succeeded me briefly in this position for the final years of funding. She convened this committee only sporadically.

15. Rinus Penninx was succeeded by Jan Rath, who had also been involved since the early days of Metropolis.

16. It should be noted that the need for infrastructure like the NMC was observed as far back as 1998, but the partnerships had not yet matured to a level where this kind of infrastructure could be used productively (see Dubois and Watson 1998, 74).

17. This last evaluation of Phase II was actually only released in the third year of Phase III for various reasons, but it was announced far earlier and thus contributed to the evaluation fatigue experienced by the network.

18. Many members of the Metropolis network have commented on the peculiarity that the major integration programs, which expend nearly a billion dollars a year, have been evaluated only twice in more than two decades of operation and that Metropolis, which costs a few million dollars a year, has been evaluated nearly a dozen times by various organizations in the last decade.

19. All dollar figures are in Canadian dollars.

20. CIC decided, as part of its Strategic Review, to sunset its investment in the Metropolis Project at the end of the project's third phase (31 March 2012). Accordingly, there will not be a fourth phase.

21. Interestingly, the provincial governments are core partners in one of the successor networks to Metropolis—the Welcoming Communities Initiative (www.welcomingcommunities.ca).

22. Since the Atlantic Centre was created midway through Phase II, the full additional funds only became available in 2004/05, so the best point of comparison is the annual core funding from that point onwards.

23. When the fifth Metropolis Centre was created in Atlantic Canada, a position was added to the Secretariat, with a small increase in operational budget, to offset the enhanced workload. Similarly, at the launch of Phase III of the project, with its increased focus on labour-intensive knowledge transfer, two more positions and a small increase in operational funds were provided. Other significant increases in operating funds include augmented allocations for translation, in order to have materials in both official languages, and for postage, to distribute materials to the 8,000-person network.

24. It is worth noting that during renewal for Phase III, a consortium of universities in 12 Ontario cities outside of Toronto asked to be considered for an expansion of Metropolis to six Centres to complete Metropolis' coverage of the Canadian cities that receive immigrants. This group argued that there was simply too much variety in Ontario for one Toronto-based Centre to cover the whole province. CIC opted not to accept this proposal. This group has gone on to secure an SSHRC-funded Community University Research Alliance grant worth $1 million over the next five years. This group is also at the heart of a proposal, "Pathways to Prosperity," to become a successor network to Metropolis after 31 March 2012. At the time of publishing, it is unknown whether this funding has been awarded.

25. The Atlantic Centre opted to retain the Gender and Immigrant Women domain that mostly maps onto the priority domain of Family, Children, and Youth. The Ontario Centre opted to maintain a Health and Well-being domain, and the British Columbia Centre added a broad domain on Settlement, Integration, and Welcoming Communities at the behest of the provincial government, which provides $100,000/year in core funding. This domain broadly maps onto the Welcoming Communities priority.

26. Ironically, interest in Metropolis from stakeholders across the country actually continued to increase even after CIC had decided to sunset the initiative. As of December 2011, membership in the Metropolis network had climbed to nearly 9,000. At least one Metropolis Centre reported a continued interest among researchers to become affiliated. This interest has been transmitted to one of the potential successor networks, the Welcoming Communities Initiative's "Pathways to Prosperity" application, which attracted unprecedented interest from partners across the country.

27. This level of activity continued in 2009, when a high-water mark of 60 Brown Bags were organized, before decreasing to under 40 in 2010 and to 25 in 2011. This decrease is connected to the departure of key personnel from the Secretariat. Interest remains high among policy-makers, and each Brown Bag in 2011 attracted approximately 20 participants, for a total of approximately 500 participants.

28. *Canadian Issues/Thèmes canadiens* magazines have included the following: Immigration: Opportunities and Challenges (April 2003); Refugees in Canada: Grant and Contributions (March 2004); Newcomers, Minorities, and Political Participation in Canada (Summer 2005); Immigration and Families (Spring 2006); Foreign Credential Recognition (Spring 2007);

Immigration and Diversity in Francophone Minority Communities (Spring 2008); Temporary Foreign Workers (Spring 2010); Mental Health (Summer 2010); and Housing and Homelessness (Fall 2010).

Canadian Diversity/Diversité canadienne magazines have included the following: Citizenship: Values and Responsibilities (Spring 2003); National Identity and Diversity (Spring 2004); Multicultural Futures? International Approaches to Pluralism (Winter 2005); Immigration and the Intersections of Diversity (Spring 2005); Canada and Japan: Identities and Values (June 2005); Negotiating Religious Pluralism: International Approaches (Fall 2005); Integration of Newcomers: International Approaches (Winter 2006); Experiences of Second Generation Canadians (Spring 2008); Immigration Futures (Summer 2008); Citizenship in the 21st Century: International Approaches (Fall 2008); and International Students (Winter 2011).

29. Since Volume 1 of *Our Diverse Cities* was posted, it has been downloaded nearly 248,000 times in English and 44,000 times in French. Volume 2 (Second- and Third-Tier Cities) has been downloaded 98,000 times in English and 43,500 times in French; Volume 3 (Rural Communities), 15,128 in English and 9,065 in French; Volume 4 (Ontario), 141,987 times in English and 28,000 times in French; Volume 5 (Atlantic Region), 51,582 times in English and 19,490 times in French; Volume 6 (Prairies), 9,000 times in English and 2,000 times in French; and Volume 7 (Quebec), 85,000 times in English and 132,000 times in French. Volume 8 (British Columbia) has only recently been posted, and Volume 9 (Toronto/Ontario) was to be posted after the final National Metropolis Conference in February/March 2012.

30. With changes to key Secretariat personnel tasked with the international aspects of the project, the final edition of this publication attempted to shift from a newsletter to a more journal-like format. It was discontinued after this failed experiment.

31. In 2008, there were 8,242,135 hits on the Metropolis websites and 2,041,923 documents viewed. In 2011, nearly 2,000,000 documents were downloaded from the Metropolis websites.

REFERENCES

Biles, J. 2008. Integration Policies in English-Speaking Canada. In *Immigration and Integration in Canada in the Twenty-first Century*, eds. J. Biles, M. Burstein, and J. Frideres, 139-186. Montreal: McGill-Queen's University Press.

Biles, J. 2011. 16 Years and What Do We Get? Immigration and Integration in Canada (1995–2011). Powerpoint Presentation for "Taking Stock of a Turbulent Decade and Looking Ahead: Immigration to North America 2000–2010" Conference, 28–30 April, London, Ontario.

Biles, J., M. Burstein, J. Frideres, E. Tolley, and R. Vineberg, eds. 2011. *Integration and Inclusion of Newcomers across Canada*. Montreal: McGill-Queen's University Press.

CERIS – The Ontario Metropolis Centre. 2008. *Annual Activities Report to SSHRC. Metropolis Project Phase Three (Year One): Fiscal year 2007/2008*. 30 June.

Citizenship and Immigration Canada (CIC). 2006. CIC Internal Review of the Metropolis Project.

Clippingdale, R. 2006. *Strategic Interviews on the Metropolis Project and on Transferring Knowledge to Policymakers*. At http://canada.metropolis.net/pdfs/strategic_Interviews_ReportMAY30_06_e.pdf (accessed 2 March 2009).

Clippingdale, R. 2009. *Metropolis and the Provinces Report*. Submitted to Metropolis Secretariat, Citizenship and Immigration Canada, February 2009.

Dubois, L., and K. Watson. 1998. *Management Review of Metropolis in Canada*. Report prepared for CIC, the Treasury Board Secretariat and SSHRC.

Esses, V.M., R. Beaujot, and B. Dodson. 2007. Graduate Training in Migration and Ethnic Relations at the University of Western Ontario. *Our Diverse Cities: Ontario*: 86-91.

Fellegi, I. 1996. *Strengthening Our Policy Capacity*. Final Report of the Deputy Minister Task Force on Strengthening Our Policy Capacity.

Government of Canada. 1997. *Citizenship and Immigration Canada Performance Report for the Period Ending March 31, 1997*. Ottawa: Canadian Government Publishing Catalogue No. BT31-4/32-1997.

Human Resources and Skills Development Canada (HRSDC). 2005. *Evaluation of the Federal Grant Provided to the Canadian Policy Research Networks Inc.—March 2005*. At http://www.hrsdc.gc.ca/eng/cs/sp/sdc/evaluation/sp-ah216e/page02.shtml (accessed 2 March 2009).

Legault, C., M. Vanderplaat, and J. Johnson. 2006. NGO Scan: Reflections on the Involvement of the NGO Settlement Sector in Metropolis. 8th National Metropolis Conference, Vancouver, 23–26 March.

Metropolis. 2002. Annexes A–H Memorandum of Understanding Between Social Sciences and Humanities Research Council and Citizenship and Immigration Canada.

Metropolis. 2007. Metropolis Phase III (2007–2012) Annexes A–L. Memorandum of Understanding Between Social Sciences and Humanities Research Council and Citizenship and Immigration Canada. At http://canada.metropolis.net/pdfs/Annexes%20A-L%20Eng.pdf (accessed 2 March 2009).

Metropolis. 2008a. Phase III Logic Model. Unpublished internal working document approved by the National Metropolis Committee.

Metropolis. 2008b. Phase III Governance Model. Unpublished internal working document produced by the Metropolis Secretariat.

Metropolis. 2008c. Knowledge Transfer Typology of CIC Staff. Unpublished internal working document produced by the Metropolis Secretariat.

Public Works and Government Services Canada (PWGSC). 2009. *Summative Evaluation of the Metropolis Project Phase II: Knowledge Transfer Activities and Impacts*. Prepared by Government Consulting Services.

Social Sciences and Humanities Research Council of Canada (SSHRC). 2006. *Report on the Mid-term Review of the Second Phase (2002–07) of the Metropolis Project Canada*. At http://canada.metropolis.net/research-policy/sshrc/mid_term_May06_Final.pdf (accessed 2 March 2009).

Weinfeld, M. n.d. *A Preliminary Stock-Taking on Immigration Research in Canada*. A synthetic overview of state-of-the-art reviews on immigration and immigrant integration in Canada from Six Disciplinary Perspectives. Prepared for the Metropolis Project and Strategic Policy, Planning and Research, Citizenship and Immigration Canada.

APPENDIX 1
Metropolis Governance Model (Phase III)

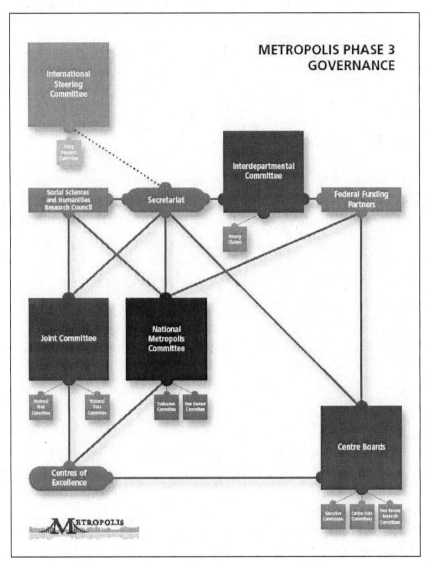

Source: Metropolis (2008b).

APPENDIX 2
Knowledge Transfer Typology for CIC Staff

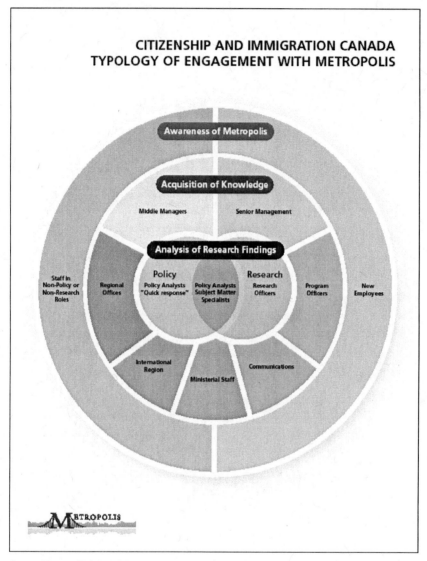

Source: Metropolis (2008c).

CHAPTER 13

Creating Spaces: Linking Migration and Diversity Research with Policy/Practice Needs

JOANNA ANNEKE RUMMENS, *Senior Scholar and Former Director of CERIS – The Ontario Metropolis Centre; Health Systems Research Scientist, The Hospital for Sick Children; Assistant Professor, Faculty of Medicine, University of Toronto*

PARADOXES AND PROMISES

We live in an information age in which knowledge about almost anything is not only widely available but also more readily accessible. Yet, it is often difficult to locate, absorb, reflect upon, and apply specific knowledge or expertise at the time of actual need, even when this information exists. This is so despite new technologies that greatly facilitate both the flow of information and knowledge management itself. Too often, there is too much information rather than too little, and the desired knowledge becomes difficult to locate within the resulting informational overload.

This raises a critical question. If our goal is to optimize policy and practice outcomes, what principles, processes, and mechanisms might be employed to better harness these vast resources? How can policy-makers

Managing Immigration and Diversity in Canada: A Transatlantic Dialogue in the New Age of Migration,
ed. D. Rodríguez-García. Montreal and Kingston: Queen's Policy Studies Series, McGill-Queen's University Press.
© 2012 The School of Policy Studies, Queen's University at Kingston. All rights reserved.

and practitioners best access the wealth of available information and expertise in knowledge-specific areas in order to optimize decision-making and implementation outcomes? How can researchers in turn best communicate and share knowledge and information that is relevant or directly pertinent to a particular policy or practice need? In brief, how can the gap between research and policy/practice be most effectively and efficiently bridged to ensure that decisions and actions are more knowledge-driven or evidence-based?

LINKING RESEARCH AND POLICY/PRACTICE: PREMISES, PROBLEMS, AND POSSIBILITIES

Policy- and practice-relevant research in the area of immigration and diversity has greater value when its findings are strategically communicated for subsequent knowledge uptake and implementation by policy-makers and practitioners. Failure to use available scientific research knowledge is inefficient and wasteful, and can be costly in both human and financial terms. This is particularly evident in the medical sciences, where lack of information sharing can readily contribute to ineffective, inefficient, and even harmful health care practices. In the area of immigration and diversity, failure to use available research findings may result in uninformed or misguided policies and practices that adversely affect the well-being of migrants and their families as well as the very social fabric of society itself.

There are, however, several barriers to effective knowledge sharing between the world of academe and that of policy-making or practice. These need first to be clearly identified before they can be directly addressed.

A first major challenge is that academe tends to favour and reward the advancement of scholarly knowledge for its own sake. There are simply very few incentives for university-based researchers to undertake policy- and practice-relevant research, and many disincentives. The format in which academic research findings are conveyed is also not conducive to information sharing relevant to decision-makers. Traditional academic research publications are often difficult for non-specialists to both access and understand. They tend to be too lengthy to read and often contain specialized terminology or disciplinary jargon. This is because academic journal articles and book publications are written for a largely academic audience usually comprised of other experts who specialize in an often narrowly defined topic area. Available primarily via university libraries and specialized Internet search engines, these scholarly publications are, generally speaking, not written for policy-makers, practitioners, and other decision-makers.

Even where research results are directly relevant to a policy area, the vast majority of academics are not trained to reflect upon the implications of their findings for policy or practice. The subsequent formulation of policy and practice recommendations per se is, moreover, informed by other considerations as well (Shields and Evans 2008); it also requires a much different skill set. In other cases, available research findings may simply be difficult to readily apply to policy or practice. Timing itself can also present a real challenge. Because of the time delay between the write-up of new research results for scientific peer review and their eventual appearance in print, most academic publications are only available months, even years, after the research itself has been completed. The subsequent timing of the dissemination of the research findings may or may not coincide with the informational needs of the policy-maker or the opening of a relevant policy window. Conversely, an immediate policy need cannot always be met with readily available research data.

In brief, as *knowledge producers,* academic researchers do not necessarily focus on policy or practice research questions, and when they do, they rarely attempt to make their findings available in terms and ways that are understandable and accessible to non-academic audiences. They often lack incentives for undertaking policy- or practice-relevant research and dissemination because such "applied" research has traditionally lacked "academic currency" within the institutional environments in which they work (Barwick et al. 2005). Beyond the simple lack of recognition, such efforts may even be met with disincentives and career penalties. Academics also do not necessarily know with whom to share research findings, nor the best ways through which to present or convey them. They also lack access to the necessary funding and other resources (ibid.) required to accomplish what in essence constitutes an additional task that is, moreover, not at all expected of them.

Policy-makers and practitioners in turn seldom turn to academic researchers when making a decision. This is because policy and practice are usually formulated in response to many other considerations and not necessarily informed by research findings at all, even where they exist (Shields 2007). As *knowledge users,* decision-makers also often have scarce or otherwise poor evidence upon which to base their decisions. They may lack awareness of existing relevant research knowledge that resides both in universities and non-governmental organizations, and even when they are aware, they do not always know where to go and whom to ask for the needed expertise. There is, moreover, not always a good fit between existing research findings and policy, programmatic, or practice needs. Nor are available research findings necessarily relevant to immediate demands. Even when research results are both relevant and timely, decision-makers may lack the capacity to access, critically evaluate, and effectively apply the available research evidence to meet existing policy or practice needs. Finally, as is the case with knowledge creators, knowledge users also often have few incentives to use the existing evidence and knowledge base (Canadian Institutes of Health Research n.d.).

So, how then might the gaps between research and policy or practice best be bridged to ensure that decisions are more knowledge-driven and/or evidence-informed?

If researchers are willing to assume multiple roles and are also willing "to act as an administrator, planner or consultant" (Goering and Wasylenki 1993); and *if* decision-makers are willing to engage in sustained interactions and discussions with researchers, and to provide or help leverage the resources needed for knowledge transfer and exchange activities (Barwick et al. 2005); and *if* community and/or non-governmental organizations are also willing to contribute their practical on-the-ground experience regarding pressing issues and needs, *then* possibilities for using findings from research to inform policy and practice are greatly increased. Collaborative partnerships among knowledge producers and users that focus on knowledge creation, transfer, exchange, uptake, and implementation with a specific area of expertise can become an effective means of reducing the gap between science and practice.

KNOWLEDGE TRANSLATION: KEY PROCESSES AND PRINCIPLES

Knowledge transfer may be defined as the process by which knowledge is shared with and communicated to people and organizations that can benefit from it. It is about reducing the gap between "what is known" and "what is used" (Zarinpoush and Gotlib Conn 2006). Knowledge transfer has as its explicit goal to provide decision-makers with the best available research findings for use in making policy and providing services so as to improve the quality of policy and practice outcomes (Dickinson 2007).

In practice, there are three models of knowledge transfer (Landry et al. 2003; Barwick et al. 2005). In the first, the knowledge producer actively *pushes* new scientific research findings out to decision-makers, often by making them more available in readily accessible language and formats. In the second, demand requests by knowledge users for specific research information actively *pulls* research findings into the realm of decision-making at moments of temporal pertinence. Most effective and efficient is the third model, namely knowledge transfer and exchange mechanisms that permit *sustained interaction* among knowledge producers and users to achieve a shared objective.

Effective knowledge transfer is not as easy to do as it may at first appear. Bridging the gap between knowledge creation and knowledge usage requires a fundamental shift in thinking, away from mere research dissemination—making information publicly available either via pushing out or pulling in—to true *knowledge exchange* through sustained interactional networks that integrally connect knowledge creators and knowledge users.

Knowledge exchange may be defined as collaborative problem-solving between researchers, decision-makers, and practitioners that happens through the linkage and exchange (Canadian Health Services Research Foundation 2005) of knowledge, information, and expertise. It speaks to *how* knowledge translation is most effectively undertaken. In essence, knowledge exchange involves ongoing interaction between decision-makers and researchers that results in mutual learning through the process of planning, producing, disseminating, and applying existing or new research in decision-making (ibid.).

While the concepts of knowledge transfer and exchange are themselves relatively simple, they require considerable thought, skill, commitment, and resources to implement effectively and efficiently. This is because effective knowledge transfer requires considerably more than mere preparation of a brief report summary of research highlights with subsequent passive delivery in report format to an array of potential knowledge users. Distilling the actual policy or practice implications of new research requires *a process of interaction and dialogue* between the knowledge producers and the targeted knowledge users to shape the very presentation, content, and format of information provided in order to facilitate optimal knowledge uptake. Having the information available, even when it is well packaged, is not enough to ensure effective translation of knowledge into policy or practice implementation.

Knowledge transfer entails specific tasks and roles, each with associated skill sets. *Knowledge mobilization*, for example, involves getting the right information to the right people in the right format at the right time, so as to optimally inform or influence decision-making (Barwick et al. 2005). It includes knowledge dissemination, transfer, and translation of knowledge that is often highly complex, technical, and discipline-specific (Shields 2008), and may be accomplished in various ways, using multiple communication formats geared towards a wide array of different stakeholder audiences. Or it may be specifically tailored to a single targeted audience of knowledge users and decision-makers.

Knowledge exchange similarly involves distinct tasks, roles, and skills. *Knowledge brokering*, for instance, is an emerging activity in the area of knowledge exchange that seeks to encourage and enhance knowledge exchange by embedding it directly in the operational culture of knowledge users. Its mandate is to link researchers and decision-makers together, facilitating their interaction so that they are able to better understand each other's goals and professional culture, influence each other's work, forge new partnerships, and share and use research-based evidence (Barwick et al. 2005). The goal of a knowledge broker is to act as a facilitating intermediary between knowledge creators and knowledge users in order to support evidence-based decision-making in the planning, organization, management, and delivery of relevant services. Such knowledge brokers may be individuals, or they may be organizational entities.

The end goal of knowledge transfer and exchange is, of course, *knowledge uptake*. *Knowledge uptake* may be defined as the incorporation of research knowledge into decision-making processes and/or its implementation into practice to affect actual behaviour. In both cases, the focus is on optimizing the impact of knowledge transfer, exchange, mobilization, or brokering on policy or practice outcomes. The scientific study of methods through which to maximize knowledge transfer uptake of both research findings and evidence-based practices to change actual behaviour is a relatively new, emerging area of inquiry known as "implementation science."

Knowledge transfer, exchange, mobilization, brokering, and uptake are all encompassed within the overall concept of *knowledge translation*, an entire area of research and expertise in its own right. *Knowledge translation* may be defined as the exchange, synthesis, and ethically sound application of knowledge—within a complex system of interactions among researchers and users—to accelerate the capture of the benefits of research for everyday citizens (CIHR n.d.). It refers to the exchange, synthesis, and subsequent uptake of information and knowledge in order to inform policy or practice. Effective knowledge translation requires the building of innovative partnership networks and knowledge transfer infrastructures that permit, facilitate, and support systematic, ongoing, and timely exchange of relevant information and knowledge between academic and non-academic stakeholders. The overall process might best be conceptualized as an active, two-way, multi-directional exchange of information, knowledge, and expertise among knowledge *creators*, knowledge *brokers*, and knowledge *users*.

FIGURE 1
Knowledge Translation Exchanges Among Knowledge Creators, Brokers, and Users

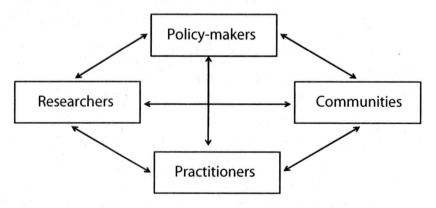

Source: Author's compilation.

Effective knowledge translation (KT) occurs through the formation of *collaborative KT partnership networks* among diverse stakeholders who share a common vision and engage in sustained interaction to achieve their shared goals and objectives. Mutual recognition and appreciation of respective areas of knowledge and expertise as both complementary and as valuable in their own right is key to the creation of these partnerships and fundamental to their very success. Representation and involvement of each type of stakeholder in governance structures, operational mechanisms, and collaborative activities is critical, as is full transparency and accountability to the collective.

To ensure that the ensuing partnership is truly meaningful, it is essential that respective areas of strength are fully articulated and operationalized in all joint initiatives and activities. Early and ongoing involvement of community members, practitioners, and policy-makers in all aspects of knowledge creation, exchange, and transfer is particularly important; this is, in and of itself, the best predictor of the final uptake and implementation of policy- and practice-relevant research findings by decision-makers and practitioners. The different partners should always feel that they are treated equitably and with respect, and the diverse needs, possibilities, and limitations that stem from the different contexts in which each works should be both acknowledged and accommodated. Rather than shy away from the various challenges that joint partnerships among diverse stakeholders and across diverse sectors inevitably entail, these should instead be embraced as truly valuable opportunities to work and learn together. Building mutual trust among the diverse partners is key and arises precisely out of such engagement.

For such knowledge translation partnerships to be both functional and sustainable, concrete incentives for participation need either to exist or be put in place for all stakeholders. This is critical if effective collaboration is to take place. These incentives may take diverse forms across the different stakeholders: Academics may derive personal satisfaction from research relevance and direct societal contributions; civic society partners may value the network's responsiveness to community needs as well as opportunities for greater capacity building; while decision-makers may see enormous benefit in being readily able to quickly access the collective's reservoir of policy- and practice-relevant information, knowledge, and expertise. The important thing is not only that these incentives exist, but also that they are acknowledged and taken into account in all joint initiatives. All parties must, at the same time, be fully willing to make the necessary investments of time, funds, and resources required for the partnership to function and be sustainable over time. Equally critical is ensuring that the various human, financial, and in-kind resources needed to support the partnership network's research and knowledge translation activities themselves have been secured, with joint investments made by all stakeholders. Finally, it is critically important to always keep in mind that knowledge translation is less an end product than an ongoing process of iterative social engagement. It is, and will always remain, a continual "work in progress." In this lies its inherent value.

PUTTING IT INTO PRACTICE: CERIS – THE ONTARIO METROPOLIS CENTRE, CANADA

The Context

Canada welcomes between 230,000 to 260,000 immigrants and refugees each year. These newcomers come from an increasingly wide range of countries, reflect diverse cultures and religions, and speak a multitude of different languages. Some are refugees fleeing famine or civil war, while others are seeking a better life for themselves and for their families. The vast majority of newcomers to Canada settle in the large urban areas of Toronto, Vancouver, and Montreal.

As one of the most multicultural metropolises in the world, Toronto is the settlement destination for approximately half of all newcomers to Canada each year (CIC n.d.). As a result, the Greater Toronto Area has become increasingly culturally, linguistically, religiously, and racially diverse over the course of the last two decades—a trend that continues. In the City of Toronto itself, at the time of the 2001 census, 49.4 percent of the population was foreign-born, and 43 percent was comprised of diverse visible minority groups; corresponding figures for the larger Census Metropolitan Area of Toronto were 43.7 percent and 37 percent respectively (Statistics Canada n.d.). More than 100 languages and dialects are spoken in Toronto on a daily basis, and a full third of the population speaks a language other than English at home (ibid.).

Responding to Societal Needs

In response to an increasing need by federal policy-makers and practitioners alike to address the various challenges and opportunities brought about by Canada's rapidly increasing socio-cultural diversity particularly in urban areas, a collaborative partnership between government, universities, and non-governmental organizations was formed in the early 1990s that would focus on the production and sharing of policy- and practice-relevant research regarding the resettlement and integration of immigrants and refugees into the economic, social, political, and cultural life of the country. The partnership arose out of a collective awareness and recognition of the pressing need for high-quality, collaborative, interdisciplinary scientific research that would directly address pressing policy issues and practice needs that arise from Canada's immigration-based population growth. This partnership became known as the Metropolis

Project, a national and international forum for research and policy on migration, diversity, and changing cities (www.canada.metropolis.net; www.international.metropolis.net).

Established in March of 1996 as the Joint Centre of Excellence for Research on Immigration and Settlement, *CERIS – The Ontario Metropolis Centre* was jointly founded by Ryerson University, the University of Toronto, and York University, in partnership with the United Way of Greater Toronto, the Community Social Planning Council of Toronto, and the Ontario Council of Agencies Serving Immigrants. CERIS brings together researchers, policy-makers, service providers, community organizations, and the media to share knowledge and information regarding pressing issues and needs in the area of migration, diversity, and civic participation within the Greater Toronto Area and the province of Ontario, across the country, as well as internationally. The Centre is jointly funded by Canada's Social Sciences and Humanities Research Council (a major academic research funding body) and 15 federal ministries and departments; it receives additional infrastructural and additional operational support from each of its three founding universities and further benefits from the considerable in-kind support of its founding community partners and numerous affiliates. These core resources are directed towards the effective operation of the CERIS research/policy/practice partnership network and its various knowledge translation activities, as well as to the internal funding of high priority area policy- and practice-relevant research initiatives by its affiliates. CERIS is one of now five such centres across Canada (in Atlantic Canada, Quebec, Ontario, the Prairies, British Columbia) that, together with the Metropolis Secretariat in Ottawa, form an integral part of the Metropolis Project, Canada (www.metropolis.net).

Shared Vision, Goal, Objectives

At its core, CERIS is a research knowledge creation and transfer network that focuses on the resettlement and integration of immigrants and refugees both within the Greater Toronto Area and across the province of Ontario (www.ceris.metropolis.net). Its research and community affiliates undertake policy- and practice-relevant research on migration, diversity, and civic participation and actively share their research findings with a broad range of interested stakeholders via a wide array of innovative knowledge transfer activities.

The Centre arose out of an overarching vision that was shared by its diverse founding partners: to jointly identify and undertake policy- and practice-relevant research that would facilitate informed decision-making and thereby optimize policy and practice outcomes. CERIS' specific goals are, *first*, to create an engaged and vibrant community of scholars and community researchers dedicated to research on migration, diversity, and civic participation; *second*, to promote innovative interdisciplinary policy- and practice-relevant research on the integration of immigrants into Canada's economic, social, political, and cultural life at the local, provincial, national, and international levels; *third*, to ensure the development of a new generation of immigration scholars and researchers through graduate student training and mentoring; and *fourth*, to disseminate research findings via effective knowledge exchange and transfer to a wide range of interested stakeholders in order to generate broad public discussion and debate, to stimulate policy development, and to inform practice.

Now in its third five-year mandate, CERIS seeks to further expand and support a highly productive *networked community* of academic and community researchers, non-governmental partners, graduate student trainees, policy-makers, practitioners, and funders interested in migration, diversity, and civic participation within the province of Ontario; to further facilitate, support, and undertake interdisciplinary policy- and practice-relevant research at the local, provincial, national, and international levels through active collaboration across the larger Metropolis Project network (www.metropolis.net; www.international.metropolis. net); and to initiate additional knowledge exchange and transfer activities across all relevant stakeholders in order to further optimize the "uptake" of research findings through knowledge mobilization to policy-makers and practitioners (Rummens, Anisef, and Shields 2007).

In brief, CERIS partners and affiliates jointly engage in (a) collaborative policy- and practice-relevant research for evidence-based decision-making, and (b) concomitant knowledge transfer and exchange in the area of migration, diversity, and civic participation.

Meaningful and Equitable Partnerships

Knowledge is not vested primarily in academia, or in government, or within civil society. Instead, it is widely distributed across universities, government ministries and departments, community groups, non-governmental organizations, and international organizations. Policy- and practice-relevant knowledge often also resides more informally within the knowledge systems and informational networks of community members within civil society itself. It does not, and cannot, always appear in the form of readily available and accessible written documents; instead, it also resides in the practical everyday experiences of those most directly affected.

From its very inception, CERIS has been deeply committed to meaningful, equitable, and productive academic-community research collaboration and effective knowledge exchange among its various stakeholders that is firmly rooted in mutual appreciation and respect. This commitment is articulated both through its overall governance and organizational structure, and the very way in which research is undertaken, shared, and mobilized by and among Centre stakeholders and affiliates.

CERIS' founding academic and community partners sought to create an academic research centre that would differ from other more traditional university-based centres, both in its focus on policy- and practice-relevant research and in its partnership between the community and university sectors, and with government. In addition to seeking to promote both informal direct connections and interactions among academics, members from civic society, and governmental representatives and concrete collaborative knowledge creation, transfer, and exchange activities, these partnership linkages were formalized to ensure that the respective stakeholders all had a recognized role in the Centre's decision-making. CERIS' semi-autonomous Governance Board was initially composed of three representatives from each of the three founding universities (Ryerson University, University of Toronto, and York University) and one representative from each of the three founding community organizations (Community Social Planning Council of Toronto, Ontario Council of Agencies Serving Immigrants, and United Way of Greater Toronto). This partnership was later expanded to include representatives from CERIS' larger Partnership Advisory Committee (subsequently rendered obsolete due to the systematic integral involvement of community partner affiliates in all aspects of Centre organizational structures and activities); representatives from various governmental departments and ministries at municipal, provincial, and federal levels; and Metropolis Project funders. All members have equal voice in decision-making; the provision of voting rights versus ex officio status is dependent entirely on absence or presence of possible conflicts of interest inherent in certain roles or statuses. The very same principle of true inclusiveness of academic, community, and policy stakeholders also extends to the Centre's Management Committee, Data Committee, Human Resources Committee, and various ad hoc committees, and is similarly reflected in all research projects and initiatives undertaken under CERIS auspices.

Central to CERIS' very success is this commitment to a true, meaningful partnership that fully recognizes and deeply values the complementary knowledge, expertise, and resources each type of stakeholder brings to the collaboration, finds ways to articulate these respective areas of strength in all initiatives and activities, and seeks ever to enhance the joint partnership to mutual benefit. Partnership is articulated through the very way in which research is undertaken and used. It begins with the collective prioritization of research needs and gaps by all stakeholders, and continues through the ensuing research project design, implementation of research methodologies and analyses, reflection upon the policy and practice implications of the findings, through to knowledge transfer, uptake, and subsequent implementation. All research undertaken under

CERIS auspices requires meaningful academic-community research partnerships, and the commitment to collaborative research and knowledge translation is such that this practice extends to all other Centre research initiatives and to affiliates' own research projects as well.

The Centre's key stakeholders are comprised of academics and graduate students; federal, provincial, and municipal ministries, departments, or offices; community associations and non-governmental organizations; other practitioners or professional bodies; and the general public. In addition to researchers based at Toronto's three universities, CERIS has affiliated academics and graduate students at 13 other universities across the province of Ontario. Its network currently includes over 332 individual affiliates. In addition to its three founding community partners, CERIS interacts with more than 150 community groups both within the Greater Toronto Area and beyond via its various research and knowledge transfer and exchange activities. Its governmental partners are drawn from the municipal, provincial, and federal levels. CERIS' very success in creating and translating policy-relevant knowledge about migration and diversity for successful social innovation is firmly embedded in its core commitment to meaningful partnership collaboration and transparent, accountable decision-making—a commitment shared and appreciated by all partners.

Joint Research Prioritization, Synthesis, Knowledge Transfer, Impact

CERIS' research and knowledge transfer objectives are very much informed by the *research priority area needs* identified by its 15 federal funders, as articulated in the Memorandum of Understanding that governs the use of the Centre's operational funds. Research activities funded through the Centre's annual internal Request for Proposals (RFP) prioritize the following six policy-research areas identified: Citizenship and Social, Cultural, and Civic Integration; Economic and Labour Market Integration; Family, Children, and Youth; Health and Well-being; Policing, Security, and Justice; and Welcoming Communities—The Role of Host Communities in Attracting, Integrating, and Retaining Newcomers and Minorities. Illustrative research questions are provided under each area by the federal knowledge users; additional research needs and gaps are collectively identified at CERIS research retreats and symposia, and by CERIS affiliates and other stakeholders themselves in their respective research activities. This collective identification and prioritization of pressing migration and resettlement issues and associated research gaps by academics, community members, policy-makers, and practitioners helps to ensure that the ensuing research initiatives are indeed policy or practice relevant. By involving decision-makers right from the start, and by involving community members directly in the research itself, researchers are ensured of increased receptivity and greater uptake of the eventual research findings by policy-makers and practitioners alike.

A key focus for CERIS is also *ongoing integrative synthesis of research findings* from work already undertaken within each of these six policy-research priority areas by CERIS affiliates as well as by other researchers and scholars. This emphasis on synthesis is integral to each CERIS research project, from its initial developmental stages (i.e., relevant literature reviews) through to the final reporting of research findings (i.e., comparison of results with those from other studies). Where possible, these cumulative syntheses also incorporate research findings recorded in the "grey literature" that includes governmental reports and community research documents, which do not always find their way into traditional academic overviews of the existing research literature. Some of the work funded through the CERIS RFP funding competition is specifically geared to such synthesis studies.

In the early states of its existence, CERIS focused on the undertaking of policy/practice-relevant research and subsequent attention to *knowledge provision*. More than a decade later, CERIS has moved well beyond this early focus on knowledge transfer alone to explore new formats and mechanisms that facilitate greater knowledge uptake, mobilization, and implementation per se. CERIS research affiliates and other stakeholders are now working collectively to further facilitate more timely and effective *knowledge uptake* by policy-makers, practitioners, and community partners through, for example, the preparation of one-page knowledge transfer briefs that succinctly outline key research findings together with their implications for policy or practice. Additional planned initiatives include the provision of professional training in knowledge translation and media training to Centre Directors, Priority Domain Leaders, and interested affiliates in order to more effectively reach a wider stakeholder audience.

The anticipated *outcomes* for the current third phase of CERIS activity include (i) prioritized research initiatives in six federally identified priority areas that are directly responsive to pressing policy and programmatic needs identified by key stakeholders; (ii) integrative research synthesis and continued knowledge transfer for CERIS research projects completed to date; cumulative synthesis and knowledge translation of current research; (iii) increased knowledge translation activity, skill building, and expertise; increased utilization of a wider range of KT tools and strategies to better meet the needs of diverse stakeholders; (iv) increased knowledge transfer by CERIS affiliates and mobilization by policy-makers and practitioners through regular monitoring and measurement to better ascertain *impact*; (v) informed policy development and programming in the area of migration, diversity, and civic participation; and (vi) a critical and sustainable mass of research knowledge and expertise in the area of migration, diversity, and civic participation vested in a sustainable networked community of experienced researchers and new trainees.

FIGURE 2
Transferring Research Knowledge for Policy and Practice Uptake

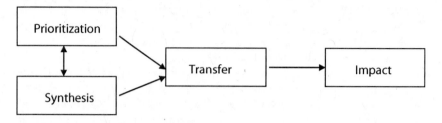

Source: Rummens, Anisef, and Shields (2007).

Creating Spaces for Mutual Engagement

Research and policy-making are both social processes. If applied knowledge creation is to be directly relevant to current policy or programmatic needs, it is best undertaken through networked partnerships among academic researchers, community members, policy-makers, and practitioners since it is in this interactional social context that policy- and practice-relevant research questions that address informational needs are more likely to arise and be successfully addressed (Anisef, Rummens, and Shields 2007). "Policy relevant research questions that can better shape research toward evidence-informed decision-making are more likely to occur in a *context of engagement*" (Shields 2008, emphasis added). This requires the intentional opening or creation of "spaces" in which such interaction can occur. Knowledge transfer and exchange are similarly more effectively accomplished via research knowledge translation networks. This is so in part because the spaces thereby created open up opportunities to share information, knowledge, and expertise "between a broader set of constituencies of interests, bringing new insights to knowledge formations," in part because they allow for a "more engaged and iterative formation of research questions and understanding of research results for public policy, public administration and service delivery" (Shields 2008).

Beyond the transformation of informal connections and relationships into equitable formal partnership structures, CERIS ensures that there is continuing dialogue across the academic, community, and policy sectors through the creation, nurturing, and fostering of multiple spaces that facilitate mutually meaningful interaction. Joint visioning and collaborative prioritizing are but the beginning of an ongoing process of "doing together"; there are many other mechanisms through which mutually beneficial engagement can be fostered. CERIS' academic, community, and governmental partners are all integrally involved in every step of the research cycle, from the initial identification of pressing research needs, the design of research projects, the adjudication of research proposals for Centre funding, data collection and analysis, the determination of implications of research findings for policy and practice, the knowledge transfer of research findings to diverse stakeholders, and subsequent implementation of research knowledge.

CERIS has built strong relationships with numerous diverse community organizations throughout its 15-year history, and these partnerships are critically important to all of its research and knowledge translation activities. Non-governmental organizations and diverse community groups participate in the identification of priority research questions for the Centre's annual internal funding competition, research retreats, and policy research symposia. They contribute as community-based researchers, research assistants, collaborators, and advisers in all research projects; are engaged as presenters, discussants, and participants at seminars, research forums, and conferences; are co-authors on various research dissemination and knowledge translation materials; and readily facilitate the effective "uptake" of research findings within their respective communities or sectors.

CERIS similarly enjoys extremely fruitful collaborations and productive working relationships with its various governmental partners. Together with the Centre's community partners, governmental representatives are directly involved in the articulation of research priorities at CERIS research retreats and policy-research symposia, in the numerous knowledge transfer and exchange activities undertaken by the Centre, and, most importantly, in the knowledge translation, brokering, mobilization, and all-important uptake of research findings to optimize policy and practice outcomes.

In large part, the very success of the Centre can be attributed to high levels of active engagement by, and interaction among, its various stakeholders. The continual creation and re-creation of interactional spaces are the very cornerstone of successful outcome impacts.

Multiple Knowledge Translation Strategies, Mechanisms, and Products

CERIS functions as a knowledge creator, a knowledge broker, and a knowledge user. Through its stakeholder partnerships, governance structures, and joint initiatives, the Centre provides an important "networked space" that facilitates effective knowledge exchange among academics, policy-makers, and civil society. Through its academic-community-policy research collaborations, it provides an effective forum for targeted policy- and practice-relevant knowledge creation and transfer within this very same network. Beyond the actual establishment of the partnership network itself, joint knowledge creation, transfer, and exchange require the development of a supporting *knowledge translation infrastructure* that employs multiple formats and seeks diverse points of contact.

CERIS' knowledge translation strategies, mechanisms, and products are all designed to facilitate ongoing and systematic exchange of both evidence-based and practical knowledge among academic and non-academic stakeholders, through an established, always expanding, collaborative partnership network in which the respective stakeholders are simultaneously active participants and targeted audiences. In this way, CERIS' research is optimally positioned to actively and effectively inform decisions about public policy, professional practice, and social programming.

a) Providing interactional contexts

As a knowledge creation and transfer initiative, CERIS has devoted considerable attention and resources to developing and implementing effective knowledge translation strategies to inform policy and practice. Unlike conventional academic research projects and units, CERIS' knowledge translation program stretches beyond traditional academic dissemination to open multiple spaces that permit ongoing and systematic exchange of policy- and practice-relevant knowledge among academic and non-academic stakeholders at the local, municipal, provincial, and federal levels.

These interactional spaces exist within the very structuring of CERIS' *Governance Board*, Management Committee, and other standing and ad hoc committees. However, as fundamentally important as this is, close interaction among CERIS' stakeholder partners does not start and end with its *network composition* and *institutional operation*. The vast majority of CERIS' academic, community, and governmental affiliates and partners interact most closely with each other when exploring common topics of interest via the *various collaborative research and knowledge translational activities* undertaken within each of six thematic priority area *CERIS Domains.* CERIS research teams are themselves also each comprised of academics, community representatives, graduate students, and community-based research assistants. CERIS Directors and Domain Leaders are, moreover, specifically tasked with planning events and facilitating collaborative initiatives that bring together members of CERIS' constituent stakeholders to explore, discuss, and pursue policy/practice-relevant topics and related initiatives of mutual interest.

Interactional spaces also exist within various knowledge exchange events that are specifically geared at collective sharing and joint planning. Each year, the Centre organizes a day-long *CERIS Research Retreat* designed to bring together CERIS affiliates to collectively determine policy- and practice-relevant research needs and gaps, and to shape effective research strategies to address pressing research questions provided by governmental funders, community partners, and academics themselves. These events serve to exchange important information, discuss research priorities, and plan for the future, and they are very important in shaping CERIS' internal open Request for Proposals (RFP) funding competition. Similarly, the annual *CERIS Policy Research Forum* provides an opportunity to present research syntheses and consider the policy implications of CERIS research findings to date within each of the priority research domains. This annual gathering of the CERIS community further serves to identify remaining gaps, consider next steps, and provide an evaluative benchmark of progress made.

Finally, interactional spaces are also created via multiple knowledge transfer forums. The monthly *CERIS Brown Bag Seminar Series* has proven to be a very popular local forum for presenting and discussing policy-relevant research undertaken by Centre affiliates. These two-hour lunchtime sessions are extremely well attended by graduate students, community members, public servants based in the Toronto area, and academics; local ethnic media also frequently attend and often publicly report on the topics and research presented. The seminar series plays an important role in knowledge transfer of research findings as well as in extending the CERIS network further to new participants.

Such knowledge transfer and exchange forums exist at the national and international level as well. The annual *National and International Metropolis Conferences* provide a context through which the major stakeholders in immigration and multicultural policy can meet and learn from each other. These conferences constitute key venues through which to communicate recent research findings and to facilitate informed discussions of public policy that include all stakeholders. At the same time, they simultaneously allow policy analysts working in government and in nongovernmental organizations to communicate their priority research needs to researchers. The National and International Metropolis Conferences bring together academics, community members, and governmental representatives from across Canada and 22 countries, respectively, for knowledge transfer, exchange, and uptake of Metropolis Project research among these core partners. They are effective in doing so because they provide a devoted time frame, location, and optimally varied format (plenary sessions, workshops, round tables, poster sessions, study tours, social events) through which academics, community members, and governmental representatives are able to meet, liaise, and plan various initiatives directly with each other.

b) Using Internet media

CERIS makes extensive use of Internet media both for "connecting with" and "sharing among" its constituent stakeholders as well as the interested public. *CERIS' website* and *Virtual Library* (www.ceris.metropolis.net) are a key portal for the Centre's research dissemination activities and linkages. As part of the larger Metropolis website network, the CERIS website provides information about the Centre and is host to many of its knowledge translation initiatives and products. It includes an extensive virtual library that contains several thousand downloadable documents. It provides linkages to demographic data sets, historical research documents, relevant institutional databases, lists of CERIS affiliates, community and governmental services providers, as well as other relevant web resources. The CERIS website is an exceptionally active site, with over 3 million visits—separate users, not individual hits—annually. The CERIS website draws a broad range of knowledge users, and analyses of website usage indicate that the number of government-based visits is high.

CERIS affiliates also make innovative use of media technology in their individual knowledge transfer activities and initiatives. One illustrative example is provided by the EMPIRICAL Project, a multimedia curriculum composed of a packaged series of pedagogical resource materials for use in courses that focus on immigration and settlement in the Canadian context. These materials are available both online and in CD-based versions that are ready to be offered through distance or on-campus education, and they may be drawn upon by teachers and learners alike.

The CERIS office itself makes extensive use of Internet technology to communicate with Centre affiliates and with other interested individuals and organizations. Email *listservs* (electronic mailing lists to targeted groups of individuals) are a key mode of regular communication with various internal groupings, for example, the members of a particular research domain or graduate students. CERIS also sends out a monthly *Electronic Bulletin* that contains information regarding CERIS events, recent publications, and other related news concerning immigration, resettlement, diversity, and integration within the Greater Toronto Area and province of Ontario. A primary vehicle for information sharing and networking, this electronic newsletter is distributed to some 1,400 subscribers each month and is also available on the CERIS website to a larger audience. It has become a vital service to the immigration research, policy, and service community in Ontario.

c) Providing access to special or unique resources

CERIS further supports knowledge creation and knowledge use through the provision of special and unique resources. *The CERIS Documentation Resource Centre* maintains a specialized collection of hard-to-find materials and is frequently consulted by researchers, graduate students, and visiting scholars. Copies of CERIS affiliate research reports, research papers, publications, knowledge transfer products, non-governmental reports, and Metropolis Project publications may all be readily accessed here. Within the collection is a large selection of difficult-to-locate and valuable "grey literature" research documents produced by community organizations in Ontario. CERIS' part-time Resource Centre Coordinator and Webmaster provides assistance in locating research materials to CERIS affiliates and visitors alike, both in person and via email inquiries. Via the CERIS Data Committee and Documentation Resource Centre, CERIS affiliates also may access *special data sets* relevant to immigration and diversity that have been provided to the Metropolis Project by Statistics Canada.

d) Developing effective outputs

CERIS knowledge transfer strategies and mechanisms allow for ready access by policy-makers and practitioners to CERIS research products. Each gives primary thought to the differential informational needs of the *diverse stakeholder audience*(s) that is targeted. Equal thought is given to the nature of the *format*(s) through which research findings and their implications are communicated in order to most effectively inform decisions regarding public policy, programmatic development, and professional practice. Attention is also given to the use of *multiple mechanisms* and *points of contact*.

The primary, but certainly not exclusive, audience to which CERIS knowledge translation activities are directed consists of federal policy-makers, in particular middle-level government policy and research professionals. These knowledge brokers within governmental departments are charged with knowledge transfer, uptake, and implementation of policy-relevant information, advice, and options to the actual government policy decision-makers, a group within the government structure that is otherwise very difficult to communicate with directly. Other key stakeholders consist of other researchers, community agencies, non-governmental organizations, and the general public.

The informational needs of each stakeholder audience are addressed either within each written product or via a separate product that is specifically tailored to their respective needs. A key challenge in such knowledge translation efforts is how "to put together in user-friendly wording and format, information, knowledge and research findings addressing a specific area of interest, and effectively and efficiently transfer this deliverable to end users" (Shields and Evans 2007). The multiple opportunities for academic and non-academic stakeholders to engage in sustained, intensive interaction that are provided via CERIS play an essential role in facilitating this transformation of research knowledge for the purposes of decision-making.

CERIS employs multiple mechanisms and formats for the dissemination and knowledge translation of its policy/practice-relevant scientific research findings, seeking always to identify diverse points of contact. CERIS researchers are actively engaged in *peer-reviewed academic publication in scholarly journals and books* and in presenting their work at various *academic conferences*. These more traditional sources of research dissemination help to ensure the scientific rigour of CERIS' research activity and form the very basis for other knowledge transfer and exchange initiatives. They are, nevertheless, only the starting point for knowledge translation itself.

All CERIS project research teams that receive internal research funding from the Centre via internal funding competitions and awards prepare concise one- to three-page *Research Summaries* of their research findings that furthermore specify the policy/practice implications of their work. These are posted directly on the CERIS website. This format and delivery mechanism was designed in consultation with policy-makers and practitioners to ensure ready access to recent research findings and to facilitate their direct uptake to inform decision-making. The *CERIS Working Papers Series* permits more extensive discussion of the relevant research literature or research project methodologies, analyses, findings, and implications and is one of the most heavily used CERIS knowledge transfer products. Like the research summaries, these working papers constitute one of the primary ways in which recent CERIS research is disseminated in both a timely and accessible fashion, often before research findings are published within academic journals.

The *CERIS Policy Matters* series provides an example of a knowledge transfer product that specifically targets a particular knowledge-user audience. The series consists of greatly abbreviated research reports that focus on key policy issues affecting migration, diversity, settlement, and integration in Canada. Their goal is to provide accessible, concise information regarding current immigration research and directly address implications for policy development so as to optimally address the needs of government knowledge users. This product is unique to CERIS and has been identified as a "best practice" within the Metropolis Project itself. Further developments along a similar line include the preparation of *one-page research-policy briefs* for use by government, civil society, and the media.

Finally, CERIS affiliates are also involved in other CERIS Metropolis Project knowledge transfer publications, which include special journal issues, monographs, and conference proceedings as well as professional magazines (www.metropolis.net). CERIS Research Summaries, Working Papers, and *Policy Matters* are all posted on the CERIS website and are downloadable in PDF format. Information regarding other dissemination and knowledge translation products prepared by Centre affiliates is readily accessible via CERIS' Virtual Library at www.ceris.metropolis.net.

e) Delivering expert consultation

Because of the way in which knowledge is absorbed within government, to ensure maximum effect, it is important that the linkages between the government knowledge brokers and users and knowledge creators and translators like CERIS be in the form of regular, strong, institutionalized, and multi-dimensional interactions. As Landry and Amara observe, "The more sustained and intense the interaction between researchers and users, the more likely utilization will occur" (quoted in Cohn 2006, 15).

Now in its 15th year of operation, CERIS continues to work closely with its government colleagues in the Metropolis Secretariat, Citizenship and Immigration Canada, in order to develop additional opportunities and avenues through which to effectively share CERIS research and priority area expertise with federal ministries and departments located in Canada's capital city. These include participation in the Ottawa-based seminars, policy research symposia, Armchair Discussions, and specific consultations. Institutional connections to federal knowledge users are further enhanced through the linking of CERIS Domain Leaders with six Metropolis Project Priority Leaders, who act as additional knowledge brokers and have as their task to help synthesize research findings that address federal research priorities across the five Canadian Metropolis Centres, while seeking to further enhance the pan-Canadian dimension of the Metropolis Project itself.

f) Committing to outreach

CERIS also seeks various ways to reach out to individuals and organizations interested in issues of migration and diversity. Its annual *CERIS Open House* is at once an opportunity for Centre affiliates to convene at an annual social event, and an opportunity for interested individuals to become directly acquainted with the Centre and its activities. It provides an opportunity for people to meet, talk, and connect with each other. CERIS Directors and Domain Leaders also engage in various outreach activities that bring together individuals and organizations interested in a particular priority area as well as the work of the Centre as a whole. Interested parties working in the area of immigration and settlement can become affiliates of the Centre through an *affiliation process* that involves either nomination or expression of interest.

Outreach also involves sharing CERIS' substantive research and accumulated knowledge translation expertise directly with various interested parties. CERIS receives a number of formal *international delegations* per year from groups who are visiting Canada to study immigration, multiculturalism, and other issues related to diversity in Canada. These delegations include government policy-makers and officials, municipal social service functionaries, private sector representatives, university professors, graduate students, and journalists, primarily from Europe, but also from other parts of the world such as the Caribbean and Asia. CERIS also regularly hosts *visiting scholars*, most recently from India, Sweden, South Korea, and the United Kingdom, and in addition receives regular shorter-term visits from professors from other parts of Ontario and Canada who are visiting the Toronto area in order to consult with colleagues, undertake research, or access the CERIS Resource Documentation Centre.

CERIS is further committed to optimally engaging both *the mainstream and ethnic media*, as this ensures knowledge translation to the general public. The print and electronic media play a leading role in establishing the agenda regarding what is considered newsworthy and publicly relevant, a role in the policy-setting and policy-making process that cannot be ignored. In the area of migration, diversity, settlement, and integration, the ethnic media has a special place, as it is able to speak to newcomer audiences with authenticity in their own languages about issues of particular concern to newcomers and ethnically diverse populations in ways the mainstream media cannot. CERIS has some important advantages in terms of access to the media, as Toronto is located at the very centre of the Canadian news media system and is home to the largest ethnic press in Canada.

Finally, a devoted on-staff *knowledge mobilization officer* trained in knowledge transfer media and strategies helps to ensure that CERIS research findings are efficiently and effectively conveyed to targeted knowledge users.

g) Mentoring the next generation

A final and critically important area of knowledge translation consists of the training and mentoring of the next generation of researchers, practitioners, and decision-makers. CERIS research publications continue to have considerable impact on curriculum development, as is most evident in the use of CERIS work in graduate course readings within Canadian universities. The Centre itself has an active Graduate Student Committee, numerous student affiliates, and a dedicated student listserv. CERIS research assistants and graduate assistants are integrally involved in CERIS research projects and knowledge translation activities, thereby gaining valuable hands-on experience. Student professional development is fostered through the provision of Graduate Student Conference Subsidies, which enable participation in National Metropolis Conferences, as well as CERIS Graduate Student Awards, which both recognize academic achievement and provide modest funds to support student research initiatives and professional development. CERIS also sponsors a one-day Graduate Student Conference, which provides an important venue for engaging young scholars and profiling their research. A Graduate Professional Development Day has also been held in conjunction with National Metropolis Conferences. CERIS' commitment to the next generation culminated in the development of a *Master of Arts Program in Immigration and Settlement Studies* at one of its partner universities; there are plans for a doctoral program in Canadian migration policy. CERIS' commitment is at once to the intergenerational transferral of knowledge and expertise, and to the sustainability of the knowledge translation network itself.

TOWARDS A COMMUNITY OF PRACTICE

CERIS – The Ontario Metropolis Centre is at its very core a dedicated network of researchers, community organizations, policy planners, and practitioners committed to "systematically moving knowledge into active service for the broadest common good" (SSHRC 2004). Over the past decade, CERIS has become a vibrant community of researchers, community organizations, service providers, and policy-makers drawn from municipal, provincial, and federal levels of government, who are jointly engaged in collaborative, interdisciplinary research initiatives and knowledge transfer and mobilization. In so doing, the Centre has successfully advanced and shared both scientific and on-the-ground knowledge that has directly helped to inform policies, programs, and practices that are critical to the successful settlement, integration, and civic participation of new Canadians in Ontario.

CERIS' experience amply demonstrates that policy- and practice-relevant information, knowledge, and expertise have far greater value when shared among interested stakeholders working together towards a common goal. The development of a *collaborative partnership* is instrumental to the creation, transfer, exchange, brokering, mobilization, and uptake of this shared knowledge into policy and practice, as is the creation of *networked spaces* through which such interface can take place. *Knowledge translation* itself involves a learning process, entails an overall trajectory, and remains ever a "work in progress." Truly collaborative partnership and effective knowledge translation both require ongoing social interaction and mutual learning. Together they result in a socially beneficial, intrinsically rewarding, and ultimately self-sustainable community of practice.

REFERENCES

Anisef, P., J.A. Rummens, and J. Shields. 2007. Diversity and the City: CERIS Research Partnerships and Knowledge Exchange for Policy Impact. *Our Diverse Cities: Ontario* 4 (Fall): 7-12.

Barwick, M., D. Butterill, D.M. Lockett, L. Buckley, and P. Goering. 2005. *Scientist Knowledge Translation Training Manual*. Toronto, Canada: The Hospital for Sick Children / Centre for Addiction and Mental Health.

Canadian Health Services Research Foundation (CHSRF). 2005. Knowledge Exchange Yields Success (KEYS). Ottawa: CHSRF. At http://www.chsrf.ca.

Canadian Institutes of Health Research (CIHR). n.d. At www.cihr.ca.

Citizenship and Immigration Canada (CIC) n.d. Canada: Immigration Overview. At www.Kanada-Canada.com/Immigration_Overview.html.

Cohn, D. 2006. Jumping into the Political Fray: Academics and Policy-Making. *IRPP Policy Matters* 7 (3), May.

Dickinson, H. (with the assistance of Paul Graham). 2007. *Knowledge Transfer and Public Policy: A Literature Review and Synthesis*. For Metropolis Canada, Ottawa, July.

Goering, P.N., and D.A. Wasylenki. 1993. Promoting the Utilization of Outcome Study Results by Assuming Multiple Roles Within the Organization. *Evaluation and Program Planning* 16: 329-334.

Landry, R., M. Lamari, and N. Amara. 2003. Extent and Determinants of Utilization of University Research in Government Agencies. *Public Administration Review* 63 (2):192-205.

Rummens, J.A., P. Anisef, and J. Shields. 2007. *CERIS - The Ontario Metropolis Centre (Phase III). A Renewed Research Agenda on Migration, Diversity and Civic Participation: Prioritization - Synthesis - Transfer – Impact*. Institutional Grant Proposal to the Social Sciences and Humanities Research Council of Canada (SSHRC).

Shields, J. 2007. Mobilizing Immigration Research for Policy Effects: The Case of CERIS. CERIS Working Paper No. 58, June. Toronto: CERIS.

Shields, J., and B. Evans. 2008. Knowledge Mobilization/Transfer, Research Partnerships, and Policymaking: Some Conceptual and Practical Considerations. *CERIS Policy Matters* (No. 33), April. Toronto: CERIS. At http://www. ceris.metropolis.net.

Social Sciences and Humanities Research Council (SSHRC). 2004. From Granting Council to Knowledge Council: Consultation Framework on SSHRC's Transformation, Vol. 1, January. Ottawa: SSHRC.

Statistics Canada. n.d. Census: Ethnocultural Portrait, Sub-provincial. At http://www12.statcan.ca/english/census01/products/analytic/companion/etoimm/subprovs.cfm.

Zarinpoush, F., and L. Gotlib Conn. 2006. Knowledge Transfer. Tip Sheet #5. Toronto: Imagine Canada. At http://www.envision.ca/cvi/docs/KnowledgeTransfer01-05-2006.pdf.

CHAPTER 14

Immigration et métropoles, Centre Métropolis du Québec (CMQ-IM) : une expérience de partenariat intersectoriel et interinstitutionnel réussie, en transition

ANNICK GERMAIN, *Professeure-chercheure titulaire, INRS-Urbanisation, Culture et Société, Montréal; Directrice, Centre Métropolis du Québec – Immigration et Métropoles (CMQ-IM)*

INTRODUCTION

L'expérience Métropolis est considérée à juste titre comme un consortium scientifique modèle, tant dans le monde académique (notamment les organismes subventionnaires) que dans celui des intervenants publics et communautaires dans le domaine de l'immigration. L'expérience des différents centres qui le composent est cependant variée, chaque centre ayant dû relever des défis particuliers liés aux contextes historiques et institutionnels spécifiques, aux cultures locales, aux couleurs régionales spécifiques que prennent les problématiques d'immigration, mais aussi

Managing Immigration and Diversity in Canada: A Transatlantic Dialogue in the New Age of Migration,
ed. D. Rodríguez-García. Montreal and Kingston: Queen's Policy Studies Series, McGill-Queen's University Press.

aux traditions académiques existantes ainsi qu'à la composition du bassin de chercheurs en immigration.

Après avoir présenté le CMQ-IM, détaillé son fonctionnement et insisté sur ses spécificités par rapport aux autres centres Métropolis, je voudrais m'attarder à quelques aspects de ce partenariat qui me semblent particulièrement marquants dans cette expérience, dans la mesure où ils en font la richesse mais aussi la fragilité. Plus exactement, je voudrais tenter de cerner les points sur lesquels se construit le dynamisme de notre centre mais aussi ceux sur lesquels se profilent ses défis. Ayant pris charge de ce navire depuis peu, mais y ayant dès le début été fortement impliquée comme chercheure et comme représentante de mon université (je faisais en effet partie des 4 mousquetaires qui ont démarré le projet), j'apprécie d'autant plus la chance qui m'est donnée de prendre ici les distances nécessaires pour mieux revisiter mon centre!

QUATRE MOUSQUETAIRES ET LE PARI
DE LA DÉCENTRALISATION

Le Centre Métropolis du Québec – Immigration et métropoles est un consortium de recherche interuniversitaire composé de six universités québécoises. L'Institut national de la recherche scientifique – Centre Urbanisation Culture Société (INRS-UCS) est l'institution-hôte et les cinq autres institutions sont : HEC Montréal, l'Université Concordia, l'Université McGill, l'Université de Montréal et l'Université de Sherbrooke.

Il est l'un des cinq centres d'excellence canadiens soutenus par le Conseil de recherche en sciences humaines (CRSH), Citoyenneté et Immigration Canada (CIC) et un consortium de partenaires publics fédéraux dans le cadre du projet national et international Métropolis. Il constitue un réseau de 82 chercheurs provenant essentiellement de dix universités québécoises.

Avant d'en expliquer le fonctionnement, il est utile de retracer l'histoire de la fondation d'Immigration et métropoles car dans le concours lancé en 1995 pour inviter des équipes de chercheurs à présenter des propositions de regroupement, aucun modèle organisationnel précis n'était imposé; chaque équipe était invitée à mettre sur pied ses propres structures administratives compte tenu des défis et des possibilités que lui offrait l'environnement dans lequel elle fonctionnait. Ainsi la dispersion géographique du Centre des Prairies contrastait avec la longue tradition de travail en équipe héritée par le Centre de Montréal. Avec le temps et au fil des phases successives du projet Métropolis, on a certes eu tendance à uniformiser les centres, tout particulièrement pour la mise en place de la phase actuelle. Mais les cinq centres canadiens du réseau Métropolis n'en demeurent pas moins distincts.

Dans le projet de Centre d'excellence sur l'immigration, l'intégration et la dynamique urbaine, présenté par les chercheurs montréalais, le consortium regroupait seulement trois universités, soit l'Université de Montréal qui en accueillait le siège social, l'Université McGill, et l'Institut national de la recherche scientifique – Urbanisation; l'INRS étant une petite université surtout consacrée à la recherche (je reviendrai plus loin sur la signification des ces 3 institutions pour notre propos). Les 56 chercheurs impliqués dans ce projet de réseau provenaient pour la plupart (mais pas exclusivement) d'universités montréalaises. La majorité d'entre eux étaient déjà regroupés plus ou moins fortement à l'intérieur d'équipes ou de centres de recherche. Le regroupement le plus important, le Centre d'Études ethniques de l'Université de Montréal (CEETUM), comprenait deux équipes qui ont été très actives dans la création d'Immigration et métropoles : le Groupe de recherche Ethnicité et Société (GRES) ainsi que le Groupe de recherche sur l'ethnicité et l'adaptation au pluralisme en éducation (GREAPE) (les deux premières directrices d'IM allaient d'ailleurs provenir de la Faculté d'éducation de l'Université de Montréal). À noter également la collaboration de divers regroupements comme le Centre de langues patrimoniales (CLP), le programme de recherche sur le racisme et la discrimination et la Chaire de recherche en relations ethniques (CRE). Du côté de l'Université McGill et de l'INRS, deux regroupements comptaient chacun une dizaine de chercheurs, soit le Groupe de recherche sur l'Immigration (GRI) à McGill et le Groupe d'étude Ville et immigration (GEVI) à l'INRS. À ces principaux noyaux s'ajoutaient des chercheurs reconnus d'autres universités (celle de Sherbrooke, celle d'Ottawa, ou de l'Université du Québec à Montréal) ou de centres de recherche comme le Centre international de criminologie comparée, ou encore des chercheurs d'institutions publiques. Les 56 chercheurs retenus avaient tous déjà à leur actif des travaux de recherche sur l'immigration et bénéficiaient, individuellement, d'une certaine réputation dans le monde académique. Ils avaient été sollicités en fonction d'un programme de recherche structuré en six volets portant sur les aspects socio-démographiques et l'intégration au travail, sur la vie de quartier, les trajectoires résidentielles et la gestion des équipements collectifs, sur l'éducation et la formation, sur la santé, les services sociaux, la sécurité et la justice, sur l'intégration linguistique et sociale, et sur la citoyenneté, la culture et le climat social.[1] En fait, chaque chercheur restait dans son institution mais acceptait de se joindre à Immigration et métropoles, en sachant que la subvention de base de chaque centre ne serait pas très élevée compte tenu du grand nombre de chercheurs impliqués. Aujourd'hui le budget, qui a été amputé pour permettre le financement de concours de recherche pancanadiens pendant la phase 3, ne permet pas de garantir à tous les chercheurs un financement même minimal. Nous verrons plus loin pourquoi dans notre Centre le financement disponible pour chaque projet de recherche est plus faible que dans les autres centres du fait du mode de fonctionnement retenu (décentralisation et partage du budget également entre les 6 domaines). C'est dire que les budgets de recherche disponibles ne justifiaient pas à eux seuls une telle mobilisation de départ et que les chercheurs se sont joints au projet en partie pour d'autres raisons, même si l'aspect budgétaire a toujours été présent dans les préoccupations des membres du Centre. Pourquoi donc tant de chercheurs ont répondu à l'appel?

La montée en puissance des questions (voire des problèmes) d'immigration, leur importance névralgique dans les politiques canadiennes et québécoises (toute la croissance de la main-d'œuvre repose actuellement sur l'immigration) qui en faisaient un moteur essentiel de développement, font certainement partie de la réponse. Mais bien d'autres aspects doivent être évoqués.

L'existence de ces divers regroupements de chercheurs sur lesquels s'est bâti le Centre Immigration et métropoles témoignait d'un important virage dans les milieux de la recherche universitaire au Québec entrepris dans les années 1980. Pour accélérer un rattrapage qui handicapait le Québec par rapport aux autres universités canadiennes ou étrangères, un fonds pour financer la recherche scientifique avait été mis en place au Québec (le FCAR) avec comme stratégie de valoriser le travail d'équipe. Les universitaires québécois ont donc pris l'habitude de former des équipes pour obtenir des fonds de recherche. Le Projet Métropolis s'inscrivait donc à cet égard en continuité avec ces habitudes de travail. Par contre, il allait induire de nouvelles dynamiques de collaboration entre chercheurs et milieux de pratique en établissant systématiquement des relations de partenariat avec tous les intervenants clés pour la formulation des politiques aux différents paliers de gouvernement et dans le secteur associatif. Ce modèle allait d'ailleurs être repris par la suite par certains organismes subventionnaires dont le CRSH avec les Alliances de recherche universités-communautés (ARUC). Cette proximité avec les milieux de pratique et de la décision était de plus déjà bien établie au sein d'un des trois membres du consortium, soit l'Institut national de la recherche scientifique.

Cette très petite institution (160 professeurs en tout, répartis dans 4 centres) est une université un peu particulière car sa mission est davantage centrée sur la recherche que sur l'enseignement. Elle fut fondée à la fin des années 1960 avec un mandat très contemporain, celui de développer la recherche fondamentale et appliquée orientée vers le développement économique, social et culturel du Québec ainsi que les études avancées. L'INRS s'est donc toujours distingué par une tradition de recherche en partenariat, se concrétisant notamment par des contrats confiés par des décideurs publics et privés (tant dans le domaine des sciences naturelles que des sciences sociales). Par ailleurs, le centre INRS mobilisé dans le consortium IM s'était spécialisé dans les thématiques tournant autour de l'urbanisation. Or pendant longtemps, les intervenants canadiens et québécois dans le domaine de l'immigration accordaient peu d'importance à ces thématiques, n'y voyant pas grande pertinence pour leur propos. Toutefois, au tournant des années 1990, la reconnaissance de l'importance des dynamiques urbaines dans l'intégration des immigrants allait devenir incontournable dans le sillage des émeutes ethniques et/ ou raciales qui allaient éclater tant aux États-Unis que dans certains pays européens. Le ministère québécois de l'immigration allait d'ailleurs financer plusieurs recherches pour explorer l'impact des dynamiques urbaines sur les questions d'immigration, et les chercheurs de l'INRS avaient été sollicités pour l'occasion. C'est dire que le choix d'inscrire les questions métropolitaines au cœur du projet Métropolis (et dans notre centre ce choix était explicite) était au fond assez innovateur. Et c'est aussi pour cette raison que ce qui était à l'époque l'INRS-Urbanisation était un des 4 joueurs dans la définition du projet de centre, (les trois autres étant l'Université McGill et deux facultés de l'Université de Montréal, celle des Arts et des Sciences et celle de l'Éducation, par ordre croissant). Aujourd'hui des questions comme les banlieues, les ghettos, les enclaves, la ségrégation, etc. défrayent l'actualité et la pertinence de l'apport des Études urbaines semble évidente (les disciplines de l'urbain sont d'ailleurs surreprésentées parmi les directeurs de centres). L'INRS venait donc compléter un consortium composé des deux plus grosses universités québécoises, l'une francophone, l'autre anglophone.

Ce réseau interuniversitaire allait de surcroît être arrimé à un réseau intersectoriel sans précédent, du niveau national au niveau micro-local, des gouvernements supérieurs aux municipalités sans oublier le tiers secteur (secteur associatif et communautaire). Cet arrimage s'est consolidé au fil des années mais ses débuts coïncidèrent pourtant à une conjoncture peu favorable où tout incitait à la division, soit celle du (second) référendum sur la souveraineté du Québec en 1995. Le processus de conception et de mise en place du centre IM se déroulait en effet dans un contexte fortement tourmenté, celui de « l'avant » et de « l'après référendum », un référendum dont l'issue fut particulièrement serrée. Les relations intergouvernementales n'étaient donc pas au beau fixe, et les relations interpersonnelles étaient elles aussi à l'occasion tendues! Ainsi, parmi les « 4 mousquetaires » associés dans la préparation de ce projet au nom de leur institution et sous le leadership énergique de Marie Mc Andrew, professeure à l'Université de Montréal, les opinions politiques sur la question de l'avenir du Québec étaient fortement divergentes!

Au fond, en y repensant bien, ce fut une excellente chose, car nous avons dû d'emblée travailler au-delà de nos différences pour construire un projet commun. La construction d'une cohésion au-delà des affiliations universitaires, et au-delà des affiliations disciplinaires (car nos centres couvrent des domaines variés, allant des sciences de l'éducation, à la médecine en passant par la sociologie, la géographie, les sciences politiques…) était indispensable pour amorcer la construction de partenariats avec des acteurs extérieurs au monde académique (le CEETUM allait d'ailleurs se transformer plus tard en Centre d'études ethniques des universités montréalaises!).

Cette cohésion s'est construite grâce à la combinaison d'un leadership énergique et d'un modèle organisationnel fortement décentralisé. Le grand défi consistait en effet à mobiliser un tel volume de chercheurs et de partenaires. Nous avons donc fait le pari d'une structure assez décentralisée où la gestion des domaines de recherche était assurée dans chacune des trois institutions universitaires partenaires de départ, de manière à garantir leur implication, et ce principe de décentralisation a été maintenu jusqu'à ce jour (nous reviendrons plus loin sur le fonctionnement actuel).

L'immigration étant au Québec un phénomène essentiellement métropolitain, les universités montréalaises étaient naturellement concernées par un programme de recherche sur le sujet, lequel a cependant assez tôt fait une certaine place à la régionalisation de l'immigration (en dehors de la métropole) et des chercheurs de la région de Sherbrooke, une des régions les plus dynamiques en matière d'attraction et de rétention d'immigrants. La géographie de l'immigration, beaucoup plus dispersée dans une province comme l'Ontario qui accueille aussi chaque année des flux d'immigrants beaucoup plus volumineux, ne simplifie pas la tâche de nos collègues du Centre de l'Ontario, alors que nous avons jusqu'à un certain point profité de la concentration des immigrants à Montréal.

La direction du Centre IM était logée à l'Université de Montréal jusqu'il y a peu, et vient d'être transférée à l'INRS, autre signe d'une bonne collaboration interuniversitaire. Au total, le consortium que représente IM a sans nul doute permis de stimuler les collaborations entre chercheurs d'universités différentes au Québec dans le domaine de l'immigration et de créer un climat d'échanges relativement conviviaux. Et le fait que notre centre repose aujourd'hui sur un consortium de six universités, et non plus trois, en est la conséquence directe.

Quelques explications s'imposent sur la structure de gestion.

UNE STRUCTURE DE GESTION À L'IMAGE DU PARTENARIAT

La direction du CMQ-IM est logée depuis le mois de mars 2008 à l'INRS-UCS qui a donc la responsabilité d'administrer la subvention de base (autour de 300 000 $ par an). Près de la moitié de cette somme sert à faire fonctionner l'infrastructure de base du Centre. L'équipe de direction est composée, en plus de la directrice (un professeur qui bénéficie pour ce faire d'une décharge de son institution pour l'équivalent d'un cours), d'une coordonnatrice et d'une secrétaire travaillant toutes deux à temps plein, ainsi que d'un webmestre à temps partiel. Cette infrastructure sert à l'ensemble des chercheurs. L'équipe de direction coordonne les activités du Centre (notamment la confection des plans de recherche) et facilite les liens entre les chercheurs, leurs partenaires et les instances centrales du projet Métropolis à Ottawa.

Comme l'indique l'organigramme ci-joint, les instances décisionnelles sont composées d'un Comité de coordination et d'un Conseil des partenaires qui reflètent le caractère inter-universitaire du Centre, mais aussi interpartenarial, puisque les chercheurs sont étroitement associés à leurs partenaires provenant des divers paliers gouvernementaux (y compris municipal) et de la société civile (ONG).

FIGURE 1
Organigramme

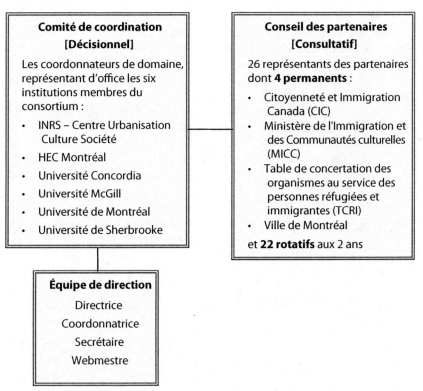

Source : compilation de l'auteur.

Notre centre couvre six domaines de recherche dont nous reparlerons plus loin et la coordination de chacun a été confiée à une des six institutions universitaires membres du consortium. Nous avons en effet partagé le budget de recherche également entre les six domaines et donc entre les six institutions universitaires. Les chercheurs relevant d'un domaine peuvent cependant provenir de différentes institutions. Les autres centres fonctionnent différemment et peuvent financer davantage chaque projet.

Le Comité de coordination est donc composé des six coordonnateurs de domaine[2] et prend les décisions ultimes relatives aux plans de recherche et aux enveloppes budgétaires particulières. Chaque institution a accepté d'octroyer à son coordonnateur une décharge pour l'équivalent d'un cours.

Le Conseil des partenaires, lui, est composé de 26 représentants des partenaires; certains y siègent d'office, d'autres ont des mandats de deux ans. Le Conseil se prononce notamment sur les plans de recherche.

Ce genre de structure est fort efficace pour s'assurer de l'implication de tous les intervenants dans les activités du Centre. Cela suppose toutefois qu'il n'y ait pas trop de roulement dans le personnel qui représente les institutions et que ces personnes soient autorisées à participer non seulement aux échanges lorsque l'on discute par exemple des plans de recherche, mais aussi à leur définition ainsi qu'à leur mise en œuvre. À l'occasion, les institutions publiques imposent à leur personnel un certain nombre de contraintes en matière de représentation publique. Ainsi les périodes électorales sont en général de bien mauvais moments pour réunir le Conseil des partenaires!

La composition du Conseil a fait l'objet d'un soin particulier car il fallait assurer une représentation permanente des partenaires principaux tout en rejoignant un éventail le plus large possible de partenaires, ce qui fut fait en leur confiant un mandat de deux ans.

FIGURE 2
Composition du Conseil des partenaires (2007–2009)*

Domaines	Citoyenneté	Économique	Famille	Collectivités d'accueil	Justice	Logement Vie de quartier	Général	TOTAL
Fédéral	▶ Patrimoine canadien	▶ Citoyenneté et Immigration Canada		▶ Secrétariat rural ▶ Développement économique Canada	▶ Sécurité publique (Consortium)	▶ Société canadienne d'hypothèques et de logement	▶ Statistique Canada	7
Provincial	▶ CSLF ▶ MICC/RI	▶ MESS ▶ Conseil des relations interculturelles	▶ MELS ▶ Santé publique ▶ CSSS		▶ CDPDJ	▶ Société d'habitation du Québec	▶ Ministère de l'Immigration et des Communautés culturelles	10
Municipal				▶ Ville de Sherbrooke	▶ Service de police de la Ville de Montréal	▶ Office municipal d'habitation de Montréal	▶ Ville de Montréal	4
ONG		▶ La Maisonnée					▶ TCRI Centraide	3
Privé		▶ Banque Nationale du Canada		▶ Fédération des Caisses Desjardins				2
Total	3	5	3	4	3	3	5	26

* Légende :
• CSLF – Conseil supérieur de la langue française
• MESS – Ministère de l'Emploi et de la Solidarité sociale du Québec
• MELS – Ministère de l'Éducation, du Loisir et du Sport du Québec
• CDPDJ – Commission des droits de la personne et des droits de la jeunesse
• TCRI – Table de concertation des organismes au service des personnes réfugiées et immigrantes
Source : compilation de l'auteur.

Le Conseil se réunit généralement deux fois par an.[3] Ces rencontres permettent aux membres de côtoyer des représentants d'institutions publiques (et des chercheurs) dans une variété de domaines (éducation, emploi, habitat, etc.), ce qui n'est pas banal, en plus de couvrir divers niveaux d'intervention et de paliers gouvernementaux. Les intervenants ont ainsi une vision intégrée de l'immigration et peuvent sensibiliser par la suite leurs ministères et organismes respectifs. Les séances du Conseil sont propices au réseautage et sont de ce fait suivies avec assiduité.

Le fait d'inclure des partenaires municipaux est aussi un trait propre au projet Métropolis; dans le cas du Québec les municipalités ont peu de prérogatives dans le domaine de l'immigration et s'en sont assez peu préoccupées jusqu'à tout récemment (à l'exception de la Ville de Montréal qui fut pionnière, mais qui paradoxalement a tendance à réduire son engagement, comme j'ai eu l'occasion d'en discuter dans un autre forum de la fondation CIDOB (Germain 2007)).

Mais chacun des six domaines a aussi son réseau de partenaires qu'il convoque deux ou trois fois par an pour préparer les plans de recherche et pour discuter des résultats. En fait, c'est vraiment à ce niveau que se construit la collaboration entre les chercheurs et leurs partenaires.

LE FONCTIONNEMENT PAR DOMAINE

Notre centre couvre six domaines de recherche alors que d'autres centres n'en couvrent que quelques-uns et ne répartissent en tout cas pas les budgets par domaine.

FIGURE 3
Les domaines de recherche

1	Citoyenneté et intégration sociale, culturelle, linguistique et civique
2	Intégration économique et marché du travail
3	Familles, enfants et jeunes
4	Rôle des collectivités d'accueil pour les nouveaux arrivants et les membres des minorités
5	Justice, police et sécurité
6	Logement, vie de quartier et environnement urbain

Source : compilation de l'auteur.

En conséquence, les sommes disponibles pour chaque domaine sont très limitées, ce qui nous a conduits très tôt à les considérer d'abord et avant tout comme des ressources à effet de levier (*seed money*). En d'autres termes, ces financements servent soit à initier de nouvelles recherches qui devront être financées par d'autres ressources, soit à ajouter un complément à des projets en cours. À l'occasion, des petits projets sont entièrement financés à même les fonds IM. On voit donc que le financement offert aux chercheurs est un financement d'appoint qui s'inscrit dans le prolongement des activités de recherche déjà menées ou prévisibles par les chercheurs.

FIGURE 4
Catégorie de projet et type de financement

	Catégorie de projet et type de financement
1	développement de nouvelles recherches dont le financement fera l'objet de demandes ultérieures à des organismes subventionnaires (*seed money*)
2	développement de nouvelles recherches dont le commanditaire principal est déjà identifié et son engagement largement assuré (*seed money*)
3	ajout d'une dimension répondant aux objectifs de Métropolis dans le cadre d'une recherche dont le financement est déjà assuré par d'autres sources
4	bilans ou initiatives de diffusion s'appuyant sur des recherches déjà réalisées
5	développement d'une nouvelle recherche ciblée et autosuffisante

Source : compilation de l'auteur.

Cette stratégie est appréciée par les jeunes chercheurs qui y voient des fonds de démarrage intéressants. Elle permet aux chercheurs plus chevronnés de bénéficier de petits financements complémentaires mais surtout de profiter d'une structure de transfert de connaissances unique, compte tenu des partenaires qui participent aux activités du domaine. Mais elle permet aussi souvent à des partenaires d'apporter des compléments de budget. Leur participation prend cependant souvent d'autres formes.

FIGURE 5
Formes de soutien des partenaires

1	Soutien financier
2	Allocation de ressources matérielles ou humaines
3	Facilitation de l'accès aux institutions concernées
4	Appui à la diffusion des résultats de recherche

Source : compilation de l'auteur.

Car chaque domaine est d'abord un lieu d'échanges sur les besoins en recherche. Chaque domaine est coordonné par un professeur qui bénéficie d'une décharge d'enseignement pour ce faire.[4] Il est aidé en cela par un agent de domaine qui est un fait un étudiant engagé spécialement pour cette tâche. Le rôle de ces agents est très important car ce sont eux qui assurent la logistique des activités du domaine. Ils deviennent aussi rapidement non seulement des relais indispensables et enthousiastes dans une organisation somme toute assez complexe où le travail de réseautage est important, mais forment aussi une véritable relève dans le domaine de la recherche sur l'immigration dans une perspective collaborative. Comme ils sont souvent impliqués dans les colloques annuels qui rassemblent une bonne partie des chercheurs (et leurs partenaires) des autres centres, ils ont l'occasion de se bâtir un réseau non négligeable qui leur sera utile dans la poursuite de leur carrière.

La formation des étudiants est d'ailleurs un des objectifs importants de l'activité des domaines. Voici le bilan à cet égard pour la période 2002–2005.

FIGURE 6
Données quantitatives pour la période 2002–2005

156 étudiants, dont 128 aux études supérieures, impliqués dans divers projets d'IM
80 sujets de thèse et de mémoire reliés à l'immigration, à la diversité et à l'intégration, dont **48** directement liés à des projets financés par IM
12 mémoires de maîtrise et 7 thèses de doctorat complétés
22 publications scientifiques et 24 autres publications
74 communications scientifiques lors des colloques de Métropolis, universitaires ou d'associations professionnelles; 17 présentations publiques ou sessions de formation

Source : compilation de l'auteur.

Revenons un instant sur l'élaboration des plans de recherche car le processus de confection et d'approbation des projets de recherche témoigne de la dynamique partenariale dans laquelle ils baignent. Ils sont évalués en fonction des critères suivants :

FIGURE 7
Critères d'évaluation des projets

Qualité scientifique des projets en cours ou à développer
Correspondance avec les besoins identifiés par les partenaires
Qualité des partenariats développés
Prise en compte des thèmes prioritaires fédéraux
Dimension comparative (un atout)

Source : compilation de l'auteur.

Les thèmes prioritaires sont définis à l'échelle canadienne au début de chaque phase suite à des échanges entre tous les chercheurs et partenaires. Ils couvrent un large éventail de questions.

Au fil des ans se sont créées dans certains domaines de fortes synergies entre chercheurs et partenaires mais aussi entre partenaires. Cette mobilisation multiscalaire de partenaires introduit beaucoup de dynamisme en matière de transfert de connaissances. Ci-dessous, on peut voir un exemple de partenariat au niveau d'un des six domaines du Centre CMQ-IM.

FIGURE 8
Partenaires du domaine *Logement, vie de quartier et environnement urbain*

Société canadienne d'hypothèques et de logement	Fédéral
Société d'habitation du Québec	Provincial
Ministère de l'Immigration et des Communautés culturelles – Direction de la recherche et de l'analyse prospective	Provincial
Commission des droits de la personne et des droits de la jeunesse	Provincial
Office municipal d'habitation de Montréal – Développement social et relations avec les locataires	Municipal
Ville de Montréal – Diversité sociale	Municipal
Ville de Montréal – Planification stratégique	Municipal
Communauté métropolitaine de Montréal – Politiques et interventions de développement	Municipal
Centraide du Grand Montréal – Impact dans la communauté	ONG

Source : compilation de l'auteur.

Dans notre centre donc, à la différence des autres centres, le partenariat s'est construit à la fois dans chacun des 6 domaines et dans les instances centrales du centre.

Chercheurs et partenaires se rencontrent plusieurs fois par an à l'occasion de réunions de domaines où se retrouvent chercheurs, représentants d'institutions publiques et d'ONG clés dans le domaine. Ces rencontres servent à la fois de lieux où sont discutés les programmations de recherches ainsi que les formes de collaboration impliquant les partenaires, mais aussi de lieux où s'échangent les demandes de dissémination et de transfert de connaissances des partenaires ainsi que les outputs (articles, conférences, working papers, etc.) planifiés par les chercheurs. Il est intéressant de noter que la continuité du projet Métropolis a permis d'établir des liens de collaboration solides, surtout dans les secteurs où le turnover du personnel n'est pas trop rapide! Ce genre de partenariat repose en effet beaucoup sur les liens de confiance qui se nouent au fil du temps entre chercheurs et partenaires, ce qui suppose une certaine pérennité des structures de collaboration… et des personnes sur lesquelles elles reposent. Par ailleurs, la fréquence des rencontres permet également des ajustements requis par les réalités particulièrement mouvantes des flux migratoires, de nouvelles questions, des problèmes inédits surgissant sans cesse.

Tous les domaines ne se prêtent cependant pas à de telles dynamiques partenariales et ce ne sont pas non plus tous les chercheurs qui y trouvent un intérêt, compte tenu de leurs objets de recherche et de leurs méthodologies. Les partenariats les plus fructueux se développent généralement à propos de questions de recherche très appliquées, supposant de nombreuses interactions avec les milieux de pratique. C'est plus difficile dans le travail proprement théorique.

Par ailleurs, au fil des ans les partenaires qui agissent aussi à titre de bailleurs de fonds ont tendance à s'assurer de plus en plus que leurs priorités sont prises en compte, surtout au niveau de l'ensemble des centres. Les bilans montrent pourtant qu'ils n'ont aucune raison d'être inquiets, comme l'indique la figure ci-dessous.

FIGURE 9
Comptabilisation des projets 2002–2005

Selon les types de partenariat*
24 projets avec des partenaires fédéraux 38 avec des provinciaux 8 avec des municipaux 27 avec des ONG
Qui répondent à un ou plusieurs thèmes prioritaires fédéraux
91 des 93 projets de recherche inscrits au programme 2002–2005

* Note : Certains projets sont le fruit de plusieurs niveaux de partenariat.
Source : compilation de l'auteur.

Mais on peut se demander si ce n'est pas un des effets pervers du mode de gestion partenariale lui-même, de pousser les attentes toujours à la hausse, surtout à l'occasion du renouvellement de la subvention de base.

Dans le cas du CMQ-IM, cette tendance est peut-être plus inquiétante du fait que les partenaires fédéraux sont les seuls bailleurs de fonds responsables de la subvention de base, alors que dans d'autres provinces, des gouvernements provinciaux participent au financement.

Pour conclure sur ces points, on peut dire que si les chercheurs ont parfois le sentiment d'une disproportion entre les investissements en temps et en énergie que requiert ce mode de gestion en partenariat, ils ont conscience d'être au cœur de synergies extrêmement précieuses pour la recherche, en plus de se sentir valorisés du fait des retombées nombreuses de leur travail dans les communautés.

Mais tout est question d'équilibre et la plus grande vigilance s'impose pour éviter de tomber dans ce qu'ils pourraient ressentir comme des contraintes bureaucratiques excessives. Il faut dire que les structures de gouvernance dans nos sociétés sont devenues singulièrement complexes et induisent à l'occasion une *network fatigue*. Il est à cet égard utile de s'arrêter un moment à ces aspects et au rôle croissant du tiers secteur dans la société civile.

LE RÔLE DU TIERS SECTEUR ET CELUI DES MÉDIAS

Une des figures historiques de la sociologie québécoise, Marcel Rioux, disait que le Québec était une société allergique au conflit, cherchant toujours à fonctionner au consensus, du fait de son statut minoritaire.

Ce trait peut peut-être expliquer pourquoi au Québec le mouvement associatif et communautaire a pris une telle importance sans que cela altère la vision d'un État interventionniste plus proche des traditions françaises qu'américaines. On a donc un réseau d'ONG très structuré, qui collaborent avec des appareils d'État au sein d'instances de concertation. Mais dans le secteur de l'immigration, la réalité est différente et les ONG ont longtemps été marginales dans le mouvement communautaire québécois. De plus, le monde associatif se présente plutôt dans ce secteur comme une nébuleuse de petits organismes composés de bénévoles coexistant avec des ONG plus importantes chargées par l'État d'administrer le gros des programmes d'aide à l'établissement et à l'intégration des immigrants. Il y a quelques années, le gouvernement provincial a tenté de contenir la prolifération d'associations ethniques (au service d'un groupe ethnique particulier) et de les encourager à travailler pour des clientèles plus larges dans le cadre des programmes d'aide à l'établissement et à l'intégration (Helly, Lavallée et Mc Andrew 2000). Par ailleurs, tous ces organismes sont portés par des personnes qui sont souvent elles-mêmes immigrantes (ce qui est vrai aussi pour une bonne partie des chercheurs académiques).

Si donc le secteur associatif est en général très structuré et regroupé notamment autour de tables de concertation, dans le domaine de l'immigration le portrait est plus complexe (Germain 2002). Il est donc plus difficile pour un centre comme le nôtre d'établir des partenariats aussi systématiques que ceux qui nous lient au secteur public. Les contraintes des acteurs associatifs ne leur permettent pas non plus d'investir autant que leurs confrères du secteur public dans les activités de partenariat du centre. Ce qui ne veut pas dire qu'ils ne jouent pas un rôle névralgique, bien au contraire.

Certains d'entre eux détiennent aussi leurs propres expertises en recherche et, dans les premières années du Centre, ils ne se sentaient pas toujours reconnus en tant que tels par les chercheurs académiques. Ces derniers hésitaient d'ailleurs à mener des recherches sur le travail des organismes communautaires, craignant que cela ne leur porte préjudice compte tenu de la précarité de leurs financements. Il a donc fallu un apprivoisement réciproque des logiques de fonctionnement des uns et des autres. Mais les relations entre les milieux associatifs et les milieux académiques feront toujours l'objet d'un équilibre fragile, comme le sont celles entre le secteur public et le secteur associatif (Edgar 2008).

Un autre type de partenariat s'est aussi établi à l'occasion avec le secteur des médias (journaux, TV, etc.) dont l'impact sur l'opinion publique est devenu plus important que prévu, forçant les chercheurs à développer des relations particulières avec les journalistes pour diffuser leurs recherches mais aussi pour discuter de questions d'actualité. Ici aussi il s'agit d'une interaction délicate, qui a d'ailleurs fait l'objet de discussions au sein de notre centre, en plus d'avoir suscité un nouveau secteur de recherche. Aujourd'hui, la présence de nos chercheurs dans les médias est regardée avec attention et fait partie des dynamiques de transfert de connaissance.

En guise de conclusion, j'identifierai quatre axes sur lesquels se définissent les défis qui nous attendent.

DE QUELQUES DÉFIS À VENIR...

Le CMQ-IM est devenu un formidable réseau de chercheurs et de partenaires. Il a cependant été mis en place par une génération de chercheurs qui sont aujourd'hui en fin de carrière et sont de ce fait plus difficiles à mobiliser. Mais surtout cette génération doit apporter aide et support à celle qui la suit et qui fait face à des conditions moins favorables du fait de l'évolution des conditions de travail en milieu académique aujourd'hui beaucoup plus exigeantes, et ce d'autant plus que le Québec a traversé dans les années 1980 et début 1990 des années difficiles pendant lesquelles les universités ont engagé peu de nouvelles ressources. La succession des générations est toujours une épreuve dans les entreprises fondées par des pionniers, et à fortiori si un certain écart d'âge les sépare!

En second lieu, le domaine de l'immigration subit des changements constants : changement des flux migratoires, changement des problèmes d'intégration, changement des politiques, etc. Surtout, les questions d'immigration ne concernent plus une minorité d'individus mais des segments de plus en plus importants de nos sociétés, surtout dans un pays comme le Canada qui accueille chaque année des volumes croissants de nouveaux arrivants. À l'échelle locale, les minorités sont souvent des majorités!

Les dynamiques d'intégration mais aussi de cohabitation se complexifient puisque se côtoient plusieurs générations de personnes issues de l'immigration, dont certaines sont amenées à jouer le rôle de l'hôte. C'est donc toute la société qui se transforme.

Mais en même temps de nouvelles dynamiques migratoires nous interpellent, notamment avec la question des migrants temporaires qui sont aujourd'hui pratiquement aussi nombreux que les immigrants indépendants sélectionnés par le système de points.

Les phénomènes qui entrent dans la mire des chercheurs se multiplient et deviennent donc d'une grande complexité. De nouvelles ressources, plus importantes, devront alors être mobilisées pour y faire face et notre mode de fonctionnement devra peut-être être revu.

En même temps, le milieu de la recherche sur les questions d'immigration s'est diversifié et nos centres devront s'adapter à cette nouvelle configuration, en investissant notamment dans des partenariats avec ...d'autres centres de recherche sur l'immigration tout en se recentrant sur ce qui fait leur force, à savoir le réseau de partenaires.

Dans le domaine de l'immigration, les partenaires locaux sont de plus en plus nombreux et les efforts de réseautage ont suivi le mouvement. Il faut alors se demander si le gouvernement fédéral acceptera encore longtemps de financer seul un réseau dont profitent de plus en plus les autres paliers de gouvernement ou s'il n'essayera pas de les convaincre de participer à l'entreprise.

NOTES

1.   Demande de 1995 du Centre de Montréal.
2.   Le Comité de coordination, constitué des coordonnateurs des domaines qui représentent d'office leur institution d'attache, est l'instance décisionnelle du Centre. Il se réunit au moins quatre fois par an. Il a le mandat de discuter et d'approuver, après évaluation du comité des pairs et après avis du Conseil des partenaires, les plans de recherche proposés par les coordonnateurs. Il décide aussi de l'allocation des enveloppes budgétaires de recherche et de rayonnement dans le meilleur intérêt du Centre, en fonction des orientations générales du programme, des priorités exprimées par l'organisme subventionnaire ou les partenaires et des opportunités stratégiques émanant du milieu. Il entérine les candidatures de nouveaux chercheurs proposées par les domaines.
3.   Le Conseil des partenaires a pour mandat de réagir aux plans de recherche proposés par les coordonnateurs de domaines et de se prononcer sur les orientations d'ensemble du Centre, en particulier ses priorités et ses stratégies de dissémination des résultats et de présence active dans la communauté.
4.   Les coordonnateurs de domaine ont le mandat de développer et de consolider les capacités de recherche, de transfert et de partage de connaissances des chercheurs et partenaires de leur domaine respectif, en lien avec leurs homologues des autres Centres Métropolis et avec les responsables des priorités nationales. Pour ce faire, ils coordonnent le développement d'un plan de recherche au sein de leur domaine. Ils rédigent le bilan annuel des activités de leur domaine. Ils proposent, reçoivent et discutent des propositions de candidatures de chercheurs en se basant sur les critères d'affiliation du Centre.

RÉFÉRENCES

Edgar, G. 2008. *Agreeing to Disagree: Maintaining Dissent in the NGO Sector.* Discussion paper n° 100. Canberra : The Australia Institute.

Germain, A. 2002. *La participation des organismes s'occupant des immigrants et/ou de communautés culturelles aux instances de concertation de quartier.* Rapport de recherche. Montréal : Institut National de la Recherche Scientifique – Centre Urbanisation Culture Société (INRS-UCS). 166 p.

Germain, A. 2007. Los desafíos de la gestión local de la diversidad etnoreligiosa en Montréal : el caso de la habilitación de los lugares de culto [Les défis de la gestion locale de la diversité ethnoreligieuse : le cas de l'aménagement des lieux de culte]. *Revista CIDOB d'Afers Internacionals* 77 : 93-110.

Helly, D., M. Lavallée et M. Mc Andrew. 2000. Citoyenneté et redéfinition des politiques publiques de gestion de la diversité : la position des organismes non gouvernementaux québécois. *Recherches sociographiques* 41 (2) : 271-298.

NOTES ON CONTRIBUTORS

Naomi Alboim
Fellow at the School of Policy Studies at Queen's University, Canada.
She is also a senior fellow at the Maytree Foundation, where she leads
its immigration policy work. Naomi Alboim is an active public policy
consultant, advising governments and NGOs across Canada and
abroad. She is on the Founding Board of the Toronto Region Immigrant
Employment Council and chairs its Intergovernmental Committee. She
worked as a civil servant at senior levels in the Canadian federal and
Ontario provincial governments for 25 years, including eight years as
Deputy Minister in three different portfolios. Her areas of responsibility
have included immigration, human rights, culture, labour market training, and workplace practices. She has authored both commissioned and
unsolicited policy papers, which have had significant impact on federal
and provincial policy. She is a member of the Order of Ontario and a
recipient of the Jubilee Gold Medal for public service.

John Biles
Special Adviser to the Director General of the Integration Branch at
Citizenship and Immigration Canada. Prior to this appointment, he was
the Director of Partnerships and Knowledge Transfer for Metropolis
(an international network for comparative research and public policy
development on migration, diversity, and immigrant integration in cities in Canada and around the world). His research interests include the
political participation of newcomers and minorities, multiculturalism,
integration, citizenship, public policy and religious pluralism, and knowledge transfer. Recent publications include *Electing a Diverse Canada: The
Representation of Immigrants, Minorities, and Women* (2008); *Immigration and
Integration in Canada in the Twenty-first Century* (2008); and *Integration and
Inclusion of Newcomers and Minorities Across Canada* (2011).

Monica Boyd

Canada Research Chair in Immigration, Inequality and Public Policy, University of Toronto. In addition to academic appointments at Carleton University and Florida State University, she has held Visiting Scholar appointments at the University of Wisconsin–Madison, Harvard University, and Statistics Canada. Dr. Boyd has served as elected presidents of the Academy of Social Sciences, Royal Society of Canada; the Canadian Sociological Association; and the Canadian Population Society; and as the Chair of the International Migration Section of the American Sociological Association. Her current research projects are on the migration of high-skilled labour, care work migration, immigrant inequality in the labour force, and the socio-economic achievements of immigrant offspring. She holds two concurrent research grants to study the socio-economic achievements, intermarriage, and acculturation of the children of immigrants in Canada (the 1.5 and 2cd generations) and to study the relationship between language proficiency and immigrant labour market integration.

Elizabeth Coelho

A former Coordinator for English as a Second Language in Toronto, Elizabeth Coelho has also taught teacher education courses at the University of Toronto and worked on policy and resource development at the Ontario Ministry of Education. She has worked with educators in schools and universities across Canada and the United States, and she is now based in Spain, where cultural diversity is a new challenge for teachers. Her book *Teaching and Learning in Multicultural Schools: An Integrated Approach* has been used in teacher education courses across Canada and has also been translated into Spanish and Catalan, while her most recent book, *Adding English: A Guide to Teaching in Multilingual Classrooms*, has become the standard resource for the training of teachers of English as a Second Language in Canada. She is now working on a new book for educators in countries or areas where immigration is a relatively new phenomenon.

Zita De Koninck

Professeure titulaire au Département de Langues, Linguistique et Traduction de la Faculté des Lettres de l'Université Laval. Elle détient un Ph.D. de l'Université de Montréal. Elle a été enseignante de français langue seconde et de français langue étrangère et superviseure de stages et conceptrice de programmes, de guides pédagogiques et d'évaluation et de matériel didactique destinés aux classes d'accueil et aux milieux pluriethniques. À l'université, elle enseigne aux 1er, 2e et 3e cycles en didactique des langues appliquée aux milieux pluriethniques, en mesure et évaluation et en méthodologie de la recherche. Associée au Centre Métropolis du Québec – Immigration et Métropoles, elle s'est penchée sur l'apprentissage de la langue seconde à des fins de scolarisation, sur les modèles mis en place pour accueillir les élèves allophones et sur la question de la sous-scolarisation et de la réussite scolaire. La majorité de ses publications sont reliées à ces questions.

Louise Fontaine

Conseillère-cadre au bureau du sous-ministre adjoint à l'immigration. Elle a été directrice des Politiques et des Programmes d'immigration au Ministère de l'Immigration et des Communautés culturelles du Québec de février 2007 à février 2010. Elle était chargée de l'élaboration, du soutien à la mise en œuvre et du suivi des orientations, des politiques et des programmes en matière d'immigration au Québec. Elle a été directrice des politiques et des programmes d'immigration familiale, sociale et humanitaire au Ministère de l'Immigration et des Communautés culturelles. Elle fût aussi agente de recherche et responsable du dossier de la sélection humanitaire et du parrainage collectif. Par ailleurs, elle a participé à plusieurs missions de sélection de réfugiés et de travailleurs qualifiés. Auparavant à la fonction publique fédérale, Mme Fontaine a travaillé comme agente de liaison et comme spécialiste des programmes d'établissement des immigrants de 1979 à 1991.

Annick Germain

Docteur en sociologie et professeure-chercheure titulaire à l'INRS – Urbanisation Culture Société. Depuis février 2008 elle dirige le Centre Métropolis du Québec – Immigration et Métropoles. Ses publications portent sur Montréal (*Montréal: A Quest for a Metropolis*, avec Damaris Rose, publié en 2000 à Londres chez John Wiley & Sons), le cosmopolitisme (« Cosmopolitanism by default: Public sociability in Montreal », avec Martha Radice, dans *Cosmopolitan Urbanism*, sous la direction de Jon Binnie, Julian Holloway, Steve Millington et Craig Young, publié en 2006 à Abingdon, Angleterre, chez Routledge); la cohabitation dans les quartiers multiethniques et la gestion municipale de la diversité, y compris religieuse (« La gestion de la diversité à l'épreuve de la métropole ou les vertus de l'adhocratisme montréalais », avec Martin Alain, dans *Les métropoles et la question de la diversité culturelle : nouveaux enjeux, nouveaux défis*, sous la direction de Bernard Jouve et Alain-G. Gagnon, publié en 2005 chez les Presses universitaires de Grenoble).

Jack Jedwab

Executive Director of the Association for Canadian Studies (ACS) and the International Association for the Study of Canada (IASC). Mr. Jedwab graduated with a Bachelor of Arts in Canadian History from McGill University and an M.A. and Ph.D. in Canadian History from Concordia University. He lectured at McGill University from 1983 to 2007 in the Quebec Studies Program, the Sociology and Political Science departments, and most recently at the McGill Institute for the Study of Canada, where he taught courses on official language minorities in Canada and sports in Canada. He has authored various publications and government reports on issues of immigration, multiculturalism, human rights, and official languages, and he is the founding editor of the publications *Canadian Issues, Canadian Diversity,* and the new *Canadian Journal for Social Research.*

Peter S. Li

Professor of Sociology at the University of Saskatchewan. He has published over 80 academic papers and ten books. Among his books are *Race and Ethnic Relations in Canada* (Oxford University Press, 1999), *The Chinese in Canada* (OUP, 1988, 1998), *Ethnic Inequality in a Class Society* (Thompson, 1988), and *Destination Canada* (OUP, 2003). He has served as a consultant and an adviser to various federal departments regarding policies of immigration, multiculturalism, race relations, and social statistics. In 2001, he was given the "Living in Harmony" Recognition Award by the City of Saskatoon, Race Relations Committee. In 2002, he received the "Outstanding Contribution" Award from the Canadian Sociology and Anthropology Association. He was president of the Canadian Sociology and Anthropology Association for 2004 to 2005. In 2009, he was inducted Fellow of the Royal Society of Canada.

Gérard Pinsonneault

Chercheur associé à la Chaire en Relations Ethniques de l'Université de Montréal. Ayant reçu une formation en histoire (M.A., Université de Sherbrooke, 1981), il a été agent du service étranger du Canada en immigration (1974–1978) et puis fonctionnaire au Gouvernement du Québec en Immigration (1978–2008). Au gouvernement du Québec, après avoir rempli diverses fonctions dans le secteur de la sélection (1978–1988), il a été conseiller aux programmes en recrutement et sélection, adjoint au sous-ministre, agent de recherche et de planification (1988–2008), chargé de projet, directeur intérimaire de la recherche et de l'analyse prospective (2006–2007). Parmi ses contributions particulières au service du Gouvernement du Québec, on note la rédaction des directives administratives sur le recrutement et la sélection, ainsi que la conception et l'aménagement d'un entrepôt de données à des fins de recherche et d'analyse. En plus, il a été chargé de projet pour différentes recherches commandées par le ministère comme l'établissement des demandeurs d'asile (1997) et l'insertion en emploi des travailleurs sélectionnés (2002), et répondant ministériel au réseau international de recherche Metropolis, sur l'immigration, l'intégration et la gestion de la diversité (2003–2008).

Yves Poisson

Former Vice-President of the Public Policy Forum (PPF), Ottawa. Yves Poisson has an M.B.A. from McGill University and a B.Sc. in Economics from the Université de Montréal. His work has focused on economic themes and the integration of immigrants, including subjects such as North American economic integration, Canada's competitiveness, immigration, regional/provincial economies, and Canada-U.S. relations. Prior to joining the PPF, Yves Poisson worked in the federal public service at Human Resources Development Canada (HRSDC), both in Montreal and Ottawa. He was Director General of the Labour Program (1996–2000). During this period, he worked on the evolving labour market and work-family issues. He represented Canada at the International Labour Organization and also participated in several international meetings. Other positions he held at HRSDC related to the Unemployment Insurance Reform (1995–1996), the Social Program Review Task Group (1993–1995), federal-provincial relations and the management of employment programs (1983–1989), and the implementation of new employment and training policies (1989–1992).

Maryse Potvin
Political scientist; sociologist; professor in Education at the Université du Québec à Montréal (UQAM); director of the Group on Media, Social Discourses, and Public Opinion and of the "Education and Ethnic Relations" new research axis at the Centre d'études ethniques des universités montréalaises (CEETUM); and researcher at the Centre Métropolis du Québec. She was an adviser in public policy at the Ministère de l'Immigration et des Communautés culturelles (2000–2002). Her research and publications deal with ethnic relations, discrimination, youth of immigrant origin, anti-racist and democratic education, social discourse analysis, and social and scholarly inequalities. Her publications include the books *Crise des accommodements raisonnables. Une fiction médiatique?* (Athéna, 2008) and *La 2e génération issue de l'immigration. Une comparaison France-Québec* (Athéna, 2007). She has published a number of articles in the *International Social Sciences Journal* and the *Journal of International Migration and Integration*, among other journals, as well as expert reports, notably on the measurement of discriminations in Canada for the European Commission (2004) and on media and reasonable accommodations for the Bouchard-Taylor Commission in 2007 to 2008.

Jeffrey G. Reitz
(Ph.D., Columbia 1972; FRSC) Professor and former Chair in the Department of Sociology, and R.F. Harney Professor of Ethnic, Immigration, and Pluralism Studies (www.utoronto.ca/ethnicstudies), University of Toronto. He was Mackenzie King Visiting Professor at Harvard University in 2000 to 2001 and received the "Outstanding Contribution" Award from the Canadian Sociological Association in 2005. His latest book is *Multiculturalism and Social Cohesion: Potentials and Challenges of Diversity* (Springer, 2009); previous books include *Host*

Societies and the Reception of Immigrants (2003) and *Warmth of the Welcome: Social Causes of Economic Success for Immigrants in Different Nations and Cities* (1998). Recent articles include "Immigrant Employment Success in Canada: Understanding the Decline" (2007); "Race, Religion, and the Social Integration of Canada's New Immigrant Minorities (*International Migration Review*, 2009); and "Comparisons of the Success of Racial Minority Immigrant Offspring in the United States, Canada and Australia (*Social Science Research*, 2011).

Dan Rodríguez-García (Editor)
Associate Professor of Social and Cultural Anthropology, Autonomous University of Barcelona (UAB), Spain. He has held research fellowships at the University of Sussex (U.K.) and at the University of Toronto. Dan Rodríguez-García is the Director of the Research Group on Immigration, Mixedness, and Social Cohesion (INMIX); is a senior researcher with the Migration Research Group, UAB; and is a member of the Network of Excellence on International Migration, Integration and Social Cohesion in Europe (IMISCOE). He regularly participates in knowledge transfer activities regarding immigration and diversity issues for different government institutions and foundations. His books include *The Immigrant Population in Catalonia, Spain: Settlement and Integration* (2012, co-authored) and *Immigration and Hybridity Today* (2004, award-winning publication). His articles include "Beyond Assimilation and Multiculturalism: A Critical Review of the Debate on Managing Diversity" (*Journal of International Migration and Integration*, 2010) and the prize-winning "Mixed Marriages and Transnational Families in the Intercultural Context" (*Journal of Ethnic and Migration Studies*, 2006). In October 2008, he was Founder and Director of the international *Managing Immigration and Diversity in Quebec and Canada Forum* (Barcelona), from which this book results.

Joanna Anneke Rummens
Health Systems Research Scientist, Community Health Systems Resource Group, Learning Institute, and Project Investigator, Child Health Evaluative Sciences, Research Institute, The Hospital for Sick Children, Toronto; Senior Scholar and former Director of CERIS – The Ontario Metropolis Centre of Excellence for Research on Immigration and Settlement; Assistant Professor in Culture, Community and Health Studies, Department of Psychiatry, Faculty of Medicine, University of Toronto. Dr. Rummens is a multilingual anthropologist and sociologist whose research explores the links between identity/diversity, health/ well-being, and life outcomes, with a special focus on vulnerable and marginalized populations, immigrant/refugee/migrant children and youth, and war-affected newcomer communities. Her work reflects a strong commitment to policy- and practice-relevant research,

collaborative research partnerships with diverse ethnocultural communities, and effective knowledge translation to a broad range of key stakeholders. Dr. Rummens also serves in an advisory capacity in the areas of identity, diversity, citizenship, integration, and health to various federal and provincial governmental departments in Canada.

Myer Siemiatycki

Professor of Politics and Public Administration at Ryerson University in Toronto. His research has explored immigrant integration and civic engagement in Canada, with a focus on the city of Toronto. Professor Siemiatycki was the founding Director of the Graduate Program in Immigration and Settlement Studies at Ryerson University. He has been active in the Metropolis Project, serving as a Research Domain Leader at CERIS – The Ontario Metropolis Centre of Excellence for Research on Immigration and Settlement. In his publications, Myer Siemiatycki has examined three dimensions of immigrant integration in Canada: immigrant political participation, immigrant transnationalism, and minority religions. He is co-editor of the book *Electing a Diverse Canada: The Representation of Immigrants, Minorities, and Women*. His publications (sole or co-authored) have examined such topics as immigrant electoral representation in Toronto, the transnationalism of Hong Kong immigrants in Canada, and the religious claims-making of Muslim and Jewish communities in Canada.

Queen's Policy Studies
Recent Publications

The Queen's Policy Studies Series is dedicated to the exploration of major public policy issues that confront governments and society in Canada and other nations.

Manuscript submission. We are pleased to consider new book proposals and manuscripts. Preliminary inquiries are welcome. A subvention is normally required for the publication of an academic book. Please direct questions or proposals to the Publications Unit by email at spspress@queensu.ca, or visit our website at: www.queensu.ca/sps/books, or contact us by phone at (613) 533-2192.

Our books are available from good bookstores everywhere, including the Queen's University bookstore (http://www.campusbookstore.com/). McGill-Queen's University Press is the exclusive world representative and distributor of books in the series. A full catalogue and ordering information may be found on their web site (http://mqup.mcgill.ca/).

School of Policy Studies

International Perspectives: Integration and Inclusion, James Frideres and John Biles (eds.) 2012. ISBN 978-1-55339-317-7

Dynamic Negotiations: Teacher Labour Relations in Canadian Elementary and Secondary Education, Sara Slinn and Arthur Sweetman (eds.) 2012. ISBN 978-1-55339-304-7

Where to from Here? Keeping Medicare Sustainable, Stephen Duckett 2012. ISBN 978-1-55339-318-4

International Migration in Uncertain Times, John Nieuwenhuysen, Howard Duncan, and Stine Neerup (eds.) 2012. ISBN 978-1-55339-308-5

Life After Forty: Official Languages Policy in Canada/Après quarante ans, les politiques de langue officielle au Canada, Jack Jedwab and Rodrigue Landry (eds.) 2011. ISBN 978-1-55339-279-8

From Innovation to Transformation: Moving up the Curve in Ontario Healthcare, Hon. Elinor Caplan, Dr. Tom Bigda-Peyton, Maia MacNiven, and Sandy Sheahan 2011. ISBN 978-1-55339-315-3

Academic Reform: Policy Options for Improving the Quality and Cost-Effectiveness of Undergraduate Education in Ontario, Ian D. Clark, David Trick, and Richard Van Loon 2011. ISBN 978-1-55339-310-8

Integration and Inclusion of Newcomers and Minorities across Canada, John Biles, Meyer Burstein, James Frideres, Erin Tolley, and Robert Vineberg (eds.) 2011. ISBN 978-1-55339-290-3

A New Synthesis of Public Administration: Serving in the 21ˢᵗ Century, Jocelyne Bourgon, 2011. Paper ISBN 978-1-55339-312-2 Cloth ISBN 978-1-55339-313-9

Recreating Canada: Essays in Honour of Paul Weiler, Randall Morck (ed.), 2011. ISBN 978-1-55339-273-6

Data Data Everywhere: Access and Accountability? Colleen M. Flood (ed.), 2011. ISBN 978-1-55339-236-1

Making the Case: Using Case Studies for Teaching and Knowledge Management in Public Administration, Andrew Graham, 2011. ISBN 978-1-55339-302-3

Canada's Isotope Crisis: What Next? Jatin Nathwani and Donald Wallace (eds.), 2010. Paper ISBN 978-1-55339-283-5 Cloth ISBN 978-1-55339-284-2

Pursuing Higher Education in Canada: Economic, Social, and Policy Dimensions, Ross Finnie, Marc Frenette, Richard E. Mueller, and Arthur Sweetman (eds.), 2010. Paper ISBN 978-1-55339-277-4 Cloth ISBN 978-1-55339-278-1

Canadian Immigration: Economic Evidence for a Dynamic Policy Environment,
Ted McDonald, Elizabeth Ruddick, Arthur Sweetman, and Christopher Worswick
(eds.), 2010. Paper ISBN 978-1-55339-281-1 Cloth ISBN 978-1-55339-282-8

Taking Stock: Research on Teaching and Learning in Higher Education, Julia Christensen
Hughes and Joy Mighty (eds.), 2010. Paper ISBN 978-1-55339-271-2
Cloth ISBN 978-1-55339-272-9

Centre for the Study of Democracy

Jimmy and Rosalynn Carter: A Canadian Tribute, Arthur Milnes (ed.), 2011.
Paper ISBN 978-1-55339-300-9 Cloth ISBN 978-1-55339-301-6

*Unrevised and Unrepented II: Debating Speeches and C̶   ̶u̶ the Right Honourable Arthur
Meighen,* Arthur Milnes (ed.), 2011 ̶P̶a̶p̶e̶r̶ ̶I̶S̶B̶N̶ ̶o̶∙̶   ̶ ̶ ̶ ̶ ̶9̶6̶-̶5̶
Cloth ISBN 978-1-55339-297-2

Centre for International and Defence Policy

Afghanistan in the Balance: Counterinsurgency, Comprehensive Approach, and Political Order,
Hans-Georg Ehrhart, Sven Bernhard Gareis, and Charles Pentland (eds.), 2012.
ISBN 978-1-55339-353-5

*Security Operations in the 21st Century: Canadian Perspectives on the Comprehensive
Approach,* Michael Rostek and Peter Gizewski (eds.), 2011. ISBN 978-1-55339-351-1

Europe Without Soldiers? Recruitment and Retention across the Armed Forces of Europe,
Tibor Szvircsev Tresch and Christian Leuprecht (eds.), 2010.
Paper ISBN 978-1-55339-246-0 Cloth ISBN 978-1-55339-247-7

Mission Critical: Smaller Democracies' Role in Global Stability Operations,
Christian Leuprecht, Jodok Troy, and David Last (eds.), 2010. ISBN 978-1-55339-244-6

John Deutsch Institute for the Study of Economic Policy

The 2009 Federal Budget: Challenge, Response and Retrospect, Charles M. Beach,
Bev Dahlby and Paul A.R. Hobson (eds.), 2010. Paper ISBN 978-1-55339-165-4
Cloth ISBN 978-1-55339-166-1

Discount Rates for the Evaluation of Public Private Partnerships, David F. Burgess and
Glenn P. Jenkins (eds.), 2010. Paper ISBN 978-1-55339-163-0 Cloth ISBN 978-1-55339-164-7

Institute of Intergovernmental Relations

The Evolving Canadian Crown, Jennifer Smith and D. Michael Jackson (eds.), 2011.
ISBN 978-1-55339-202-6

The Federal Idea: Essays in Honour of Ronald L. Watts, Thomas J. Courchene, John R. Allan,
Christian Leuprecht, and Nadia Verrelli (eds.), 2011. Paper ISBN 978-1-55339-198-2
Cloth ISBN 978-1-55339-199-9

Canada: The State of the Federation 2009, vol. 22, *Carbon Pricing and Environmental
Federalism,* Thomas J. Courchene and John R. Allan (eds.), 2010.
Paper ISBN 978-1-55339-196-8 Cloth ISBN 978-1-55339-197-5

Our publications may be purchased at leading bookstores, including the Queen's University Bookstore (http://www.campusbookstore.com/) or can be ordered online from:
McGill-Queen's University Press, at **http://mqup.mcgill.ca/ordering.php**

For more information about new and backlist titles from Queen's Policy Studies, visit
http://www.queensu.ca/sps/books or visit the McGill-Queen's University Press
web site at: **http://mqup.mcgill.ca/**